SuperMutant Magic Academy

Jillian Tamaki

Drawn & Quarterly

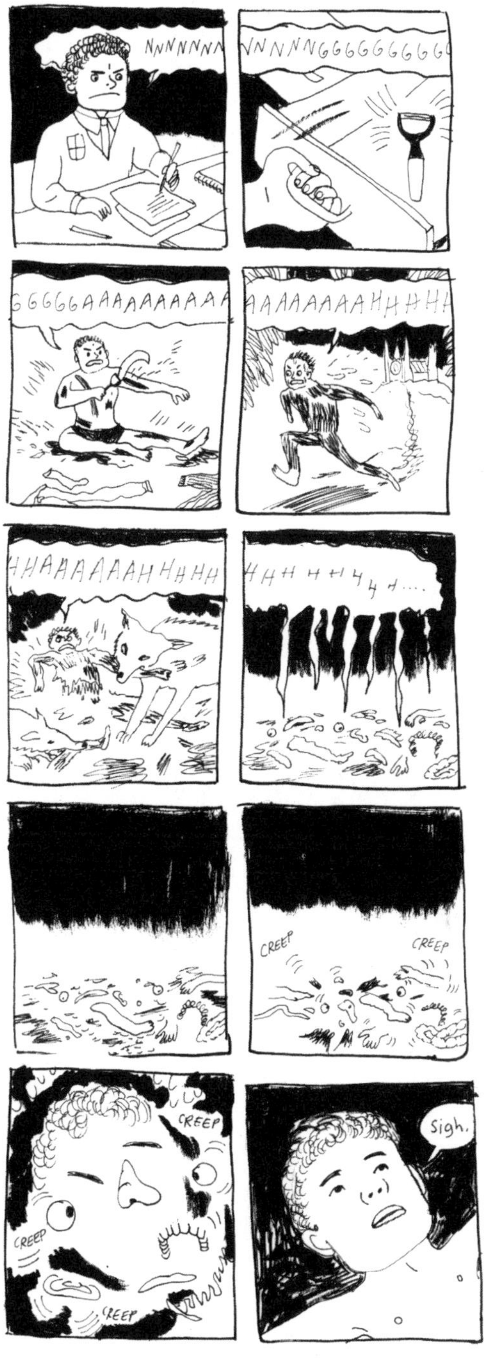

NNNNNNN
NNNNNGGGGGGGGGG
GGGGGAAAAAAAAAA
AAAAAAAAAHHHHH
HHAAAAAAAHHHHH
HHHHHHHHH....
CREEP
CREEP
CREEP
CREEP
CREEP
Sigh.

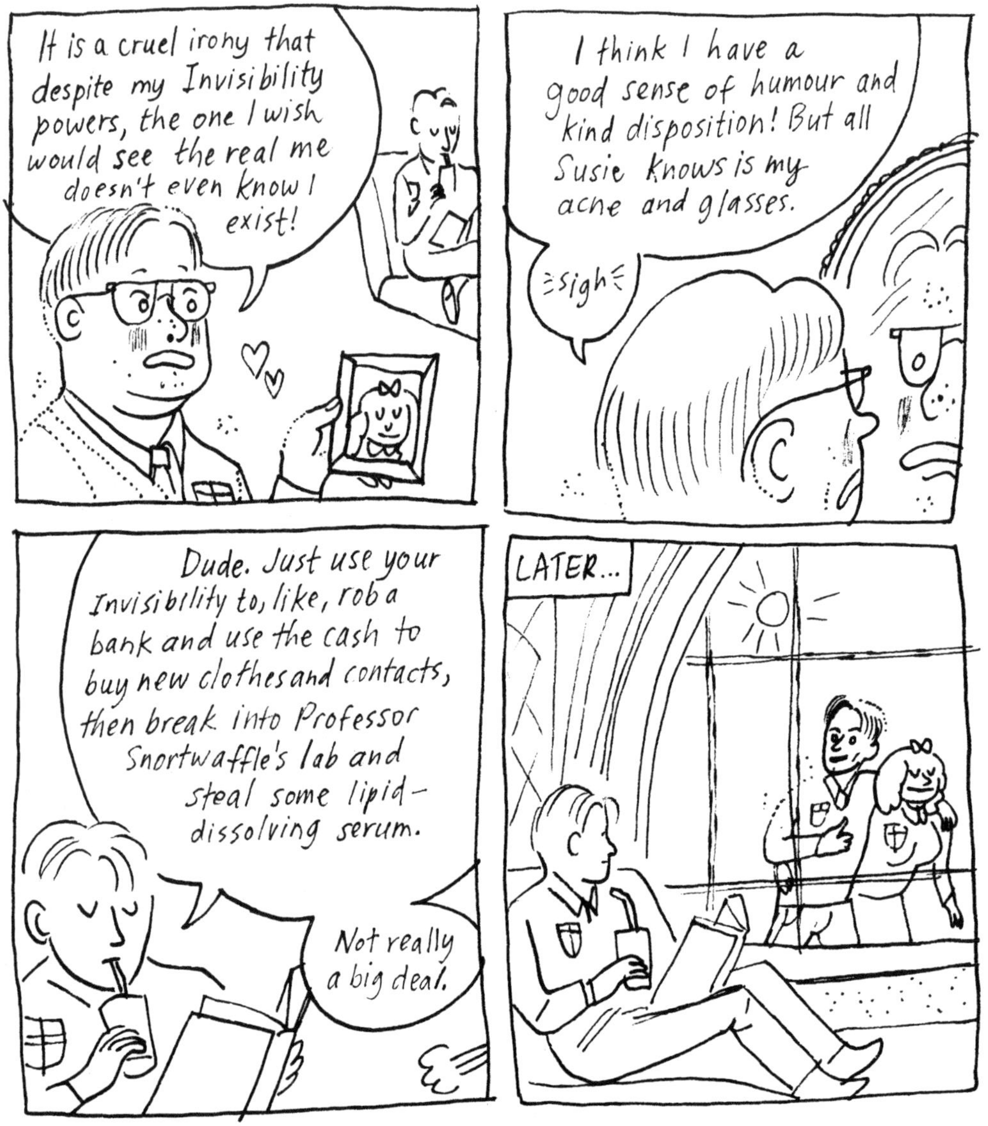
It is a cruel irony that despite my Invisibility powers, the one I wish would see the real me doesn't even know I exist!
I think I have a good sense of humour and kind disposition! But all Susie knows is my acne and glasses.
sigh
Dude. Just use your Invisibility to, like, rob a bank and use the cash to buy new clothes and contacts, then break into Professor Snortwaffle's lab and steal some lipid-dissolving serum.
Not really a big deal.
LATER...

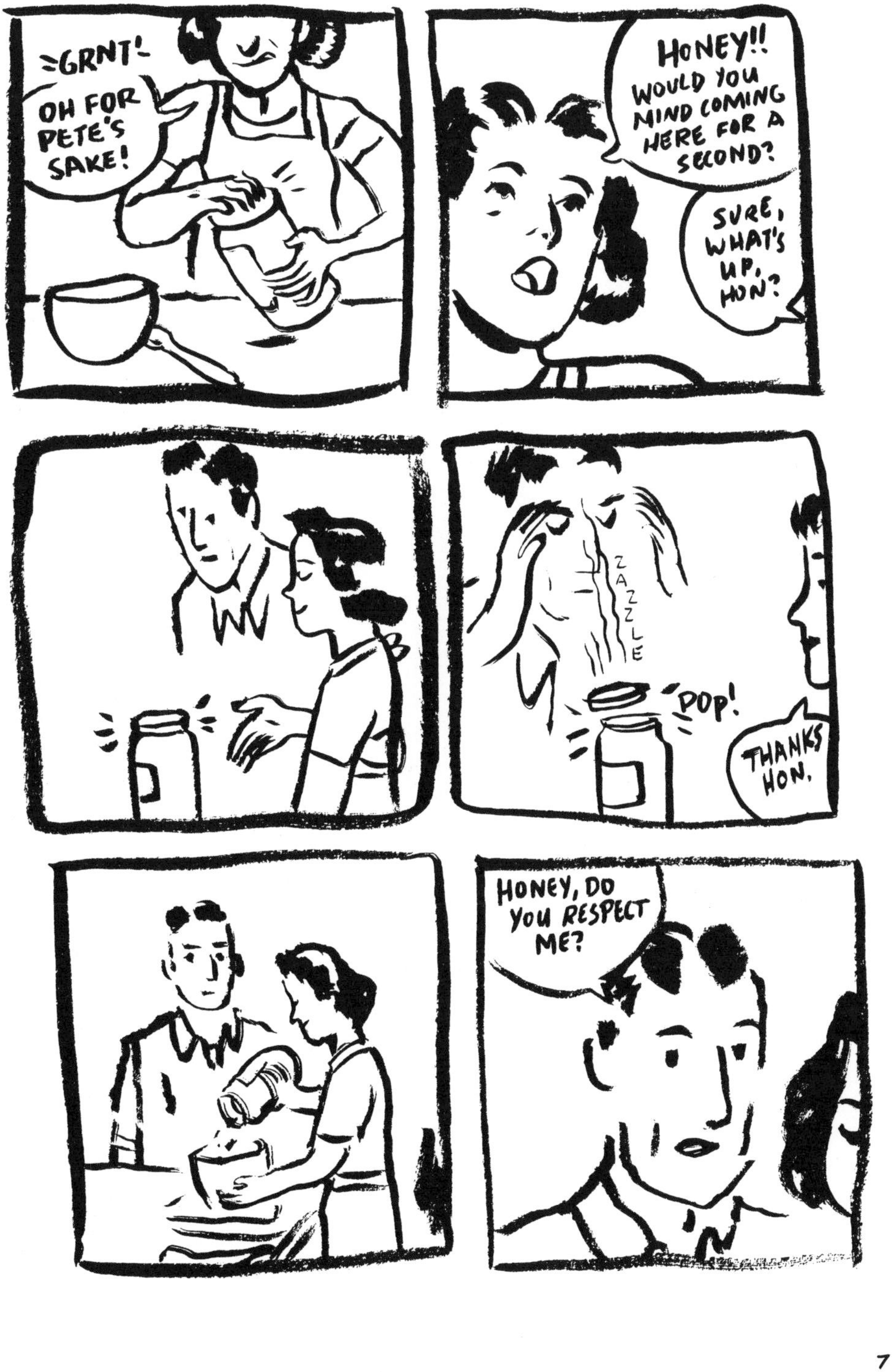

GRNT!
OH FOR PETE'S SAKE!
HONEY!! WOULD YOU MIND COMING HERE FOR A SECOND?
SURE, WHAT'S UP, HON?
ZAZZLE
POP!
THANKS HON.
HONEY, DO YOU RESPECT ME?

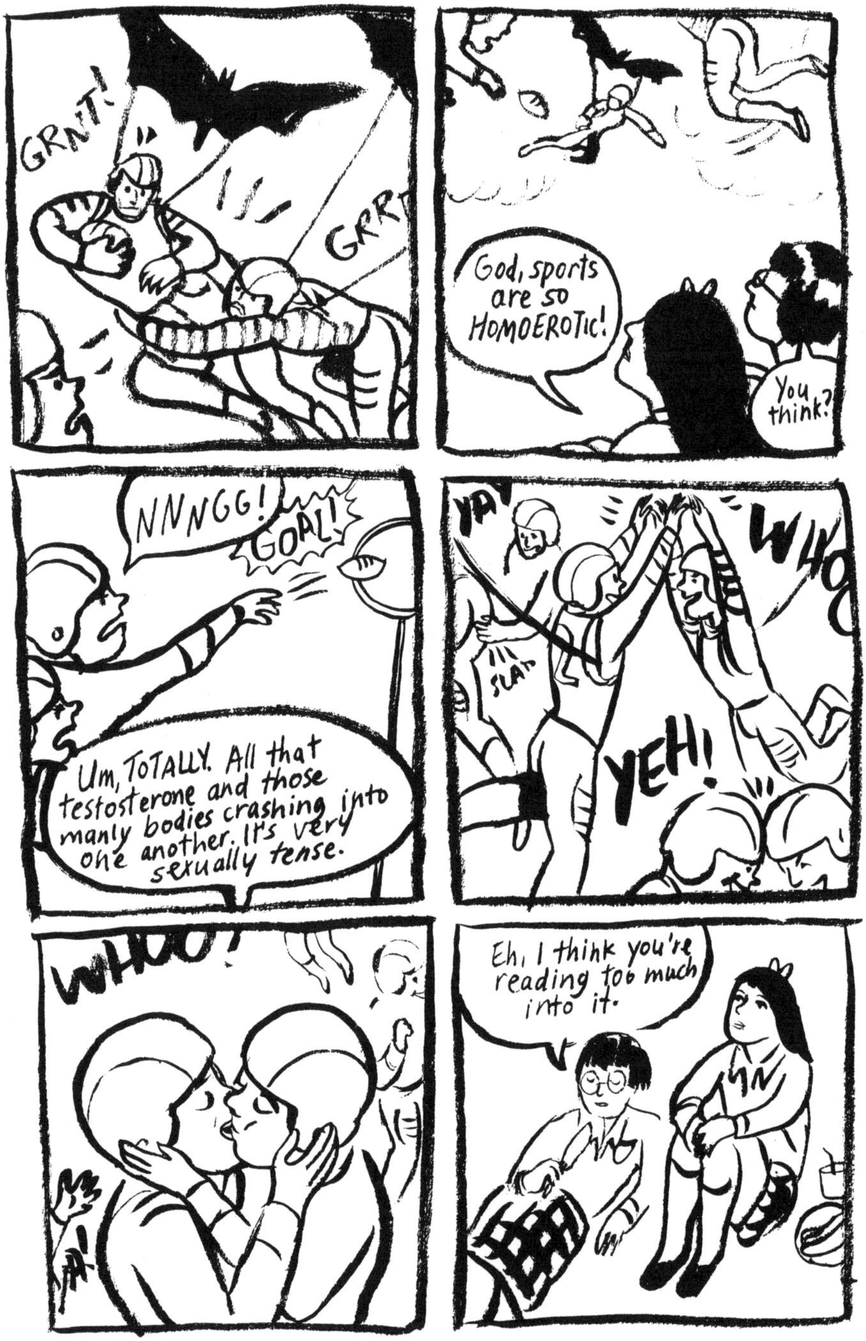
GRNT!
God, sports are so HOMOEROTIC!
You think?
NNNGG!
GOAL!
Um, TOTALLY. All that testosterone and those manly bodies crashing into one another. It's very sexually tense.
YEH!
WHOO!
Eh, I think you're reading too much into it.

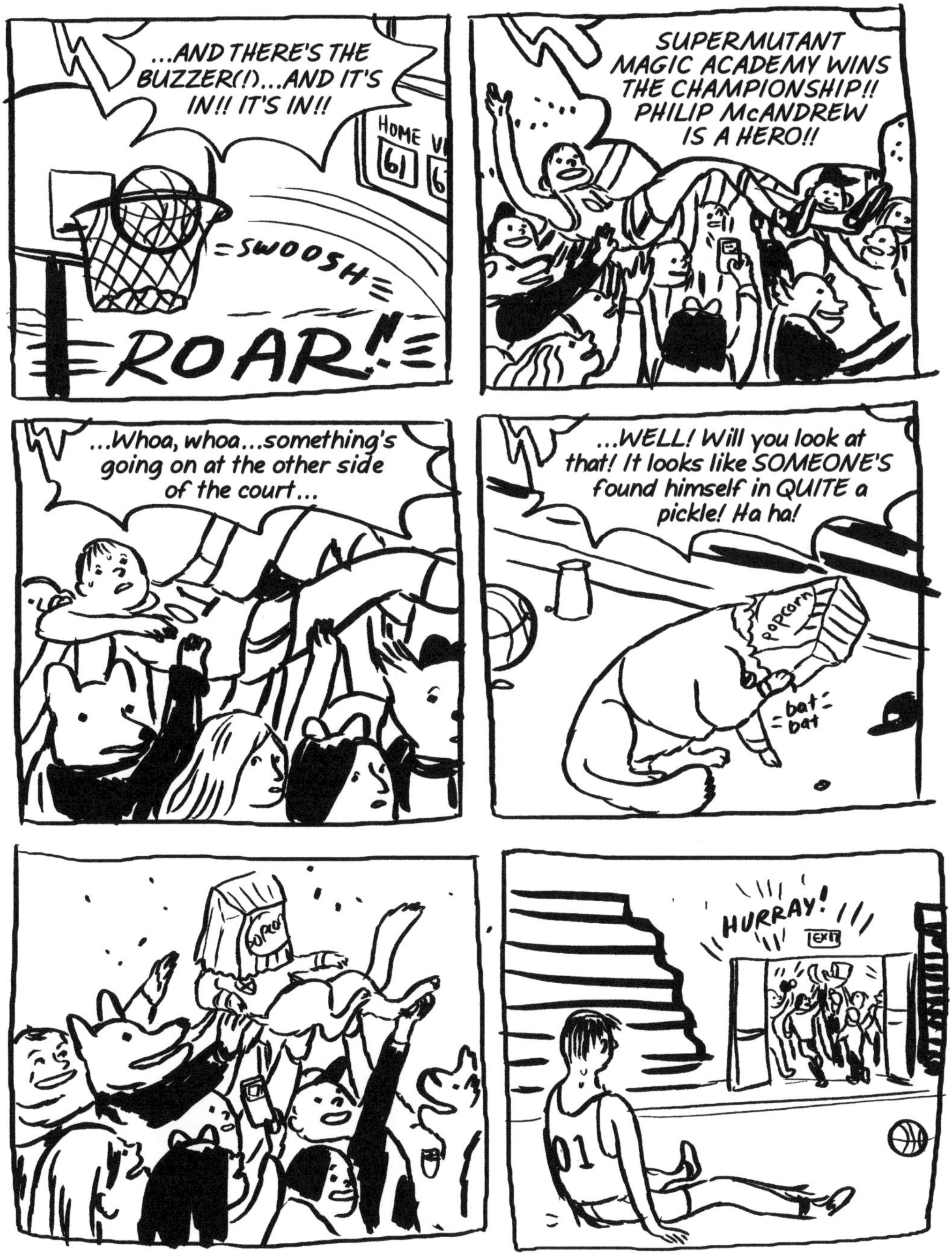
...AND THERE'S THE BUZZER(!)...AND IT'S IN!! IT'S IN!!
HOME
61
SWOOSH
ROAR!!
SUPERMUTANT MAGIC ACADEMY WINS THE CHAMPIONSHIP!! PHILIP McANDREW IS A HERO!!
...Whoa, whoa...something's going on at the other side of the court...
...WELL! Will you look at that! It looks like SOMEONE'S found himself in QUITE a pickle! Ha ha!
popcorn
bat bat
HURRAY!
EXIT
01

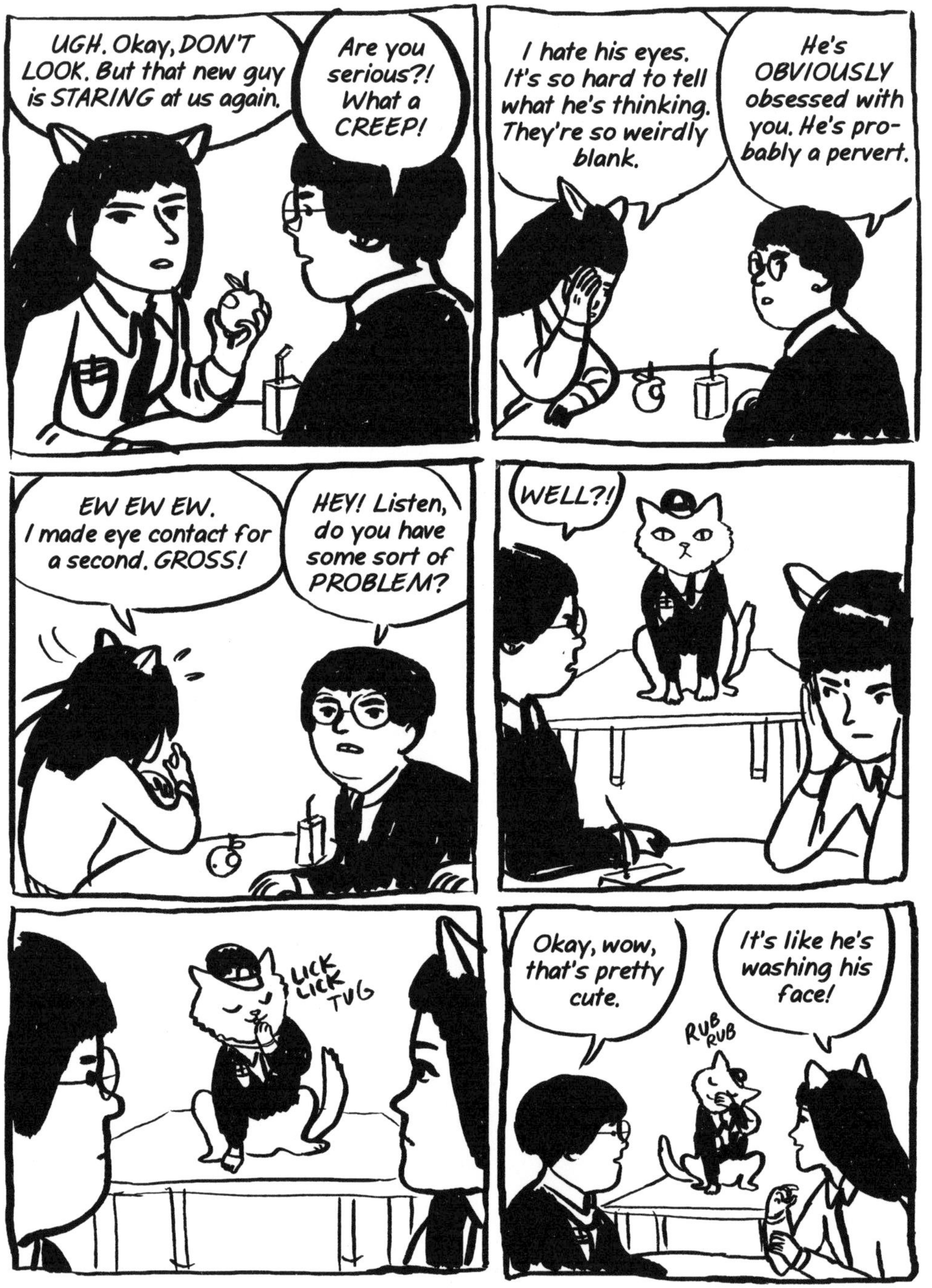
UGH. Okay, DON'T LOOK. But that new guy is STARING at us again.
Are you serious?! What a CREEP!
I hate his eyes. It's so hard to tell what he's thinking. They're so weirdly blank.
He's OBVIOUSLY obsessed with you. He's probably a pervert.
EW EW EW. I made eye contact for a second. GROSS!
HEY! Listen, do you have some sort of PROBLEM?
WELL?!
LICK LICK TUG
Okay, wow, that's pretty cute.
It's like he's washing his face!
RUB RUB

I still don't see why a CAT gets to attend the Super-Mutant Magic Academy. It doesn't even have a Superability! Not fair.
z z z
Grimdorff says that he'll play a pivotal part of a future epic battle between the forces of Good and Evil.
I hardly think we're in a position to argue.
I guess.
OH COME ON!
Ew.
SOP SOP

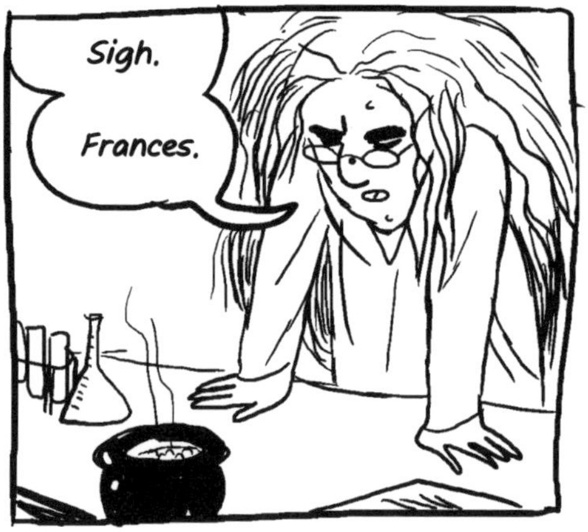
Sigh.
Frances.

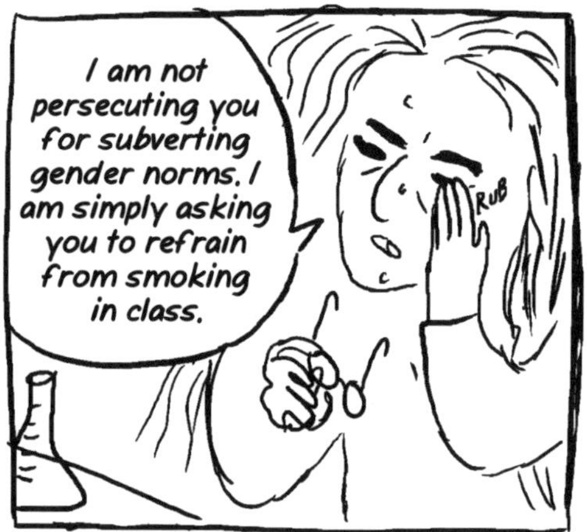
I am not persecuting you for subverting gender norms. I am simply asking you to refrain from smoking in class.
RUB

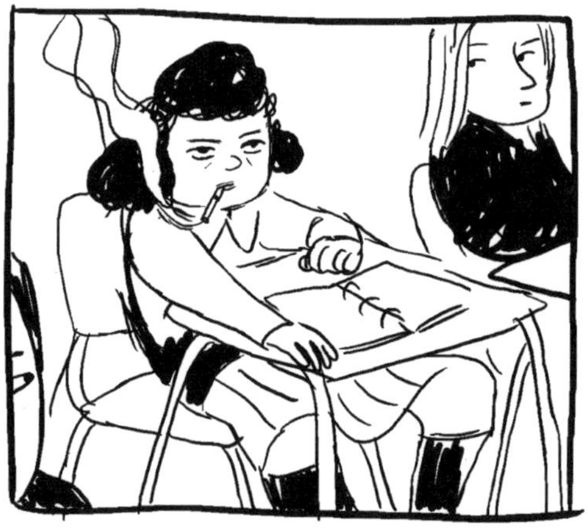

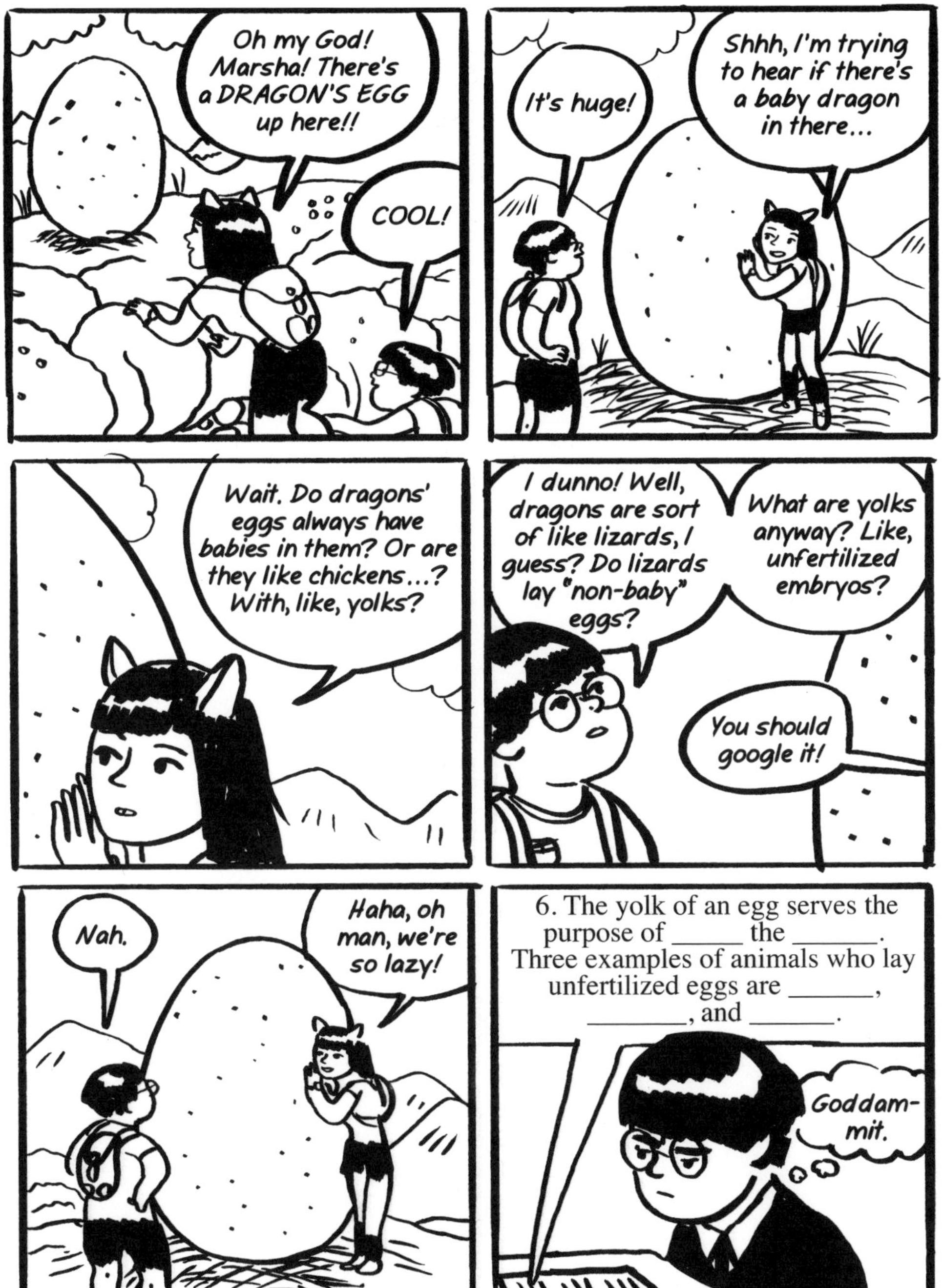
Oh my God! Marsha! There's a DRAGON'S EGG up here!!
COOL!
It's huge!
Shhh, I'm trying to hear if there's a baby dragon in there...
Wait. Do dragons' eggs always have babies in them? Or are they like chickens...? With, like, yolks?
I dunno! Well, dragons are sort of like lizards, I guess? Do lizards lay "non-baby" eggs?
What are yolks anyway? Like, unfertilized embryos?
You should google it!
Nah.
Haha, oh man, we're so lazy!
6. The yolk of an egg serves the purpose of _____ the ______. Three examples of animals who lay unfertilized eggs are ______, _______, and ______.
Goddammit.

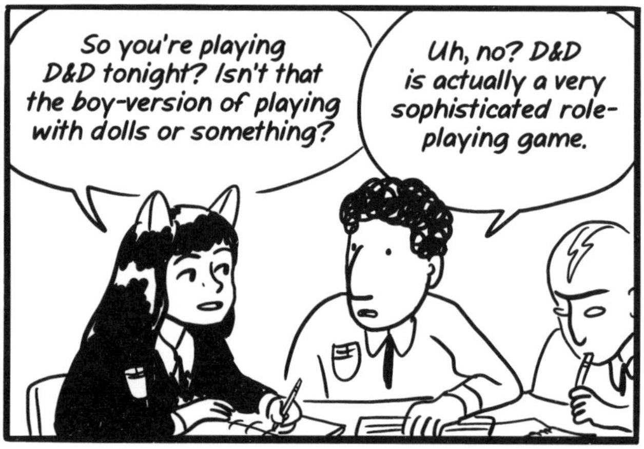
So you're playing D&D tonight? Isn't that the boy-version of playing with dolls or something?
Uh, no? D&D is actually a very sophisticated role-playing game.

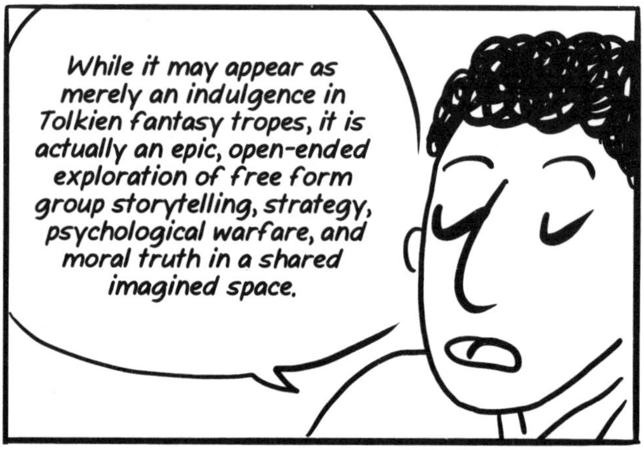
While it may appear as merely an indulgence in Tolkien fantasy tropes, it is actually an epic, open-ended exploration of free form group storytelling, strategy, psychological warfare, and moral truth in a shared imagined space.

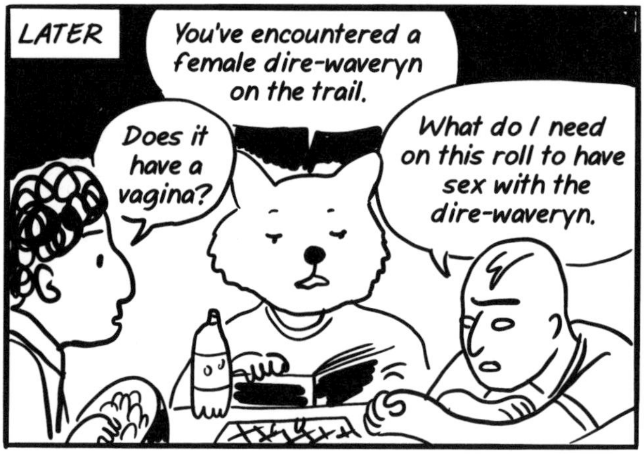
LATER
You've encountered a female dire-waveryn on the trail.
Does it have a vagina?
What do I need on this roll to have sex with the dire-waveryn.

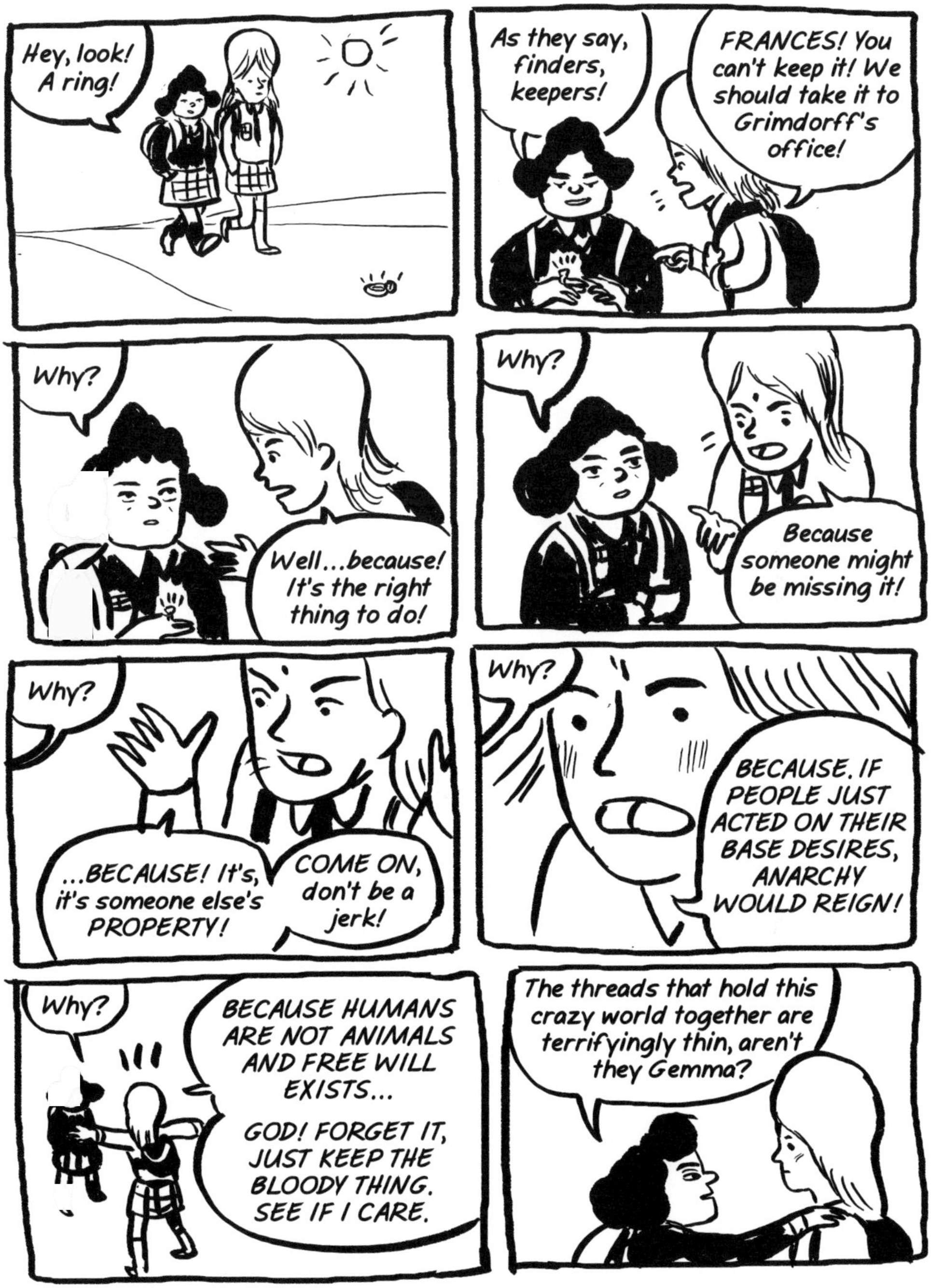
Hey, look! A ring!
As they say, finders, keepers!
FRANCES! You can't keep it! We should take it to Grimdorff's office!
Why?
Well...because! It's the right thing to do!
Why?
Because someone might be missing it!
Why?
...BECAUSE! It's, it's someone else's PROPERTY!
COME ON, don't be a jerk!
Why?
BECAUSE. IF PEOPLE JUST ACTED ON THEIR BASE DESIRES, ANARCHY WOULD REIGN!
Why?
BECAUSE HUMANS ARE NOT ANIMALS AND FREE WILL EXISTS...
GOD! FORGET IT, JUST KEEP THE BLOODY THING. SEE IF I CARE.
The threads that hold this crazy world together are terrifyingly thin, aren't they Gemma?

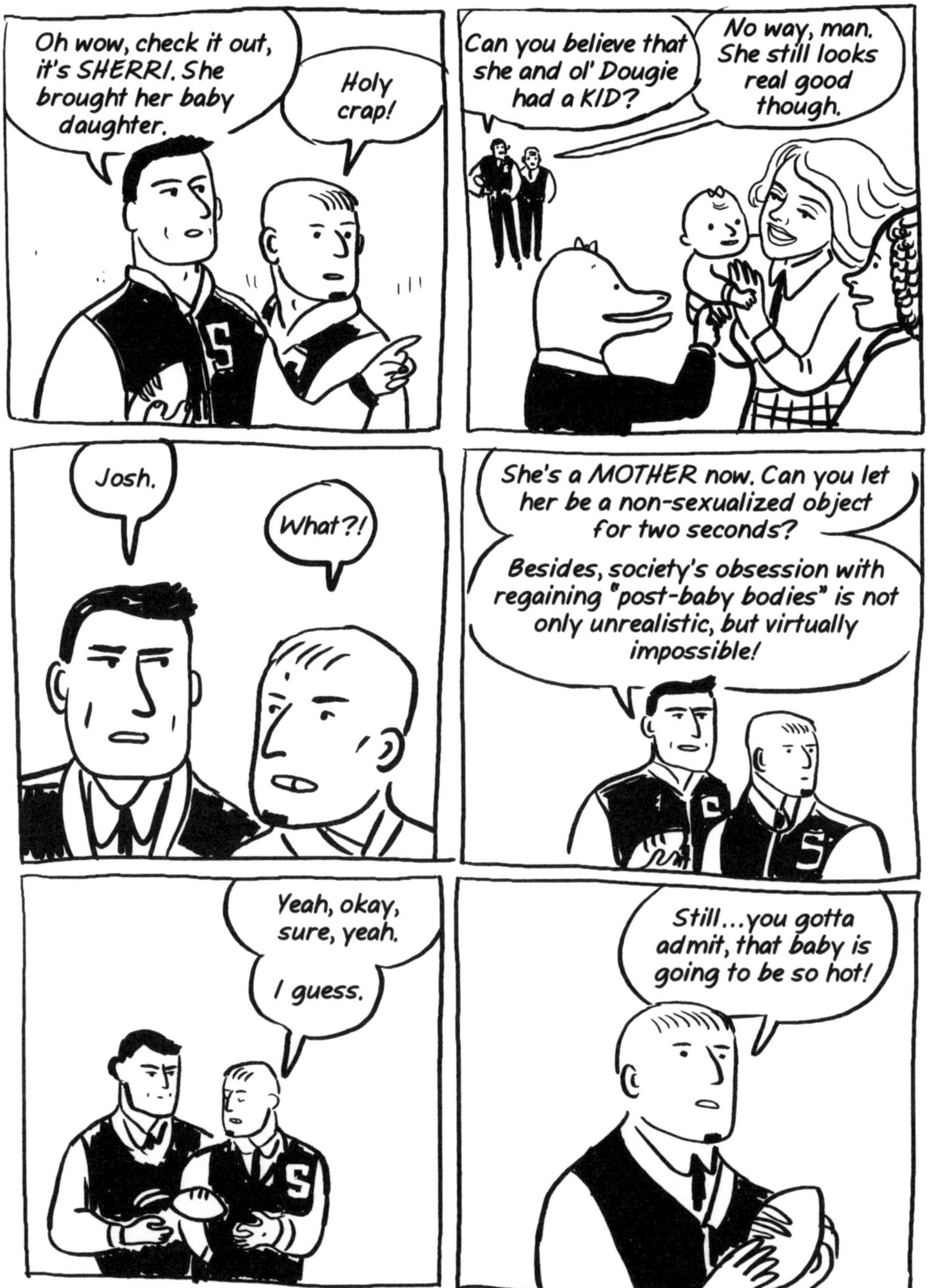
Oh wow, check it out, it's SHERRI. She brought her baby daughter.
Holy crap!
Can you believe that she and ol' Dougie had a KID?
No way, man. She still looks real good though.
Josh.
What?!
She's a MOTHER now. Can you let her be a non-sexualized object for two seconds?
Besides, society's obsession with regaining "post-baby bodies" is not only unrealistic, but virtually impossible!
Yeah, okay, sure, yeah.
I guess.
Still...you gotta admit, that baby is going to be so hot!

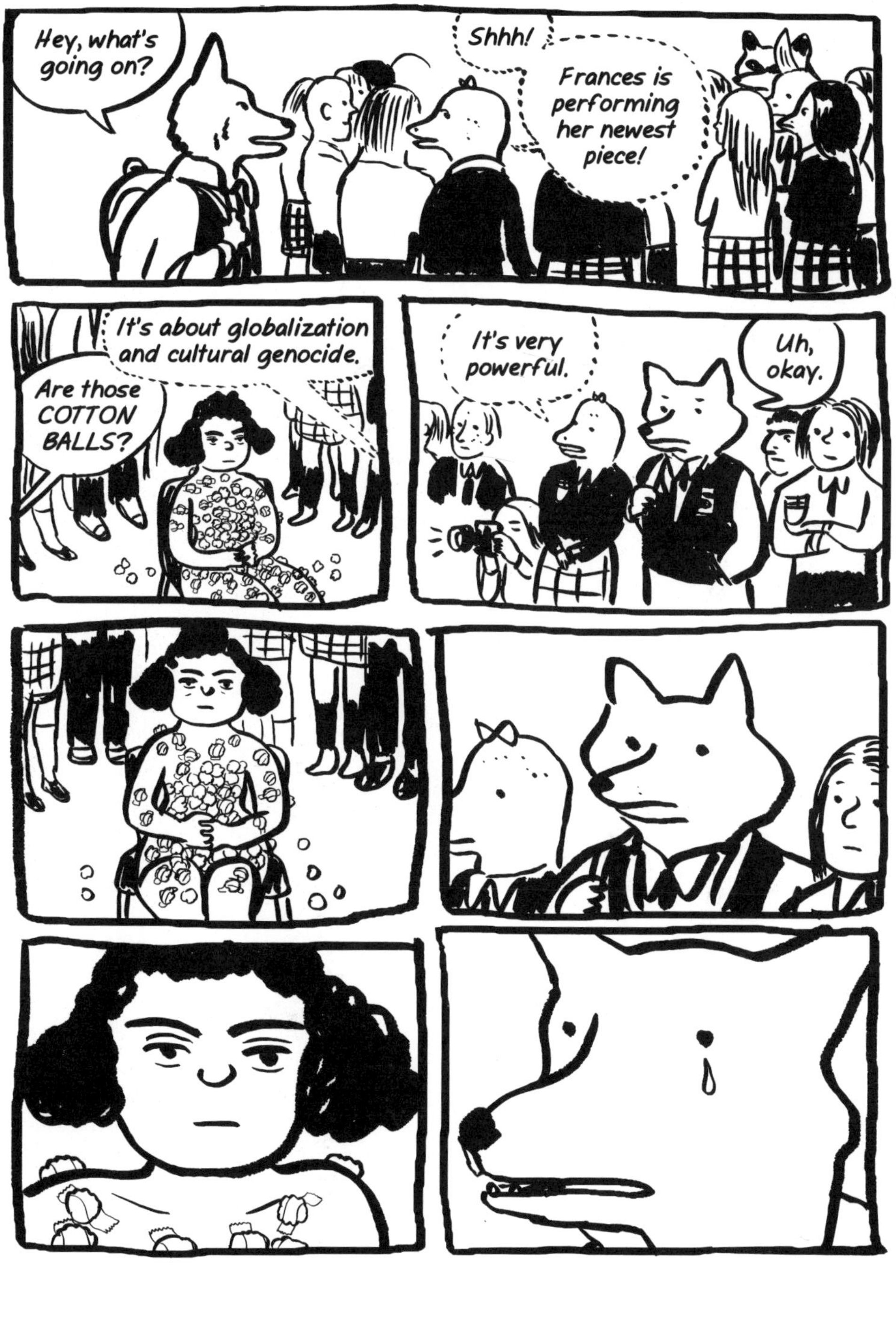
Hey, what's going on?
Shhh!
Frances is performing her newest piece!
It's about globalization and cultural genocide.
Are those COTTON BALLS?
It's very powerful.
Uh, okay.

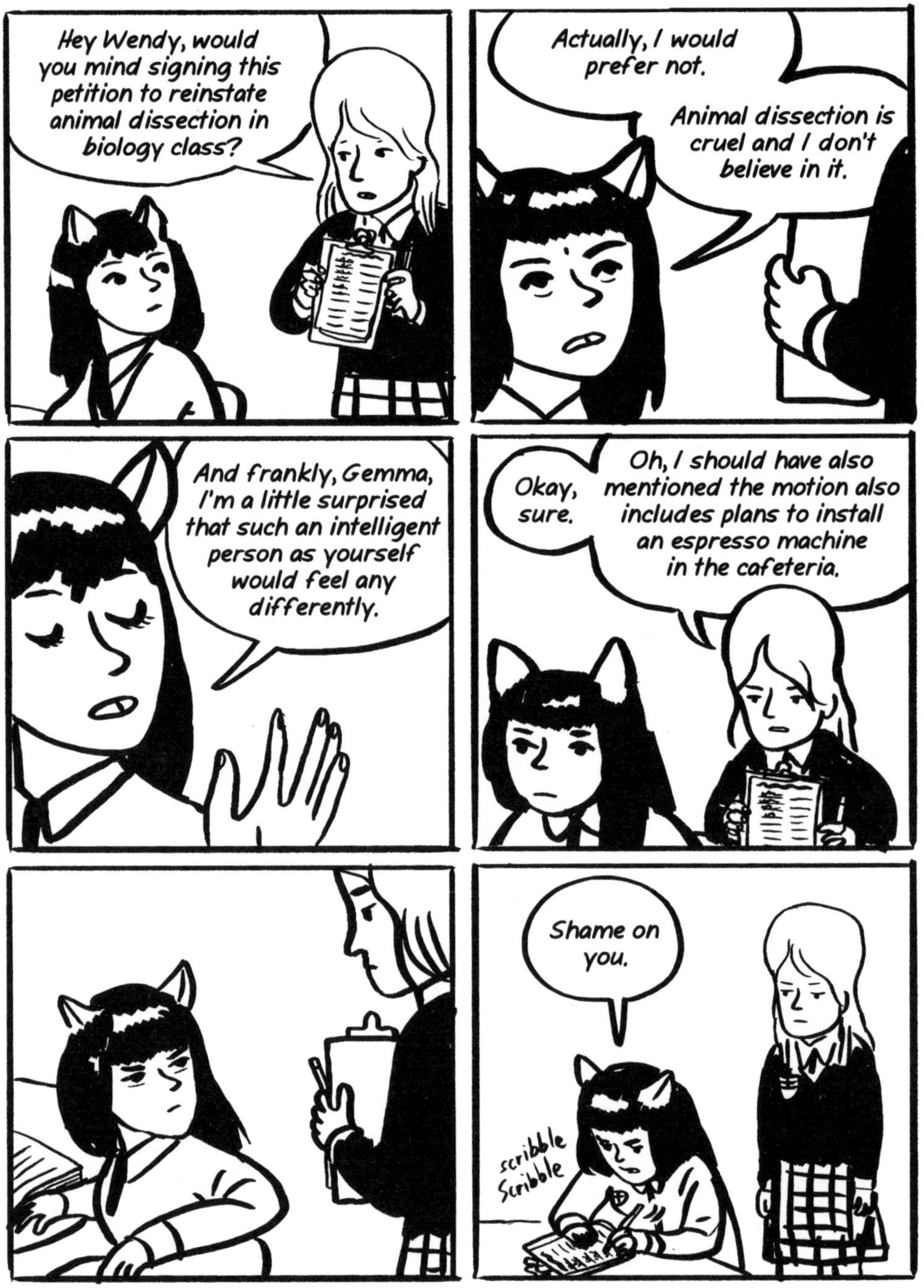

Hey Wendy, would you mind signing this petition to reinstate animal dissection in biology class?
Actually, I would prefer not.
Animal dissection is cruel and I don't believe in it.
And frankly, Gemma, I'm a little surprised that such an intelligent person as yourself would feel any differently.
Oh, I should have also mentioned the motion also includes plans to install an espresso machine in the cafeteria.
Okay, sure.
Shame on you.
scribble
Scribble

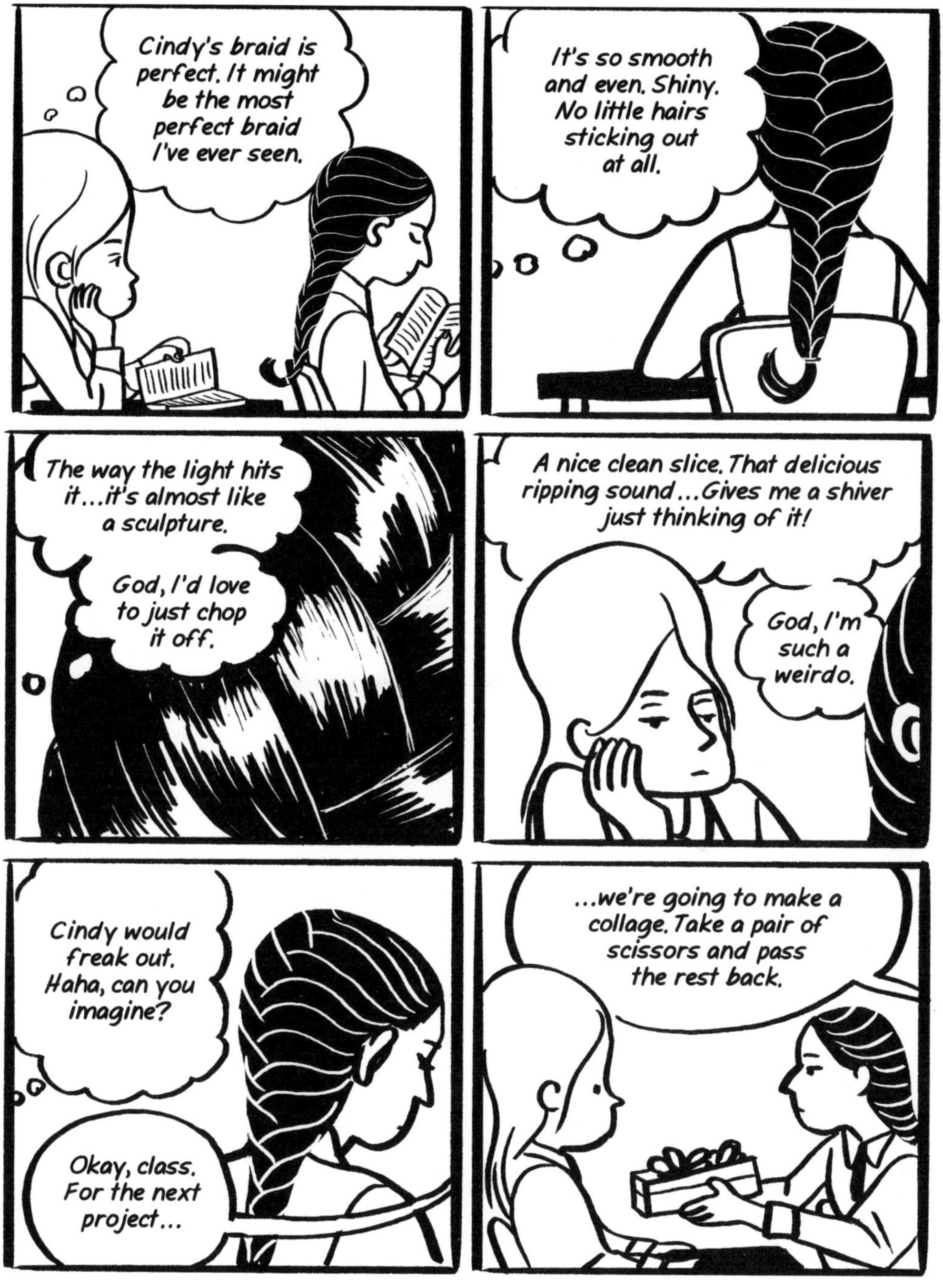
Cindy's braid is perfect. It might be the most perfect braid I've ever seen.
It's so smooth and even. Shiny. No little hairs sticking out at all.
The way the light hits it...it's almost like a sculpture.
God, I'd love to just chop it off.
A nice clean slice. That delicious ripping sound...Gives me a shiver just thinking of it!
God, I'm such a weirdo.
Cindy would freak out. Haha, can you imagine?
Okay, class. For the next project...
...we're going to make a collage. Take a pair of scissors and pass the rest back.

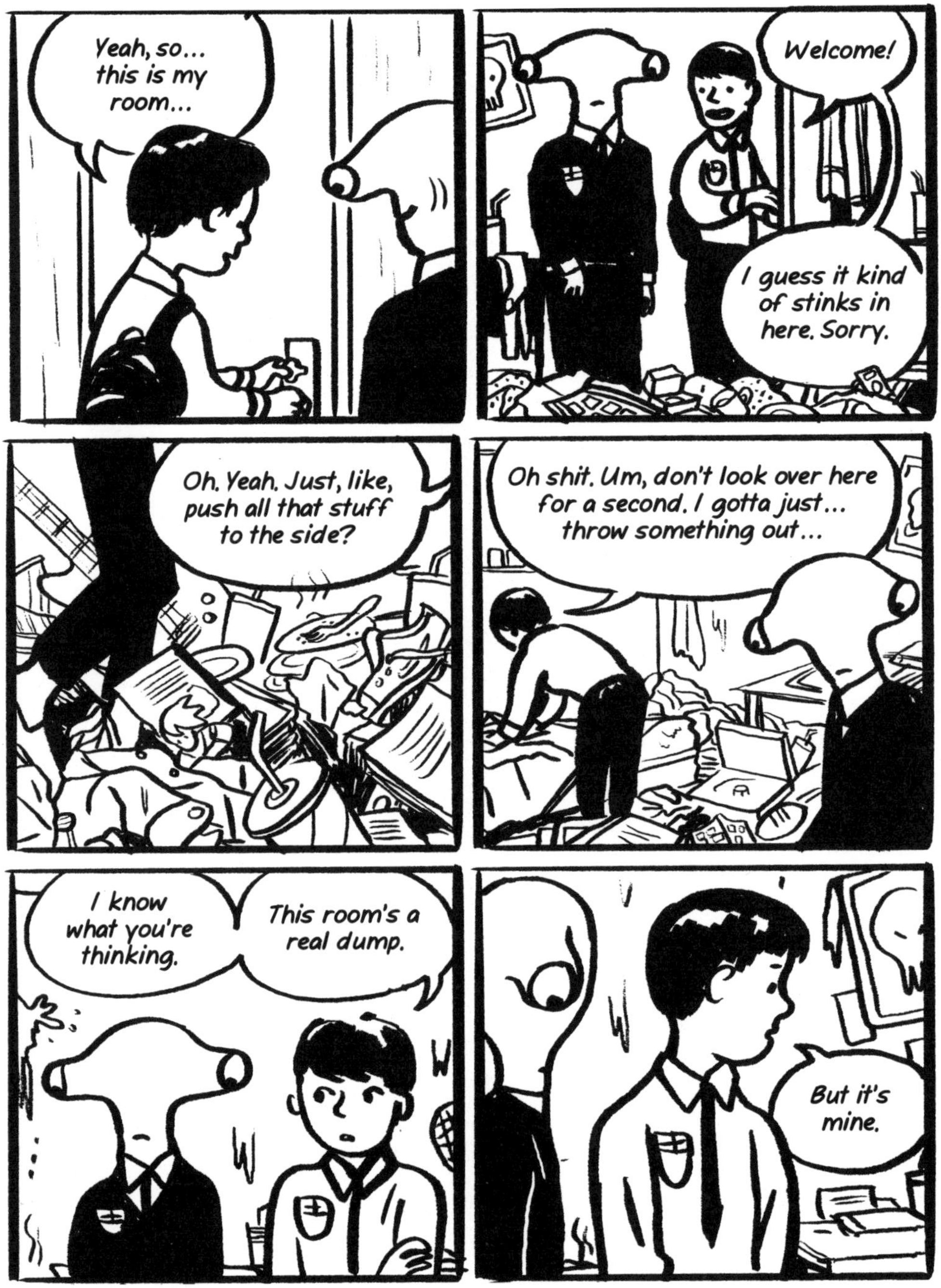
Yeah, so... this is my room...
Welcome!
I guess it kind of stinks in here. Sorry.
Oh. Yeah. Just, like, push all that stuff to the side?
Oh shit. Um, don't look over here for a second. I gotta just... throw something out...
I know what you're thinking.
This room's a real dump.
But it's mine.

UGH! GOD, I hate the Internet!

SLAM

The Internet is like a sex party where you think you're going to meet some cute, cool people, share a bit of yourself, learn a bit about yourself. Maybe make some new friends, keep it casual...

But in reality it's this orgiastic frenzy of... UNSATIABLENESS. Ill-mannered brutes hungrily consuming. Taking what they want and tossing you aside once they've had their fill! The collective mind has the attention span of a gnat!

It started off so thrilling and new. Now we're all addicts looking for junk, our junk being attention and approval.

Sex party?

Is that a real place?

God, I'm such a hypo-crite.

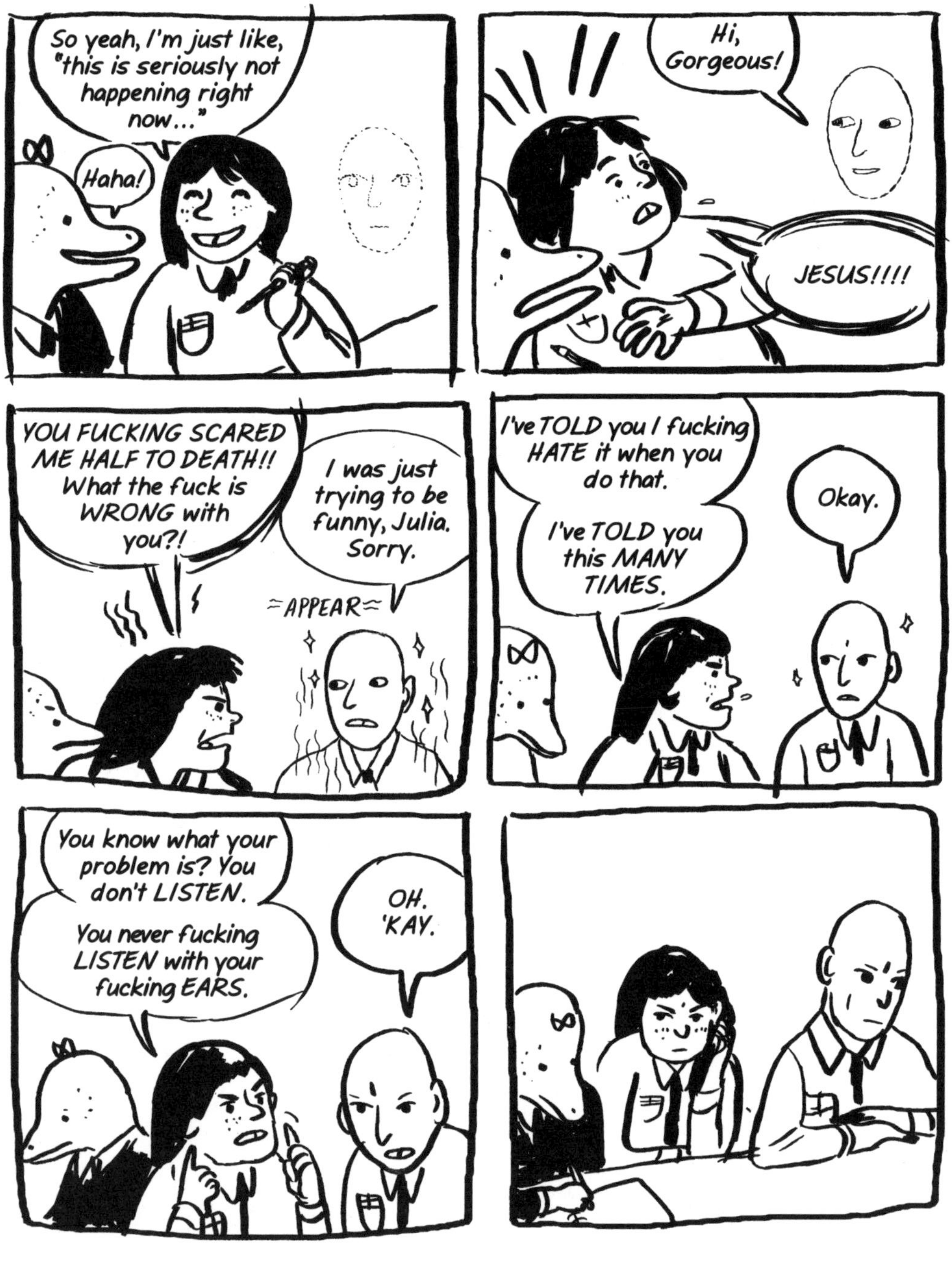
So yeah, I'm just like, "this is seriously not happening right now..."
Haha!
Hi, Gorgeous!
JESUS!!!!
YOU FUCKING SCARED ME HALF TO DEATH!! What the fuck is WRONG with you?!
I was just trying to be funny, Julia. Sorry.
≈APPEAR≈
I've TOLD you I fucking HATE it when you do that.
I've TOLD you this MANY TIMES.
Okay.
You know what your problem is? You don't LISTEN.
You never fucking LISTEN with your fucking EARS.
OH. 'KAY.

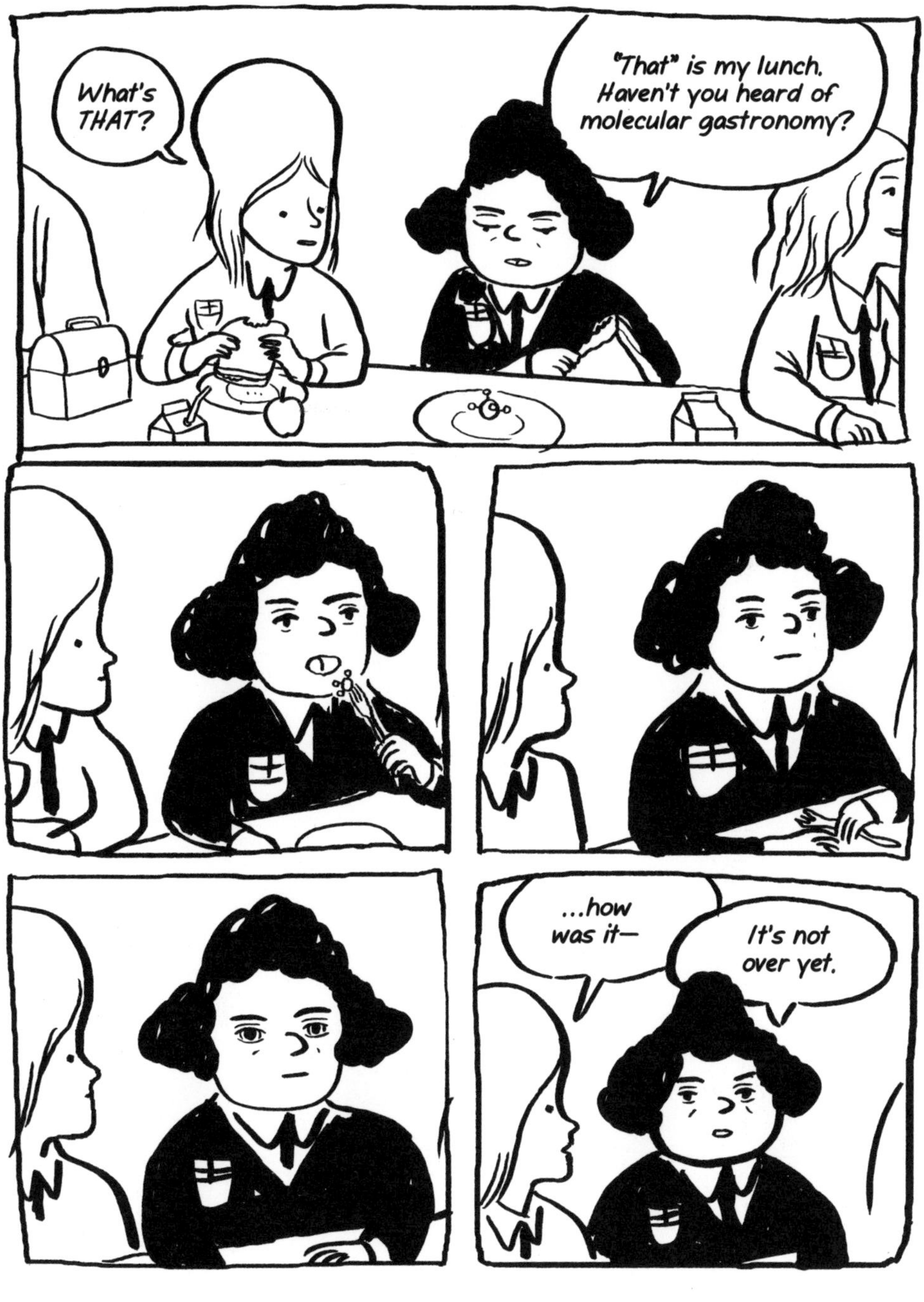
What's THAT?
"That" is my lunch. Haven't you heard of molecular gastronomy?
...how was it—
It's not over yet.

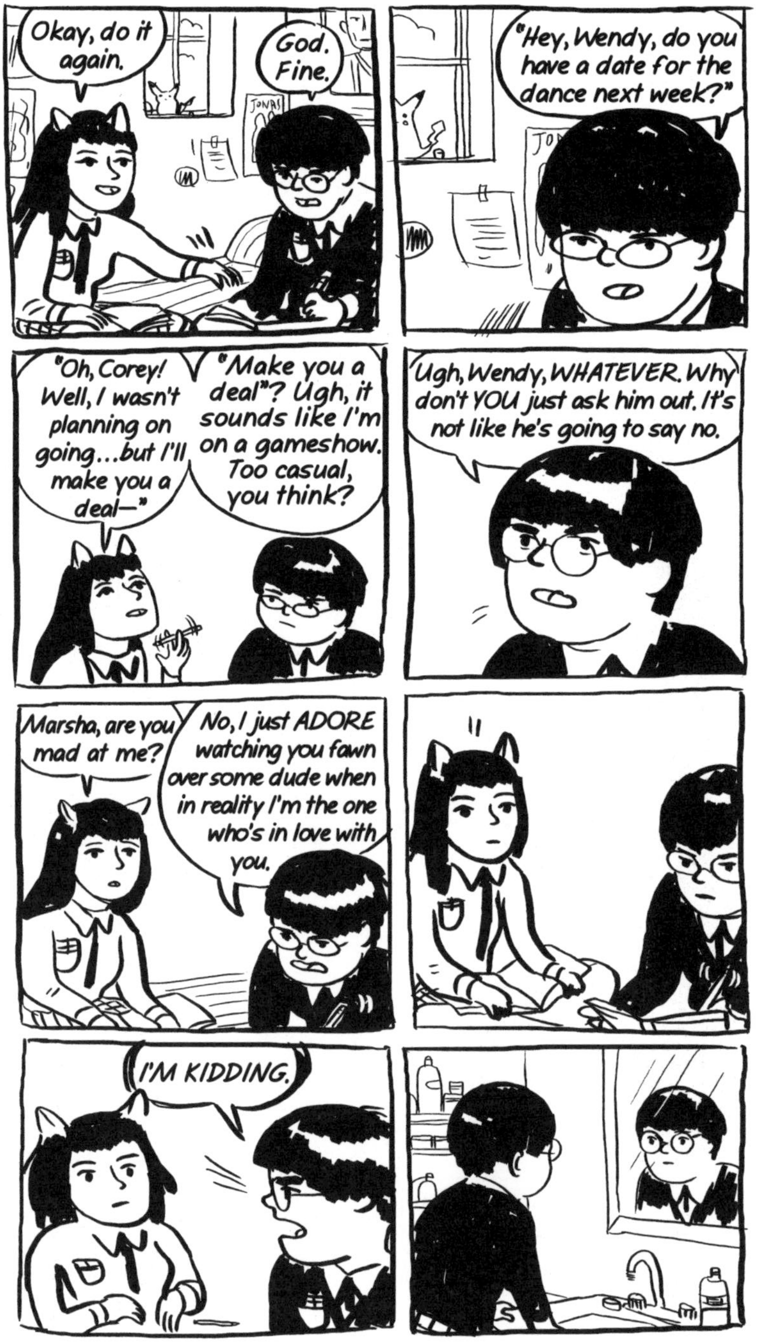
Okay, do it again.
God. Fine.
"Hey, Wendy, do you have a date for the dance next week?"
"Oh, Corey! Well, I wasn't planning on going...but I'll make you a deal—"
"Make you a deal"? Ugh, it sounds like I'm on a gameshow. Too casual, you think?
Ugh, Wendy, WHATEVER. Why don't YOU just ask him out. It's not like he's going to say no.
Marsha, are you mad at me?
No, I just ADORE watching you fawn over some dude when in reality I'm the one who's in love with you.
I'M KIDDING.

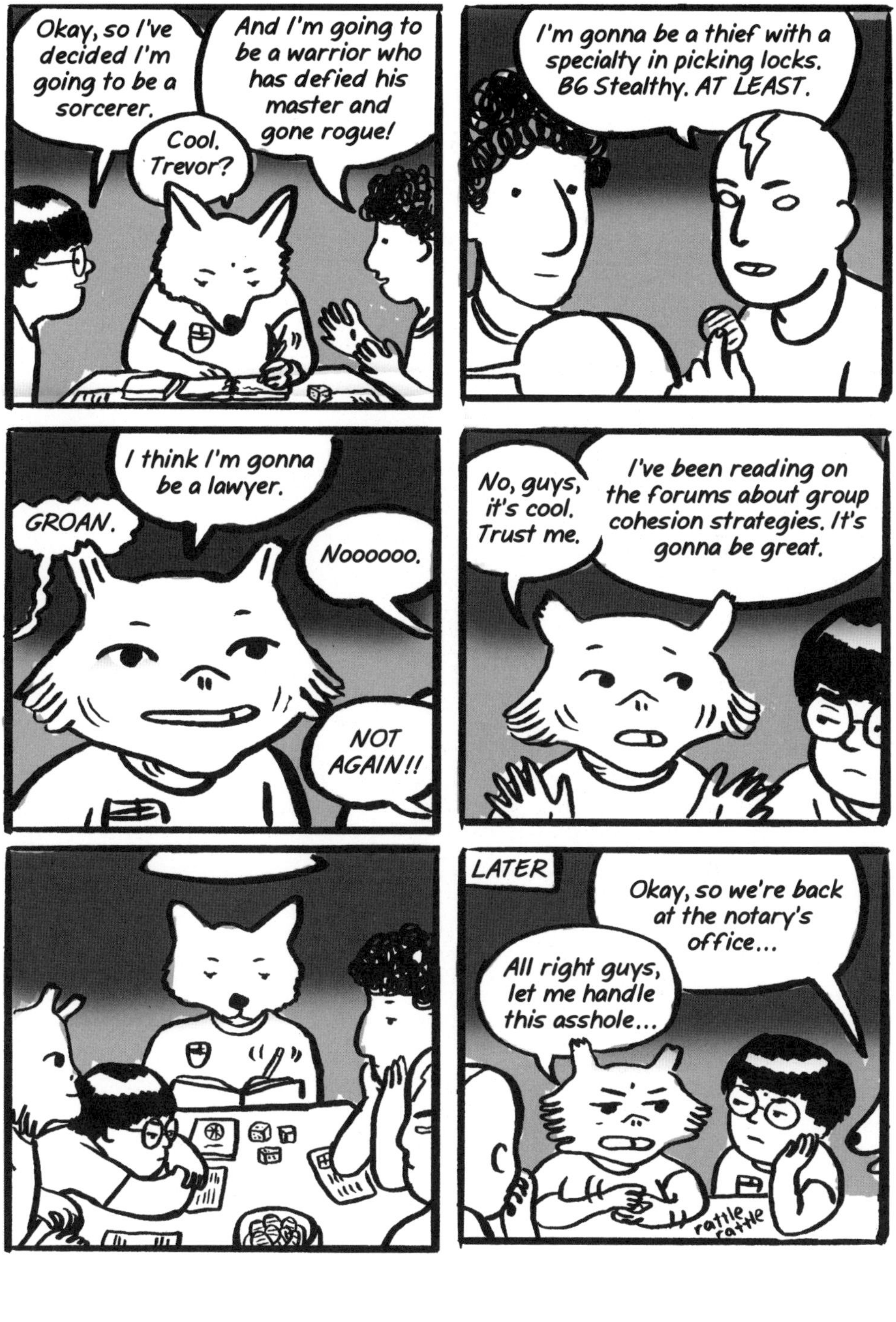
Okay, so I've decided I'm going to be a sorcerer.
Cool. Trevor?
And I'm going to be a warrior who has defied his master and gone rogue!
I'm gonna be a thief with a specialty in picking locks. B6 Stealthy. AT LEAST.
I think I'm gonna be a lawyer.
GROAN.
Noooooo.
NOT AGAIN!!
No, guys, it's cool. Trust me.
I've been reading on the forums about group cohesion strategies. It's gonna be great.
LATER
Okay, so we're back at the notary's office...
All right guys, let me handle this asshole...
rattle rattle

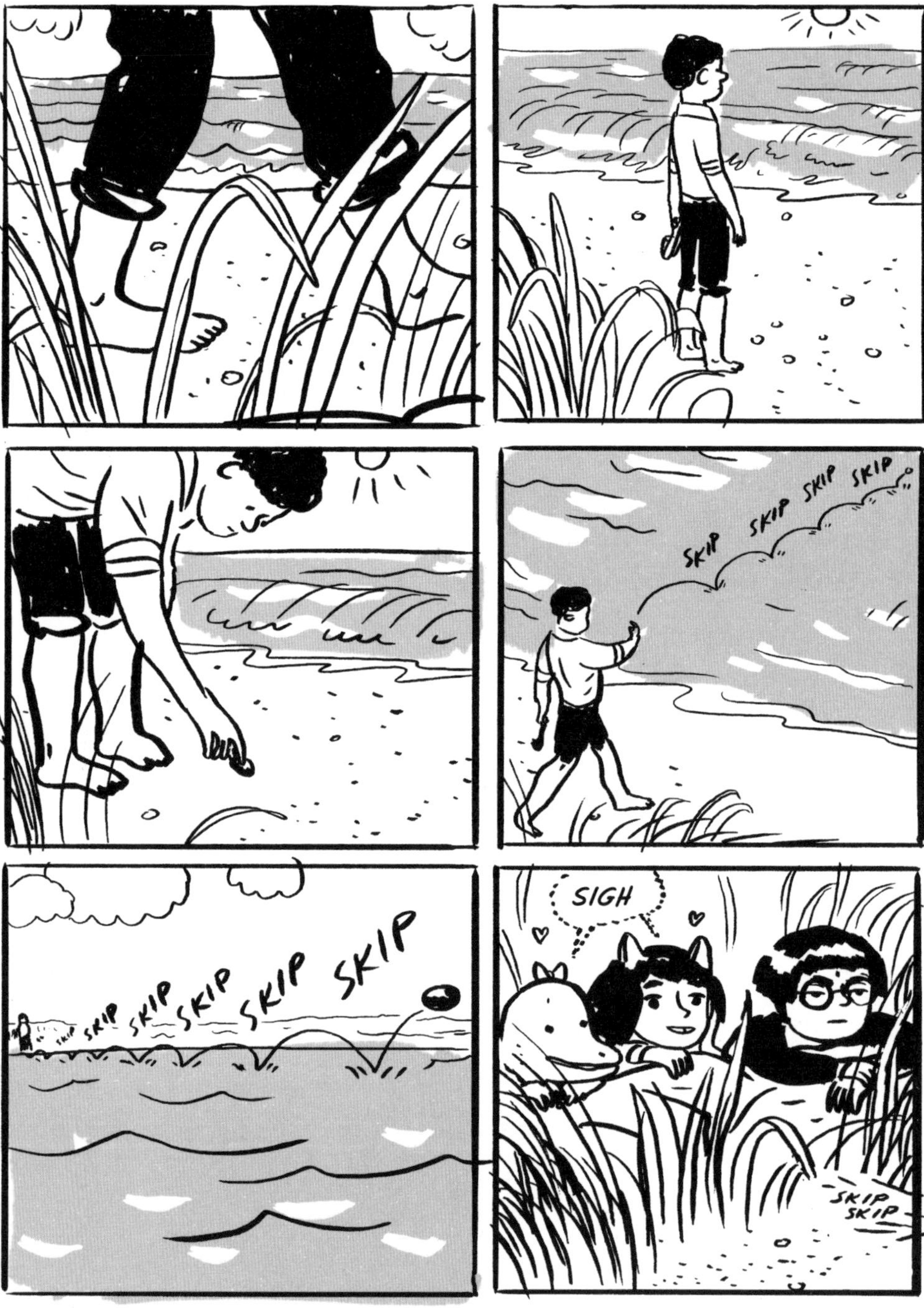
SKIP SKIP SKIP SKIP
SKIP SKIP SKIP SKIP SKIP SKIP
SIGH
SKIP SKIP

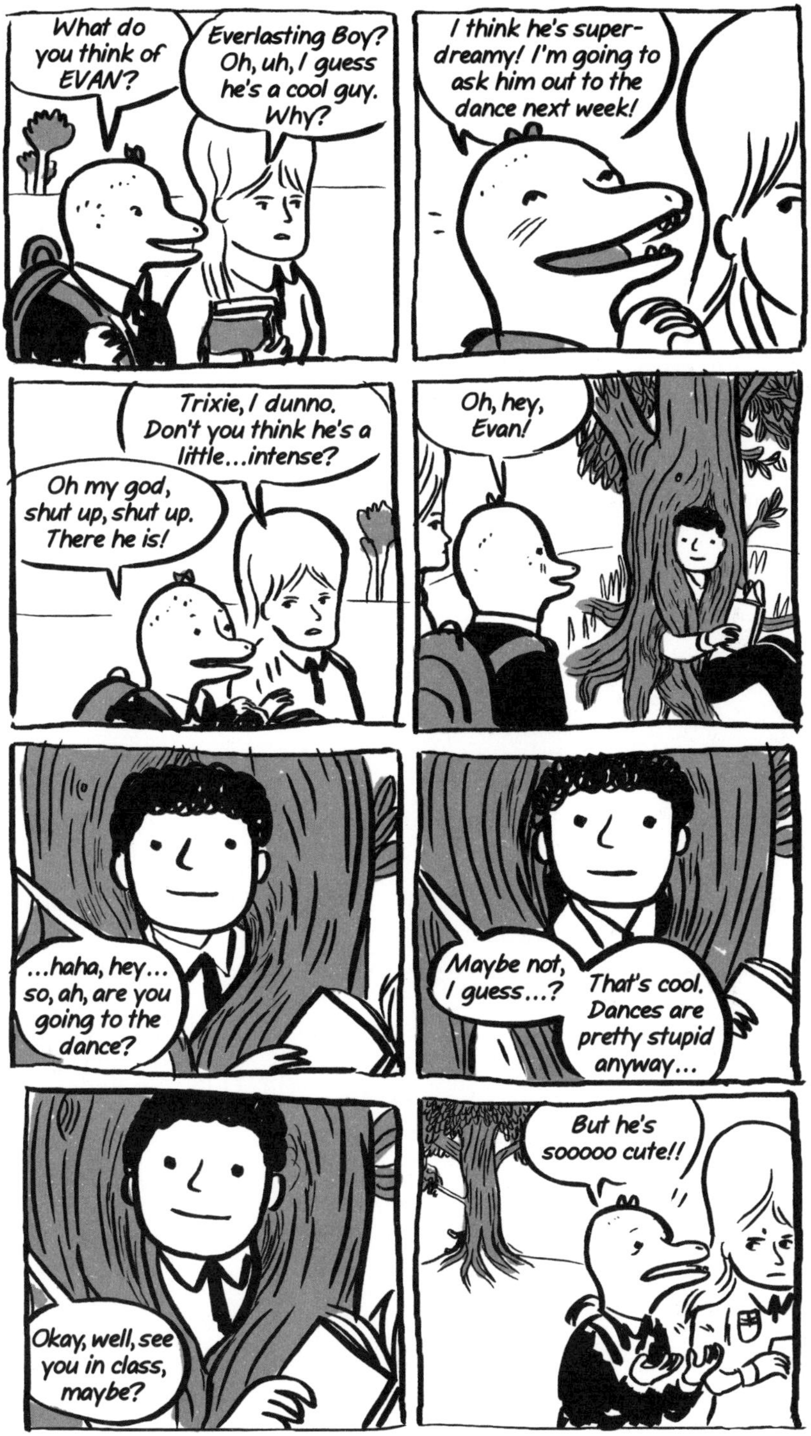

What do you think of EVAN?
Everlasting Boy? Oh, uh, I guess he's a cool guy. Why?
I think he's super-dreamy! I'm going to ask him out to the dance next week!
Trixie, I dunno. Don't you think he's a little...intense?
Oh my god, shut up, shut up. There he is!
Oh, hey, Evan!
...haha, hey... so, ah, are you going to the dance?
Maybe not, I guess...?
That's cool. Dances are pretty stupid anyway...
Okay, well, see you in class, maybe?
But he's sooooo cute!!

I free my hand and reach out for Gwendolyn. Do I grab her in time?

<rattle> ...three successes. You do.

You grab her hand and pull her off from the cliff face. You feel her shaking with fear. Her eyes are filled with terror.

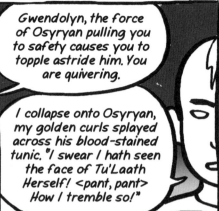

Gwendolyn, the force of Osyryan pulling you to safety causes you to topple astride him. You are quivering.

I collapse onto Osyryan, my golden curls splayed across his blood-stained tunic. "I swear I hath seen the face of Tu'Laath Herself! <pant, pant> How I tremble so!"

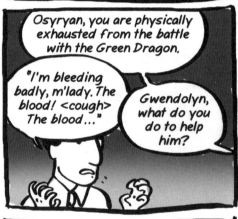

Osyryan, you are physically exhausted from the battle with the Green Dragon.

"I'm bleeding badly, m'lady. The blood! <cough> The blood..."

Gwendolyn, what do you do to help him?

Riiiiiip! I rip some of my fabric from my bodice. I gently dress the wound and touch his brow. It's cold. So, so very cold.

He's lost too much blood. His eyelids are fluttering.

"No. NO! You cannot leave me, Osyryan! For... for...I am with child!"

Okay, guys! That seems like a good place to end tonight's sesh! Good one.

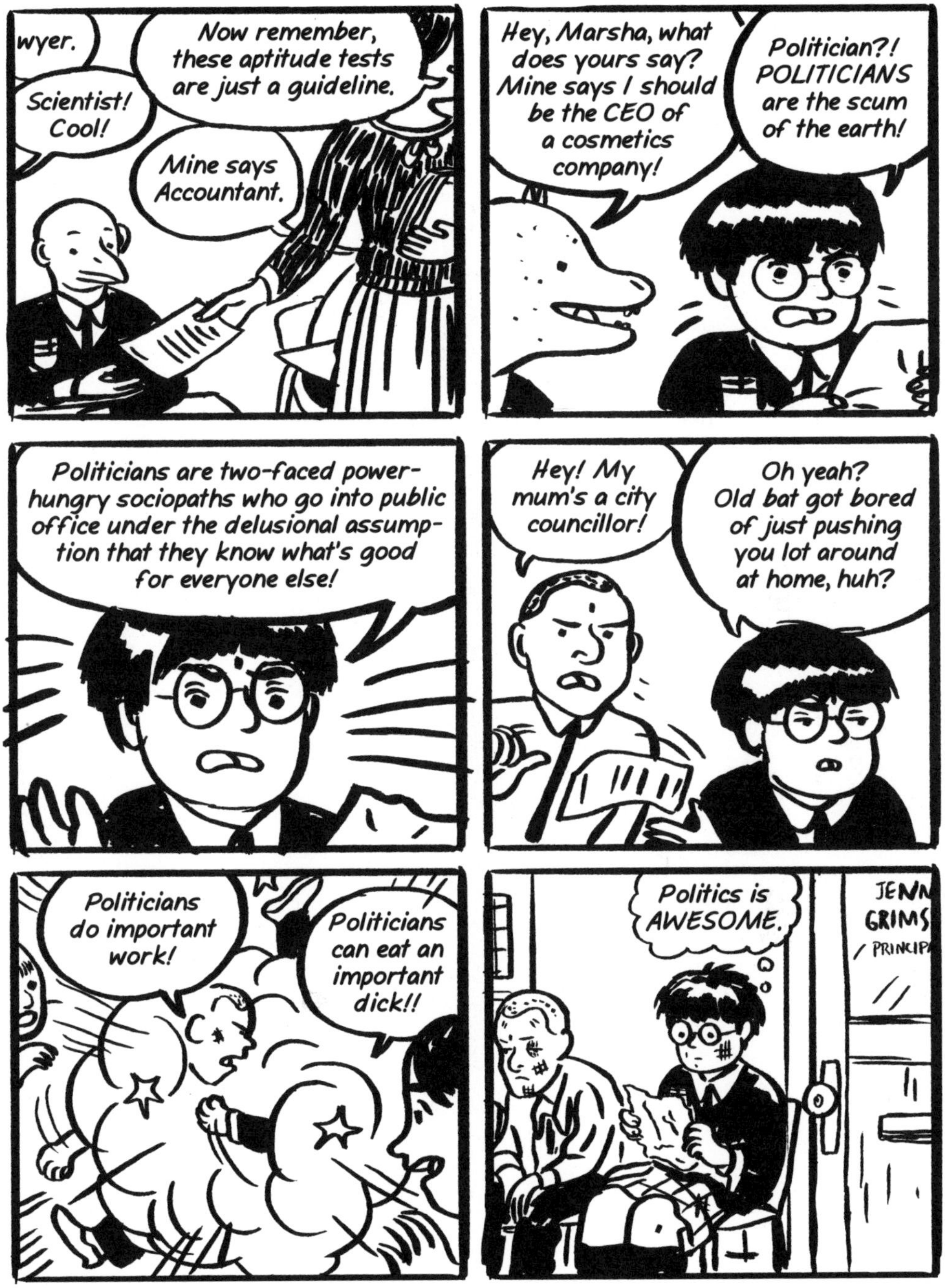
wyer.
Now remember, these aptitude tests are just a guideline.
Scientist! Cool!
Mine says Accountant.
Hey, Marsha, what does yours say? Mine says I should be the CEO of a cosmetics company!
Politician?! POLITICIANS are the scum of the earth!
Politicians are two-faced power-hungry sociopaths who go into public office under the delusional assumption that they know what's good for everyone else!
Hey! My mum's a city councillor!
Oh yeah? Old bat got bored of just pushing you lot around at home, huh?
Politicians do important work!
Politicians can eat an important dick!!
Politics is AWESOME.
JENN
GRIMS
/ PRINCIP

Hey, you look really pretty today.
Hahahaha! P'shaw, no I don't! Oh you're such a LIAR! Hee hee!
You really need to learn to take a compliment.

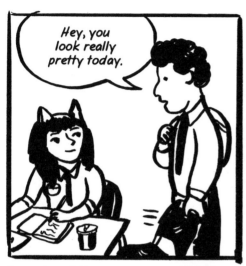

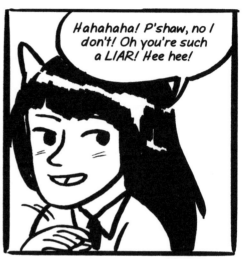

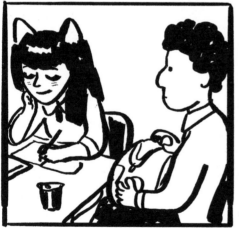

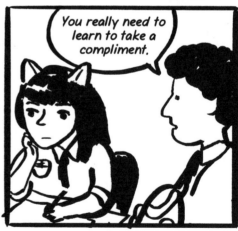

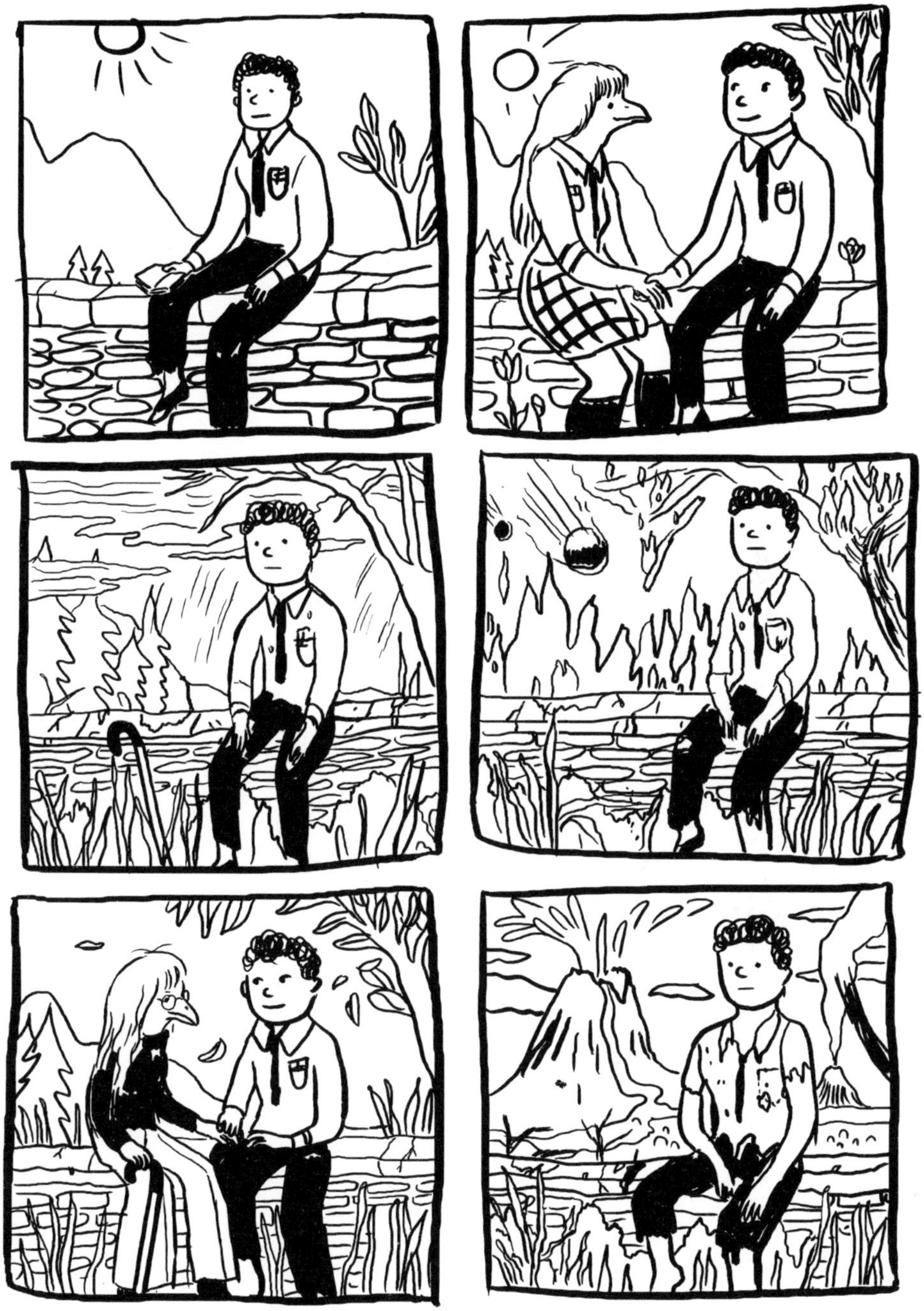

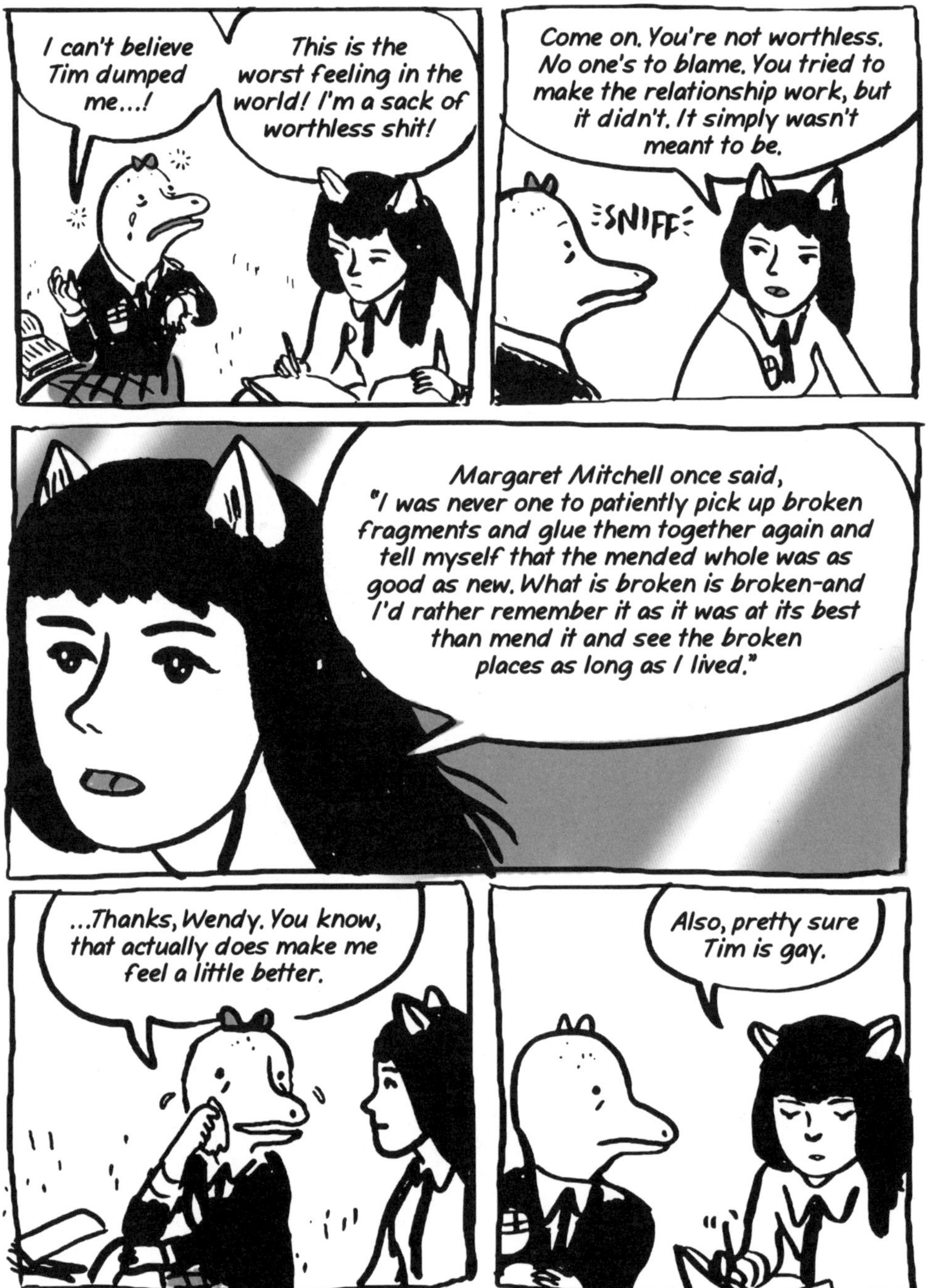
I can't believe Tim dumped me...!
This is the worst feeling in the world! I'm a sack of worthless shit!
Come on. You're not worthless. No one's to blame. You tried to make the relationship work, but it didn't. It simply wasn't meant to be.
SNIFF
Margaret Mitchell once said, "I was never one to patiently pick up broken fragments and glue them together again and tell myself that the mended whole was as good as new. What is broken is broken-and I'd rather remember it as it was at its best than mend it and see the broken places as long as I lived."
...Thanks, Wendy. You know, that actually does make me feel a little better.
Also, pretty sure Tim is gay.

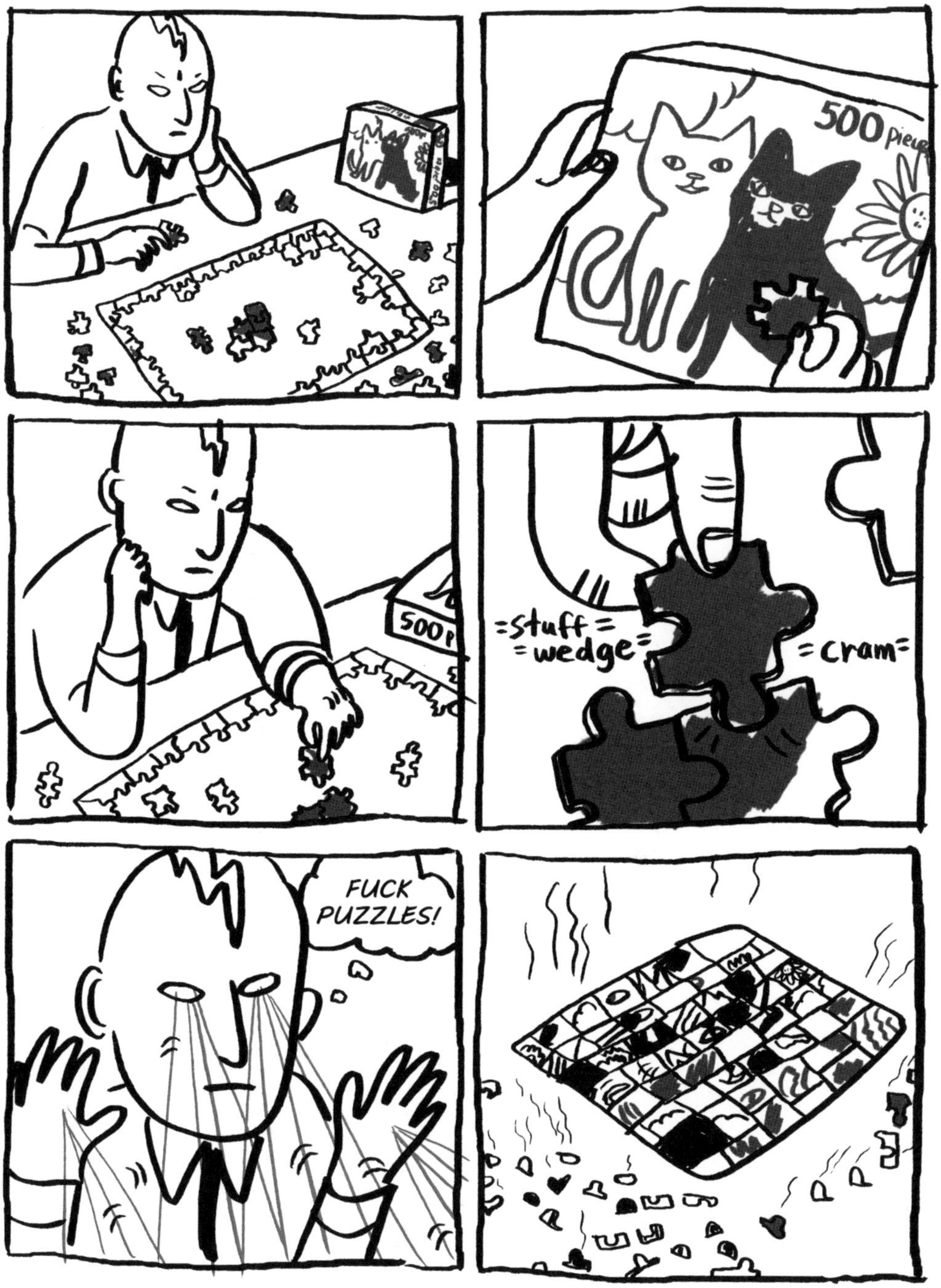
500 pieces
500 p
=stuff=
=wedge=
=cram=
FUCK PUZZLES!

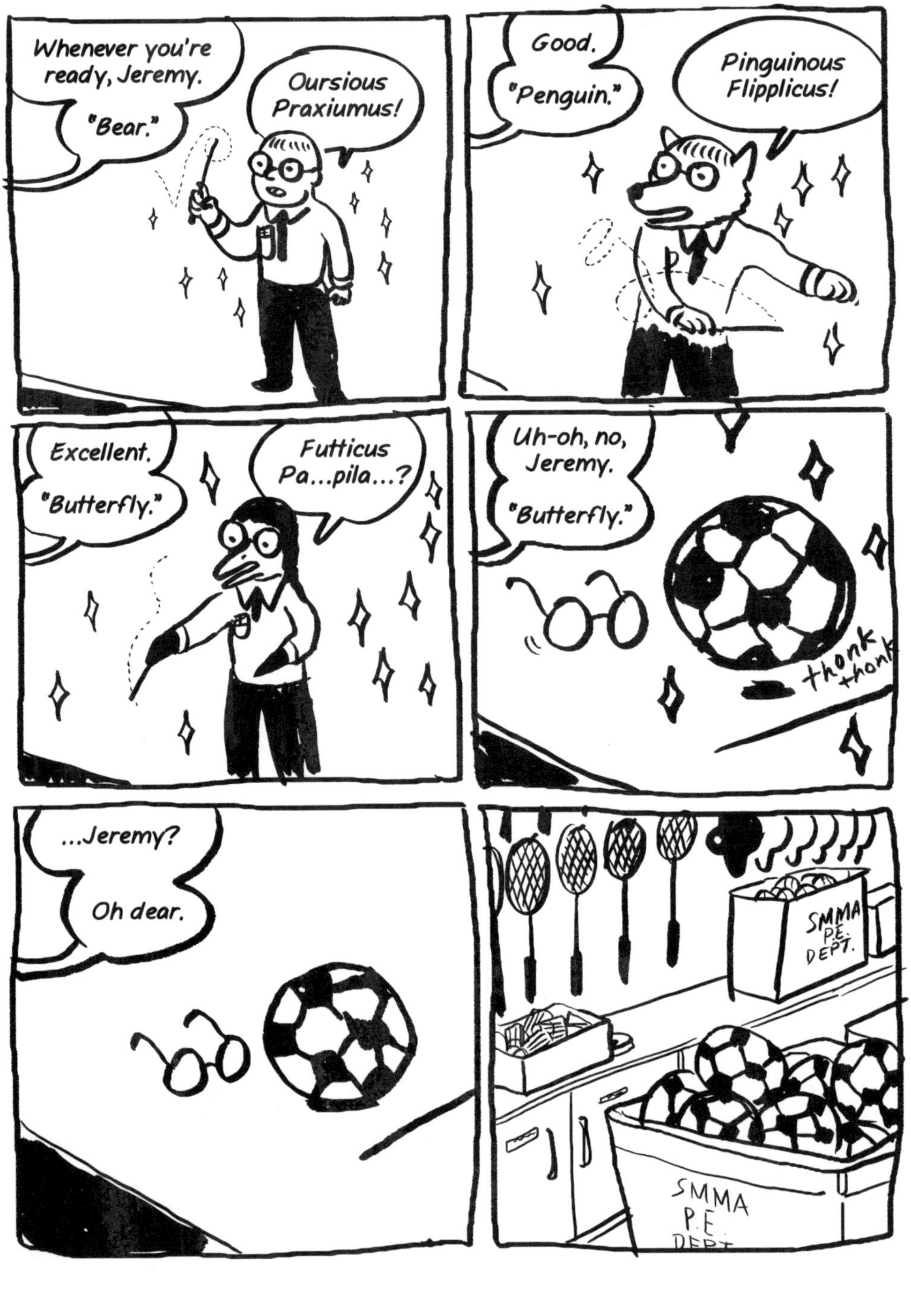
Whenever you're ready, Jeremy.
"Bear."
Oursious Praxiumus!
Good.
"Penguin."
Pinguinous Flipplicus!
Excellent.
"Butterfly."
Futticus Pa...pila...?
Uh-oh, no, Jeremy.
"Butterfly."
thonk thonk
...Jeremy?
Oh dear.
SMMA P.E. DEPT.
SMMA P.E.

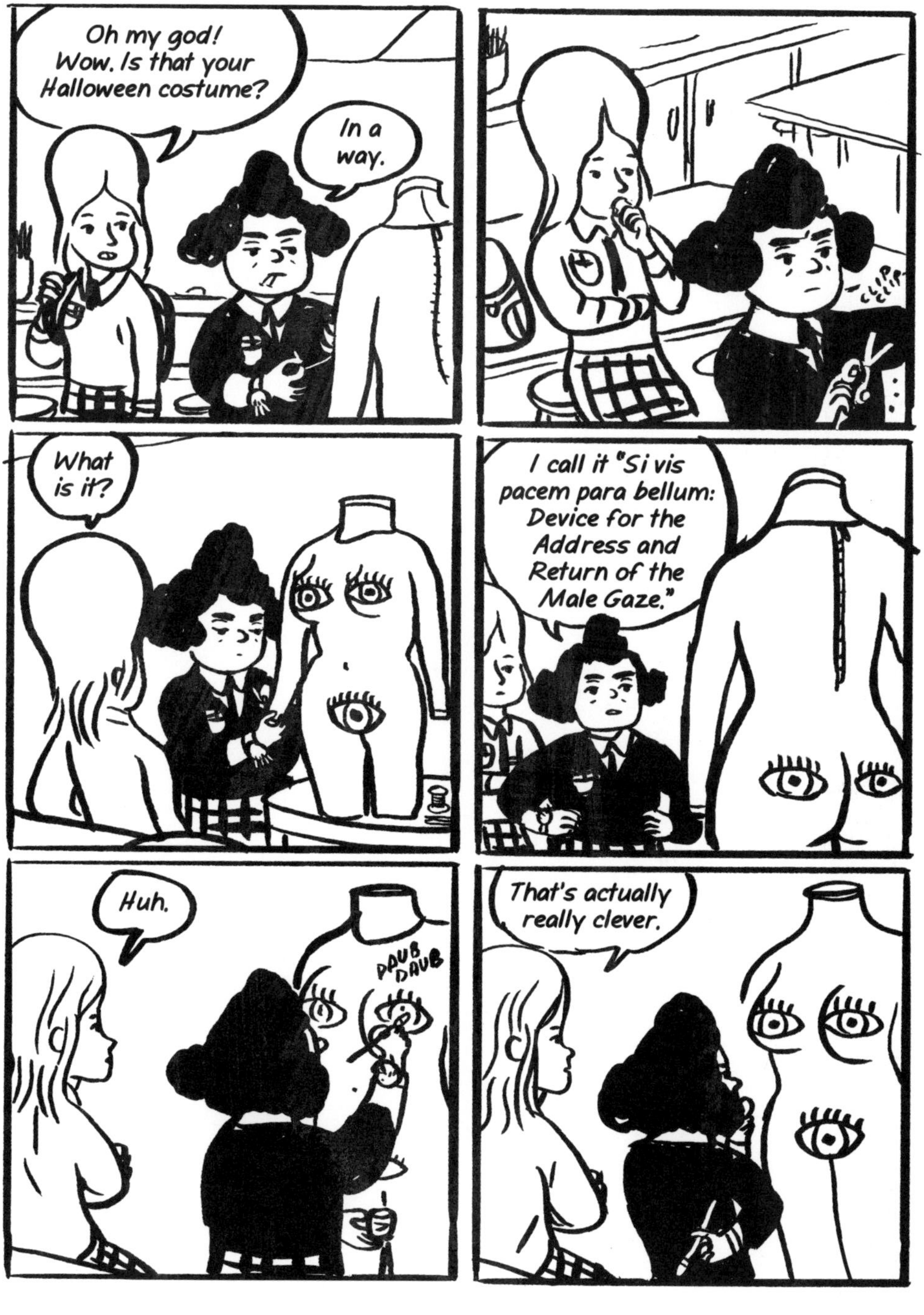
Oh my god! Wow. Is that your Halloween costume?
In a way.
CLIPP CLIPP
What is it?
I call it "Si vis pacem para bellum: Device for the Address and Return of the Male Gaze."
Huh.
DAUB DAUB
That's actually really clever.

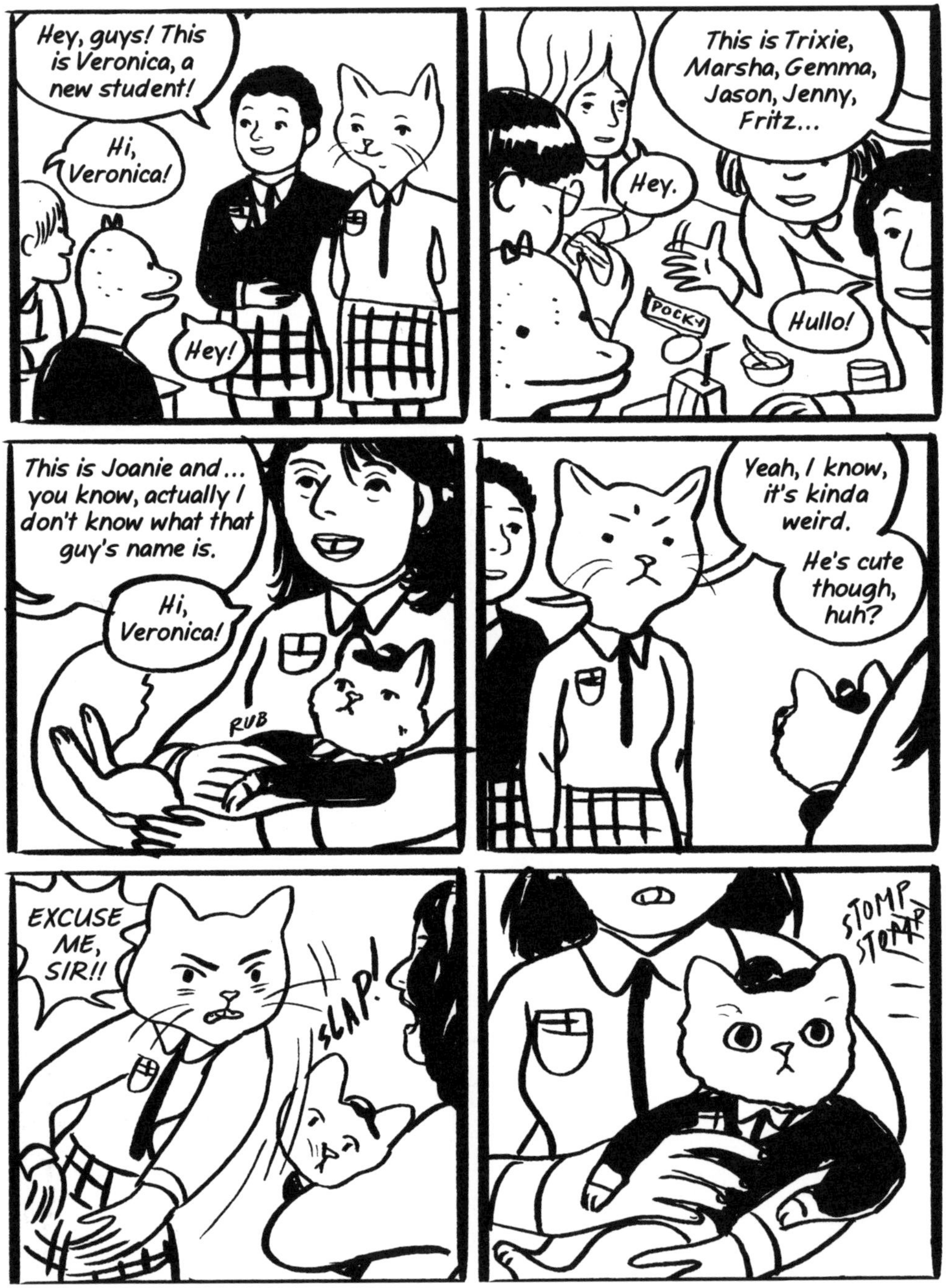
Hey, guys! This is Veronica, a new student!
Hi, Veronica!
Hey!
This is Trixie, Marsha, Gemma, Jason, Jenny, Fritz...
Hey.
POCKY
Hullo!
This is Joanie and... you know, actually I don't know what that guy's name is.
Hi, Veronica!
RUB
Yeah, I know, it's kinda weird.
He's cute though, huh?
EXCUSE ME, SIR!!
SLAP!
STOMP STOMP

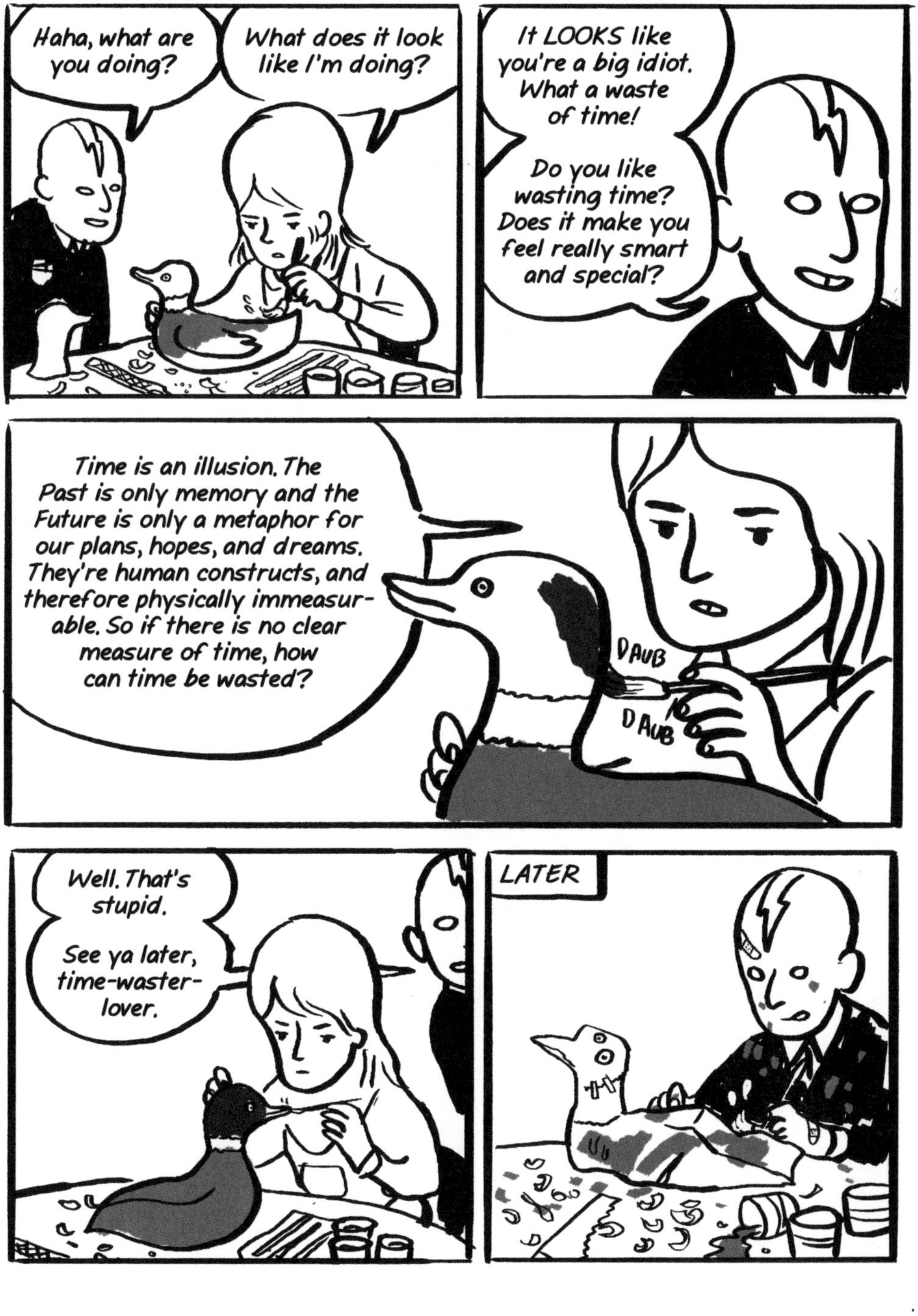
Haha, what are you doing?
What does it look like I'm doing?
It LOOKS like you're a big idiot. What a waste of time!
Do you like wasting time? Does it make you feel really smart and special?
Time is an illusion. The Past is only memory and the Future is only a metaphor for our plans, hopes, and dreams. They're human constructs, and therefore physically immeasurable. So if there is no clear measure of time, how can time be wasted?
DAUB
DAUB
Well. That's stupid.
See ya later, time-waster-lover.
LATER

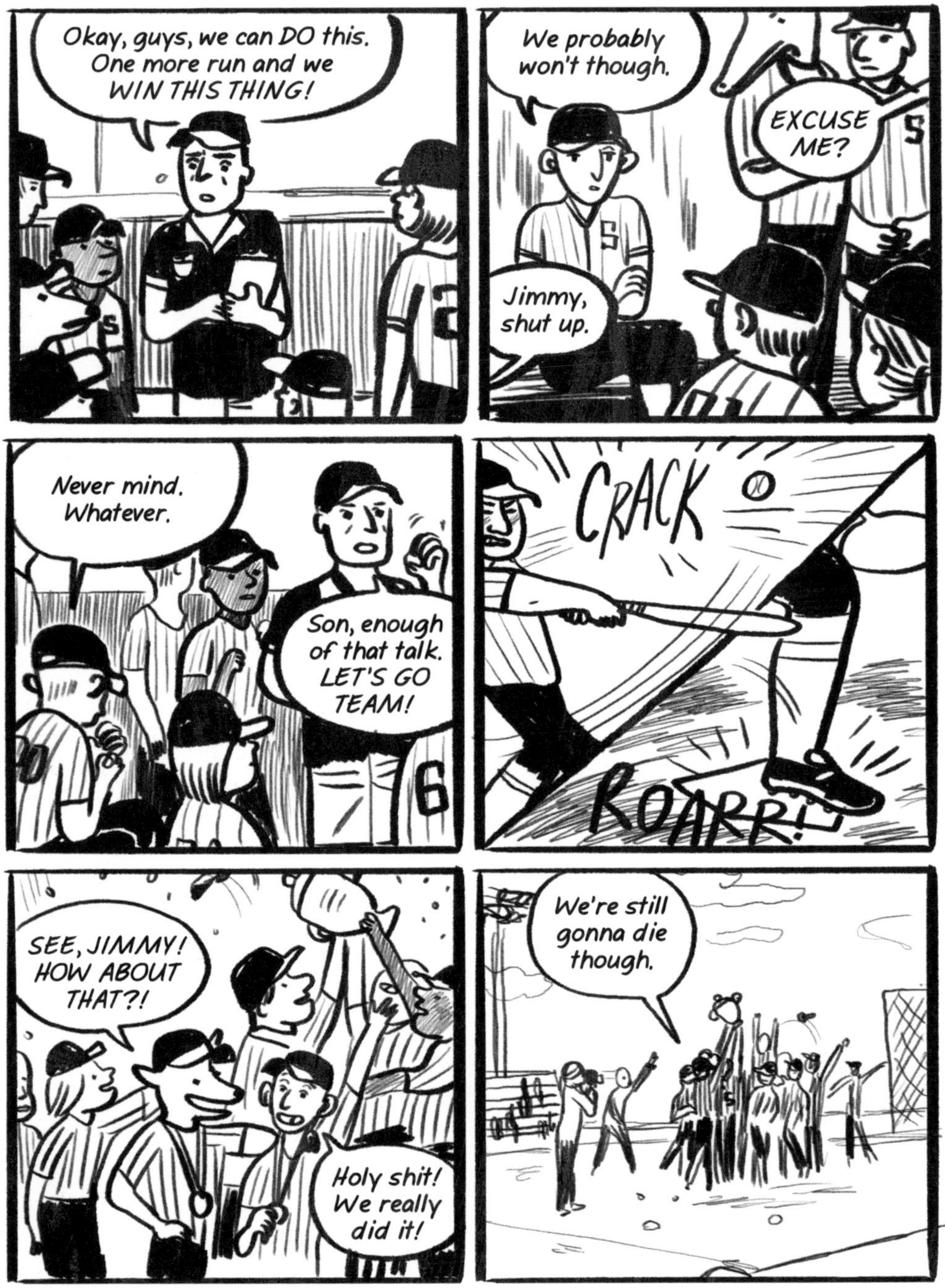
Okay, guys, we can DO this. One more run and we WIN THIS THING!
We probably won't though.
EXCUSE ME?
Jimmy, shut up.
Never mind. Whatever.
Son, enough of that talk. LET'S GO TEAM!
CRACK
ROARR!
SEE, JIMMY! HOW ABOUT THAT?!
Holy shit! We really did it!
We're still gonna die though.

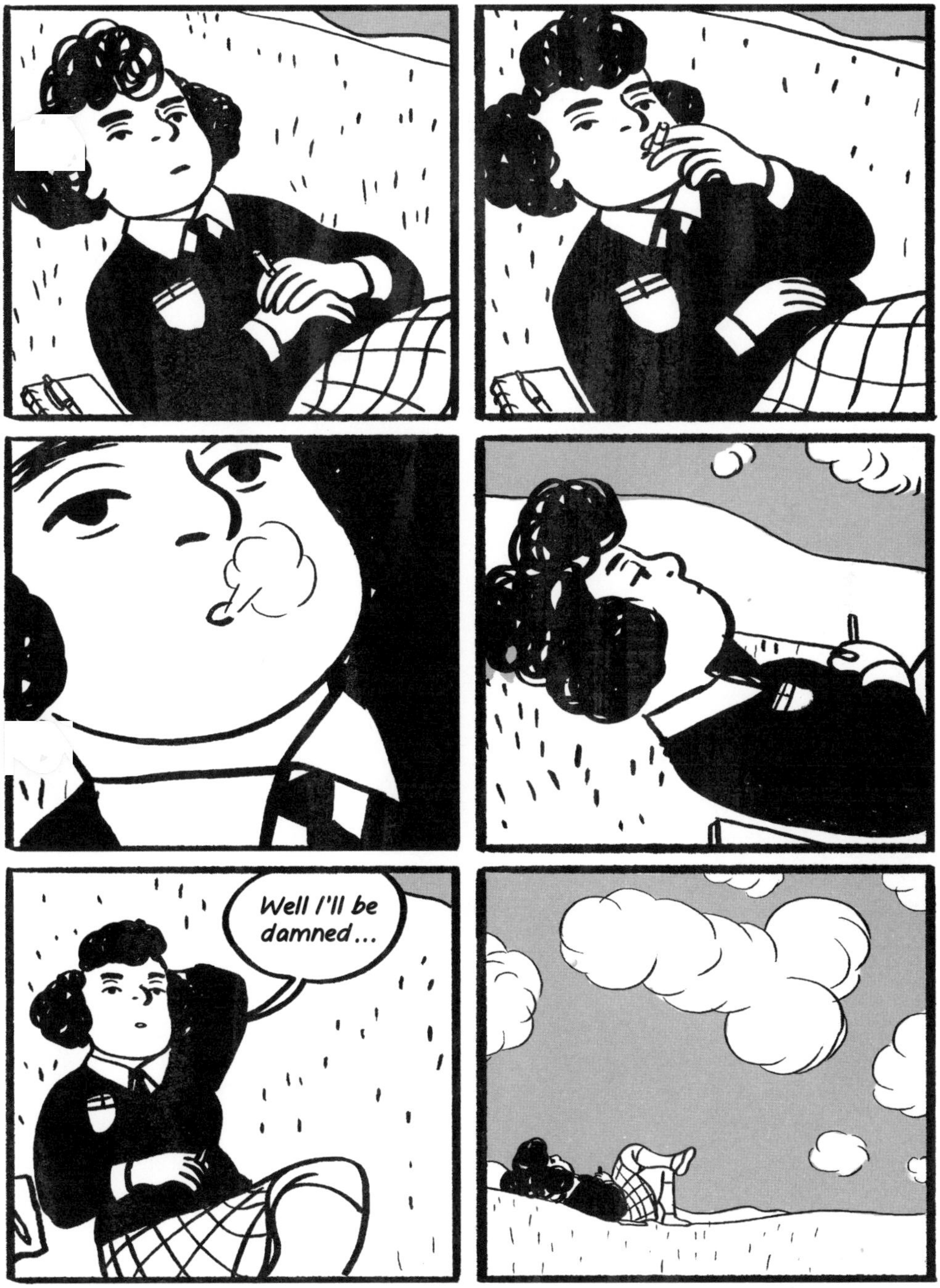
Well I'll be damned...

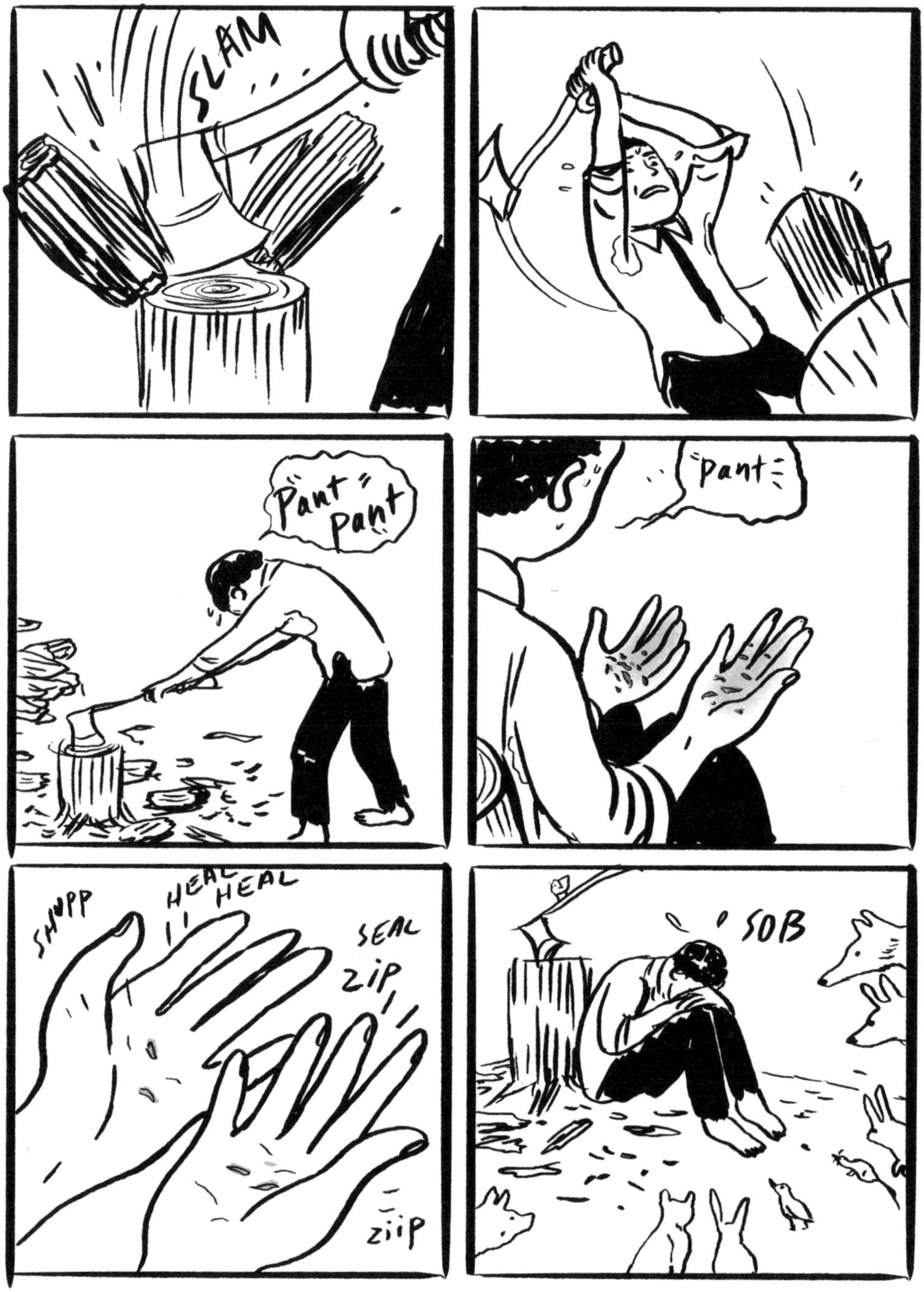
SLAM
Pant pant
pant
SHUPP
HEAL HEAL
SEAL
ZIP
ziip
SOB

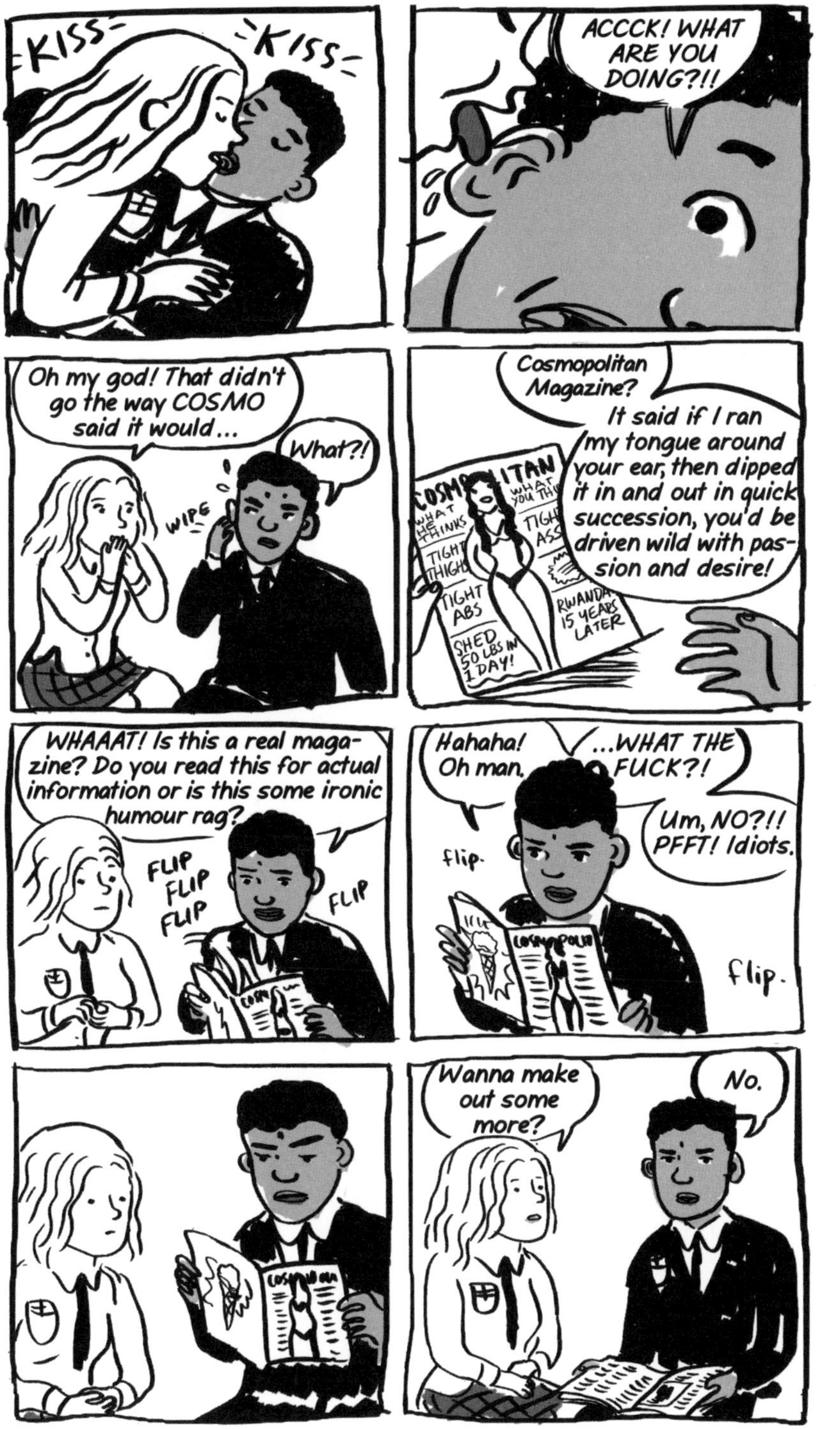
KISS
KISS
ACCCK! WHAT ARE YOU DOING?!!
Oh my god! That didn't go the way COSMO said it would...
What?!
WIPE
Cosmopolitan Magazine?
It said if I ran my tongue around your ear, then dipped it in and out in quick succession, you'd be driven wild with passion and desire!
COSMOPOLITAN
TIGHT ABS
SHED 50 LBS IN 1 DAY!
RWANDA 15 YEARS LATER
WHAAAT! Is this a real magazine? Do you read this for actual information or is this some ironic humour rag?
FLIP FLIP FLIP
FLIP
Hahaha! Oh man.
...WHAT THE FUCK?!
Um, NO?!! PFFT! Idiots.
flip.
flip.
Wanna make out some more?
No.

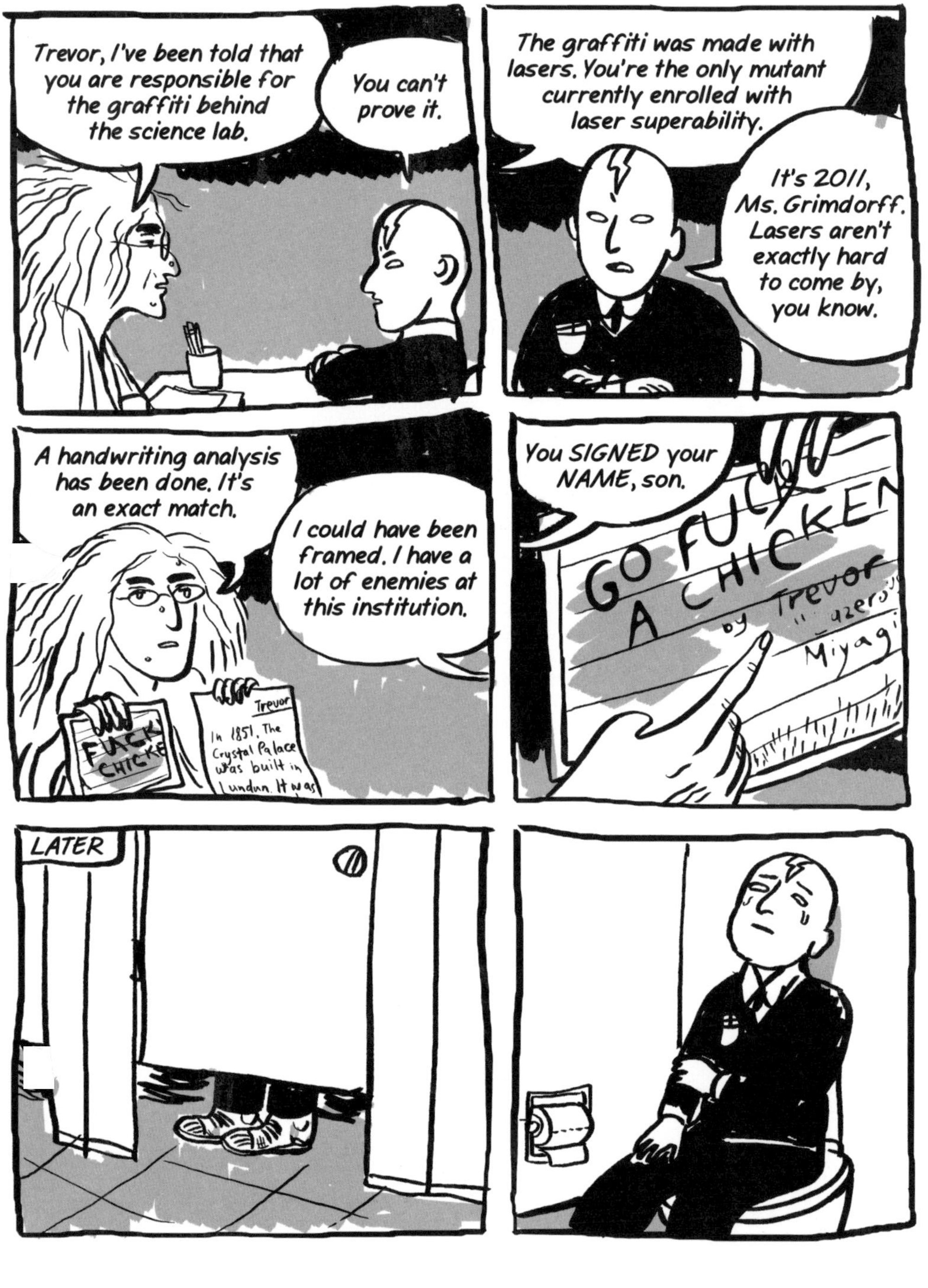
Trevor, I've been told that you are responsible for the graffiti behind the science lab.
You can't prove it.
The graffiti was made with lasers. You're the only mutant currently enrolled with laser superability.
It's 2011, Ms. Grimdorff. Lasers aren't exactly hard to come by, you know.
A handwriting analysis has been done. It's an exact match.
I could have been framed. I have a lot of enemies at this institution.
Trevor
In 1851, The Crystal Palace was built in Lundun. It was
You SIGNED your NAME, son.
A CHICKEN
by Trevor
Miyagi
LATER

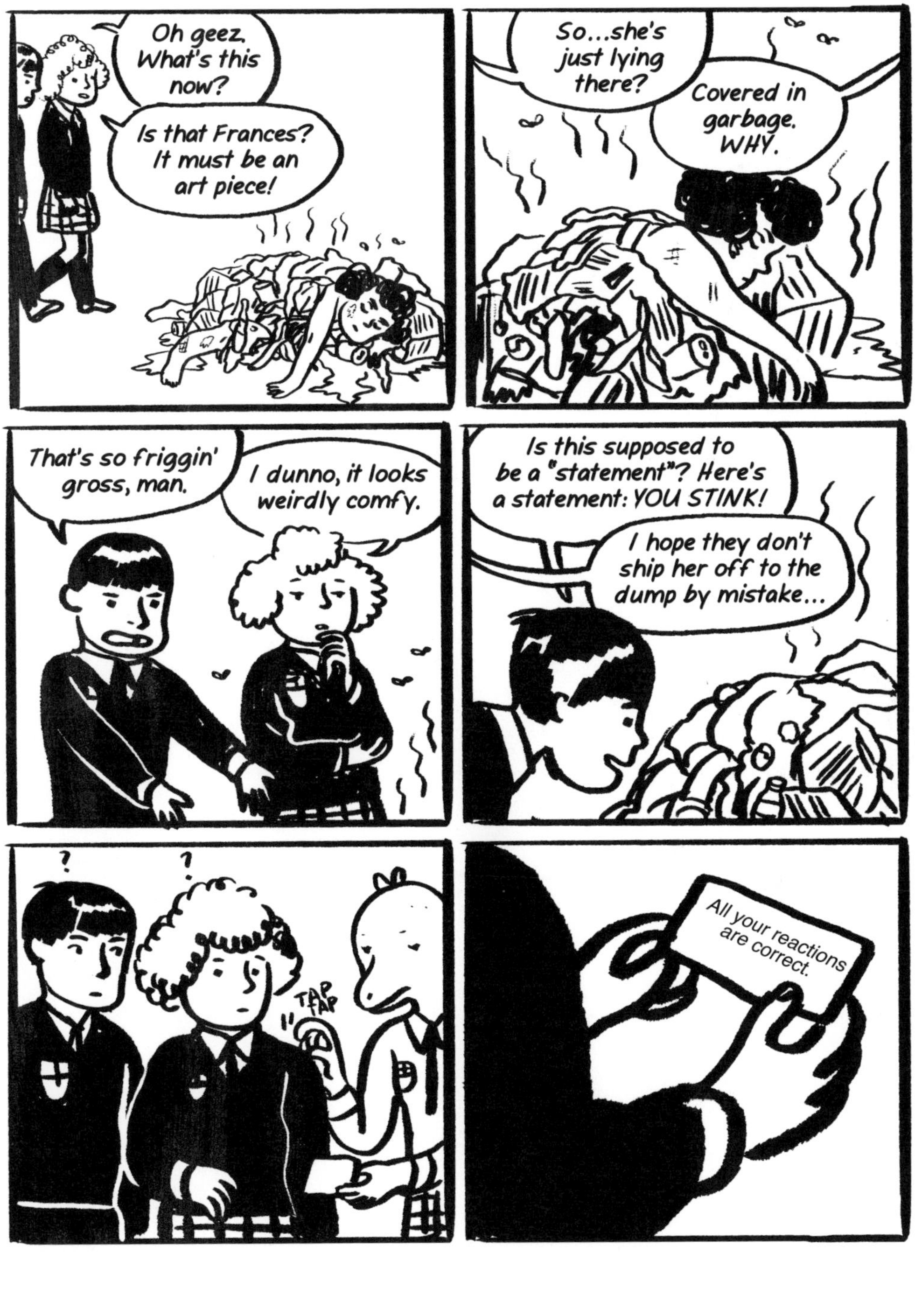
Oh geez. What's this now?
Is that Frances? It must be an art piece!
So...she's just lying there?
Covered in garbage. WHY.
That's so friggin' gross, man.
I dunno, it looks weirdly comfy.
Is this supposed to be a "statement"? Here's a statement: YOU STINK!
I hope they don't ship her off to the dump by mistake...
?
?
TAP TAP
All your reactions are correct.

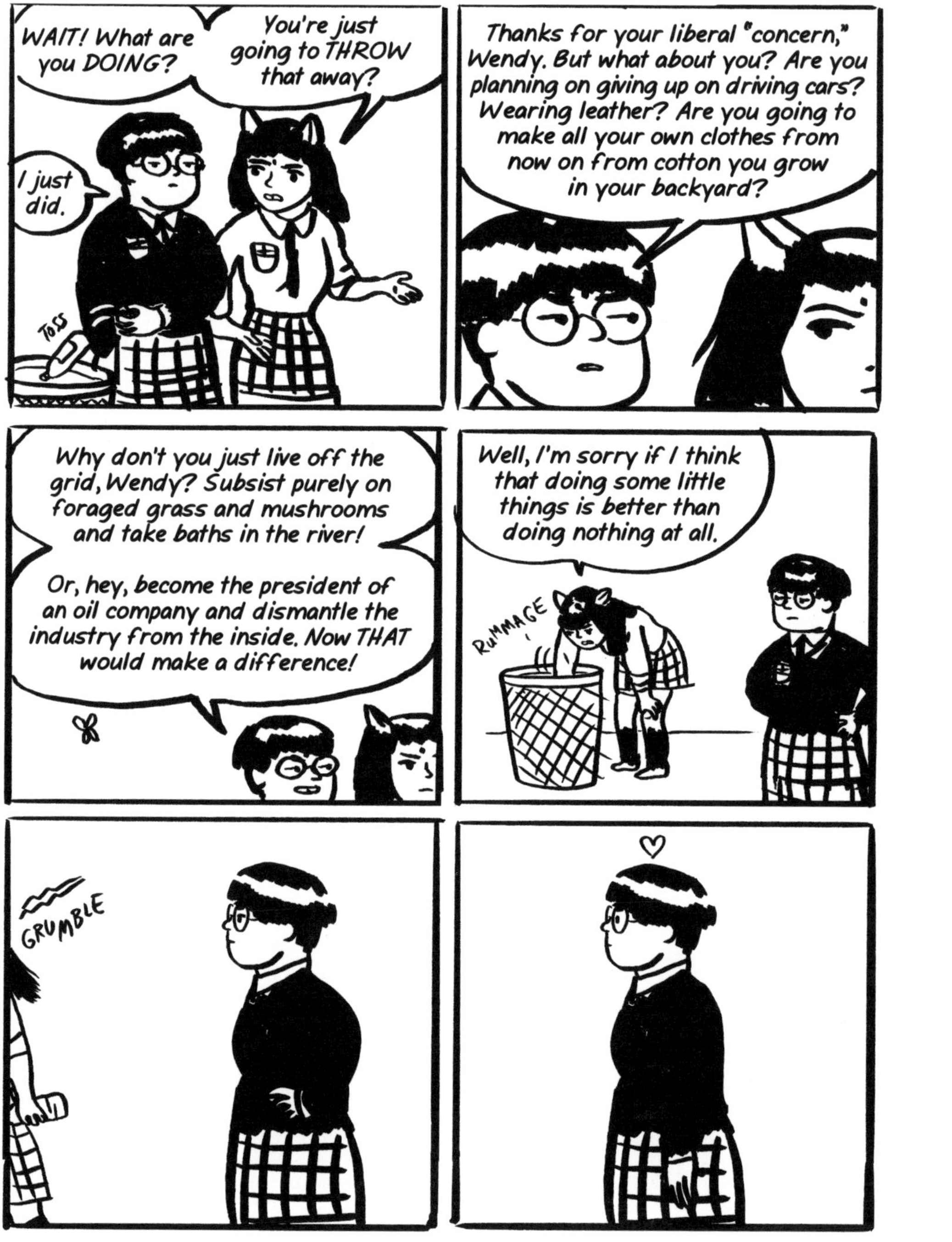
WAIT! What are you DOING?
You're just going to THROW that away?
I just did.
TOSS
Thanks for your liberal "concern," Wendy. But what about you? Are you planning on giving up on driving cars? Wearing leather? Are you going to make all your own clothes from now on from cotton you grow in your backyard?
Why don't you just live off the grid, Wendy? Subsist purely on foraged grass and mushrooms and take baths in the river!
Or, hey, become the president of an oil company and dismantle the industry from the inside. Now THAT would make a difference!
Well, I'm sorry if I think that doing some little things is better than doing nothing at all.
RUMMAGE
GRUMBLE

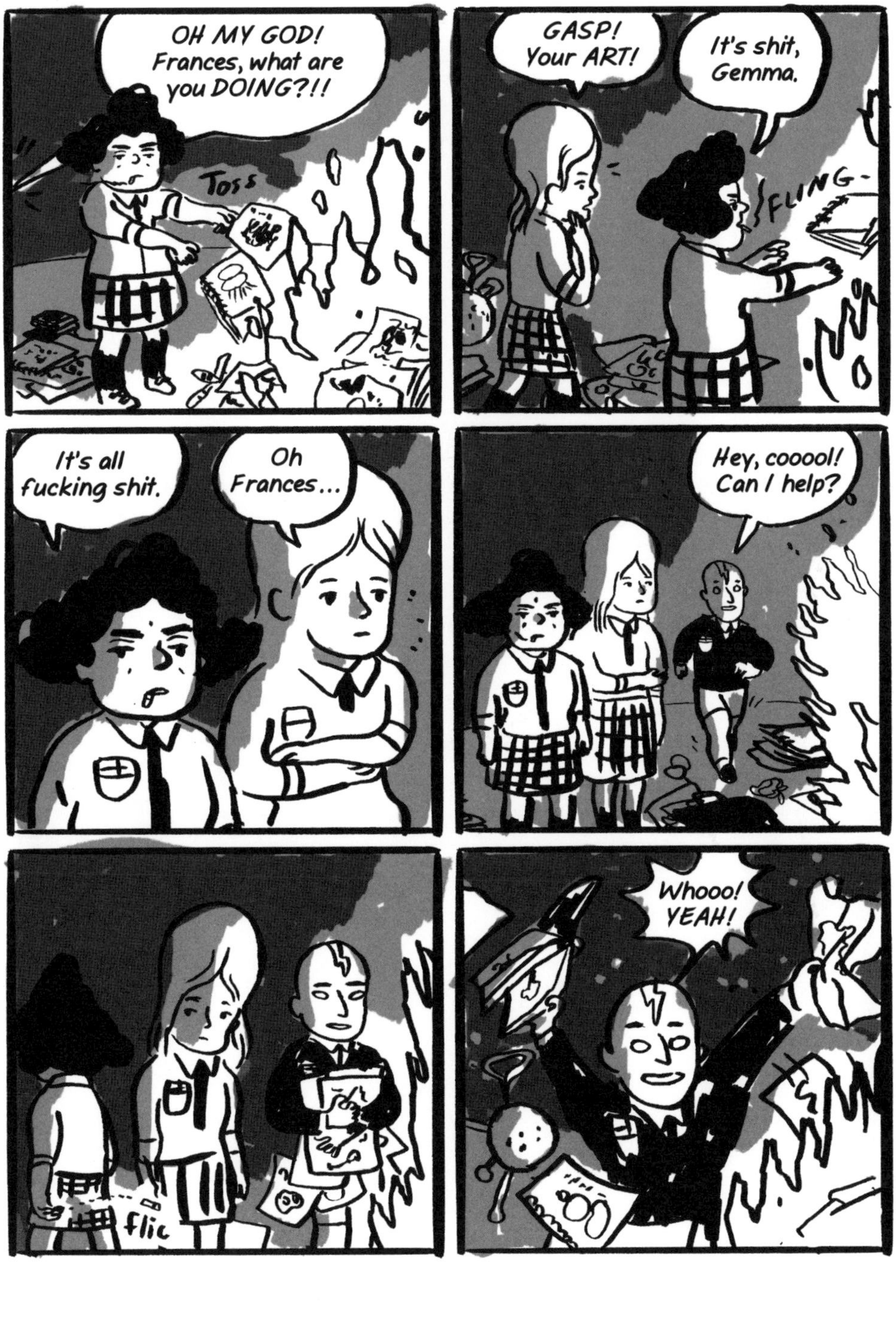
OH MY GOD! Frances, what are you DOING?!!
TOSS
GASP! Your ART!
It's shit, Gemma.
FLING
It's all fucking shit.
Oh Frances...
Hey, cooool! Can I help?
flic
Whooo! YEAH!

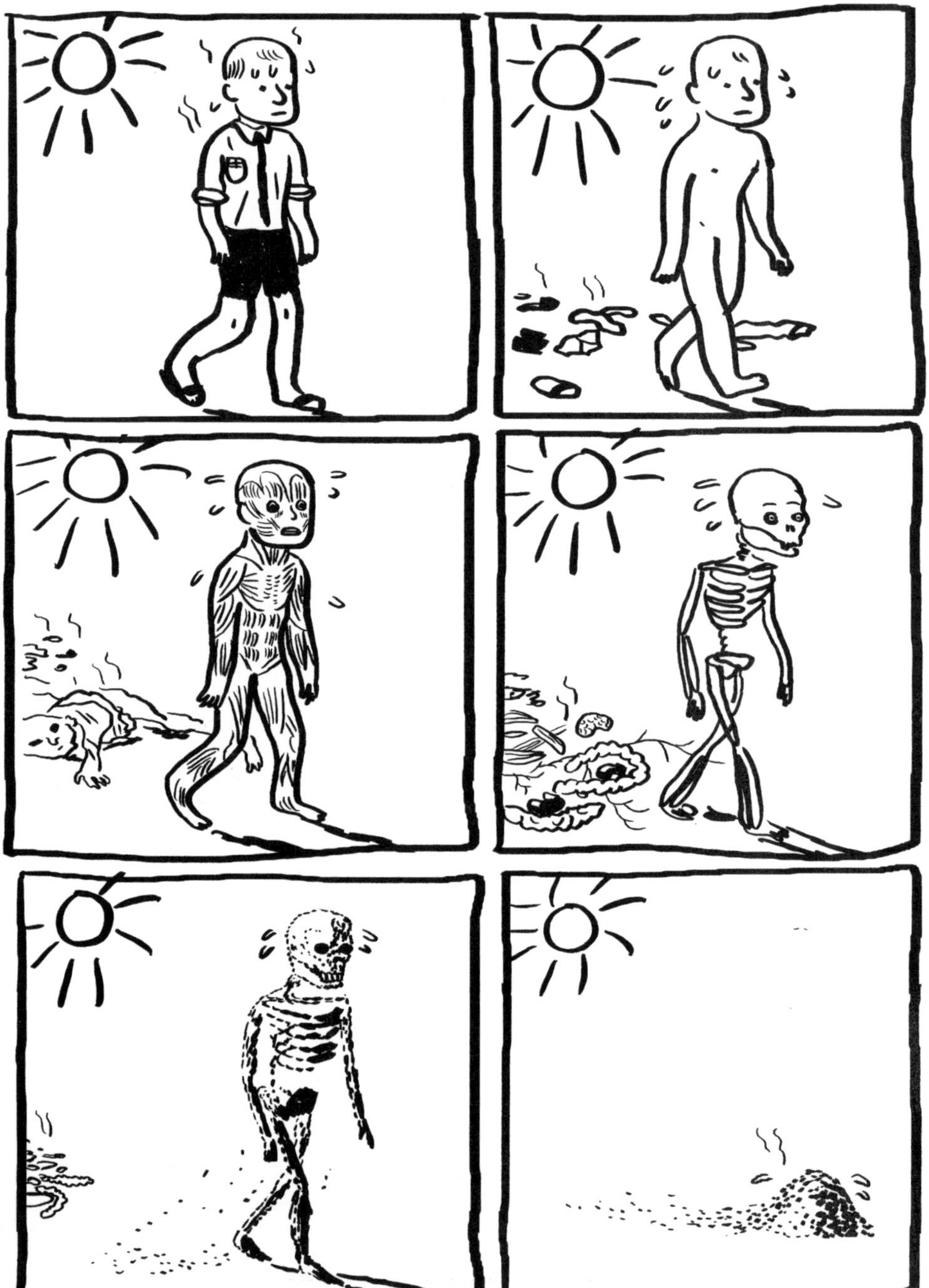

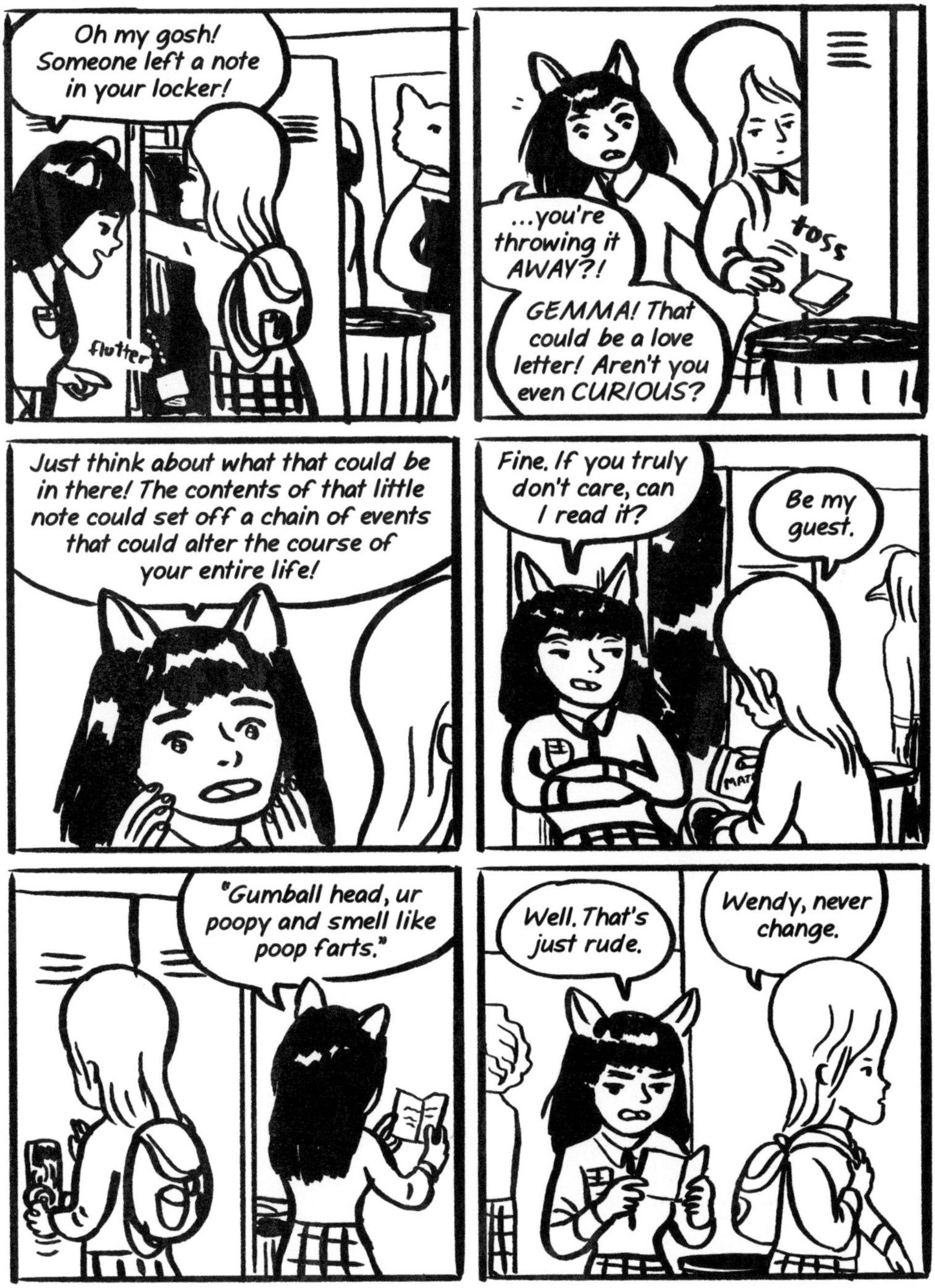
Oh my gosh! Someone left a note in your locker!
flutter
...you're throwing it AWAY?!
toss
GEMMA! That could be a love letter! Aren't you even CURIOUS?
Just think about what that could be in there! The contents of that little note could set off a chain of events that could alter the course of your entire life!
Fine. If you truly don't care, can I read it?
Be my guest.
"Gumball head, ur poopy and smell like poop farts."
Well. That's just rude.
Wendy, never change.

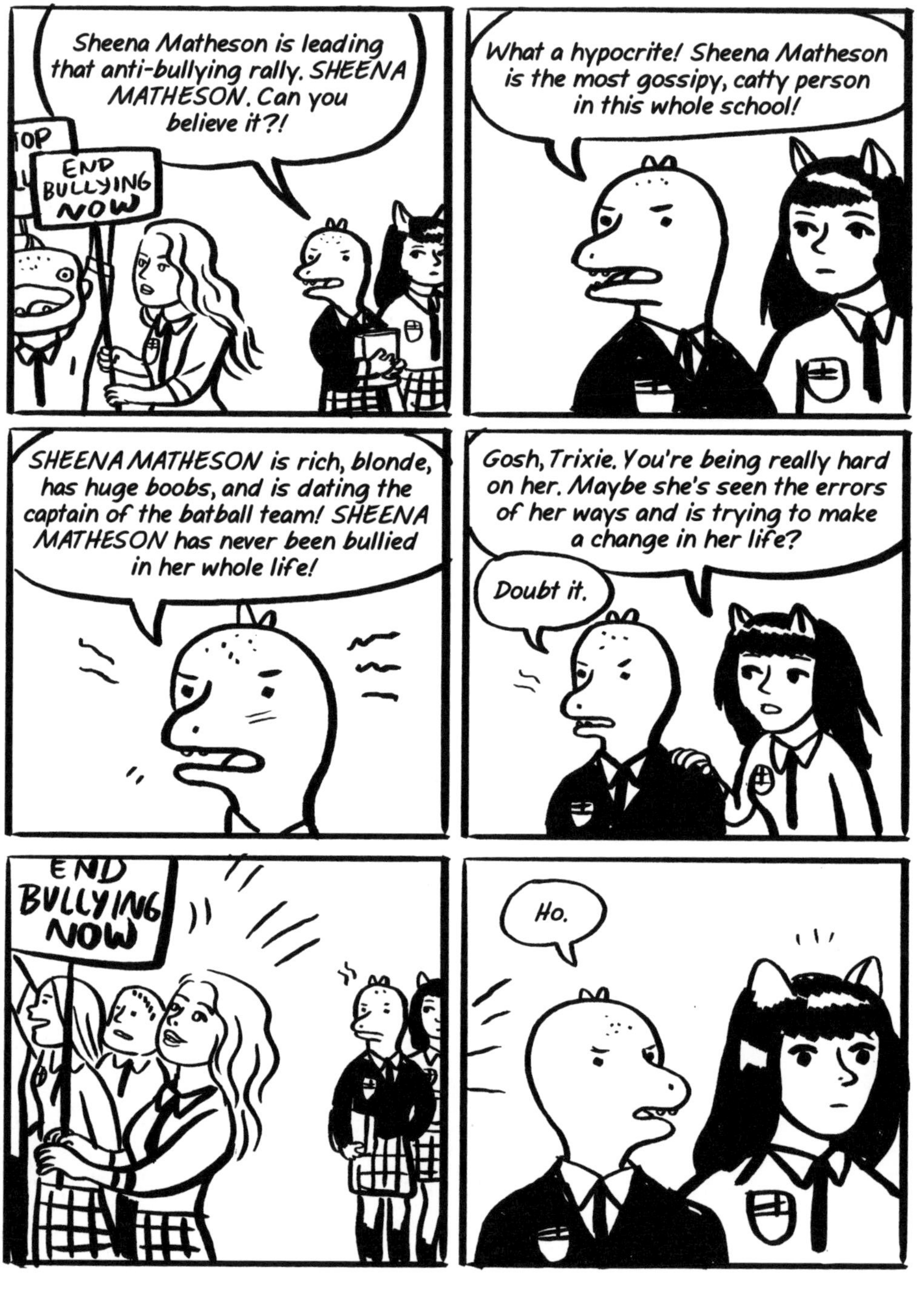
Sheena Matheson is leading that anti-bullying rally. SHEENA MATHESON. Can you believe it?!
END BULLYING NOW
What a hypocrite! Sheena Matheson is the most gossipy, catty person in this whole school!
SHEENA MATHESON is rich, blonde, has huge boobs, and is dating the captain of the batball team! SHEENA MATHESON has never been bullied in her whole life!
Gosh, Trixie. You're being really hard on her. Maybe she's seen the errors of her ways and is trying to make a change in her life?
Doubt it.
END BULLYING NOW
Ho.

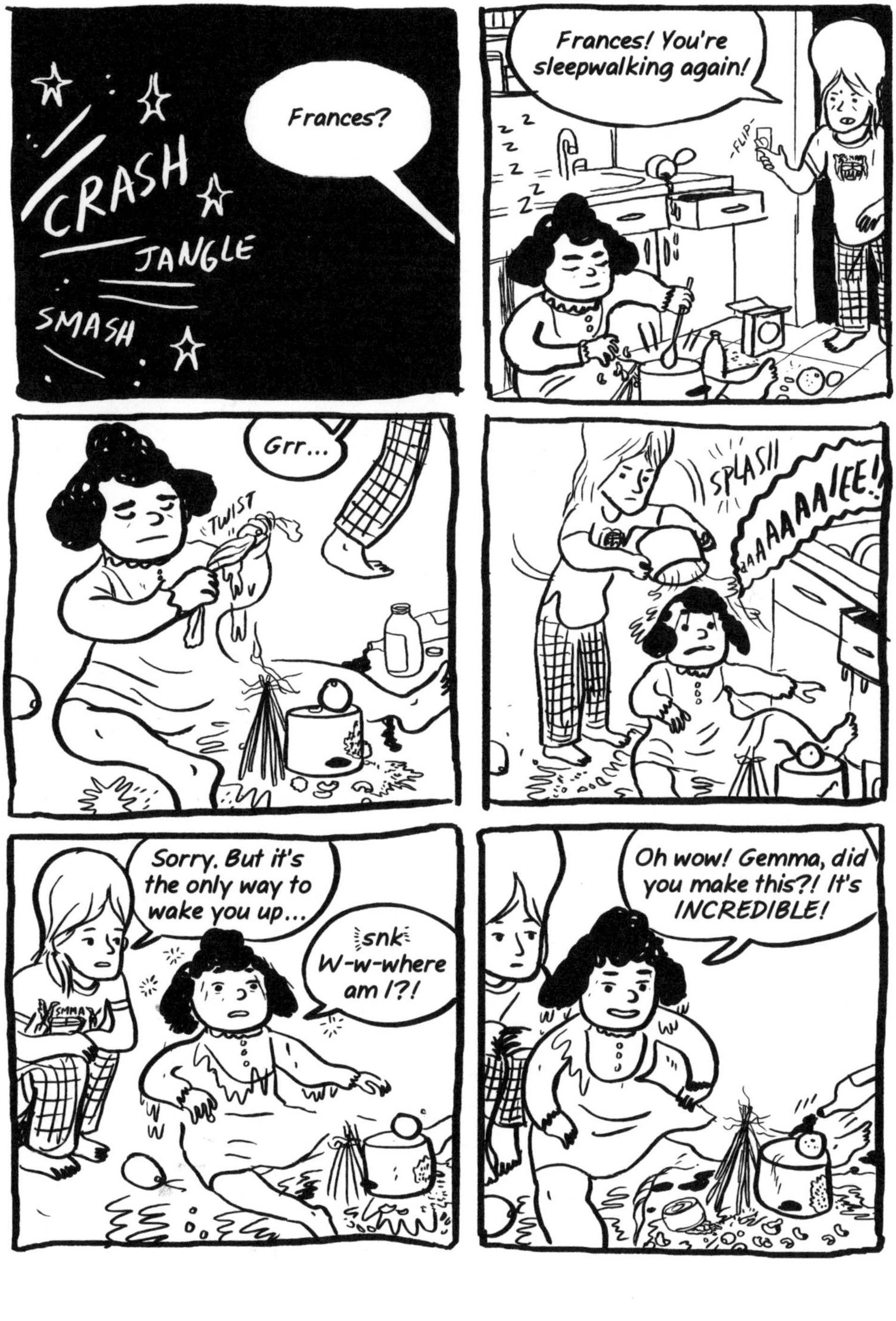
CRASH
JANGLE
SMASH
Frances?
Frances! You're sleepwalking again!
Z Z Z Z Z Z
-FLIP-
Grr...
TWIST
SPLASH
aaAAAAAAIEE!!
Sorry. But it's the only way to wake you up...
snk W-w-where am I?!
Oh wow! Gemma, did you make this?! It's INCREDIBLE!

OFFICE
Good morning, Mrs. McDouggle.
Do you have a garbage can?
Well, good morning, Trevor! Yes, of course. It's in the next room around the corner there.
Thanks!
Hm. What a nice boy.
tak tak
READ
tak tak tak

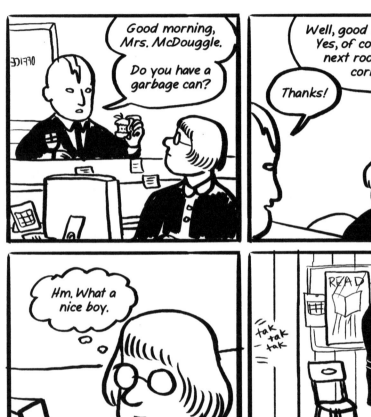

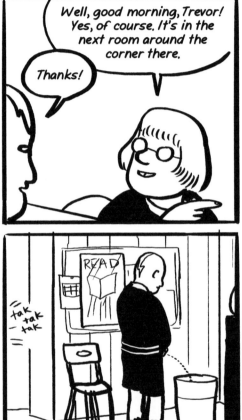

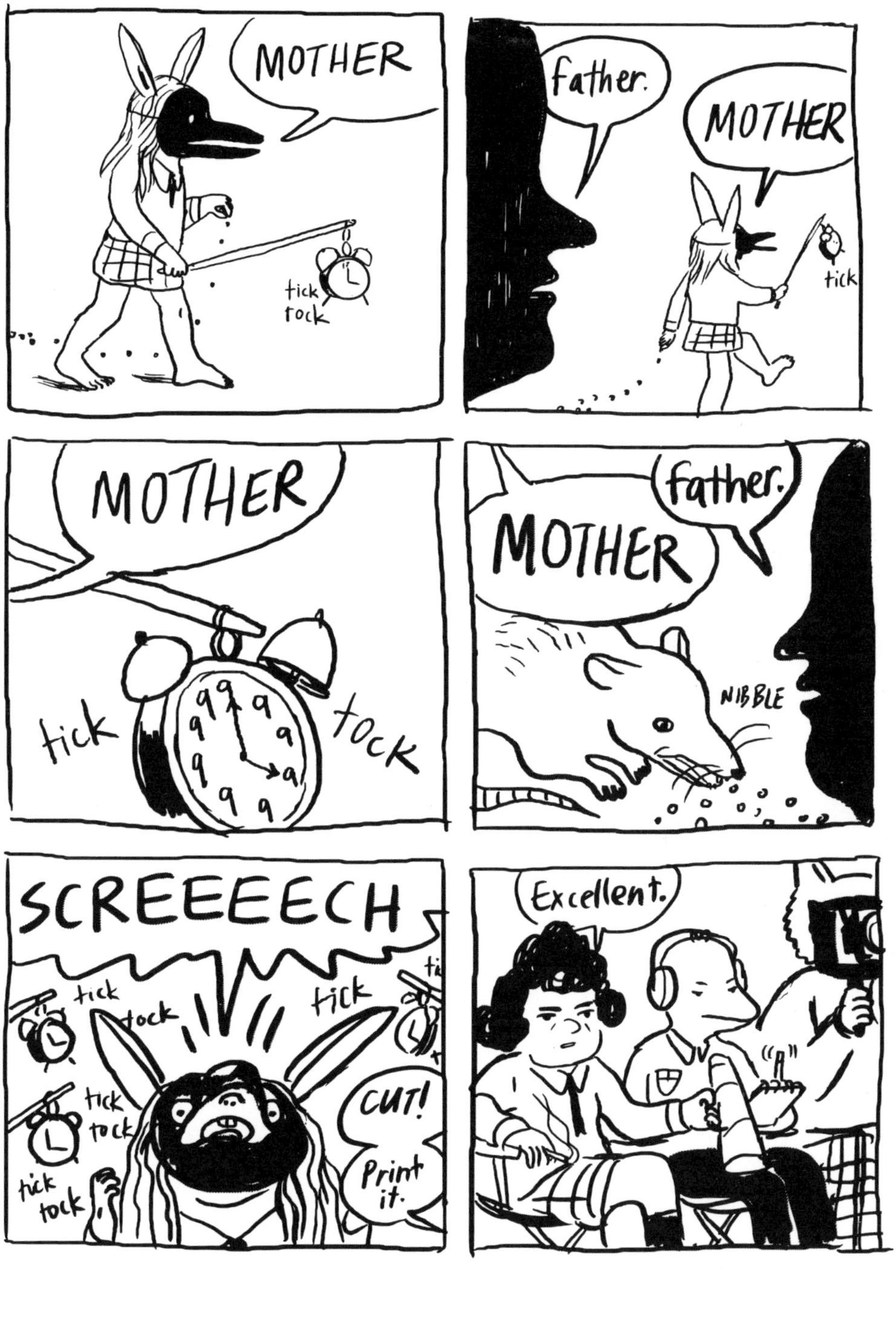
MOTHER
tick
tock
father.
MOTHER
tick
MOTHER
tick
tock
MOTHER
father.
NIBBLE
SCREEEEECH
tick
tock
tick
tock
tick
tock
tick
CUT!
Print it.
Excellent.

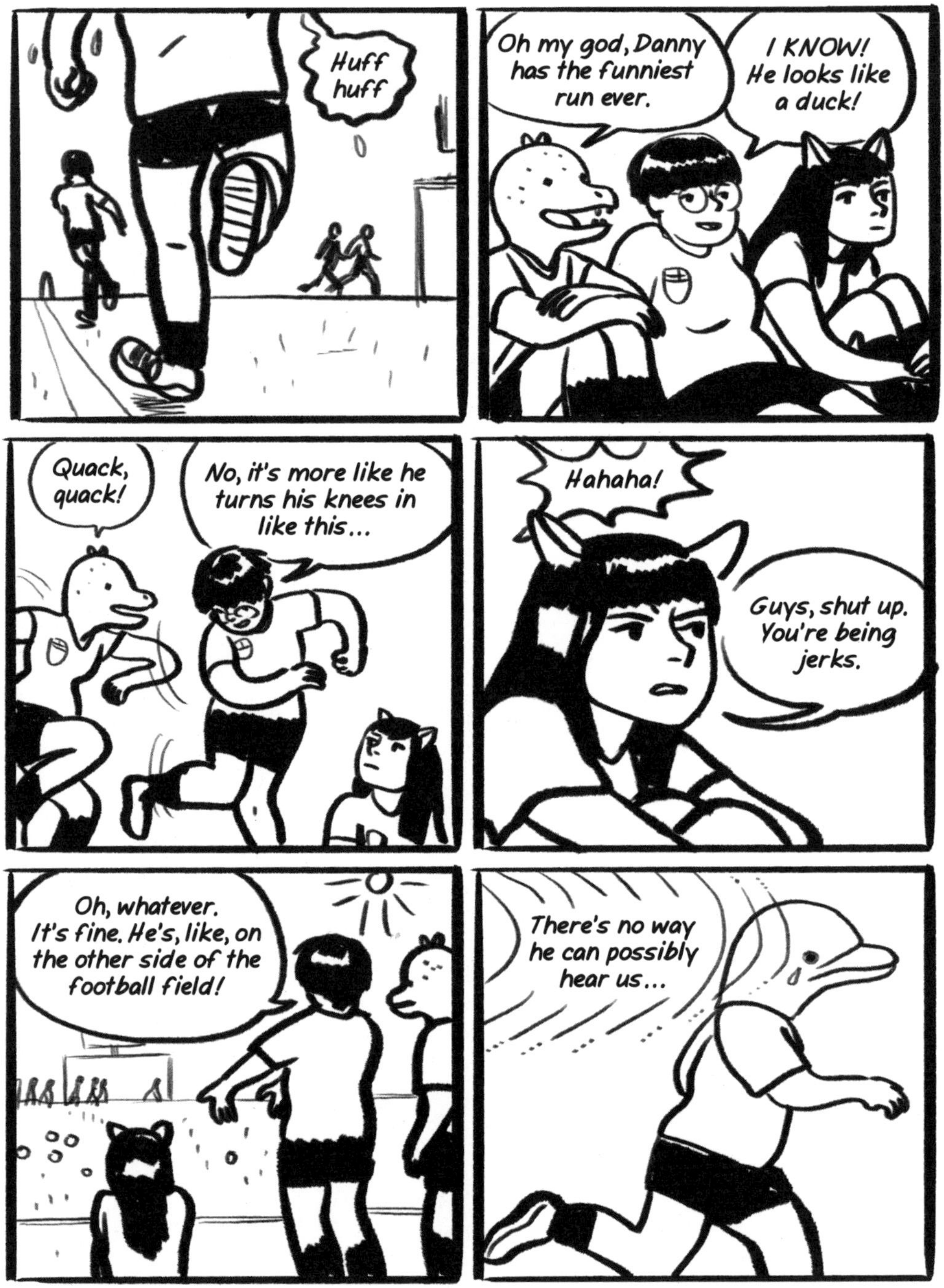
Huff huff
Oh my god, Danny has the funniest run ever.
I KNOW! He looks like a duck!
Quack, quack!
No, it's more like he turns his knees in like this...
Hahaha!
Guys, shut up. You're being jerks.
Oh, whatever. It's fine. He's, like, on the other side of the football field!
There's no way he can possibly hear us...

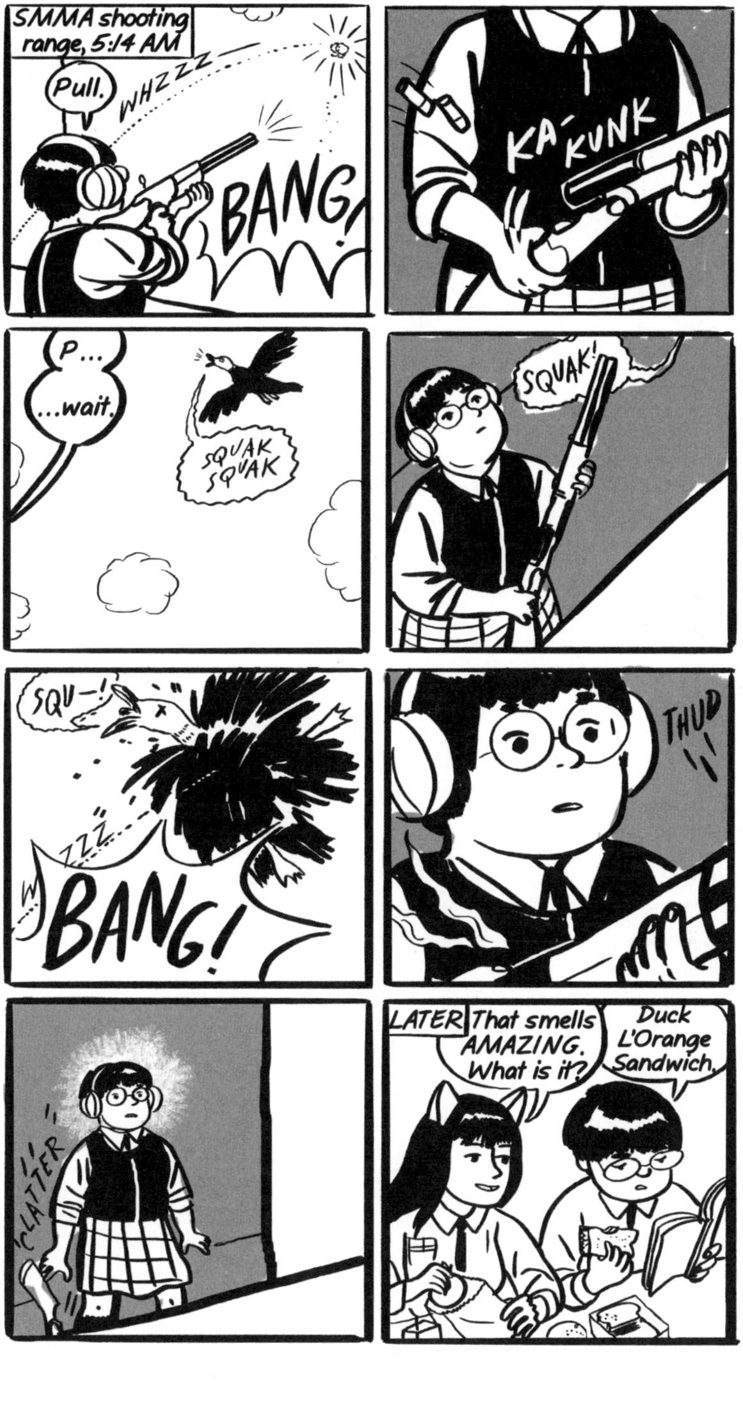
SMMA shooting range, 5:14 AM
Pull.
WHZZZ
BANG!
KA-KUNK
P...
...wait.
SQUAK SQUAK
SQUAK!
SQU—!
WZZZ
BANG!
THUD
CLATTER
LATER
That smells AMAZING. What is it?
Duck L'Orange Sandwich.

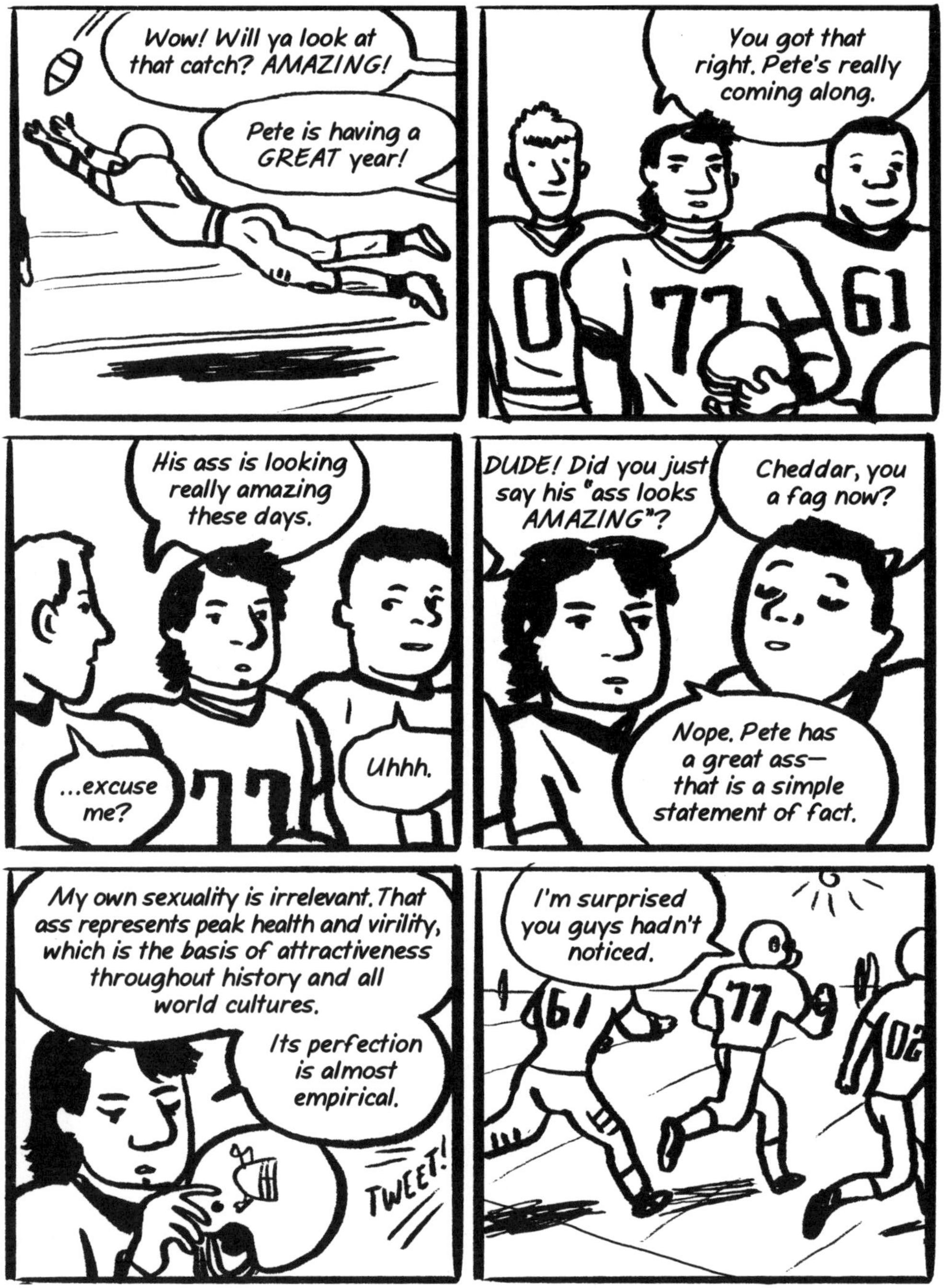
Wow! Will ya look at that catch? AMAZING!
Pete is having a GREAT year!
You got that right. Pete's really coming along.
His ass is looking really amazing these days.
...excuse me?
Uhhh.
DUDE! Did you just say his "ass looks AMAZING"?
Cheddar, you a fag now?
Nope. Pete has a great ass— that is a simple statement of fact.
My own sexuality is irrelevant. That ass represents peak health and virility, which is the basis of attractiveness throughout history and all world cultures.
Its perfection is almost empirical.
TWEET!
I'm surprised you guys hadn't noticed.

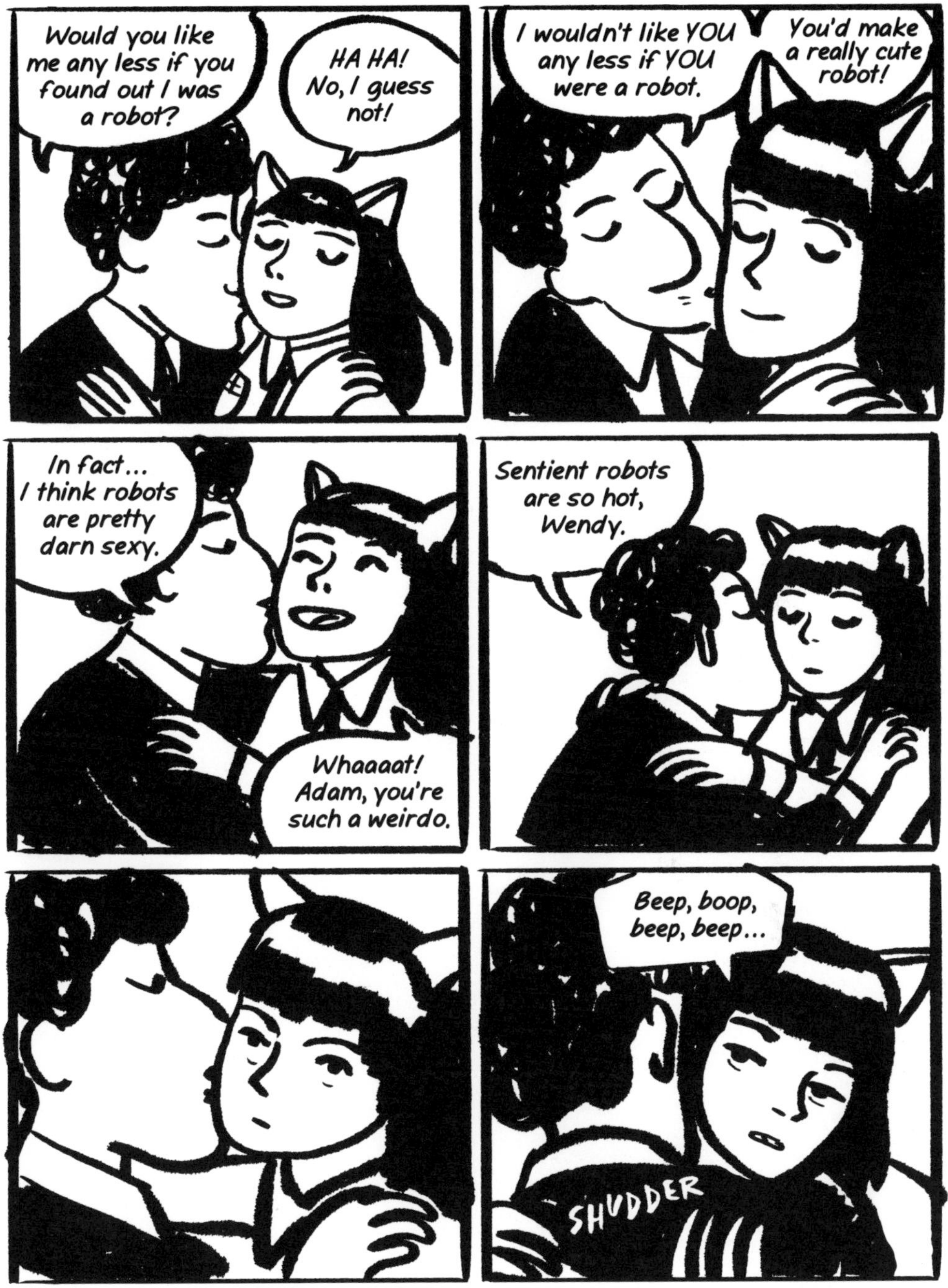
Would you like me any less if you found out I was a robot?
HA HA! No, I guess not!
I wouldn't like YOU any less if YOU were a robot.
You'd make a really cute robot!
In fact... I think robots are pretty darn sexy.
Whaaaat! Adam, you're such a weirdo.
Sentient robots are so hot, Wendy.
Beep, boop, beep, beep...
SHUDDER

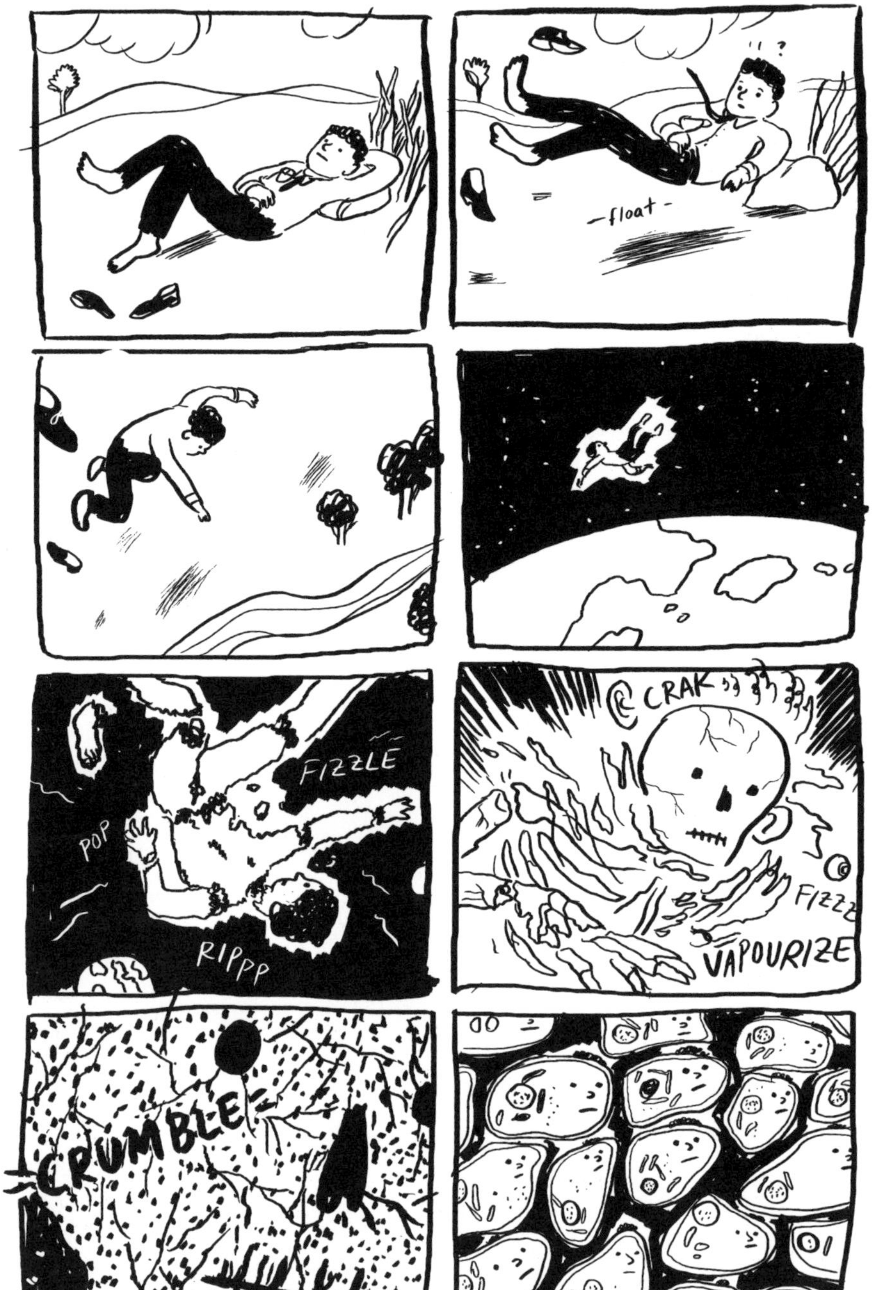

!! ?
-float-
FIZZLE
POP
RIPPP
CRAK
FIZZZ
VAPOURIZE
CRUMBLE

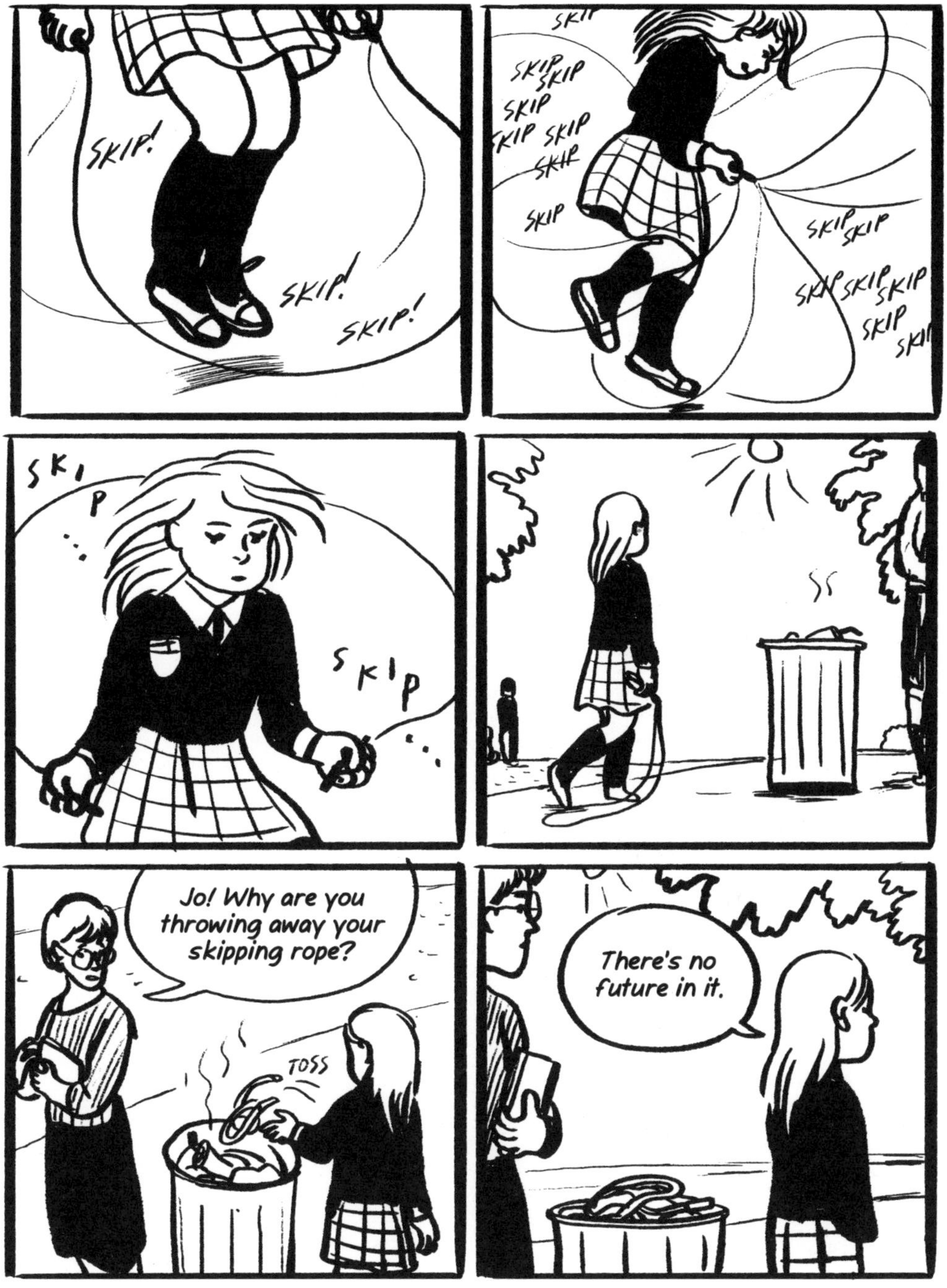
SKIP!
SKIP!
SKIP!
SKIP
SKIP SKIP
SKIP
SKIP SKIP
SKIP
SKIP
SKIP SKIP
SKIP SKIP SKIP
SKIP
S K I P . . .
S K I P . . .
Jo! Why are you throwing away your skipping rope?
TOSS
There's no future in it.

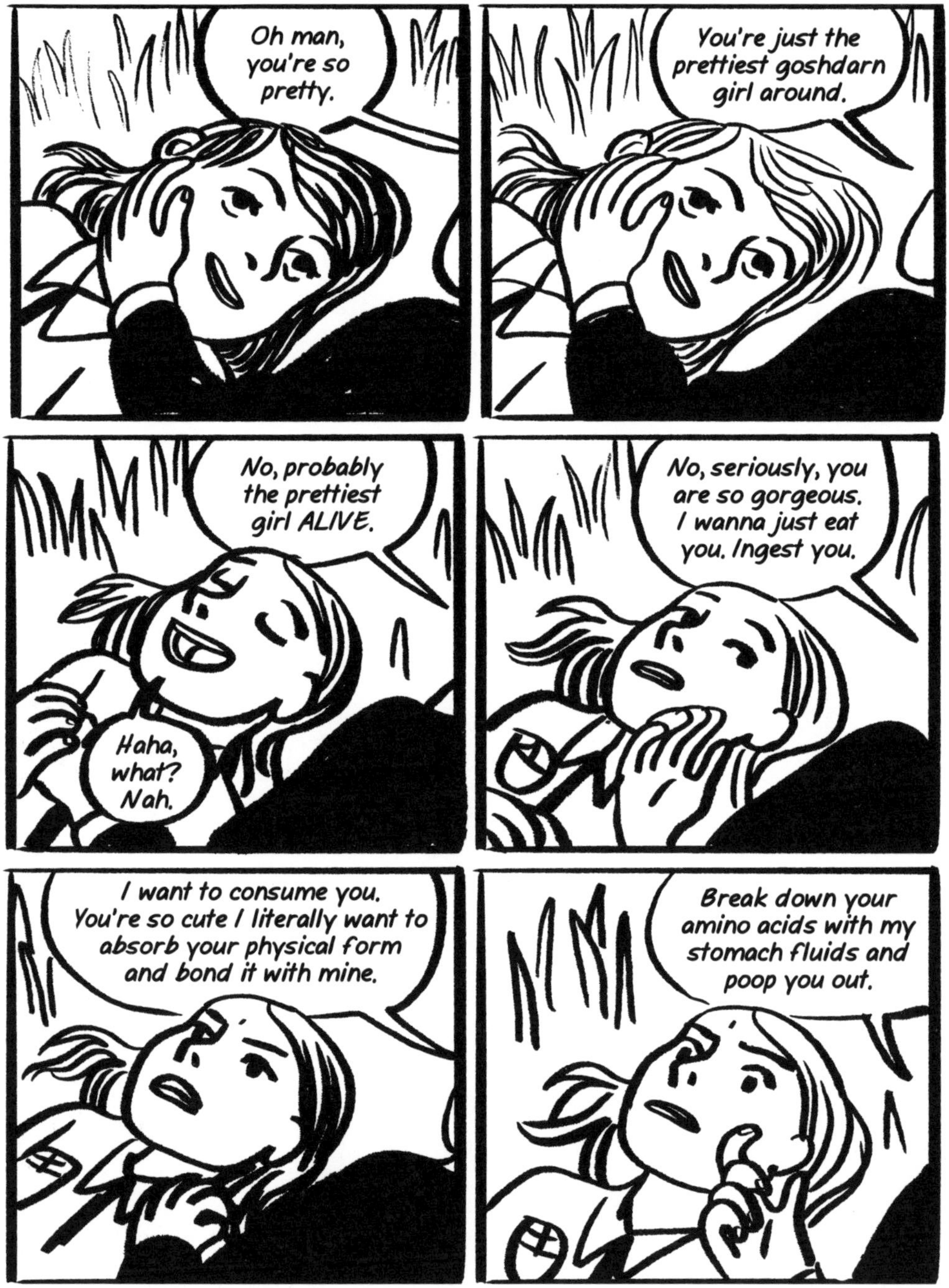
Oh man, you're so pretty.
You're just the prettiest goshdarn girl around.
No, probably the prettiest girl ALIVE.
Haha, what? Nah.
No, seriously, you are so gorgeous. I wanna just eat you. Ingest you.
I want to consume you. You're so cute I literally want to absorb your physical form and bond it with mine.
Break down your amino acids with my stomach fluids and poop you out.

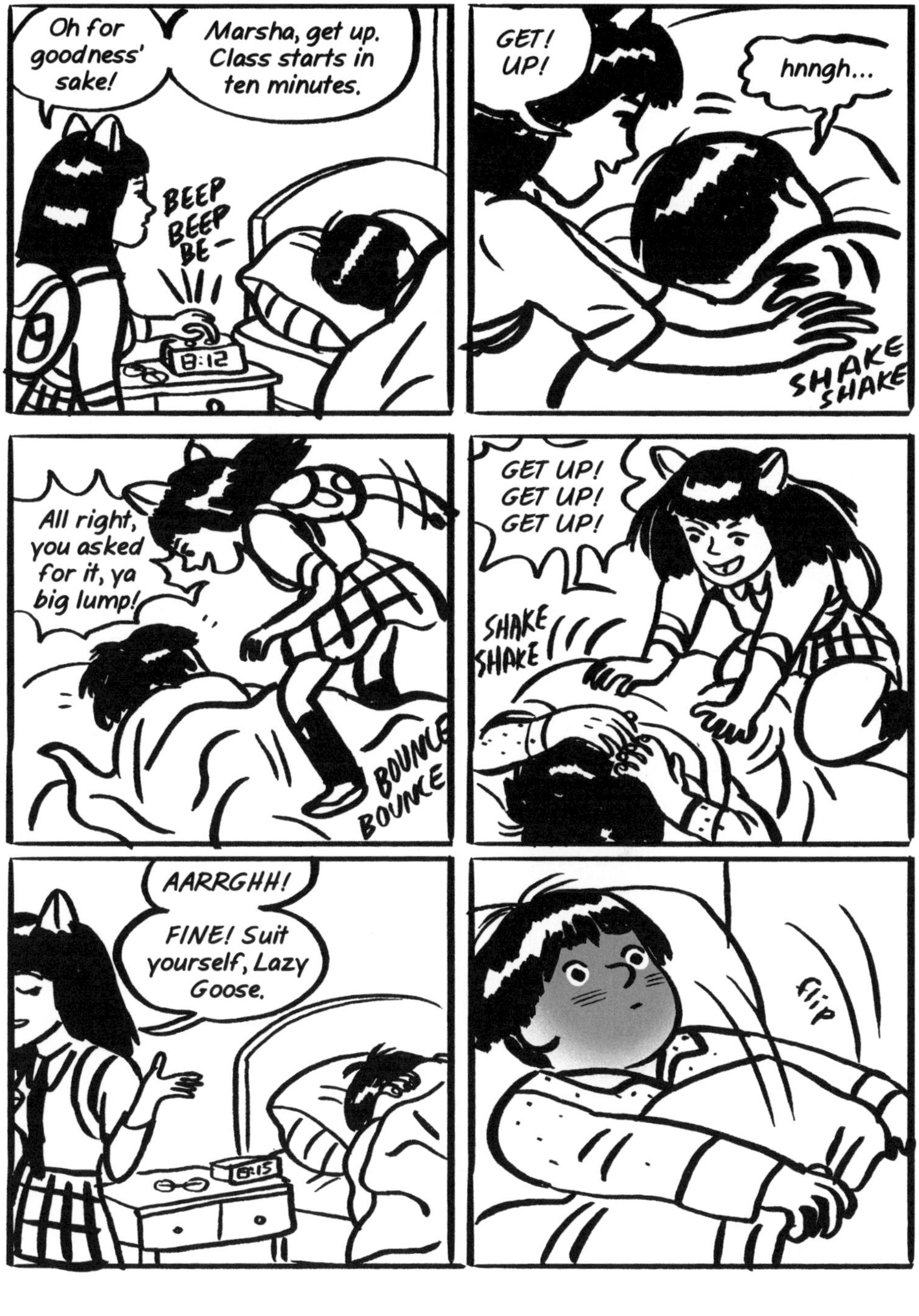

Oh for goodness' sake!
Marsha, get up. Class starts in ten minutes.
BEEP BEEP BE-
8:12
GET! UP!
hnngh...
SHAKE SHAKE
All right, you asked for it, ya big lump!
BOUNCE BOUNCE
GET UP! GET UP! GET UP!
SHAKE SHAKE
AARRGHH!
FINE! Suit yourself, Lazy Goose.
8:15
flip

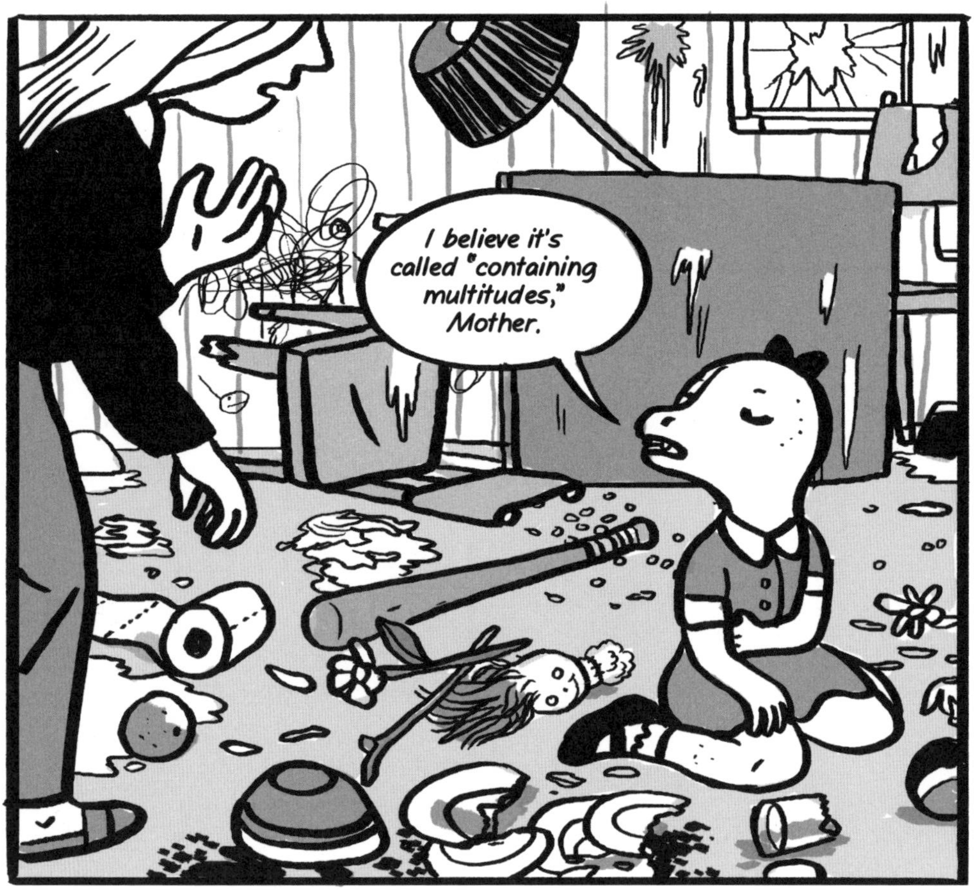
I believe it's called "containing multitudes," Mother.

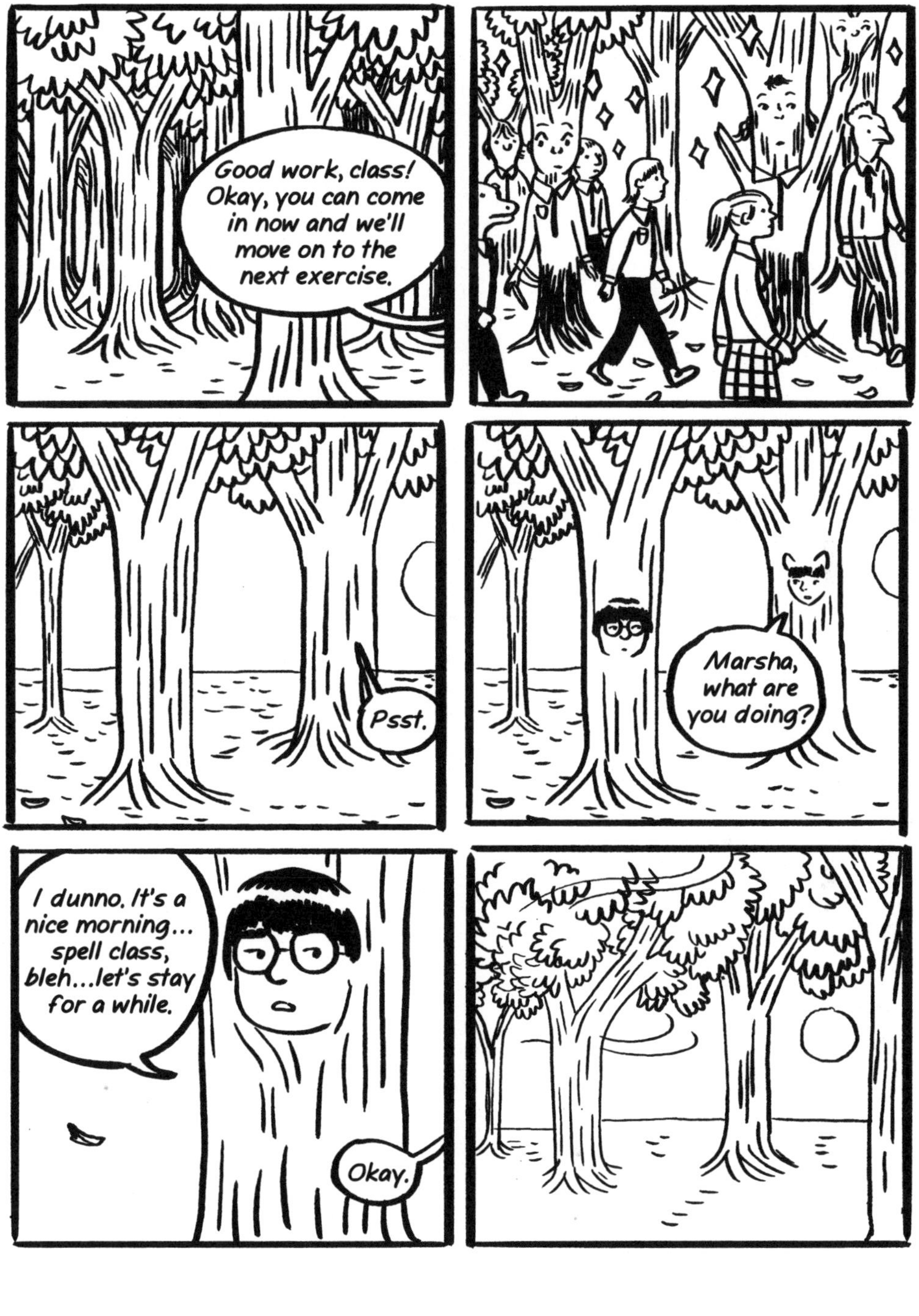
Good work, class! Okay, you can come in now and we'll move on to the next exercise.
Psst.
Marsha, what are you doing?
I dunno. It's a nice morning... spell class, bleh...let's stay for a while.
Okay.

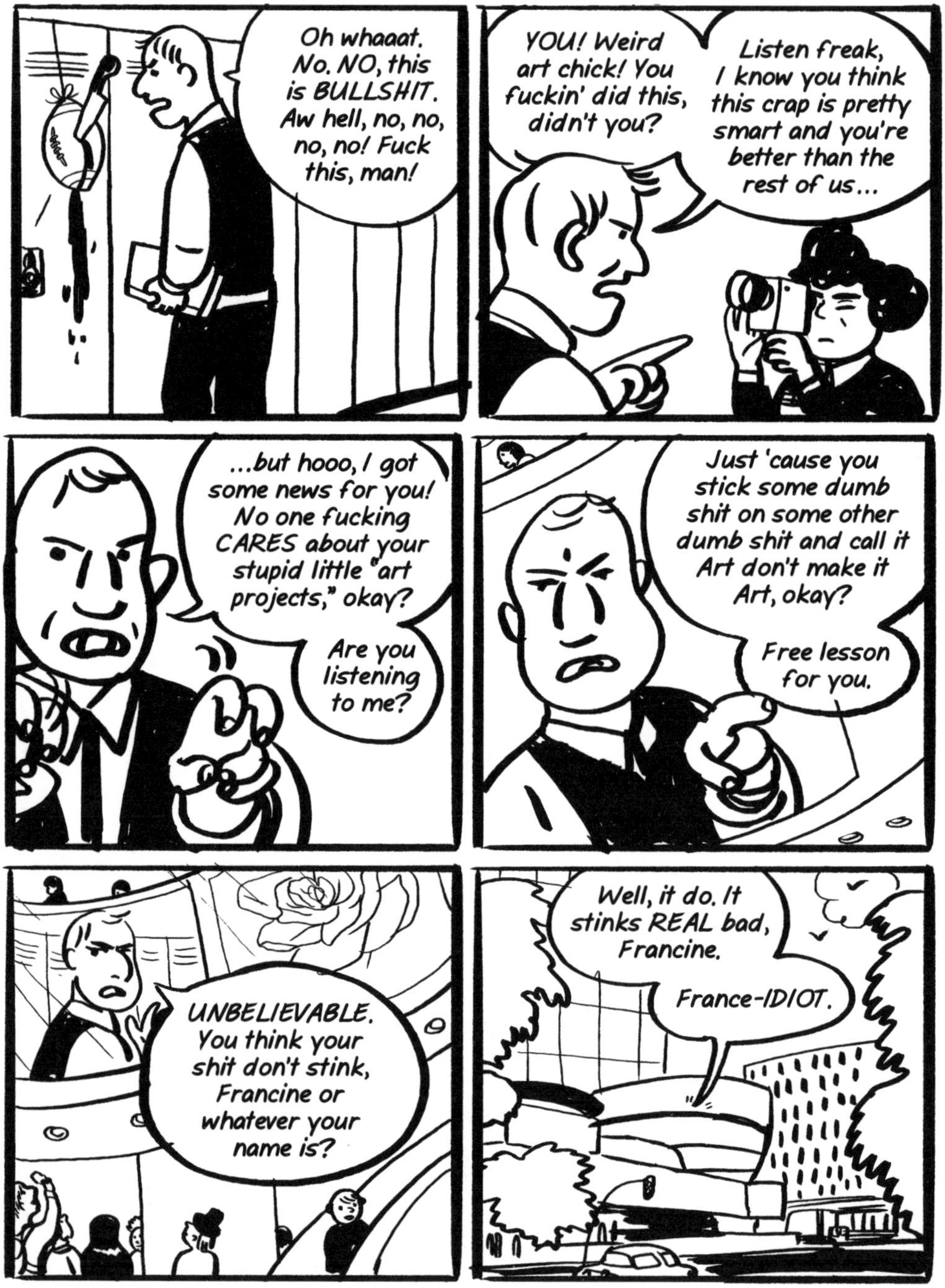
Oh whaaat. No. NO, this is BULLSHIT. Aw hell, no, no, no, no! Fuck this, man!
YOU! Weird art chick! You fuckin' did this, didn't you?
Listen freak, I know you think this crap is pretty smart and you're better than the rest of us...
...but hooo, I got some news for you! No one fucking CARES about your stupid little "art projects," okay?
Are you listening to me?
Just 'cause you stick some dumb shit on some other dumb shit and call it Art don't make it Art, okay?
Free lesson for you.
UNBELIEVABLE. You think your shit don't stink, Francine or whatever your name is?
Well, it do. It stinks REAL bad, Francine.
France-IDIOT.

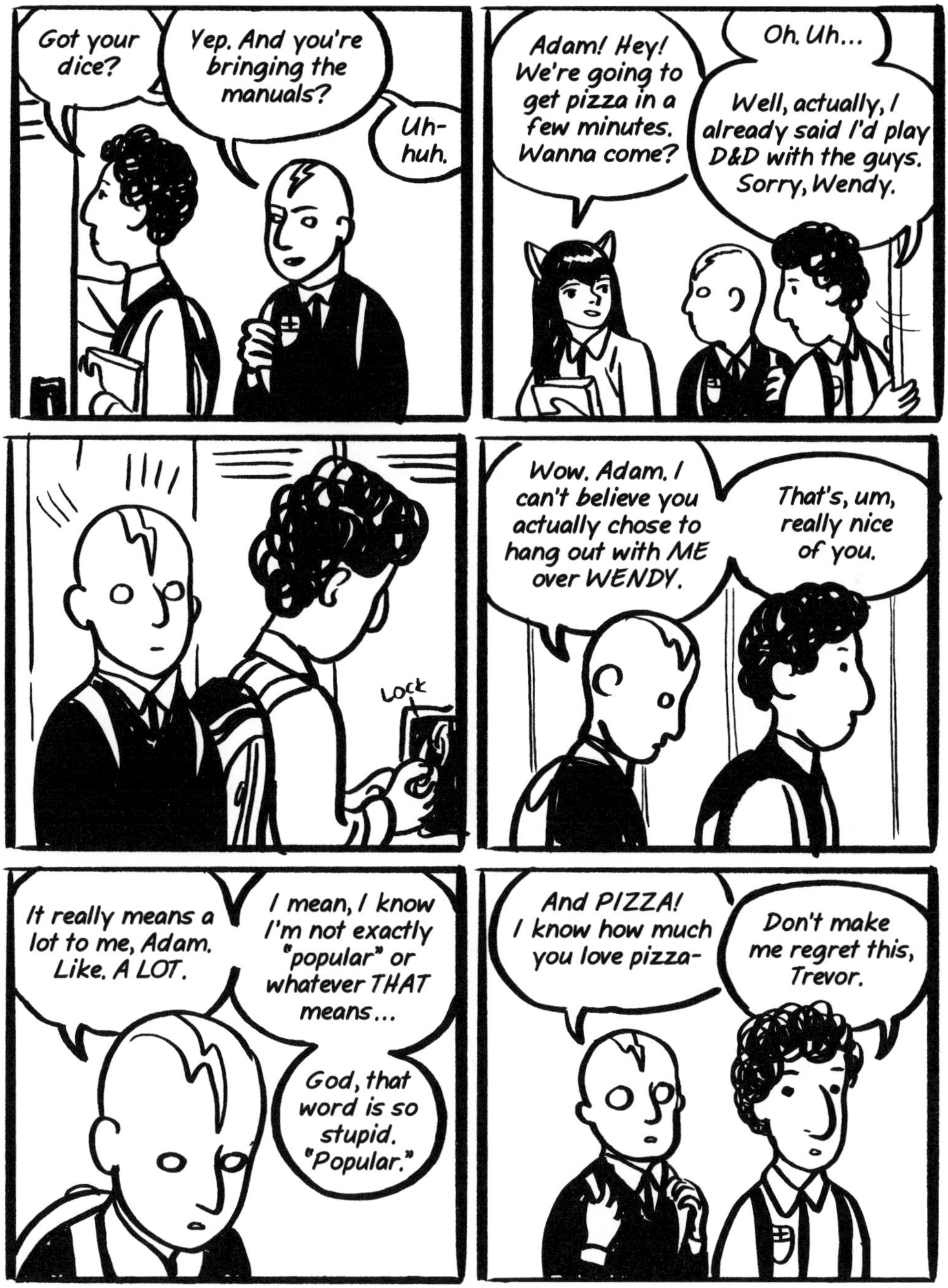

Got your dice?
Yep. And you're bringing the manuals?
Uh-huh.
Adam! Hey! We're going to get pizza in a few minutes. Wanna come?
Oh. Uh...
Well, actually, I already said I'd play D&D with the guys. Sorry, Wendy.
LOCK
Wow. Adam. I can't believe you actually chose to hang out with ME over WENDY.
That's, um, really nice of you.
It really means a lot to me, Adam. Like. A LOT.
I mean, I know I'm not exactly "popular" or whatever THAT means...
God, that word is so stupid. "Popular."
And PIZZA! I know how much you love pizza-
Don't make me regret this, Trevor.

Nice stamp collection.
Har har. Is this the part where I say "thanks" and you mock me mercilessly for being a dork or something?
Not exactly.

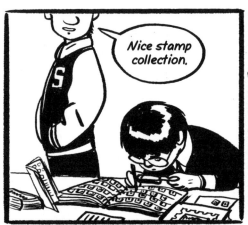

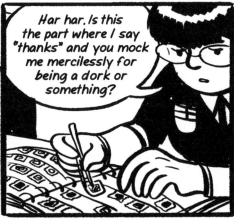

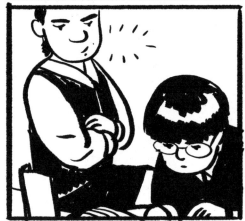

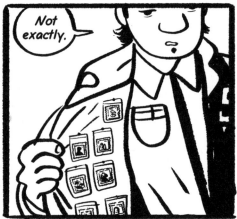

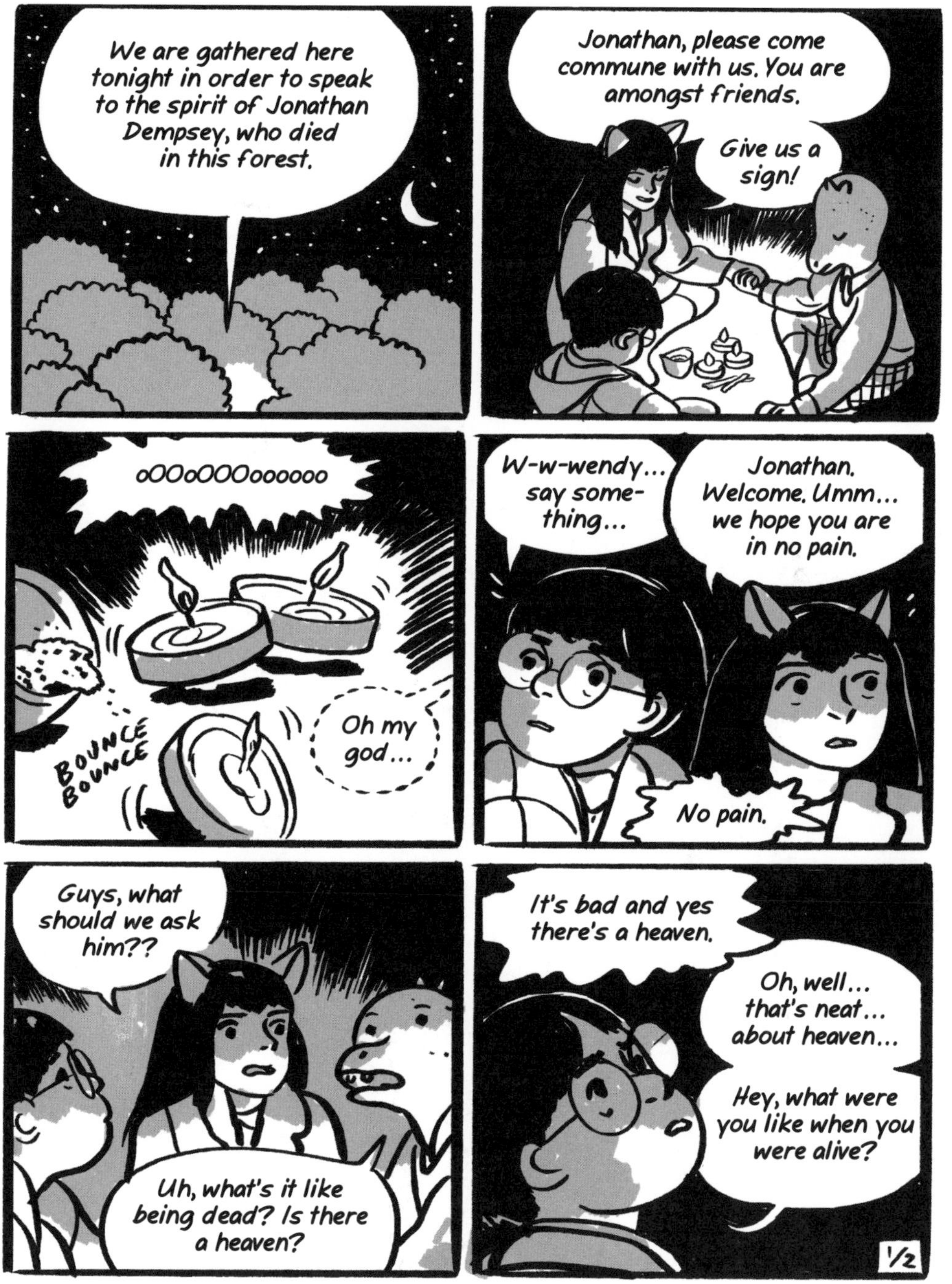

We are gathered here tonight in order to speak to the spirit of Jonathan Dempsey, who died in this forest.
Jonathan, please come commune with us. You are amongst friends.
Give us a sign!
oOOoOOOoooooo
BOUNCE BOUNCE
Oh my god...
W-w-wendy... say some-thing...
Jonathan. Welcome. Umm... we hope you are in no pain.
No pain.
Guys, what should we ask him??
Uh, what's it like being dead? Is there a heaven?
It's bad and yes there's a heaven.
Oh, well... that's neat... about heaven...
Hey, what were you like when you were alive?
1/2

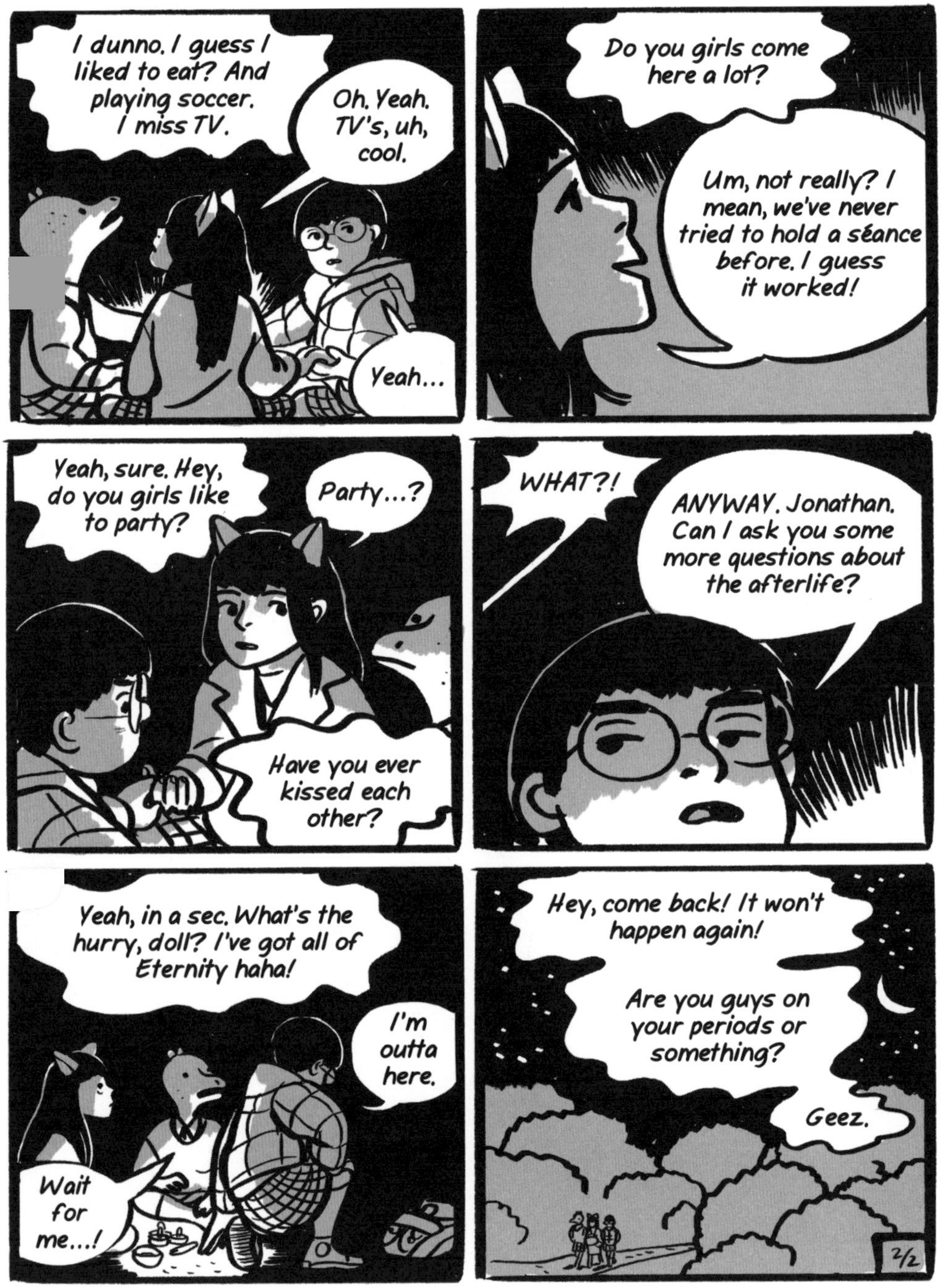
I dunno. I guess I liked to eat? And playing soccer. I miss TV.
Oh. Yeah. TV's, uh, cool.
Yeah...
Do you girls come here a lot?
Um, not really? I mean, we've never tried to hold a séance before. I guess it worked!
Yeah, sure. Hey, do you girls like to party?
Party...?
Have you ever kissed each other?
WHAT?!
ANYWAY. Jonathan. Can I ask you some more questions about the afterlife?
Yeah, in a sec. What's the hurry, doll? I've got all of Eternity haha!
I'm outta here.
Wait for me...!
Hey, come back! It won't happen again!
Are you guys on your periods or something?
Geez.
2/2

God, I hate the saxophone.

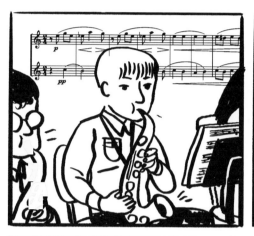

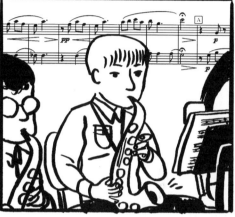

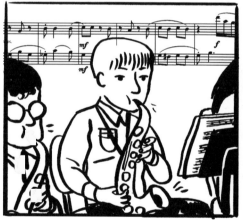

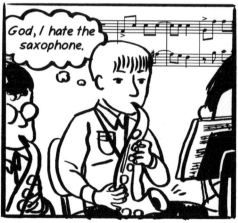

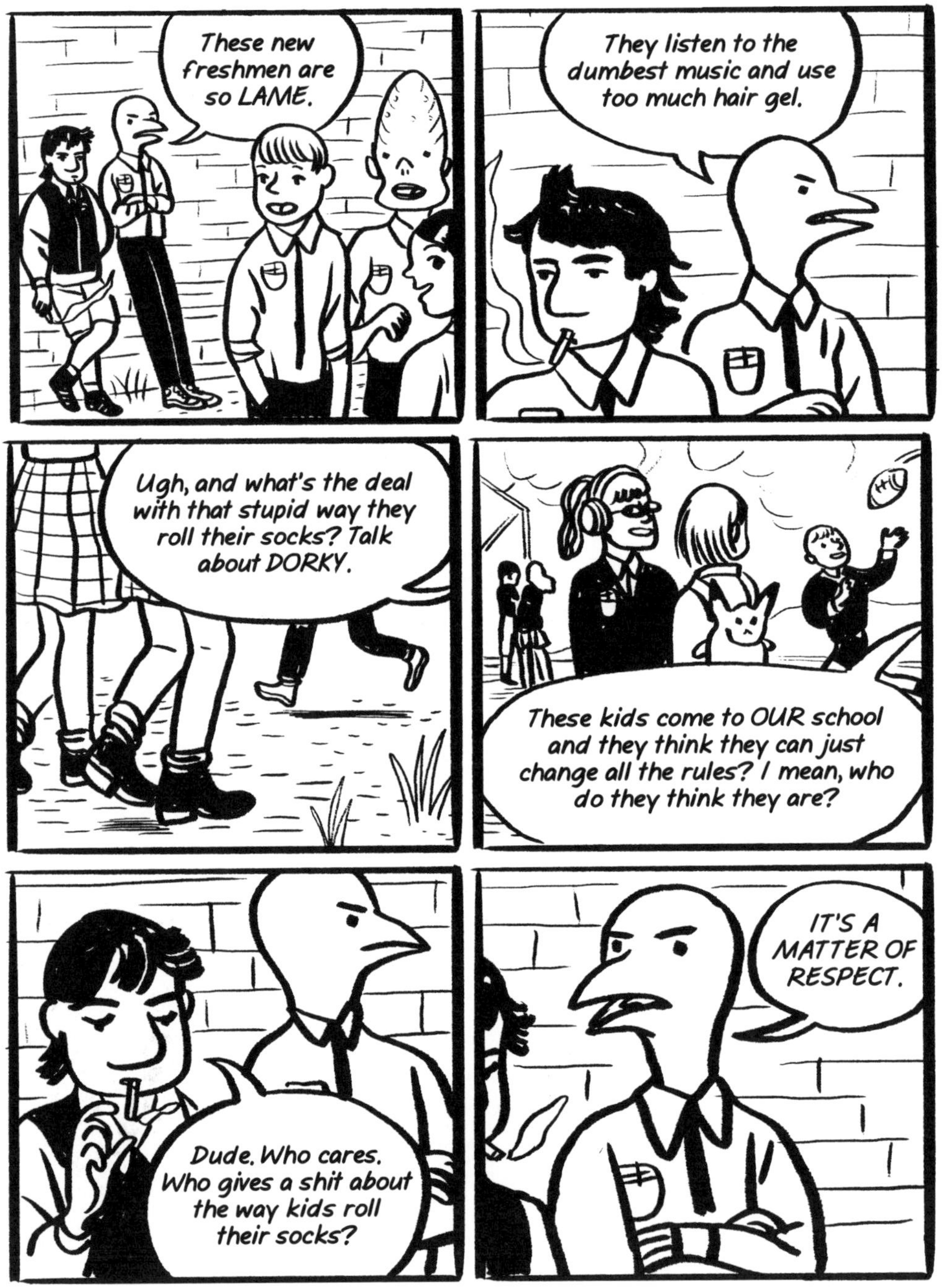
These new freshmen are so LAME.
They listen to the dumbest music and use too much hair gel.
Ugh, and what's the deal with that stupid way they roll their socks? Talk about DORKY.
These kids come to OUR school and they think they can just change all the rules? I mean, who do they think they are?
Dude. Who cares. Who gives a shit about the way kids roll their socks?
IT'S A MATTER OF RESPECT.

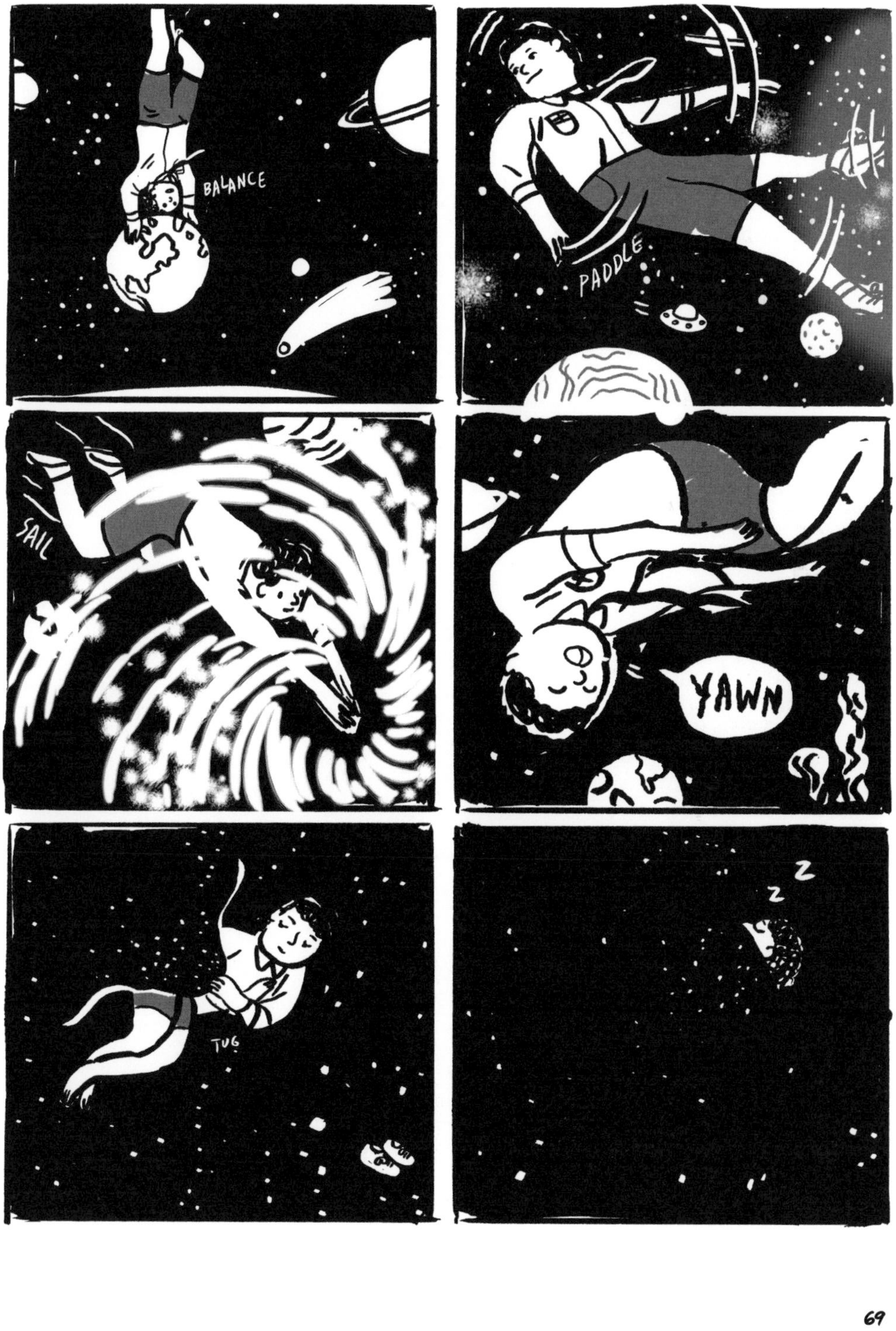
BALANCE
PADDLE
SAIL
YAWN
TUG
Z
Z

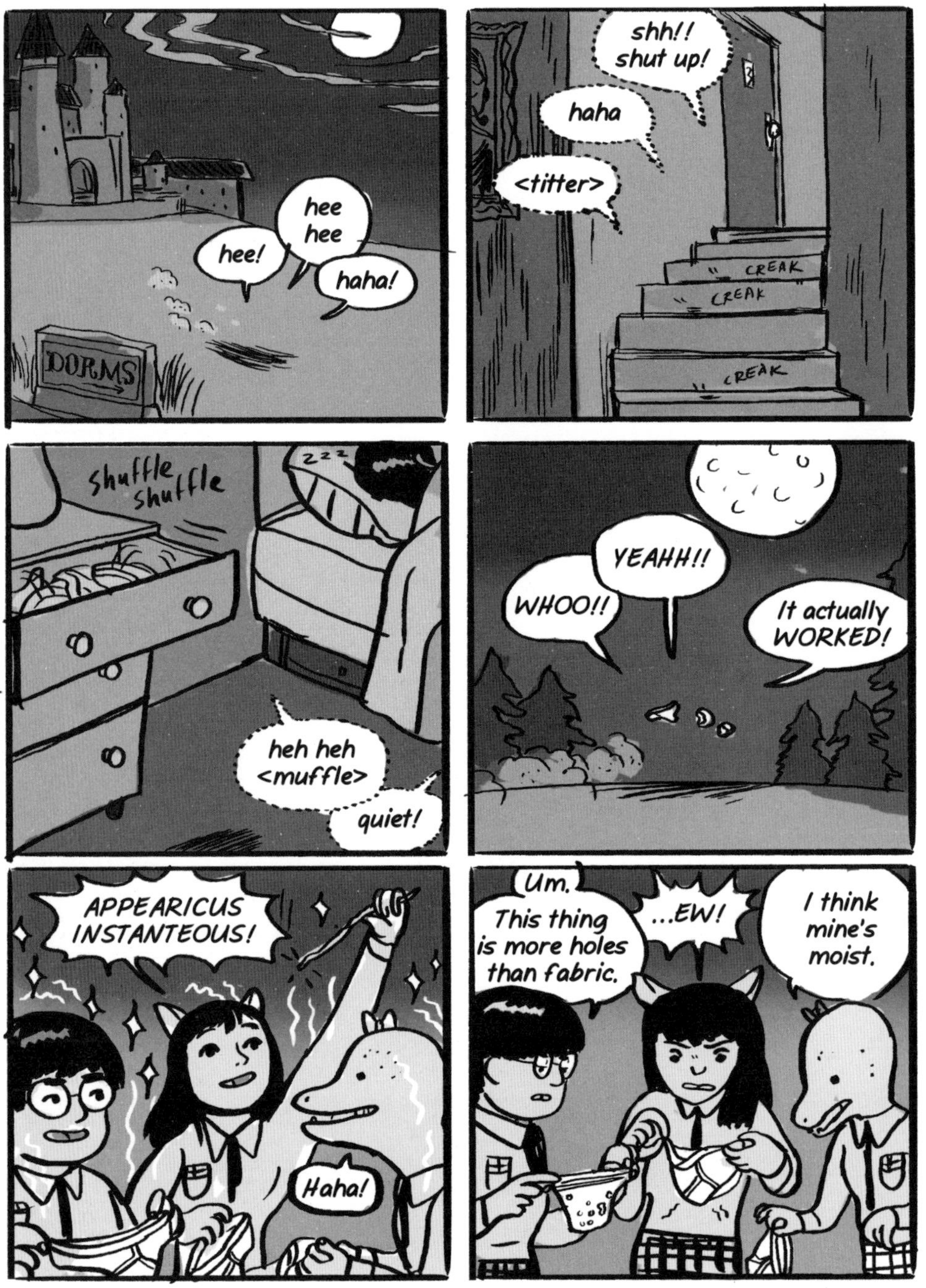
DORMS
hee!
hee hee
haha!
shh!! shut up!
haha
<titter>
CREAK
CREAK
CREAK
shuffle shuffle
zzz
heh heh <muffle>
quiet!
WHOO!!
YEAHH!!
It actually WORKED!
APPEARICUS INSTANTEOUS!
Haha!
Um.
This thing is more holes than fabric.
...EW!
I think mine's moist.

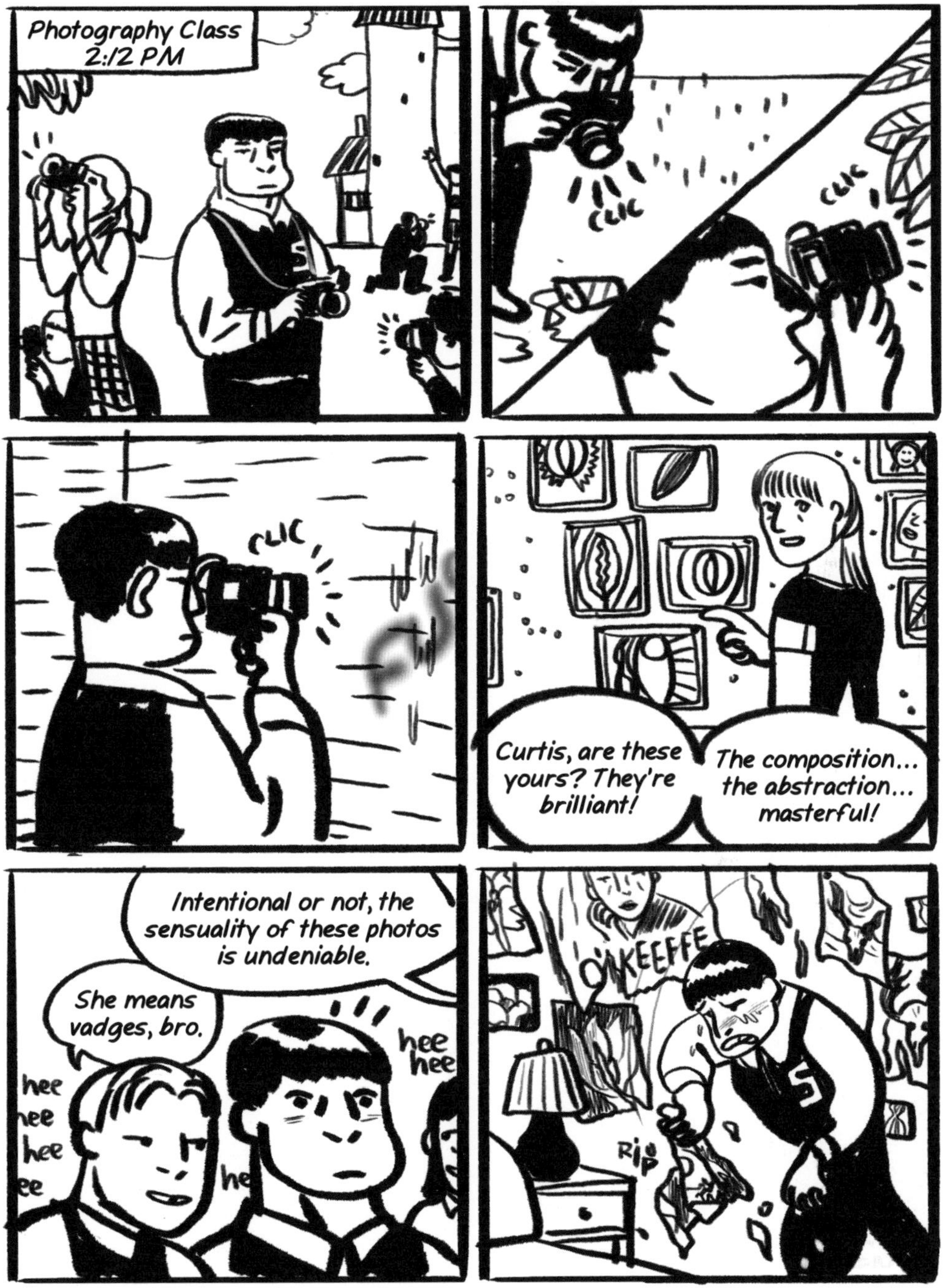
Photography Class 2:12 PM
CLIC
CLIC
CLIC
Curtis, are these yours? They're brilliant!
The composition... the abstraction... masterful!
Intentional or not, the sensuality of these photos is undeniable.
She means vadges, bro.
hee hee
hee hee hee hee
he
O'KEEFFE
RIP

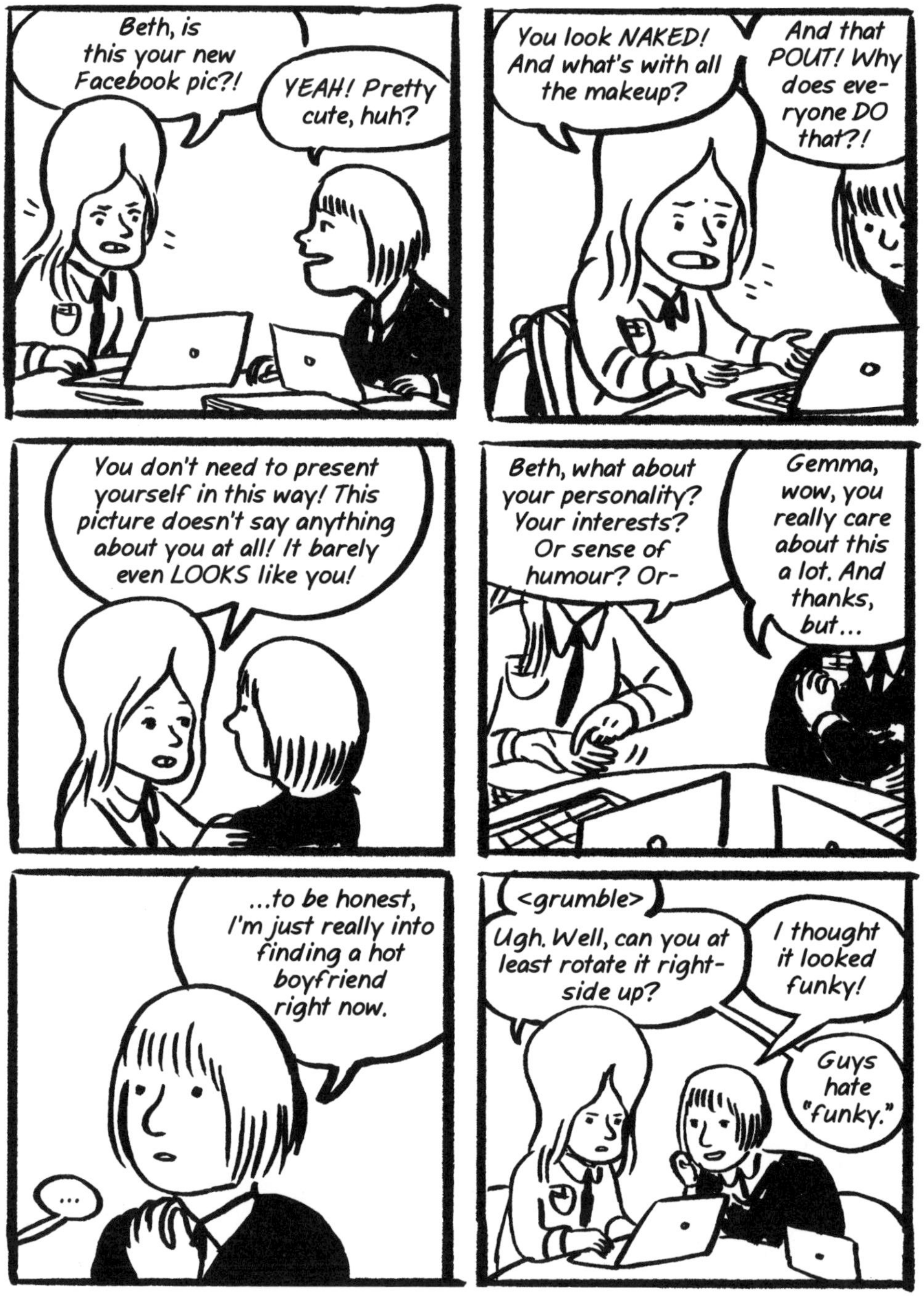
Beth, is this your new Facebook pic?!
YEAH! Pretty cute, huh?
You look NAKED! And what's with all the makeup?
And that POUT! Why does everyone DO that?!
You don't need to present yourself in this way! This picture doesn't say anything about you at all! It barely even LOOKS like you!
Beth, what about your personality? Your interests? Or sense of humour? Or-
Gemma, wow, you really care about this a lot. And thanks, but...
...to be honest, I'm just really into finding a hot boyfriend right now.
...
<grumble>
Ugh. Well, can you at least rotate it right-side up?
I thought it looked funky!
Guys hate "funky."

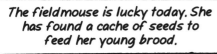

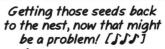

The fieldmouse is lucky today. She has found a cache of seeds to feed her young brood.

Getting those seeds back to the nest, now that might be a problem! [♪♪♪]

OH-!!

sqk!

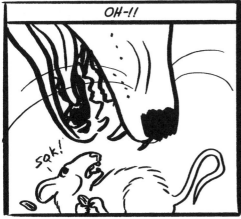

Wendy? Hello?

We're going for lunch now.

Go ahead without me. I'm not hungry...

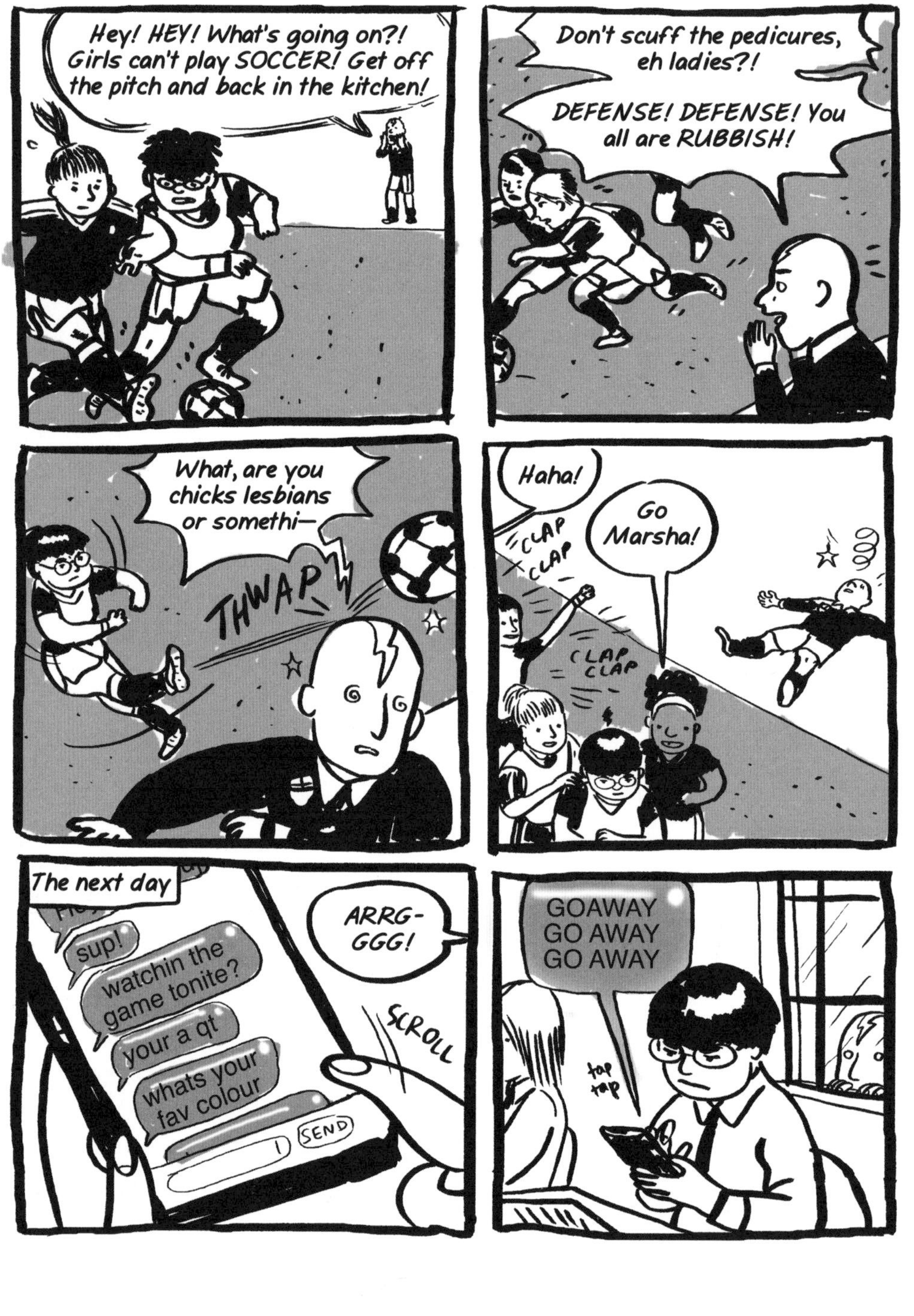
Hey! HEY! What's going on?! Girls can't play SOCCER! Get off the pitch and back in the kitchen!
Don't scuff the pedicures, eh ladies?!
DEFENSE! DEFENSE! You all are RUBBISH!
What, are you chicks lesbians or somethi—
THWAP
Haha!
CLAP CLAP
Go Marsha!
CLAP CLAP
The next day
sup!
watchin the game tonite?
your a qt
whats your fav colour
SEND
ARRG-GGG!
SCROLL
GOAWAY
GO AWAY
GO AWAY
tap tap

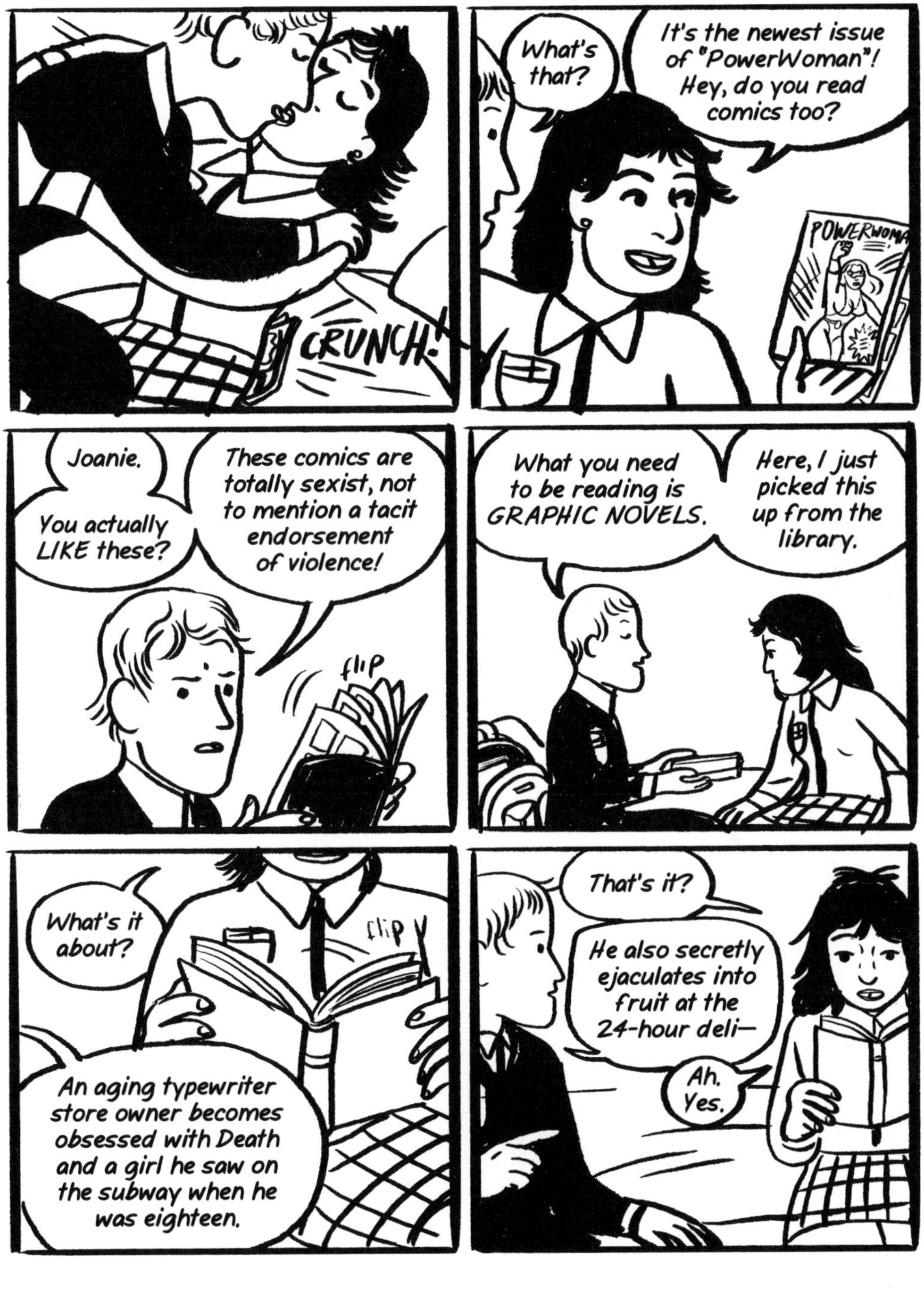
CRUNCH!
What's that?
It's the newest issue of "PowerWoman"! Hey, do you read comics too?
POWERWOMA
Joanie.
You actually LIKE these?
These comics are totally sexist, not to mention a tacit endorsement of violence!
flip
What you need to be reading is GRAPHIC NOVELS.
Here, I just picked this up from the library.
What's it about?
flip
An aging typewriter store owner becomes obsessed with Death and a girl he saw on the subway when he was eighteen.
That's it?
He also secretly ejaculates into fruit at the 24-hour deli—
Ah. Yes.

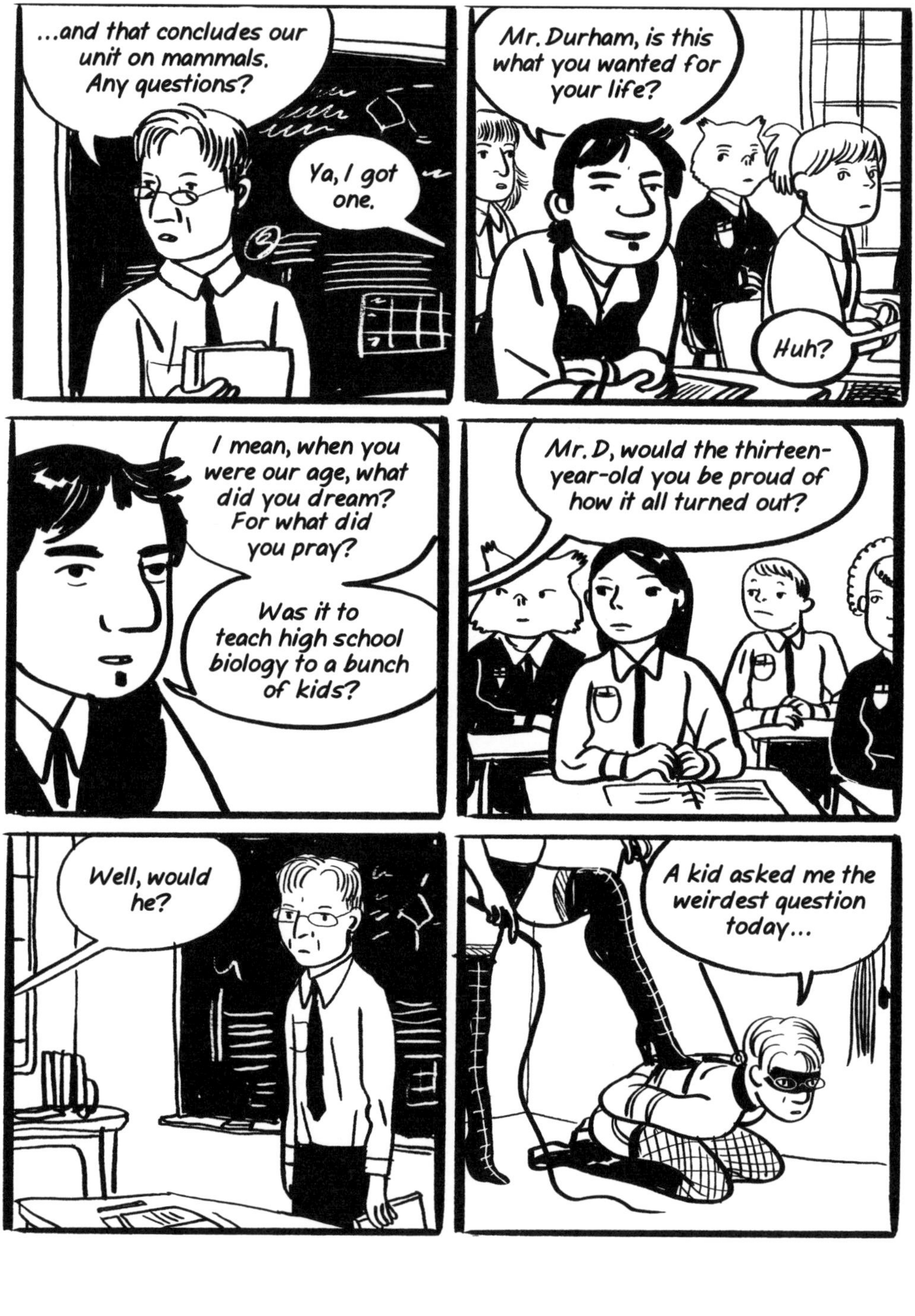
...and that concludes our unit on mammals. Any questions?
Ya, I got one.
Mr. Durham, is this what you wanted for your life?
Huh?
I mean, when you were our age, what did you dream? For what did you pray?
Was it to teach high school biology to a bunch of kids?
Mr. D, would the thirteen-year-old you be proud of how it all turned out?
Well, would he?
A kid asked me the weirdest question today...

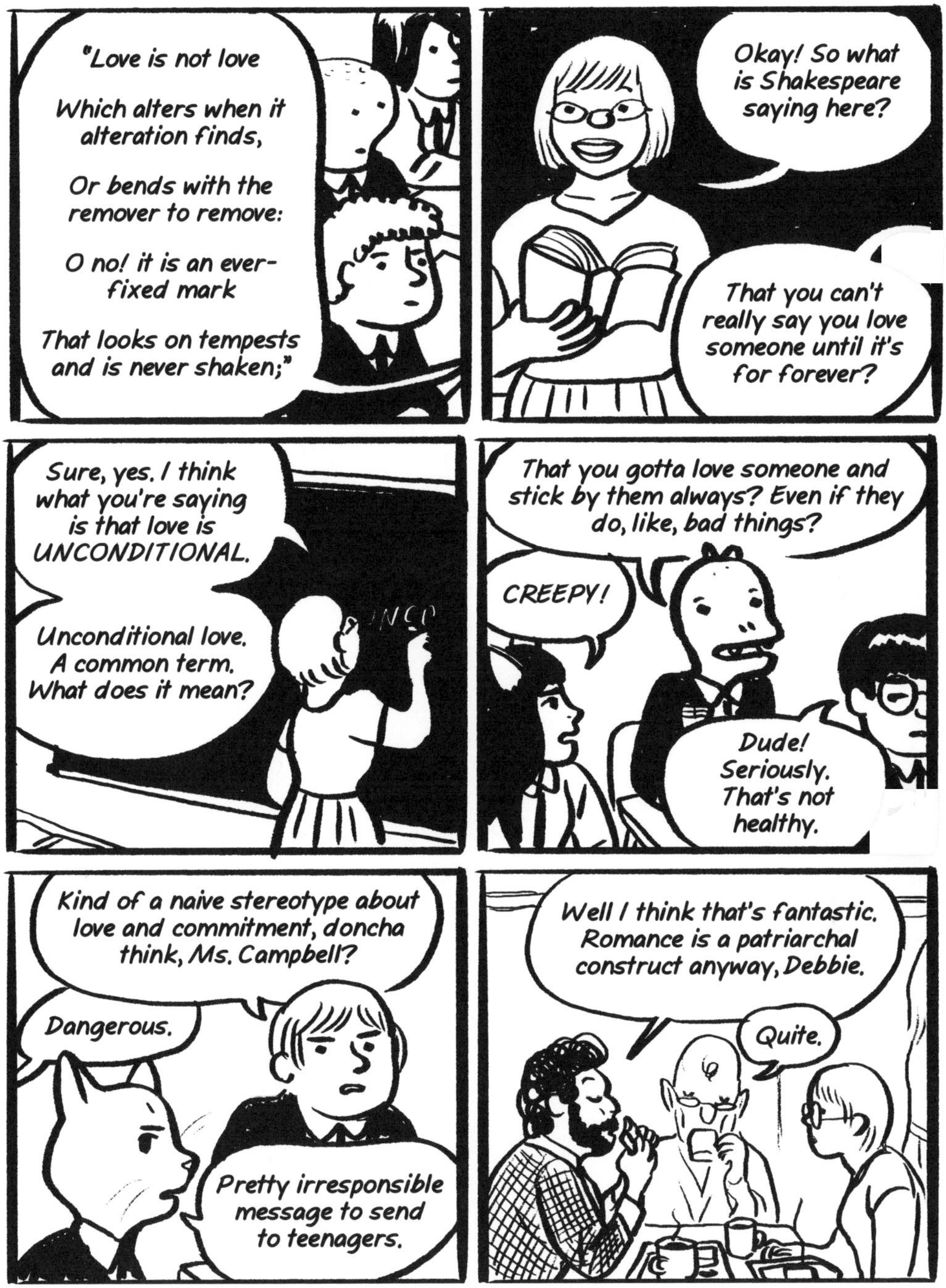
"Love is not love
Which alters when it alteration finds,
Or bends with the remover to remove:
O no! it is an ever-fixed mark
That looks on tempests and is never shaken;"
Okay! So what is Shakespeare saying here?
That you can't really say you love someone until it's for forever?
Sure, yes. I think what you're saying is that love is UNCONDITIONAL.
Unconditional love. A common term. What does it mean?
That you gotta love someone and stick by them always? Even if they do, like, bad things?
CREEPY!
Dude! Seriously. That's not healthy.
Kind of a naive stereotype about love and commitment, doncha think, Ms. Campbell?
Dangerous.
Pretty irresponsible message to send to teenagers.
Well I think that's fantastic. Romance is a patriarchal construct anyway, Debbie.
Quite.

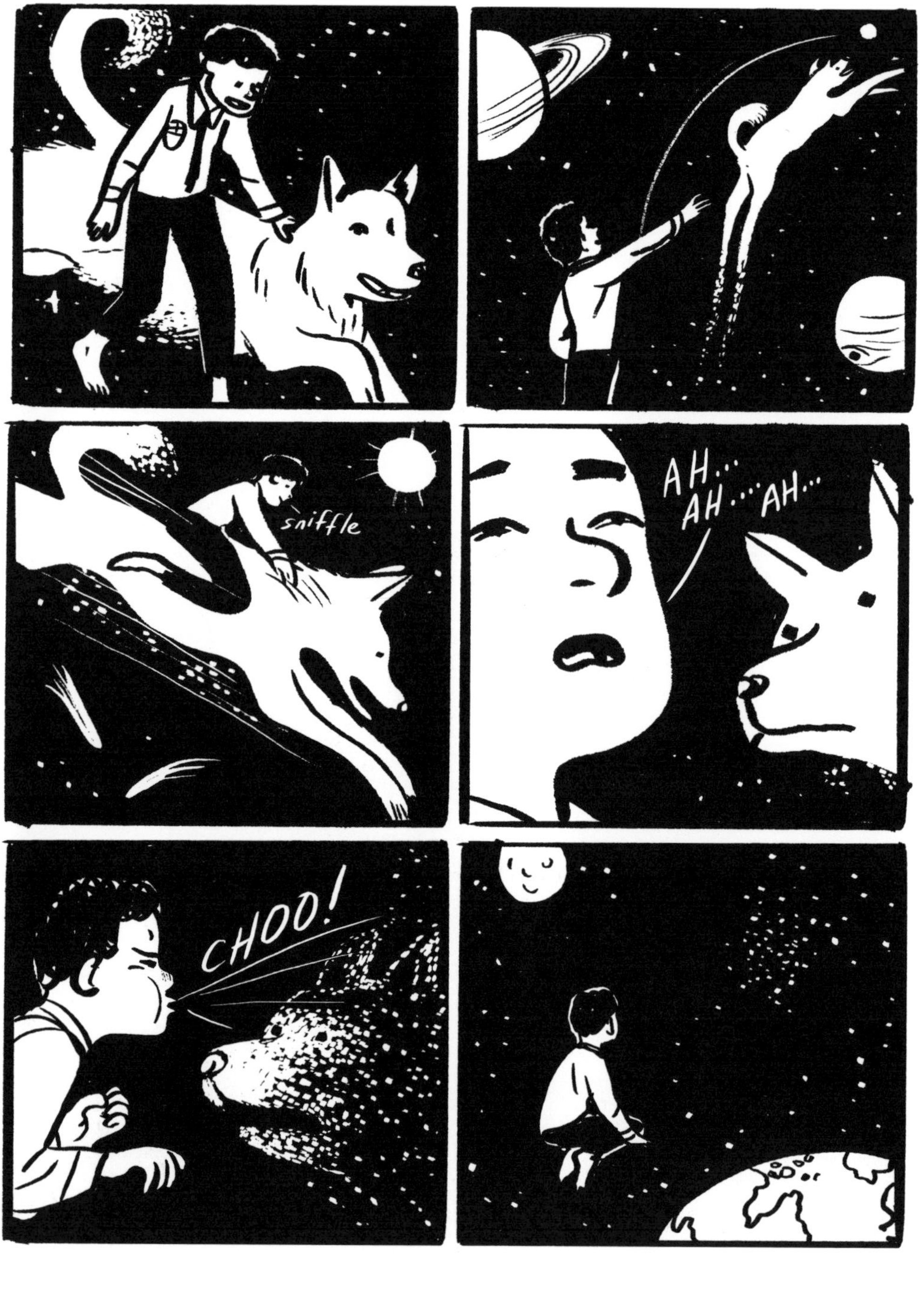
sniffle
AH... AH.... AH...
CHOO!

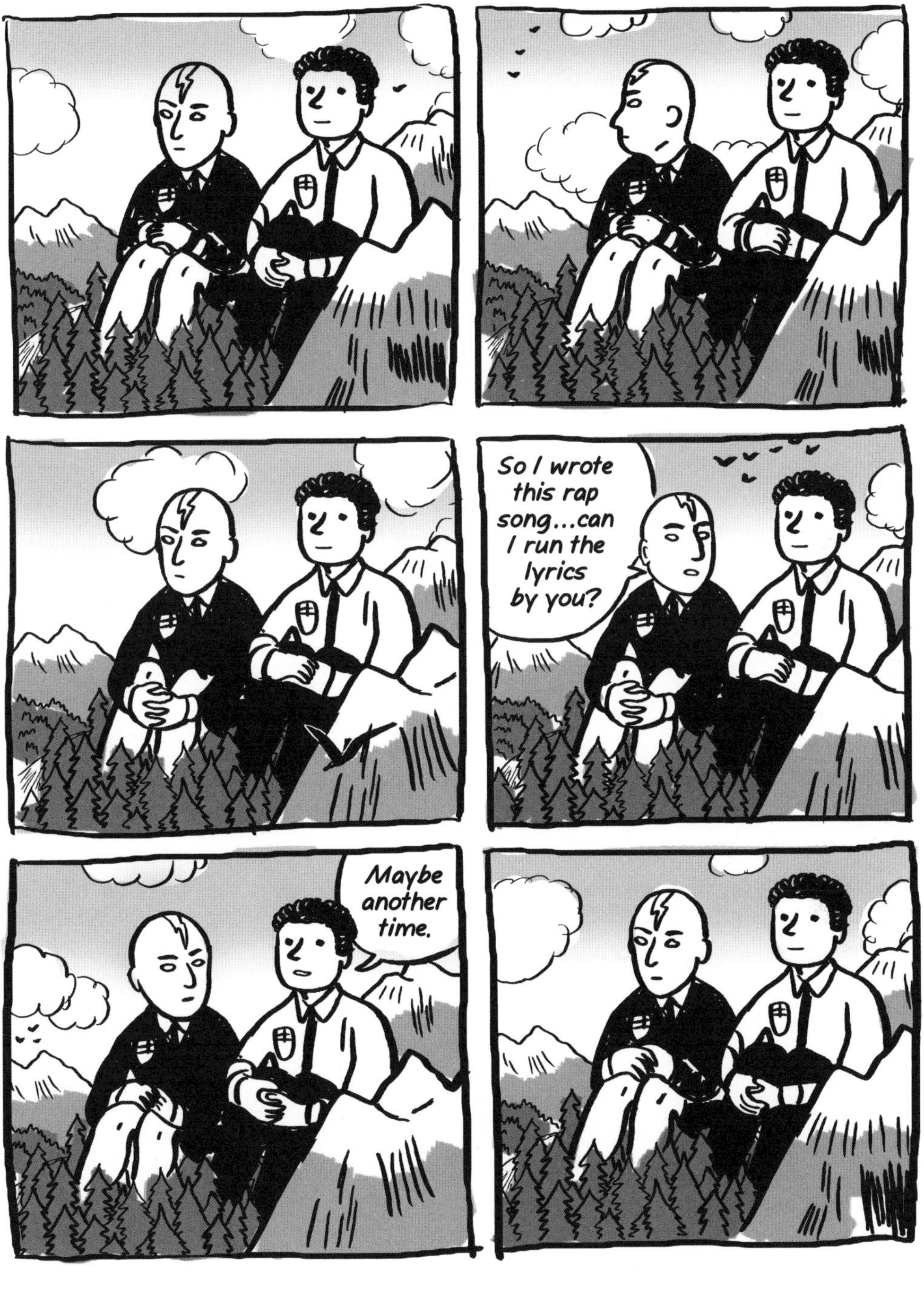
So I wrote this rap song...can I run the lyrics by you?
Maybe another time.

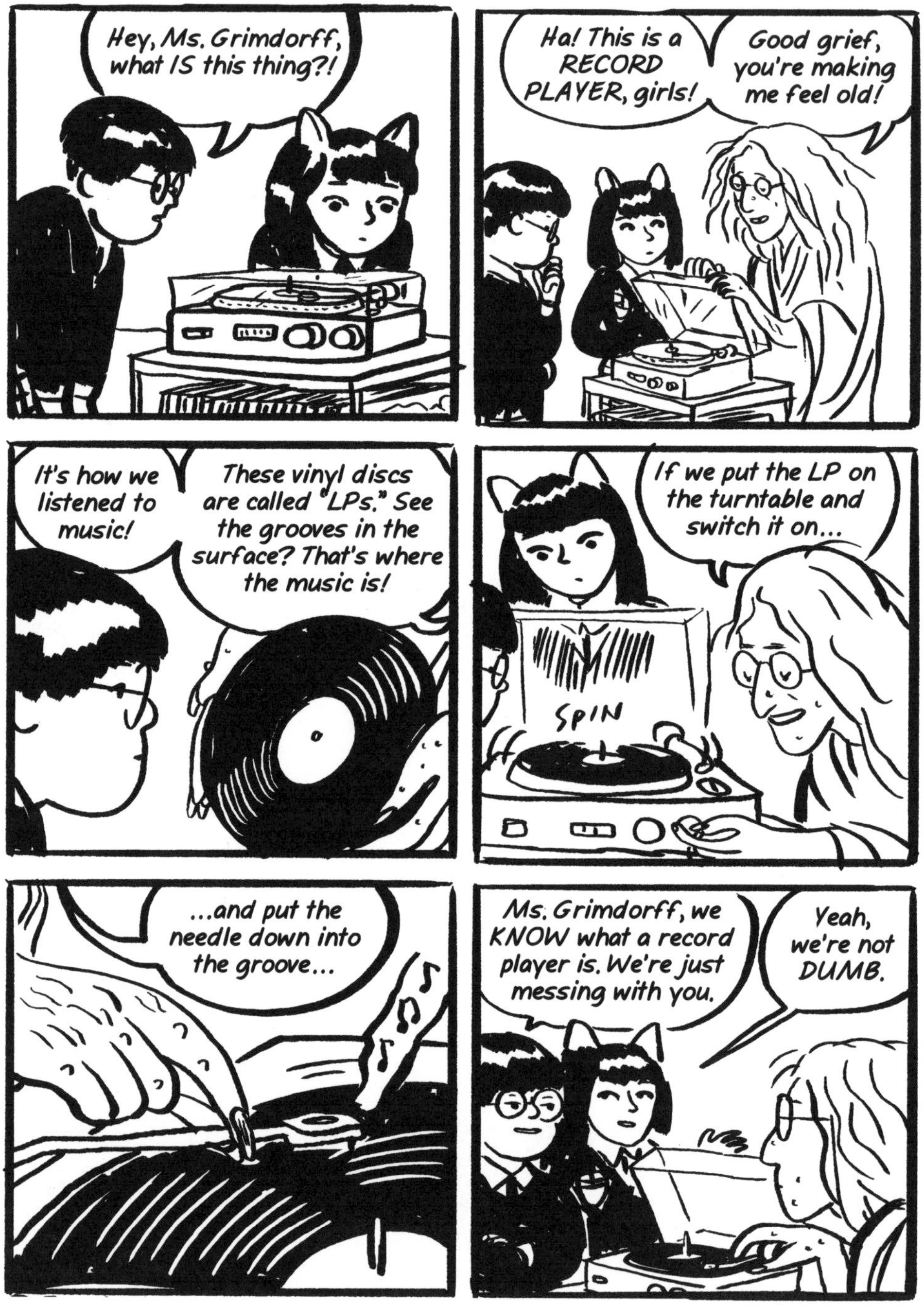
Hey, Ms. Grimdorff, what IS this thing?!
Ha! This is a RECORD PLAYER, girls!
Good grief, you're making me feel old!
It's how we listened to music!
These vinyl discs are called "LPs." See the grooves in the surface? That's where the music is!
If we put the LP on the turntable and switch it on...
SPIN
...and put the needle down into the groove...
Ms. Grimdorff, we KNOW what a record player is. We're just messing with you.
Yeah, we're not DUMB.

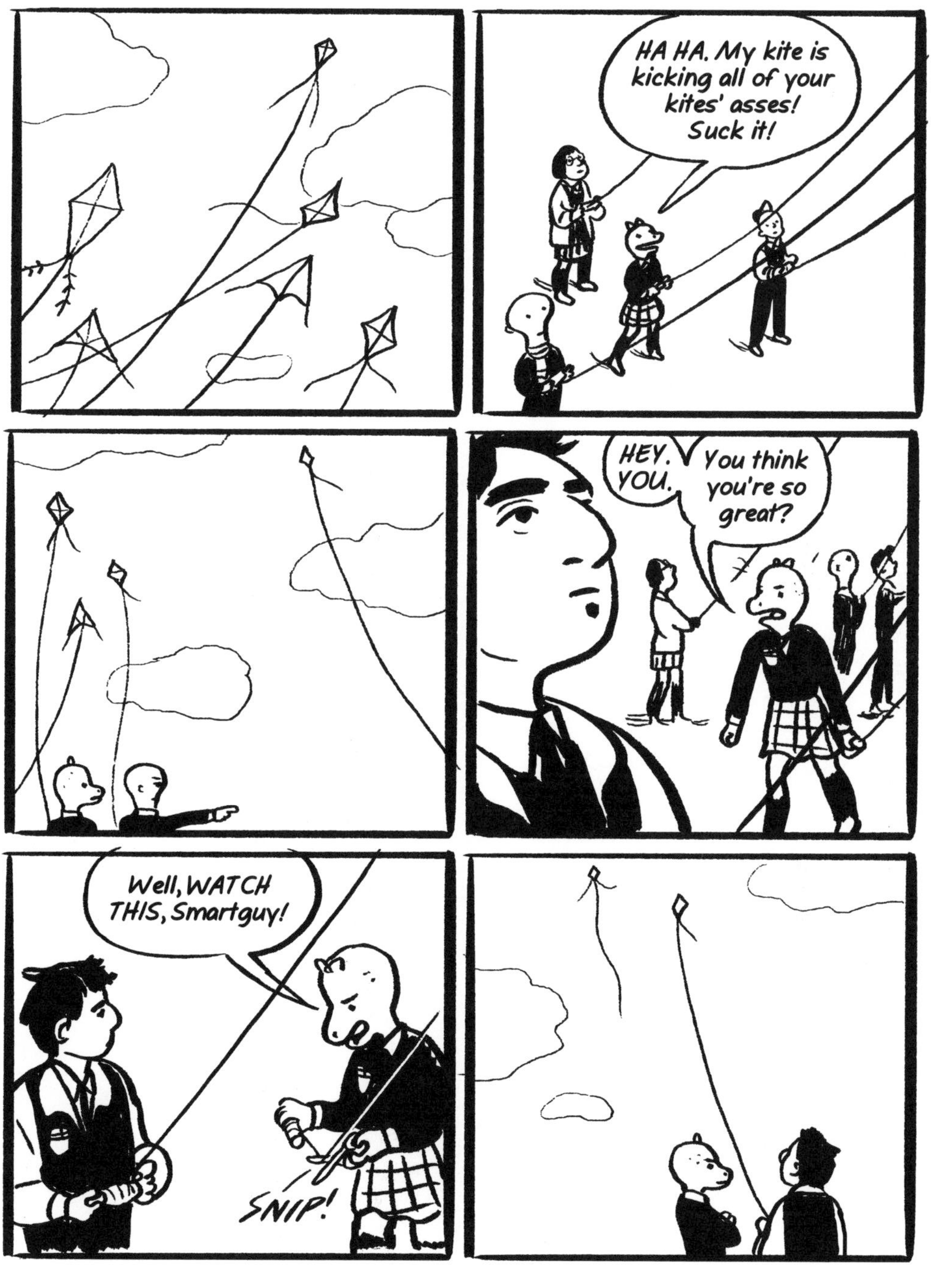
HA HA. My kite is kicking all of your kites' asses! Suck it!
HEY. YOU.
You think you're so great?
Well, WATCH THIS, Smartguy!
SNIP!

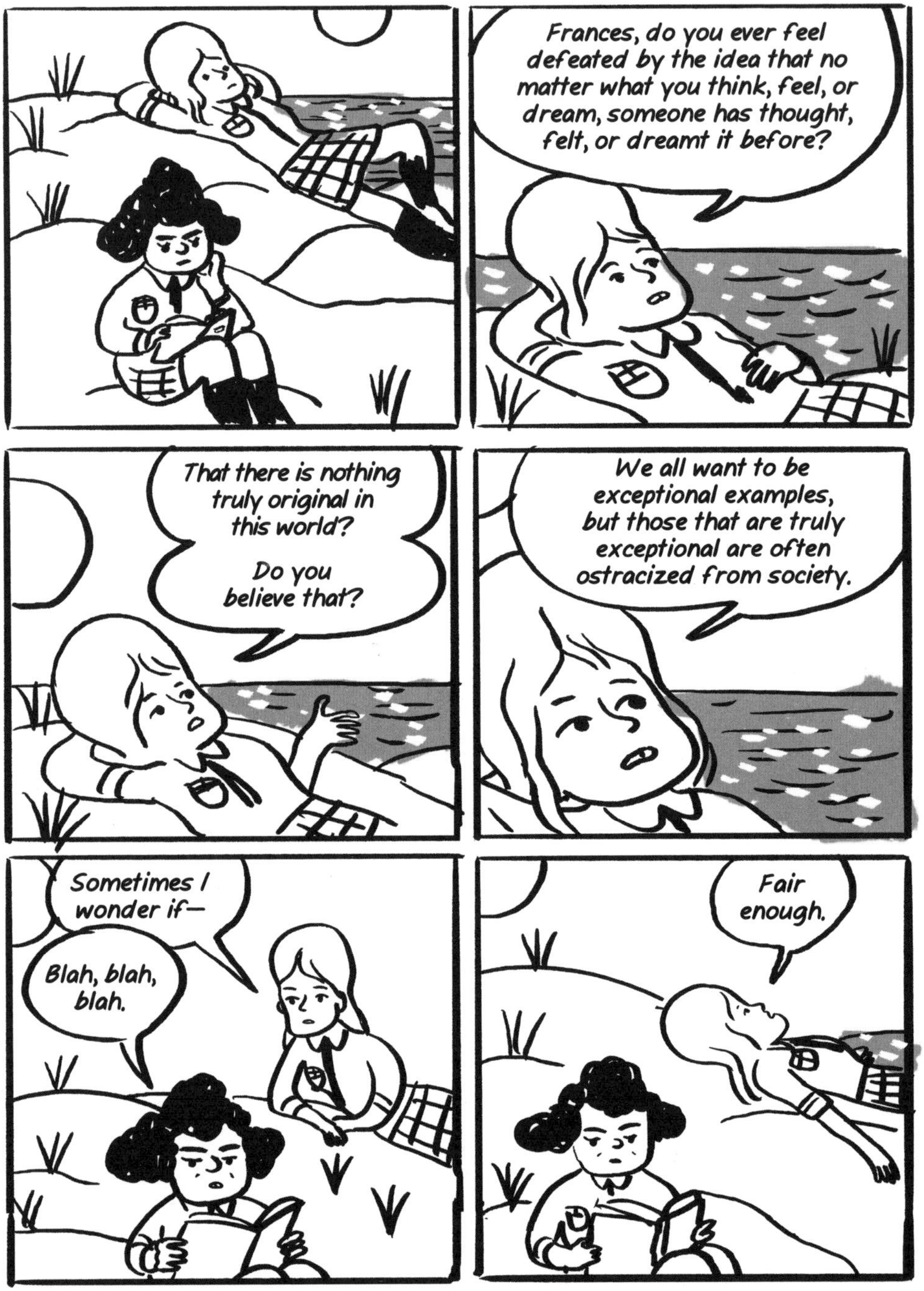
Frances, do you ever feel defeated by the idea that no matter what you think, feel, or dream, someone has thought, felt, or dreamt it before?
That there is nothing truly original in this world?
Do you believe that?
We all want to be exceptional examples, but those that are truly exceptional are often ostracized from society.
Sometimes I wonder if—
Blah, blah, blah.
Fair enough.

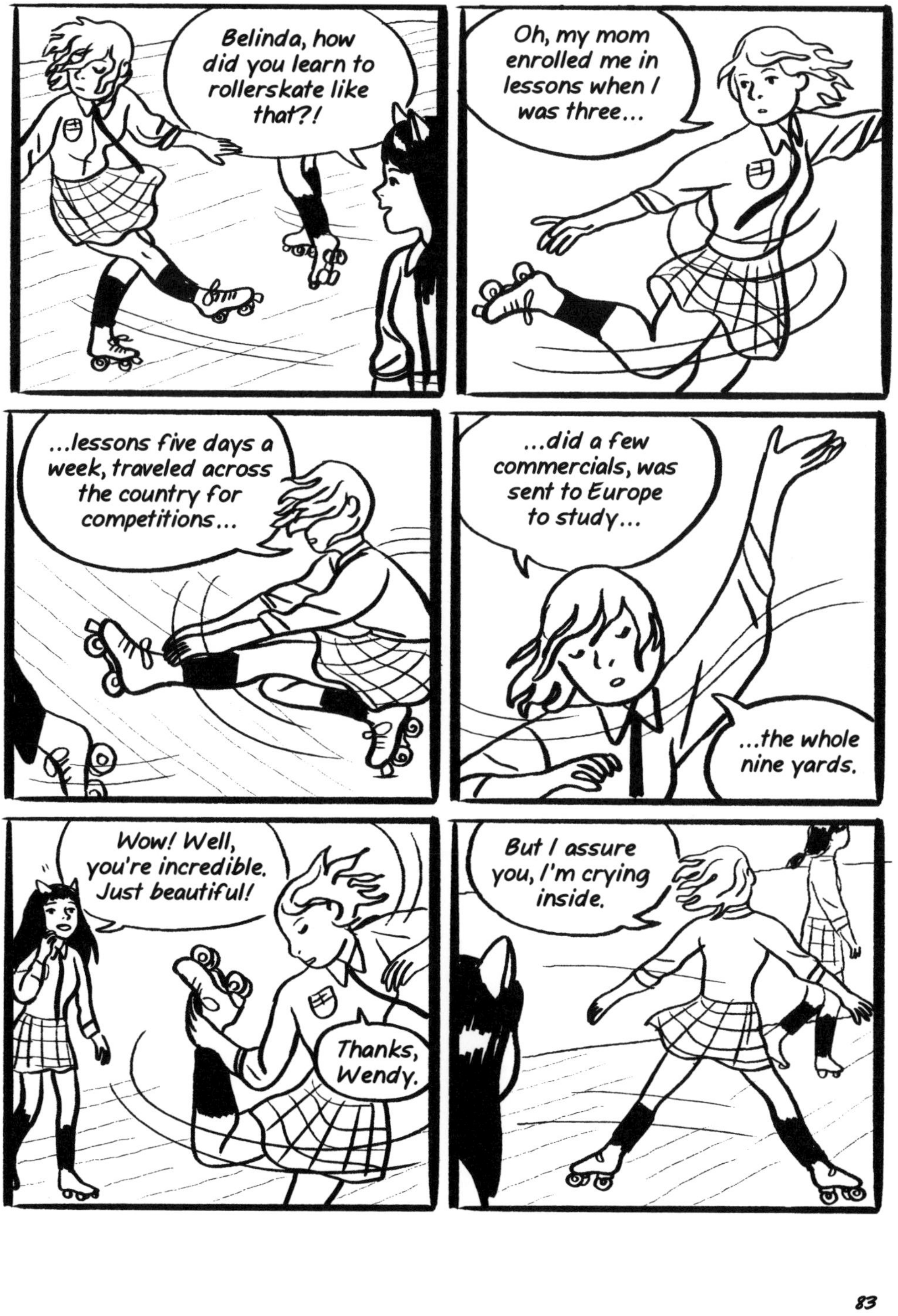
Belinda, how did you learn to rollerskate like that?!
Oh, my mom enrolled me in lessons when I was three...
...lessons five days a week, traveled across the country for competitions...
...did a few commercials, was sent to Europe to study...
...the whole nine yards.
Wow! Well, you're incredible. Just beautiful!
Thanks, Wendy.
But I assure you, I'm crying inside.

Art is all about context.
See this empty beer can? This can be Art.
Haha, you don't believe me?
Well, you see, one is used to observing a beer can on the street. Discarded. Worthless.
But what if I were to place the can somewhere else? What if I put it here in the gallery, on this pillow?
This new environment forges new meanings.
That's CONTEXT!

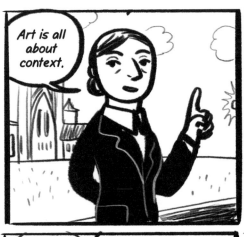

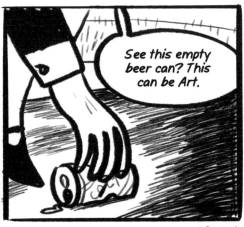

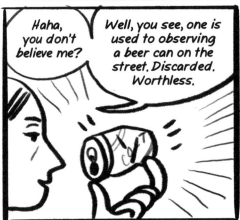

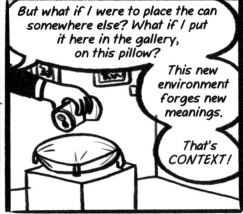

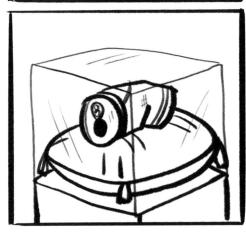

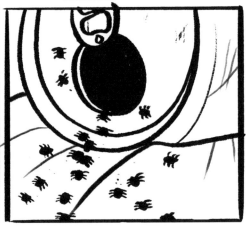

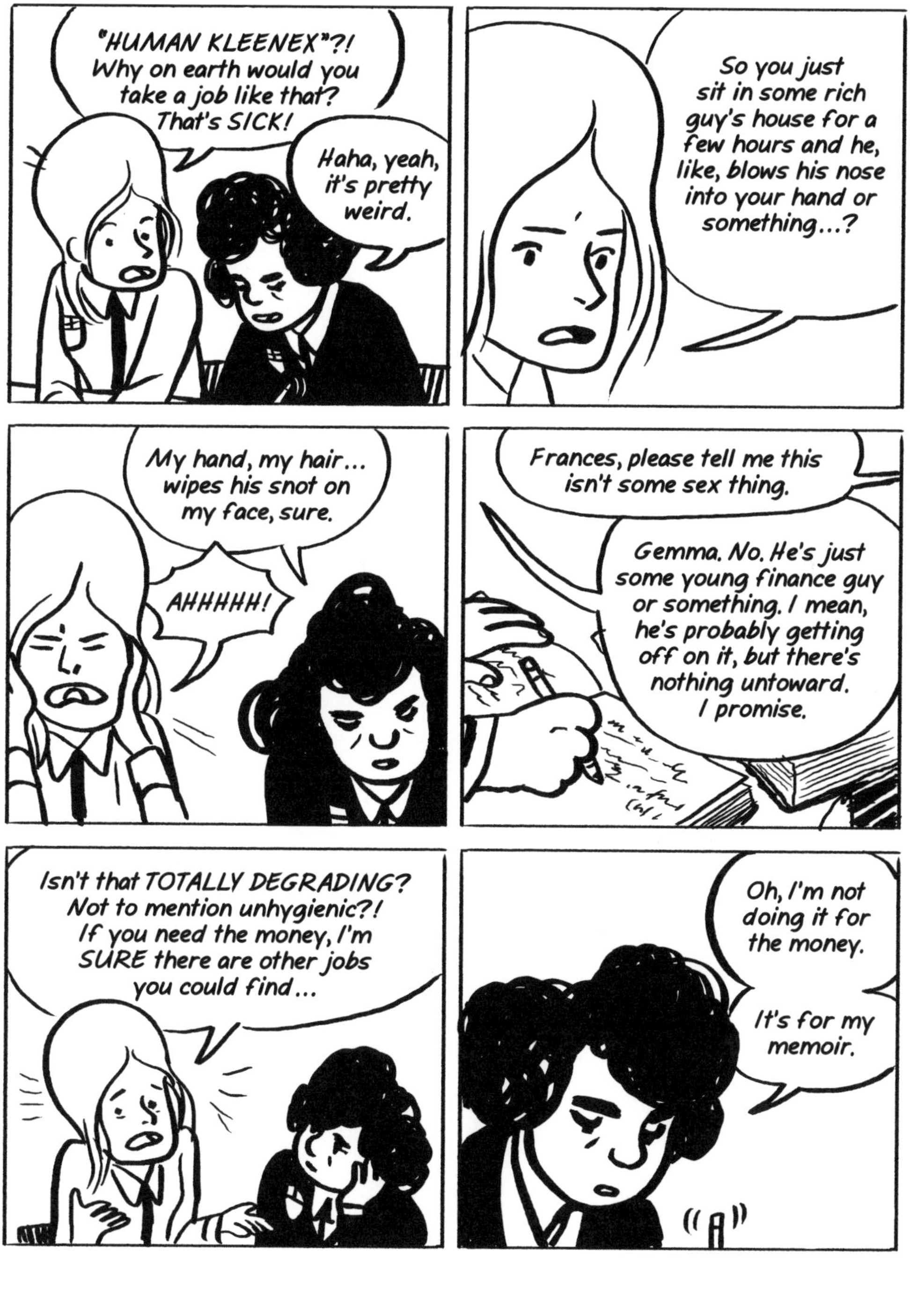
"HUMAN KLEENEX"?! Why on earth would you take a job like that? That's SICK!
Haha, yeah, it's pretty weird.
So you just sit in some rich guy's house for a few hours and he, like, blows his nose into your hand or something...?
My hand, my hair... wipes his snot on my face, sure.
AHHHHH!
Frances, please tell me this isn't some sex thing.
Gemma. No. He's just some young finance guy or something. I mean, he's probably getting off on it, but there's nothing untoward. I promise.
Isn't that TOTALLY DEGRADING? Not to mention unhygienic?! If you need the money, I'm SURE there are other jobs you could find...
Oh, I'm not doing it for the money.
It's for my memoir.

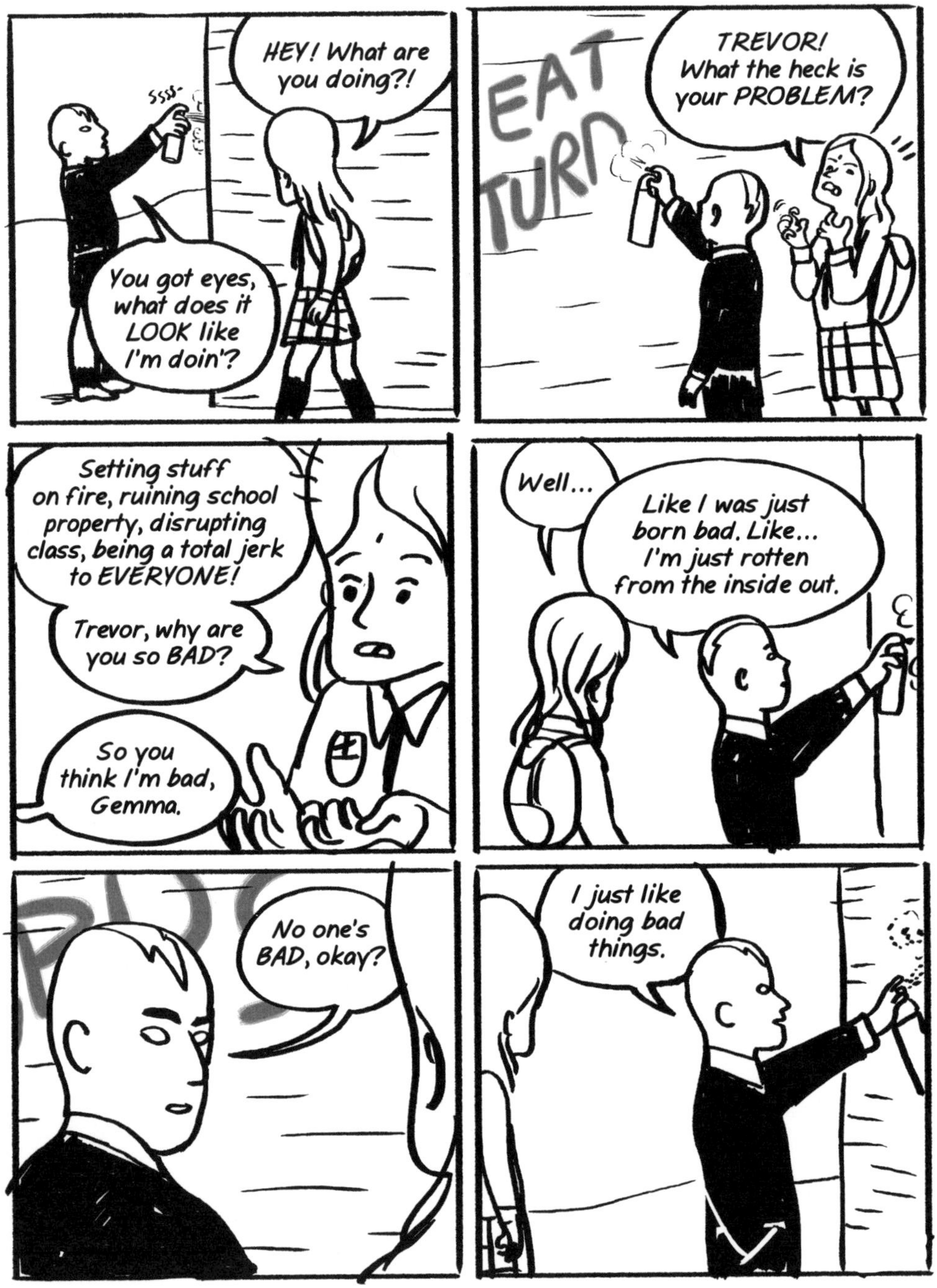
SSSS-
HEY! What are you doing?!
You got eyes, what does it LOOK like I'm doin'?
EAT TURD
TREVOR! What the heck is your PROBLEM?
Setting stuff on fire, ruining school property, disrupting class, being a total jerk to EVERYONE!
Trevor, why are you so BAD?
So you think I'm bad, Gemma.
Well...
Like I was just born bad. Like... I'm just rotten from the inside out.
No one's BAD, okay?
I just like doing bad things.

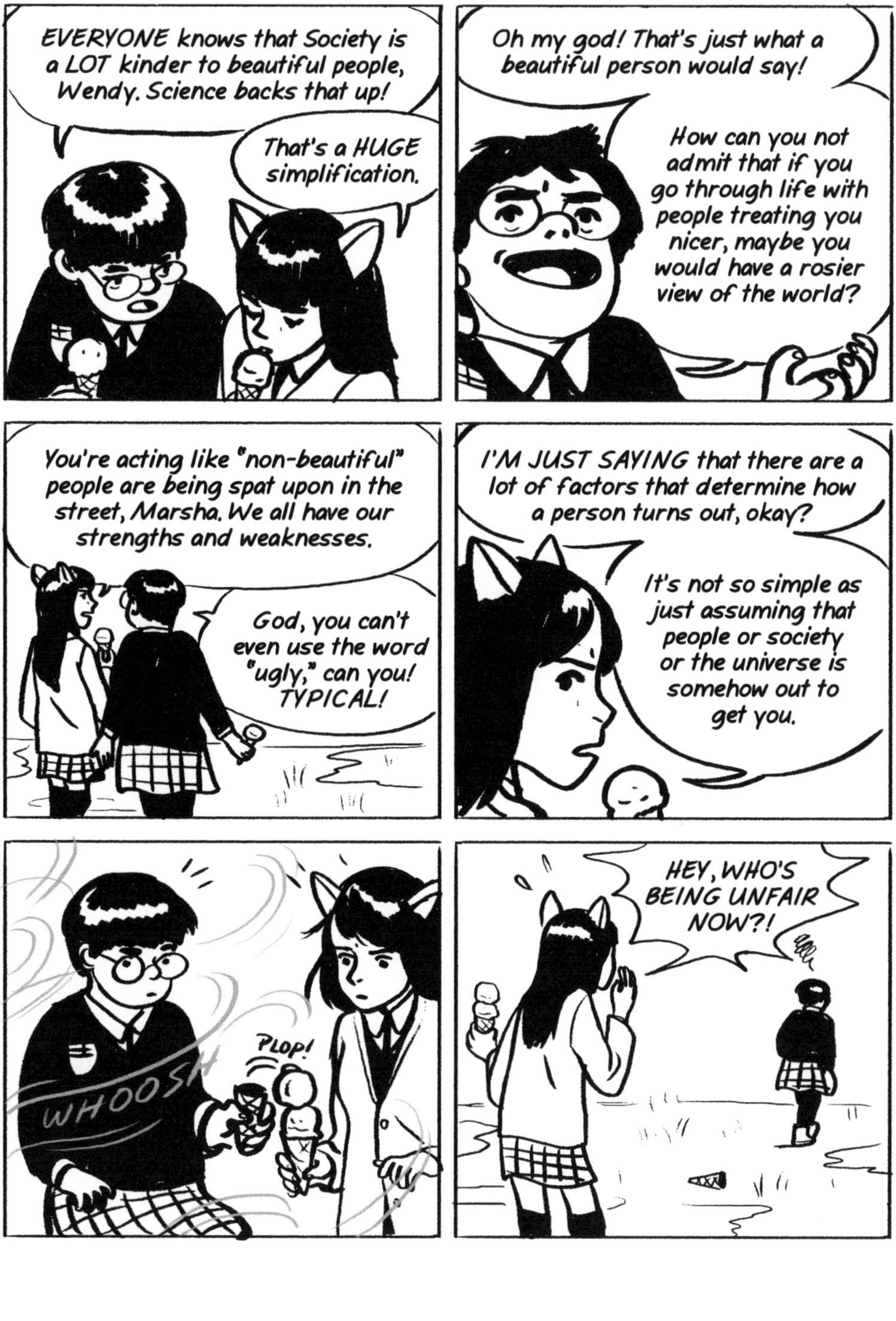
EVERYONE knows that Society is a LOT kinder to beautiful people, Wendy. Science backs that up!
That's a HUGE simplification.
Oh my god! That's just what a beautiful person would say!
How can you not admit that if you go through life with people treating you nicer, maybe you would have a rosier view of the world?
You're acting like "non-beautiful" people are being spat upon in the street, Marsha. We all have our strengths and weaknesses.
God, you can't even use the word "ugly," can you! TYPICAL!
I'M JUST SAYING that there are a lot of factors that determine how a person turns out, okay?
It's not so simple as just assuming that people or society or the universe is somehow out to get you.
PLOP!
WHOOSH
HEY, WHO'S BEING UNFAIR NOW?!

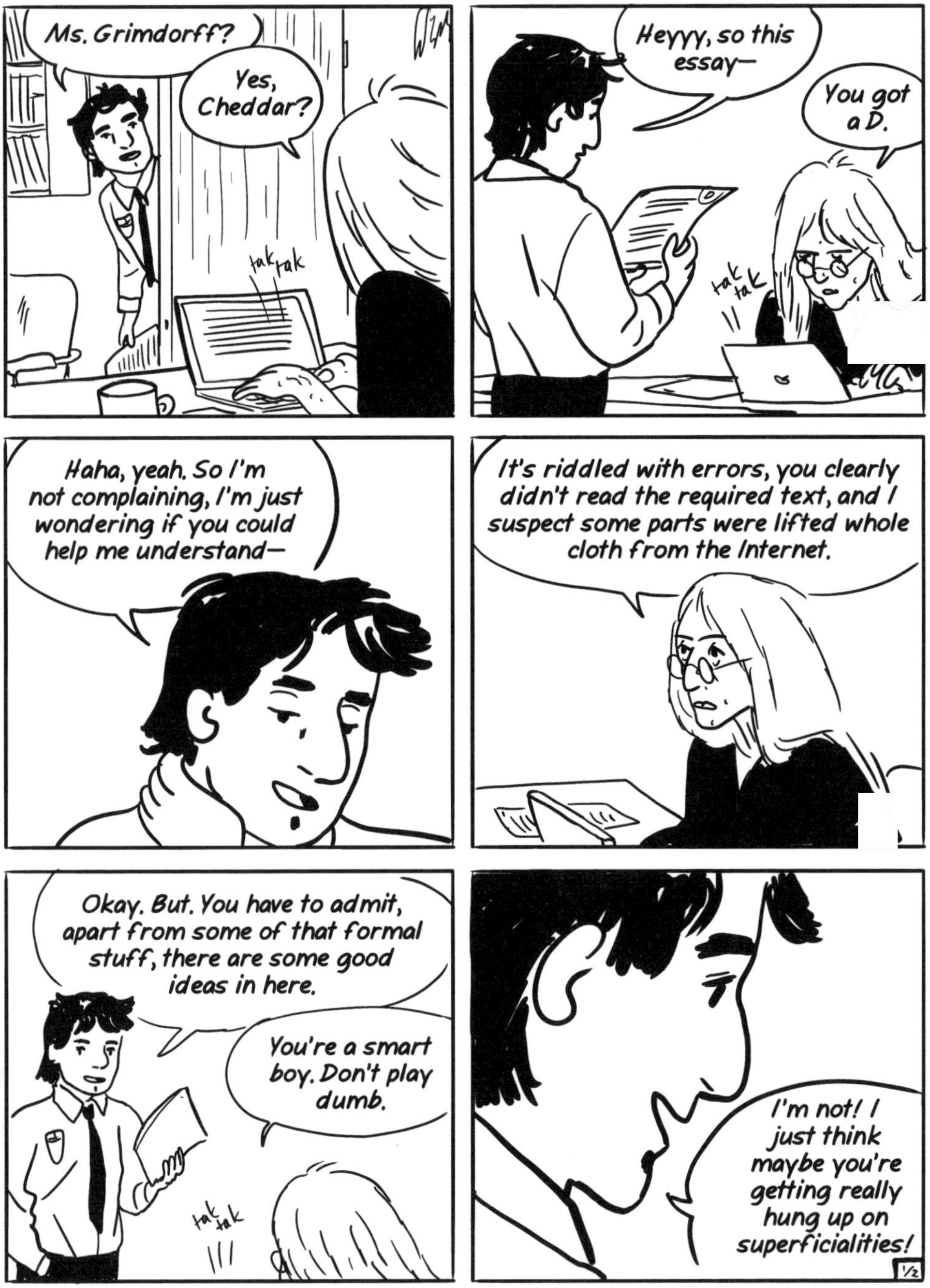
Ms. Grimdorff?
Yes, Cheddar?
tak tak
Heyyy, so this essay—
You got a D.
tak tak
Haha, yeah. So I'm not complaining, I'm just wondering if you could help me understand—
It's riddled with errors, you clearly didn't read the required text, and I suspect some parts were lifted whole cloth from the Internet.
Okay. But. You have to admit, apart from some of that formal stuff, there are some good ideas in here.
You're a smart boy. Don't play dumb.
tak tak
I'm not! I just think maybe you're getting really hung up on superficialities!
1/2

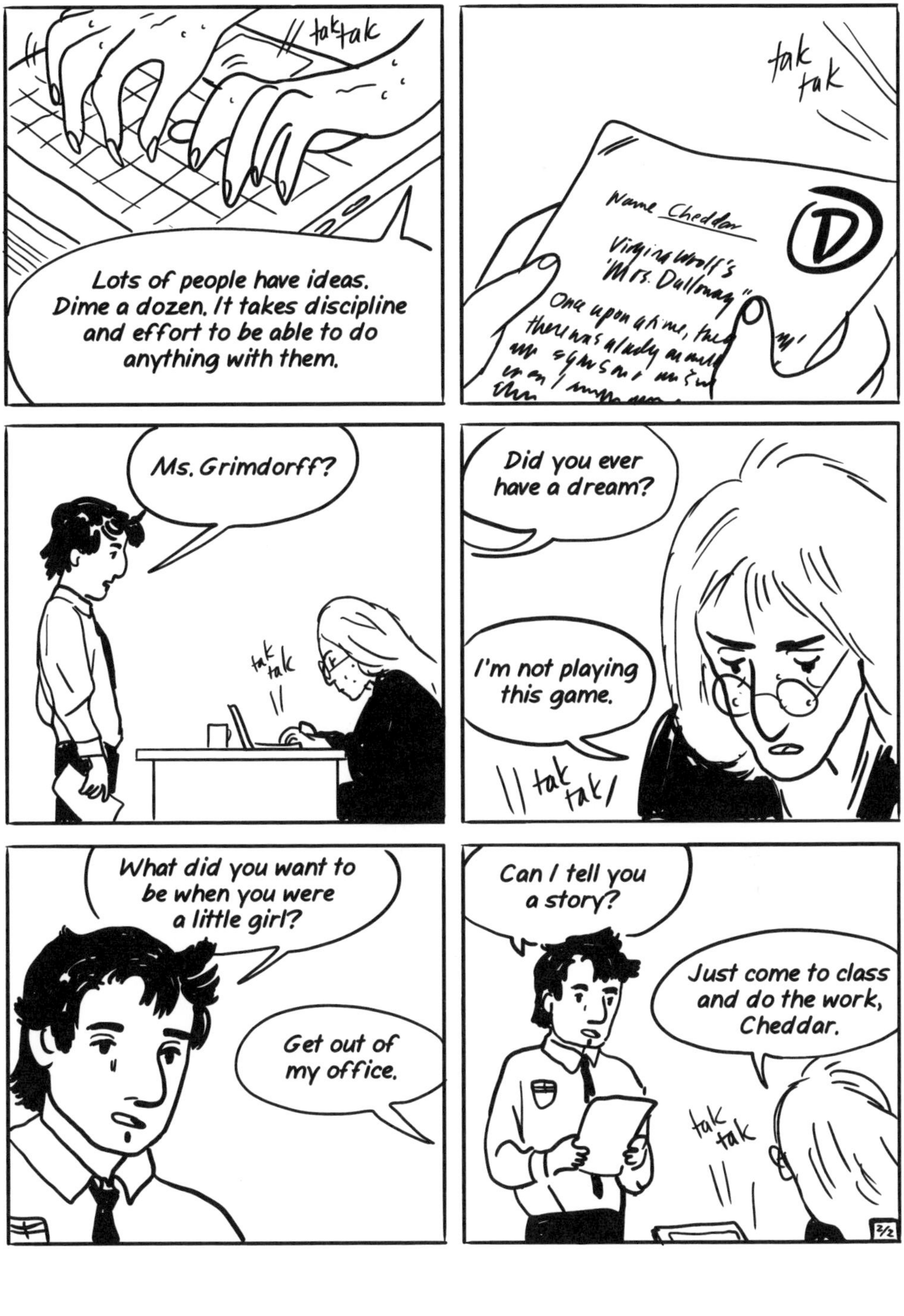

tak tak
Lots of people have ideas. Dime a dozen. It takes discipline and effort to be able to do anything with them.
tak tak
Name Cheddar
D
Virginia Woolf's 'Mrs. Dalloway'
Ms. Grimdorff?
tak tak
Did you ever have a dream?
I'm not playing this game.
tak tak
What did you want to be when you were a little girl?
Get out of my office.
Can I tell you a story?
Just come to class and do the work, Cheddar.
tak tak
2/2

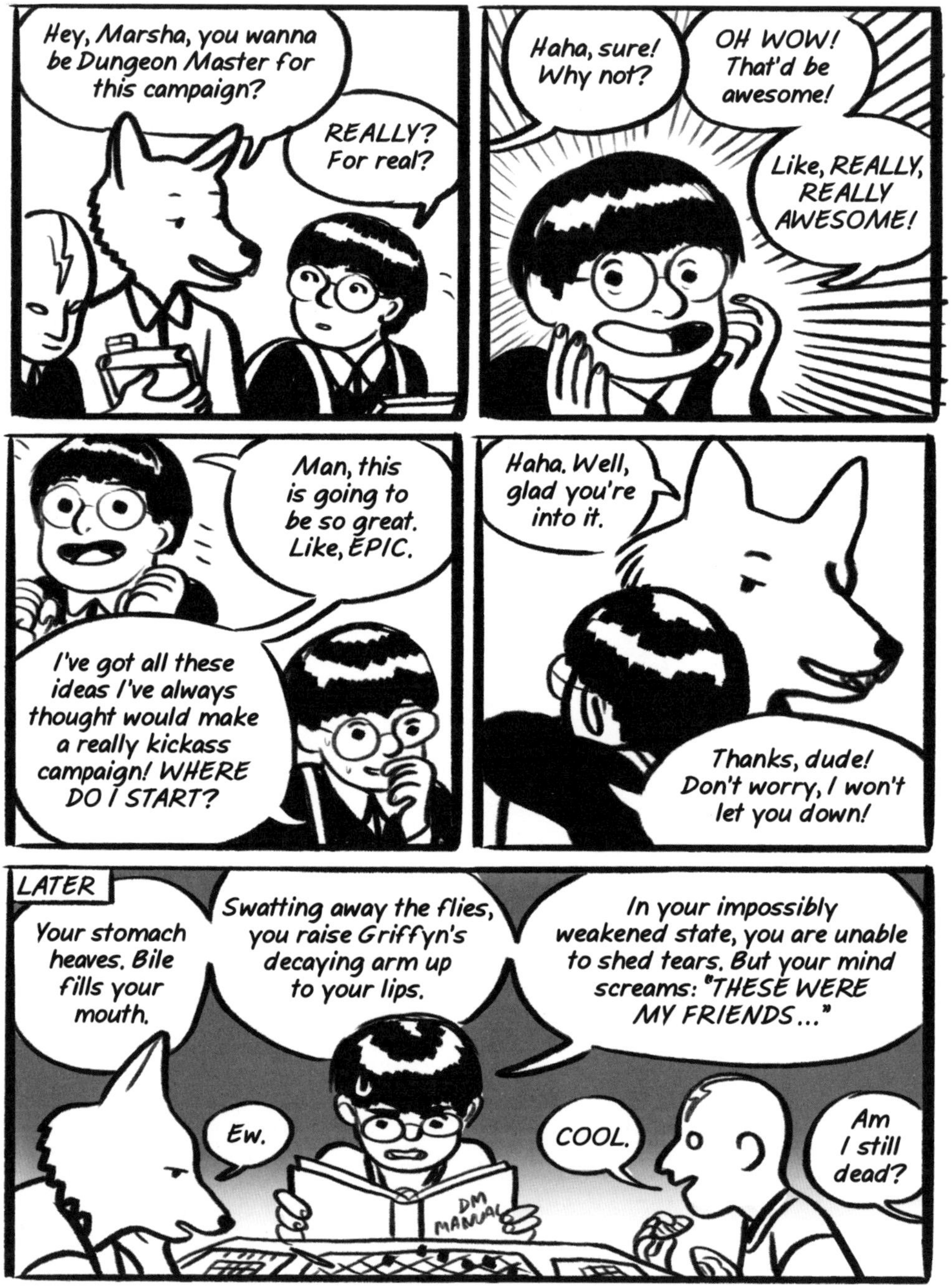
Hey, Marsha, you wanna be Dungeon Master for this campaign?
REALLY? For real?
Haha, sure! Why not?
OH WOW! That'd be awesome!
Like, REALLY, REALLY AWESOME!
Man, this is going to be so great. Like, EPIC.
I've got all these ideas I've always thought would make a really kickass campaign! WHERE DO I START?
Haha. Well, glad you're into it.
Thanks, dude! Don't worry, I won't let you down!
LATER
Your stomach heaves. Bile fills your mouth.
Swatting away the flies, you raise Griffyn's decaying arm up to your lips.
In your impossibly weakened state, you are unable to shed tears. But your mind screams: "THESE WERE MY FRIENDS..."
Ew.
COOL.
Am I still dead?
DM MANUAL

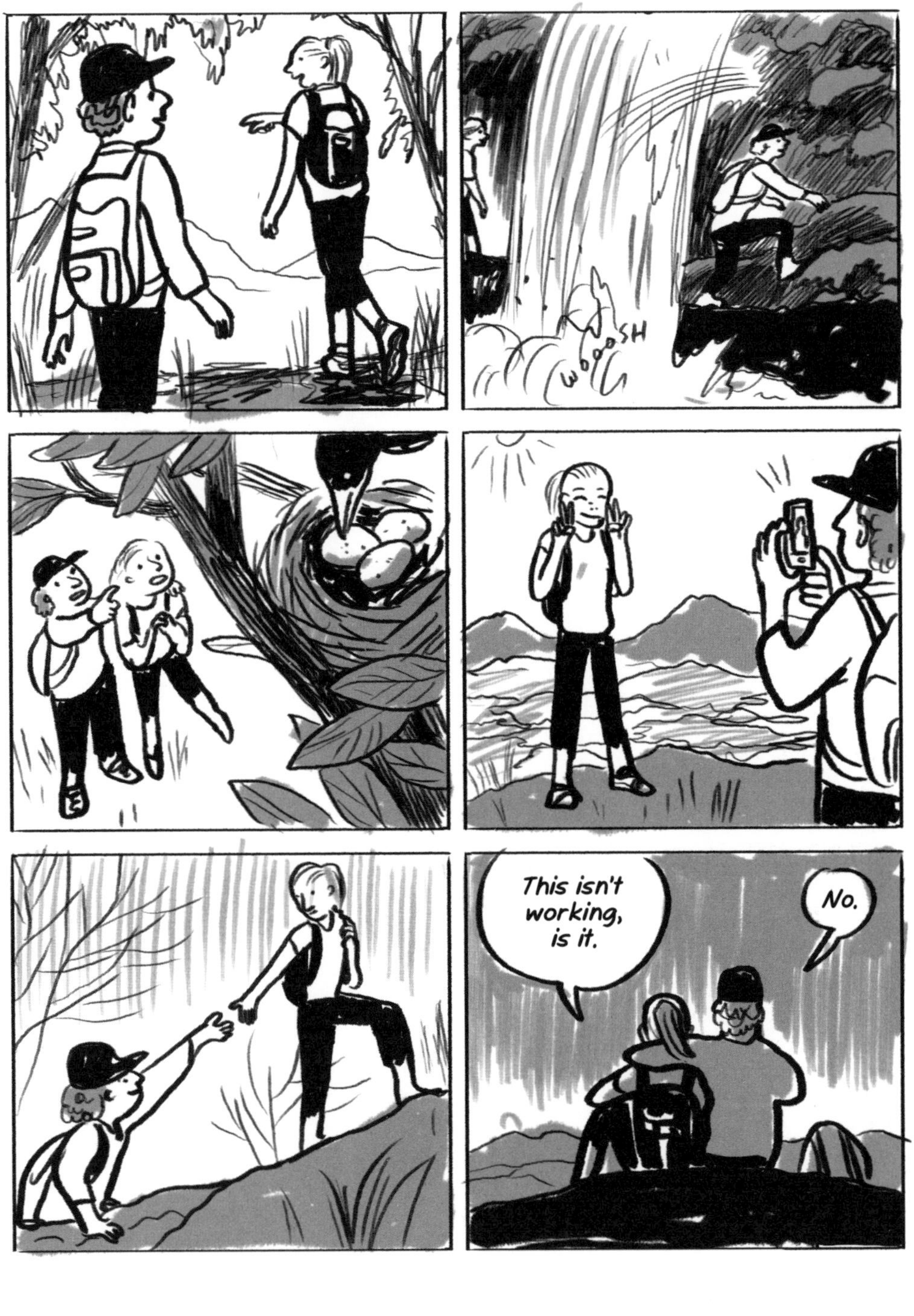
WOOOSH
This isn't working, is it.
No.

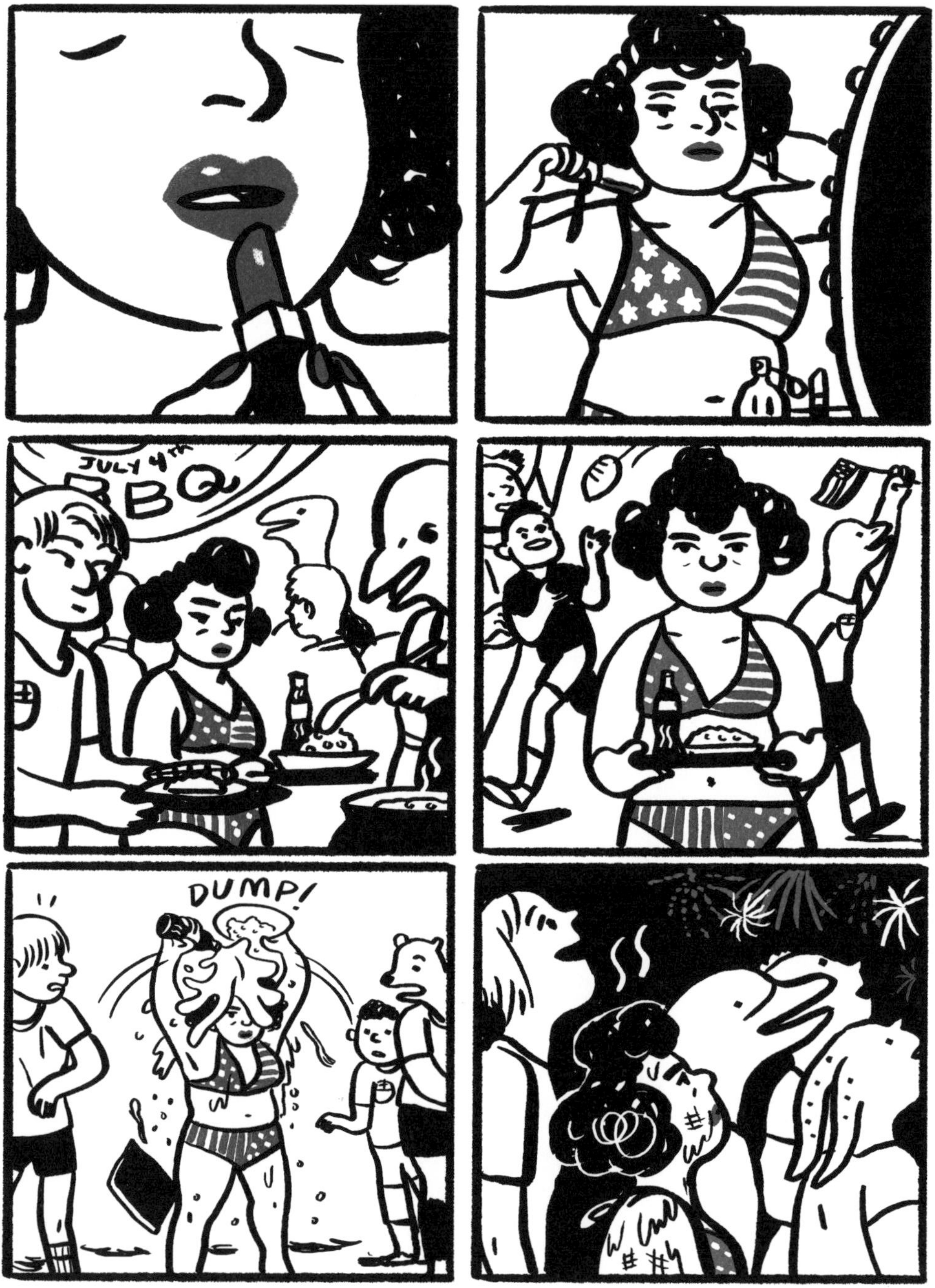
JULY 4th
BBQ
DUMP!

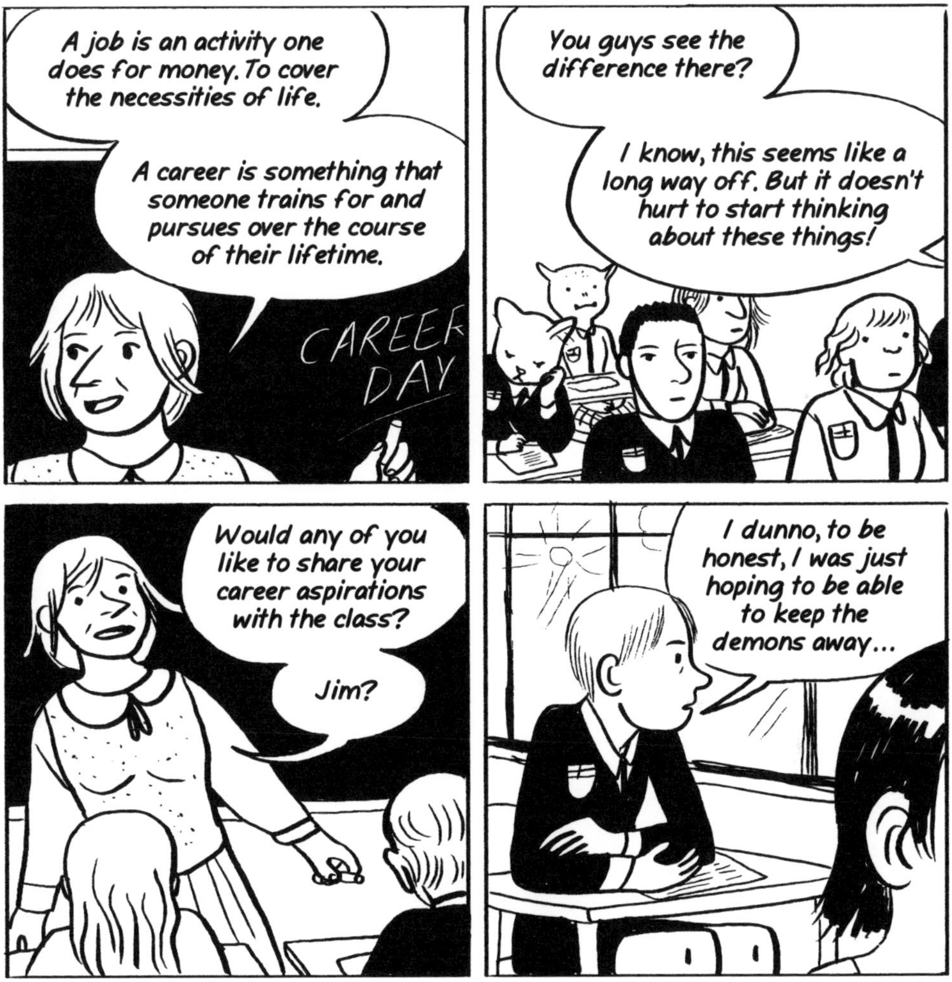
A job is an activity one does for money. To cover the necessities of life.
A career is something that someone trains for and pursues over the course of their lifetime.
CAREER DAY
You guys see the difference there?
I know, this seems like a long way off. But it doesn't hurt to start thinking about these things!
Would any of you like to share your career aspirations with the class?
Jim?
I dunno, to be honest, I was just hoping to be able to keep the demons away...

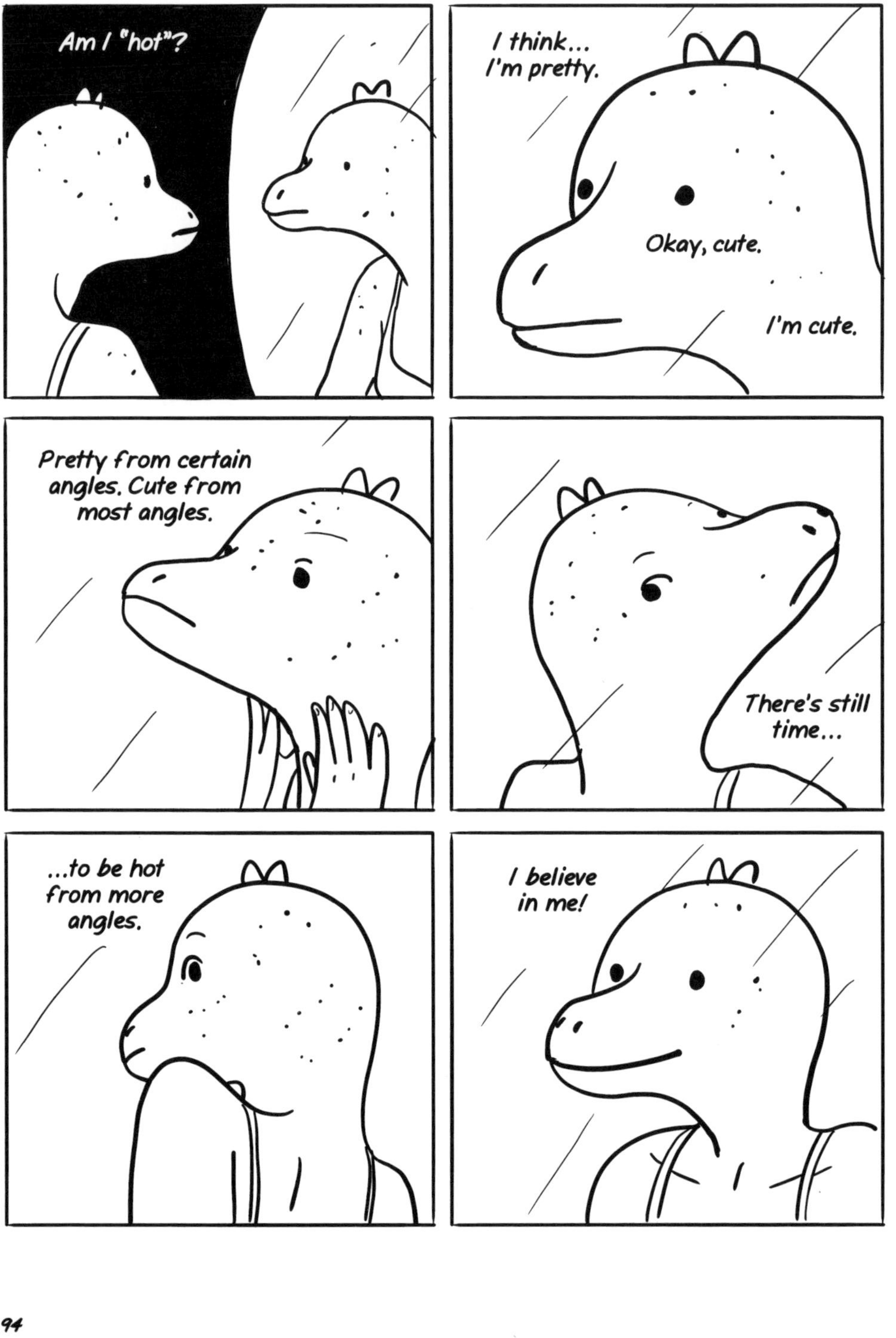
Am I "hot"?
I think... I'm pretty.
Okay, cute.
I'm cute.
Pretty from certain angles. Cute from most angles.
There's still time...
...to be hot from more angles.
I believe in me!

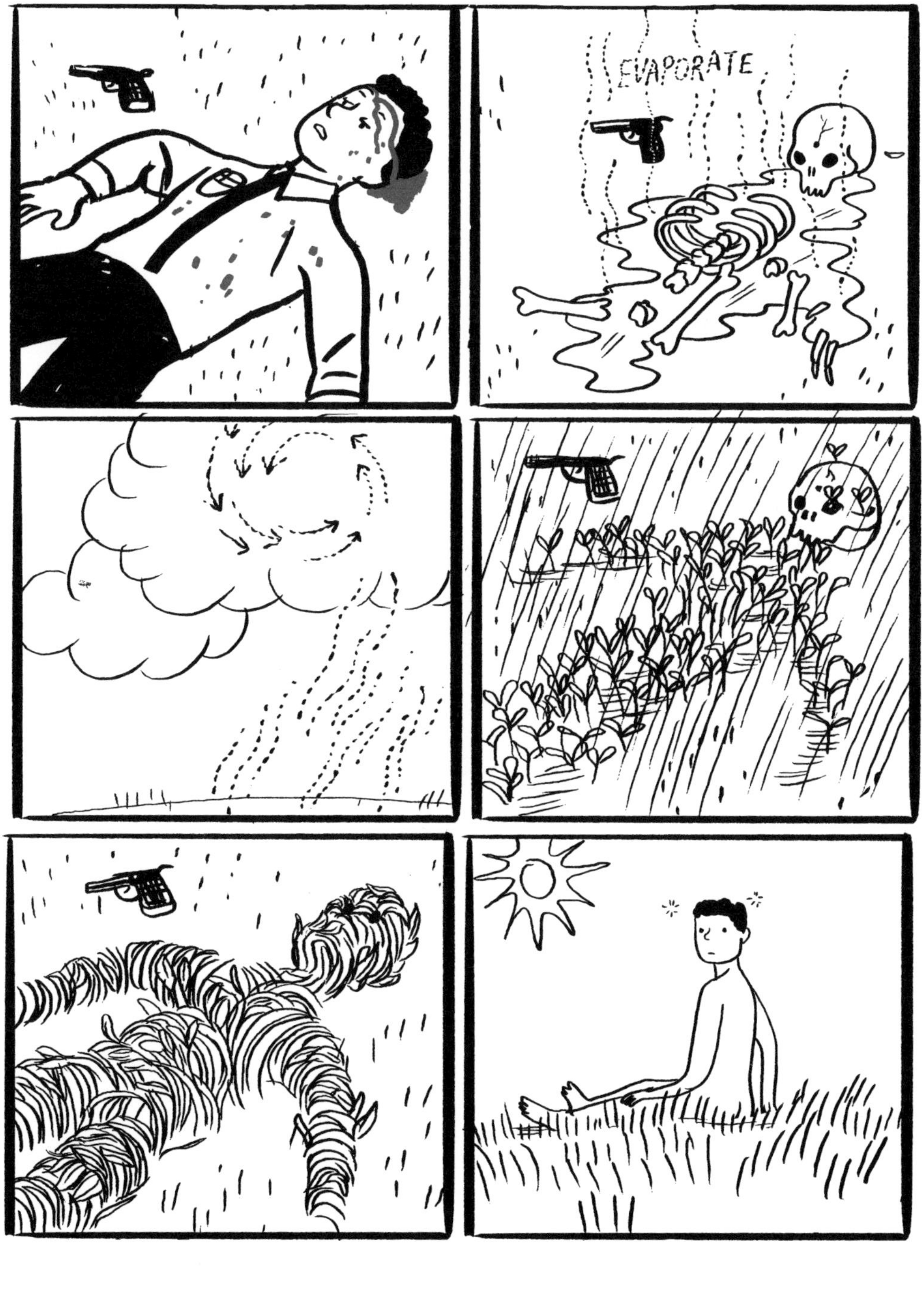
EVAPORATE

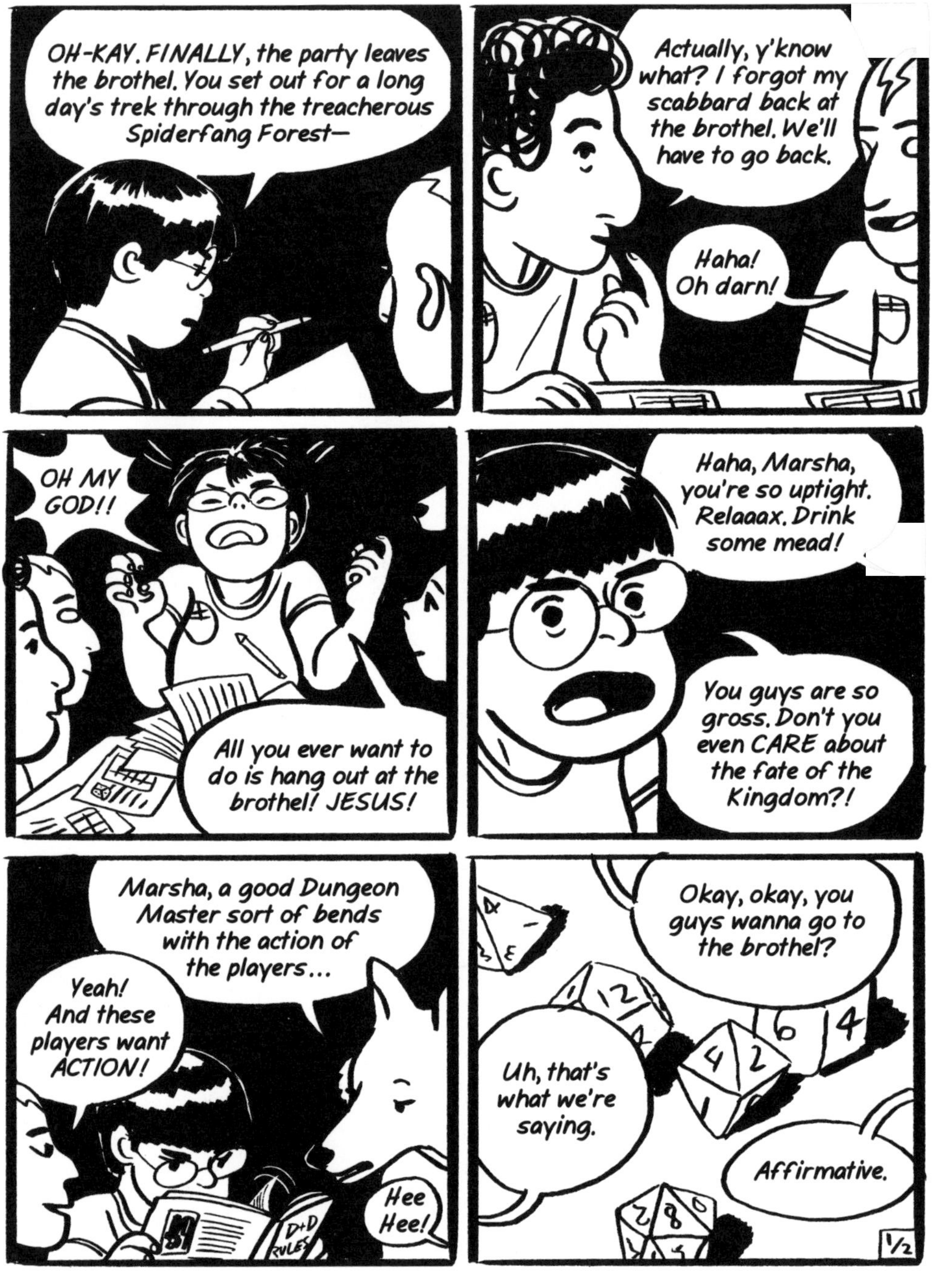
OH-KAY. FINALLY, the party leaves the brothel. You set out for a long day's trek through the treacherous Spiderfang Forest—
Actually, y'know what? I forgot my scabbard back at the brothel. We'll have to go back.
Haha! Oh darn!
OH MY GOD!!
All you ever want to do is hang out at the brothel! JESUS!
Haha, Marsha, you're so uptight. Relaaax. Drink some mead!
You guys are so gross. Don't you even CARE about the fate of the Kingdom?!
Marsha, a good Dungeon Master sort of bends with the action of the players...
Yeah! And these players want ACTION!
Hee Hee!
D+D RULES
Okay, okay, you guys wanna go to the brothel?
Uh, that's what we're saying.
Affirmative.

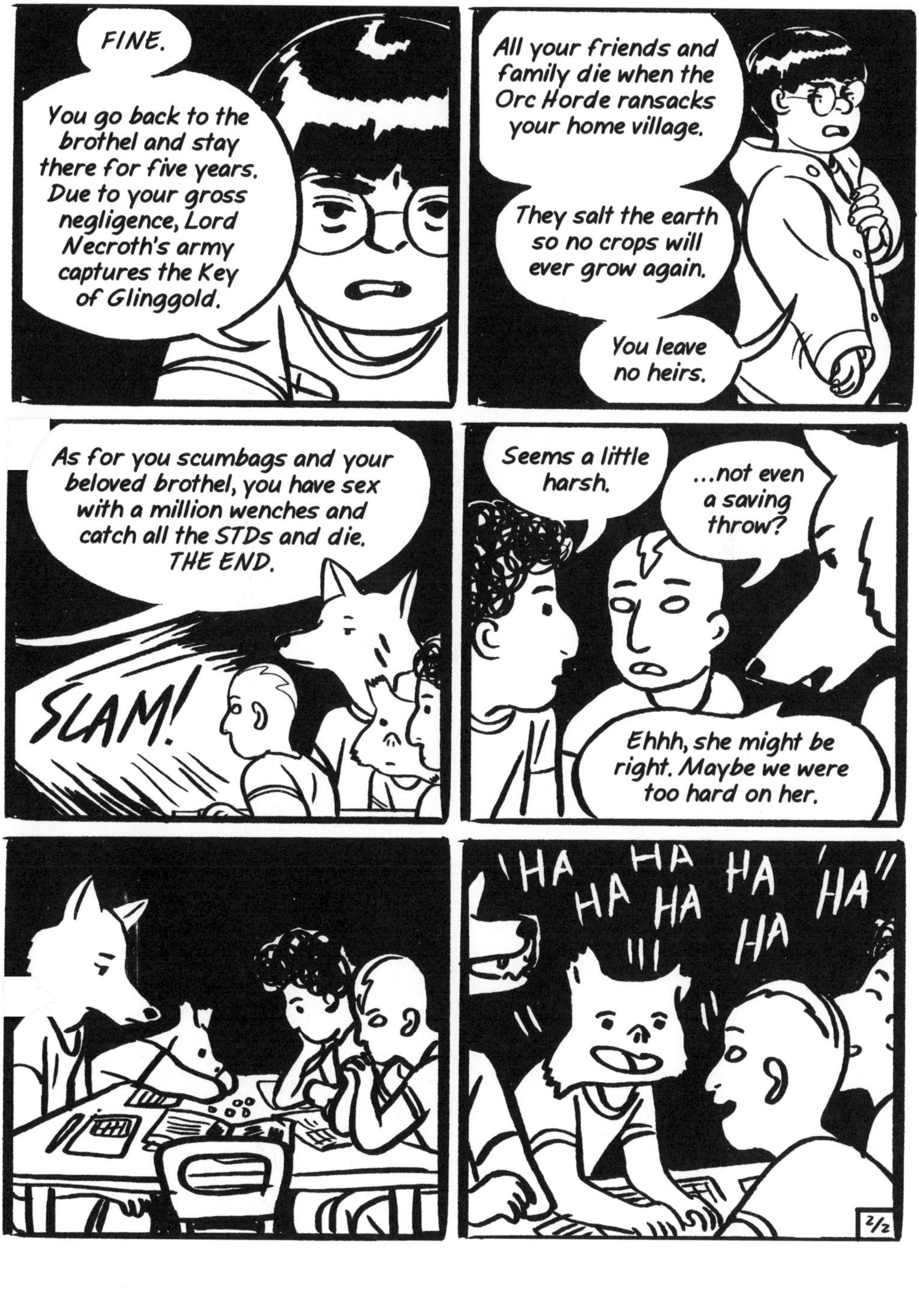
FINE.
You go back to the brothel and stay there for five years. Due to your gross negligence, Lord Necroth's army captures the Key of Glinggold.
All your friends and family die when the Orc Horde ransacks your home village.
They salt the earth so no crops will ever grow again.
You leave no heirs.
As for you scumbags and your beloved brothel, you have sex with a million wenches and catch all the STDs and die. THE END.
SLAM!
Seems a little harsh.
...not even a saving throw?
Ehhh, she might be right. Maybe we were too hard on her.
"HA HA HA HA HA HA HA HA"
2/2

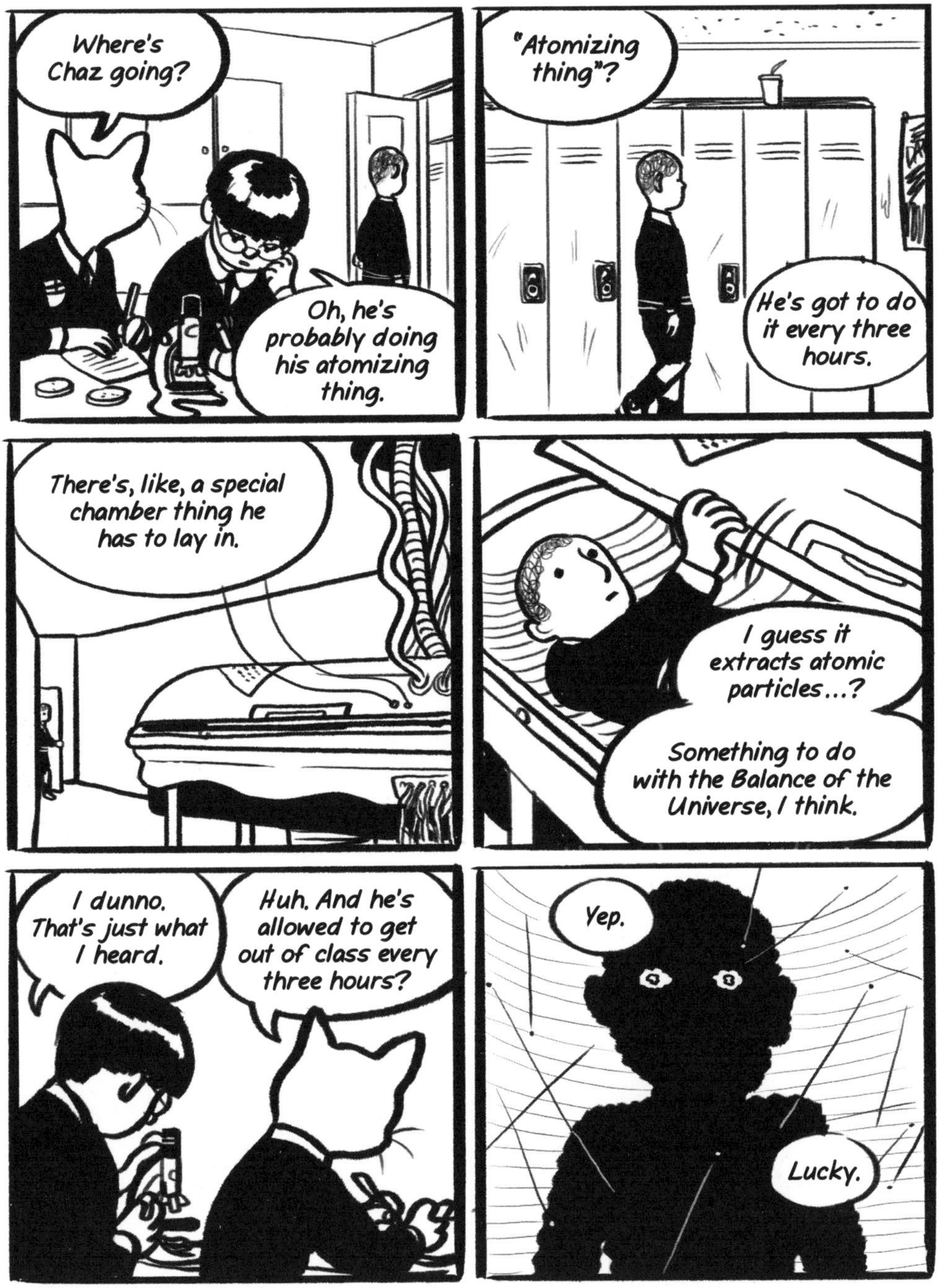

Where's Chaz going?
Oh, he's probably doing his atomizing thing.
"Atomizing thing"?
He's got to do it every three hours.
There's, like, a special chamber thing he has to lay in.
I guess it extracts atomic particles...?
Something to do with the Balance of the Universe, I think.
I dunno. That's just what I heard.
Huh. And he's allowed to get out of class every three hours?
Yep.
Lucky.

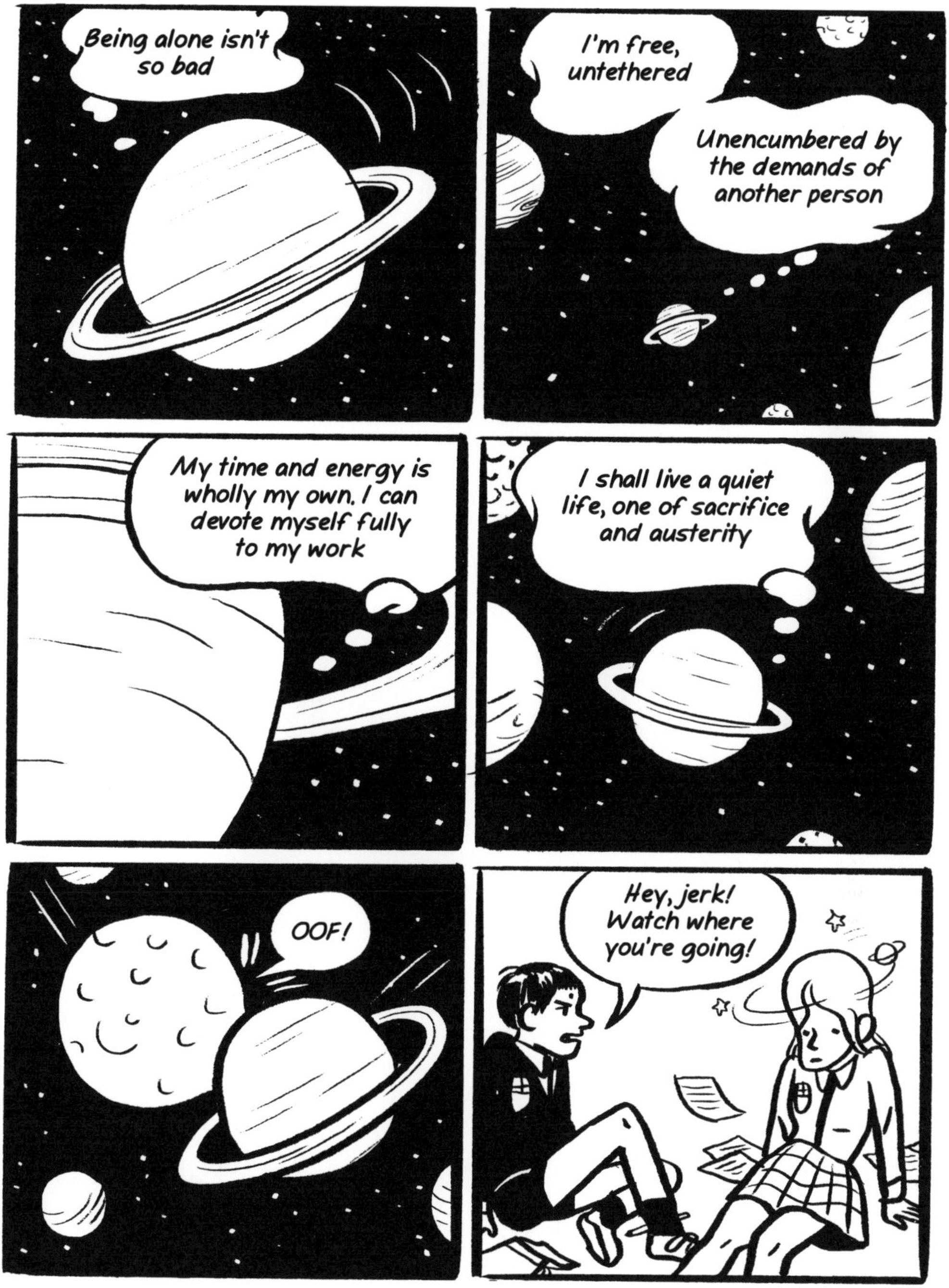
Being alone isn't so bad
I'm free, untethered
Unencumbered by the demands of another person
My time and energy is wholly my own. I can devote myself fully to my work
I shall live a quiet life, one of sacrifice and austerity
OOF!
Hey, jerk! Watch where you're going!

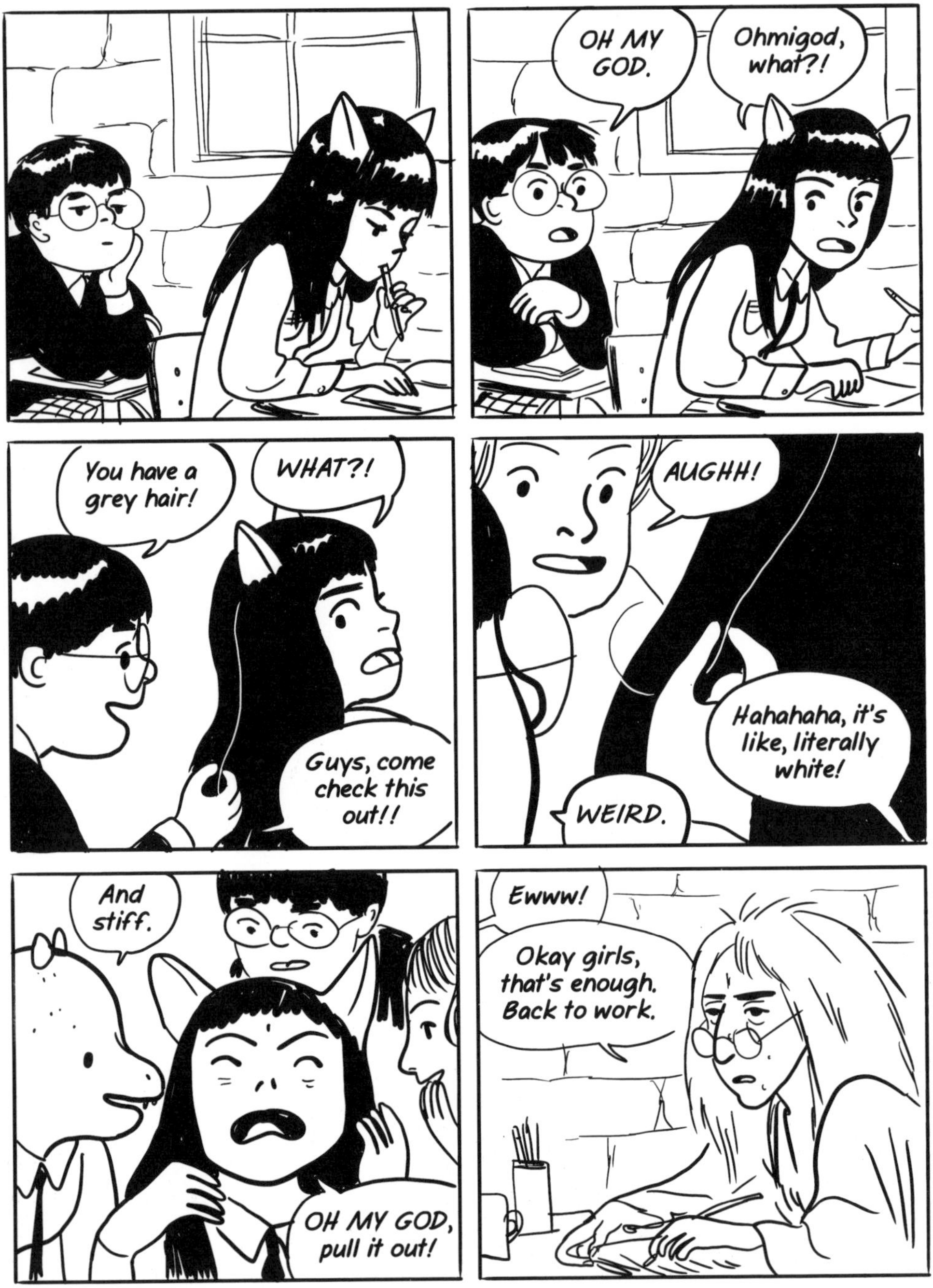
OH MY GOD.
Ohmigod, what?!
You have a grey hair!
WHAT?!
Guys, come check this out!!
AUGHH!
Hahahaha, it's like, literally white!
WEIRD.
And stiff.
OH MY GOD, pull it out!
Ewww!
Okay girls, that's enough. Back to work.

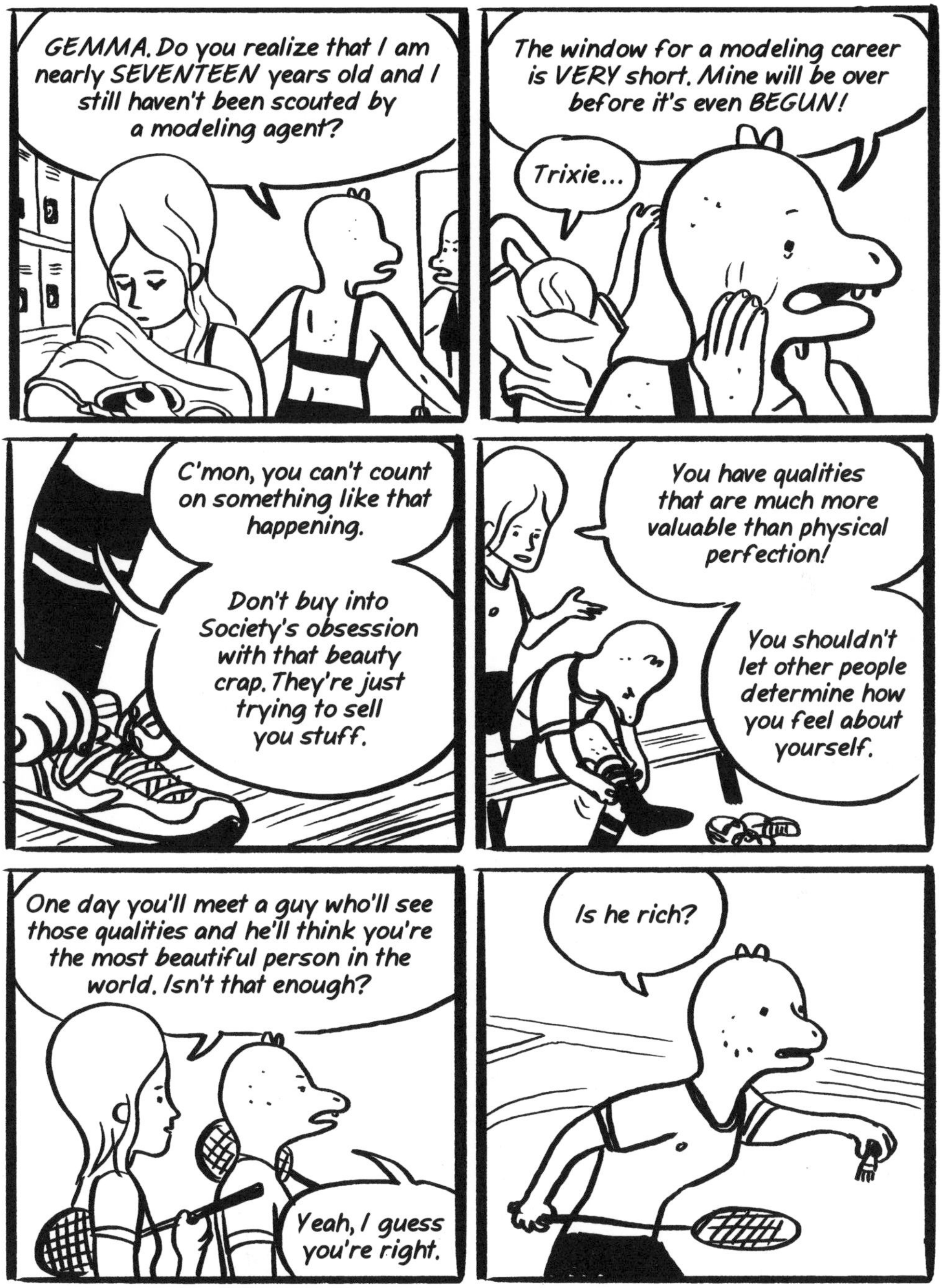
GEMMA. Do you realize that I am nearly SEVENTEEN years old and I still haven't been scouted by a modeling agent?
The window for a modeling career is VERY short. Mine will be over before it's even BEGUN!
Trixie...
C'mon, you can't count on something like that happening.
Don't buy into Society's obsession with that beauty crap. They're just trying to sell you stuff.
You have qualities that are much more valuable than physical perfection!
You shouldn't let other people determine how you feel about yourself.
One day you'll meet a guy who'll see those qualities and he'll think you're the most beautiful person in the world. Isn't that enough?
Yeah, I guess you're right.
Is he rich?

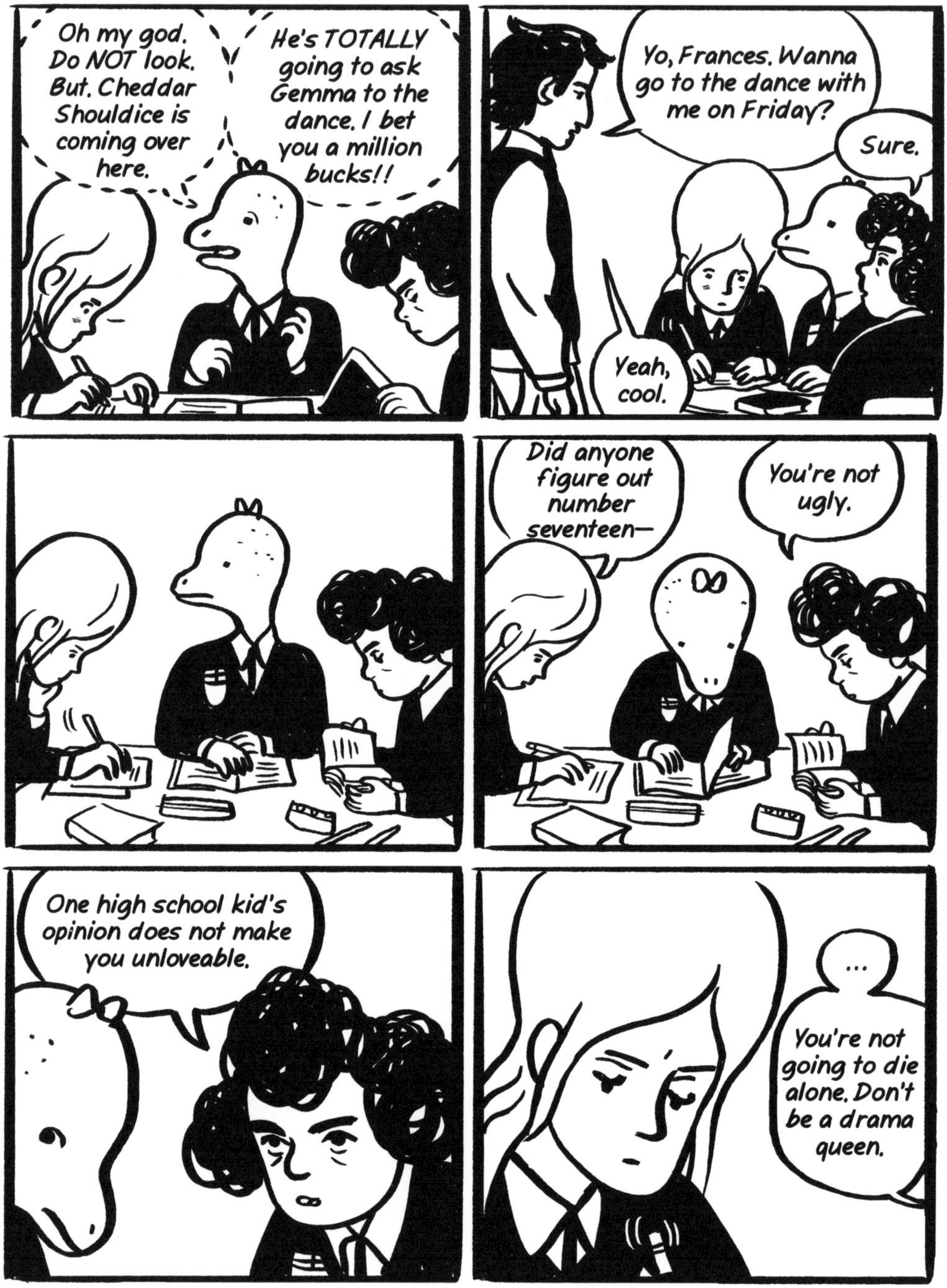
Oh my god. Do NOT look. But. Cheddar Shouldice is coming over here.
He's TOTALLY going to ask Gemma to the dance. I bet you a million bucks!!
Yo, Frances. Wanna go to the dance with me on Friday?
Sure.
Yeah, cool.
Did anyone figure out number seventeen—
You're not ugly.
One high school kid's opinion does not make you unloveable.
...
You're not going to die alone. Don't be a drama queen.

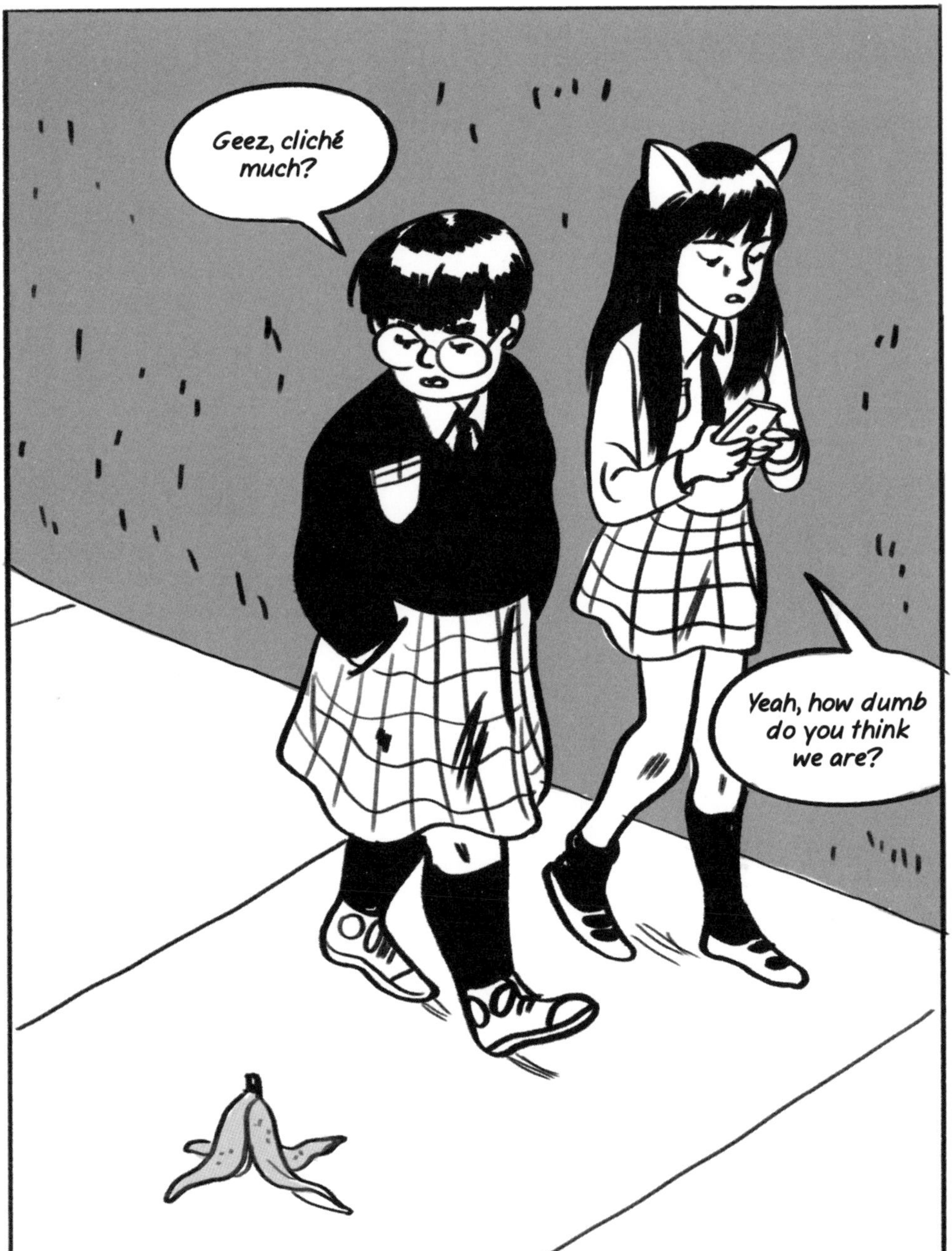
Geez, cliché much?
Yeah, how dumb do you think we are?

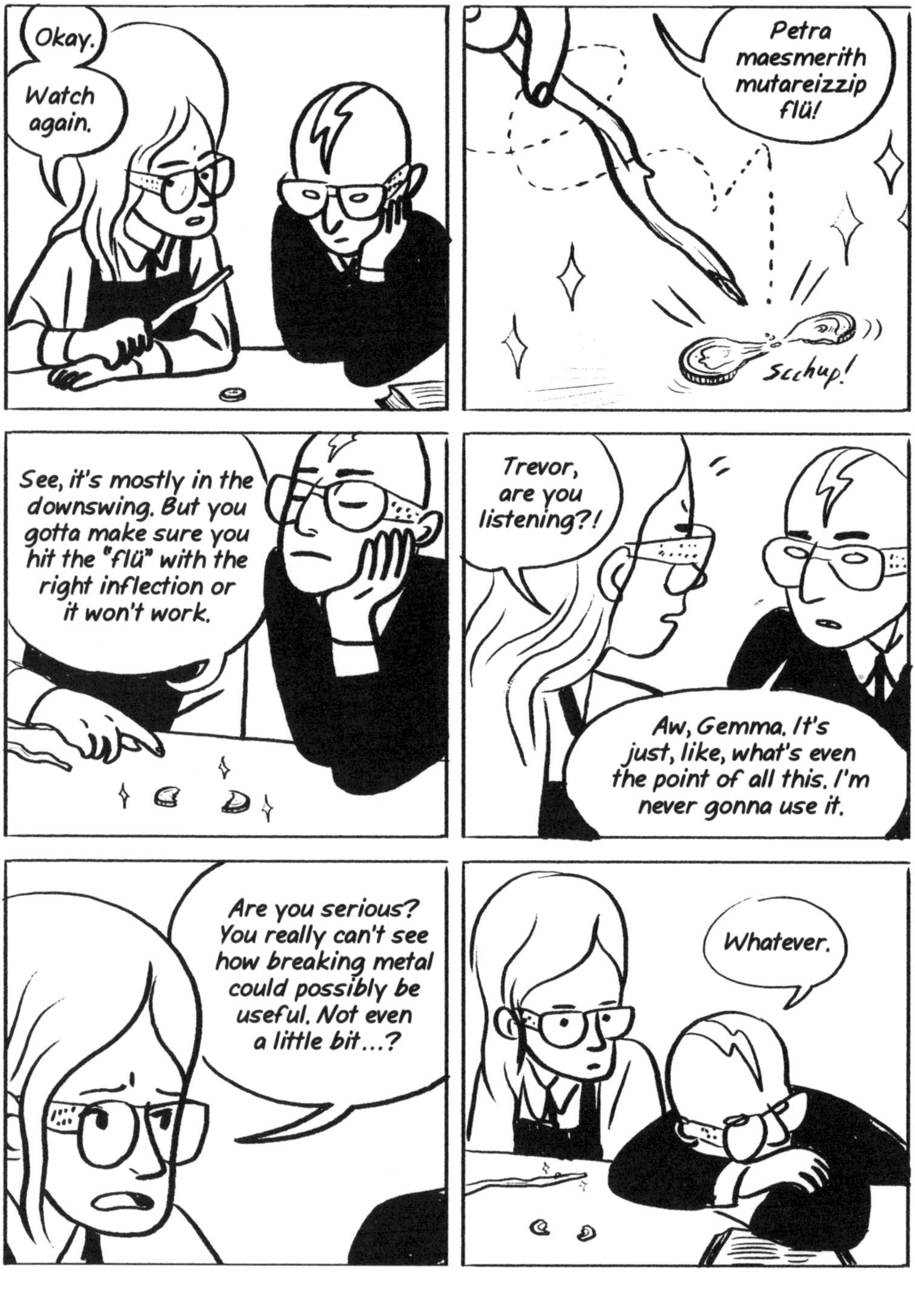
Okay.
Watch again.
Petra maesmerith mutareizzip flü!
Scchup!
See, it's mostly in the downswing. But you gotta make sure you hit the "flü" with the right inflection or it won't work.
Trevor, are you listening?!
Aw, Gemma. It's just, like, what's even the point of all this. I'm never gonna use it.
Are you serious? You really can't see how breaking metal could possibly be useful. Not even a little bit...?
Whatever.

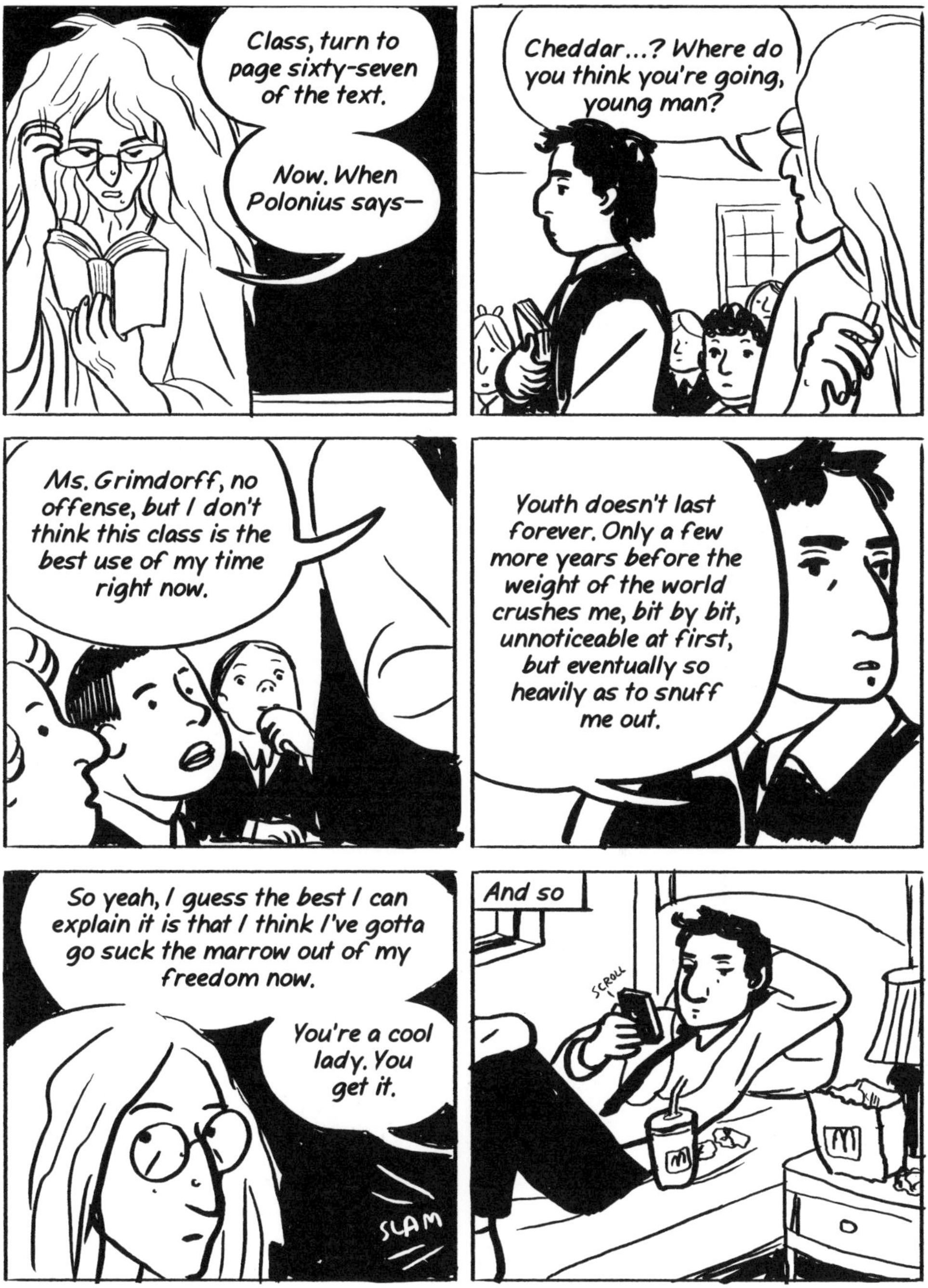

Class, turn to page sixty-seven of the text.
Now. When Polonius says—
Cheddar...? Where do you think you're going, young man?
Ms. Grimdorff, no offense, but I don't think this class is the best use of my time right now.
Youth doesn't last forever. Only a few more years before the weight of the world crushes me, bit by bit, unnoticeable at first, but eventually so heavily as to snuff me out.
So yeah, I guess the best I can explain it is that I think I've gotta go suck the marrow out of my freedom now.
You're a cool lady. You get it.
SLAM
And so
SCROLL

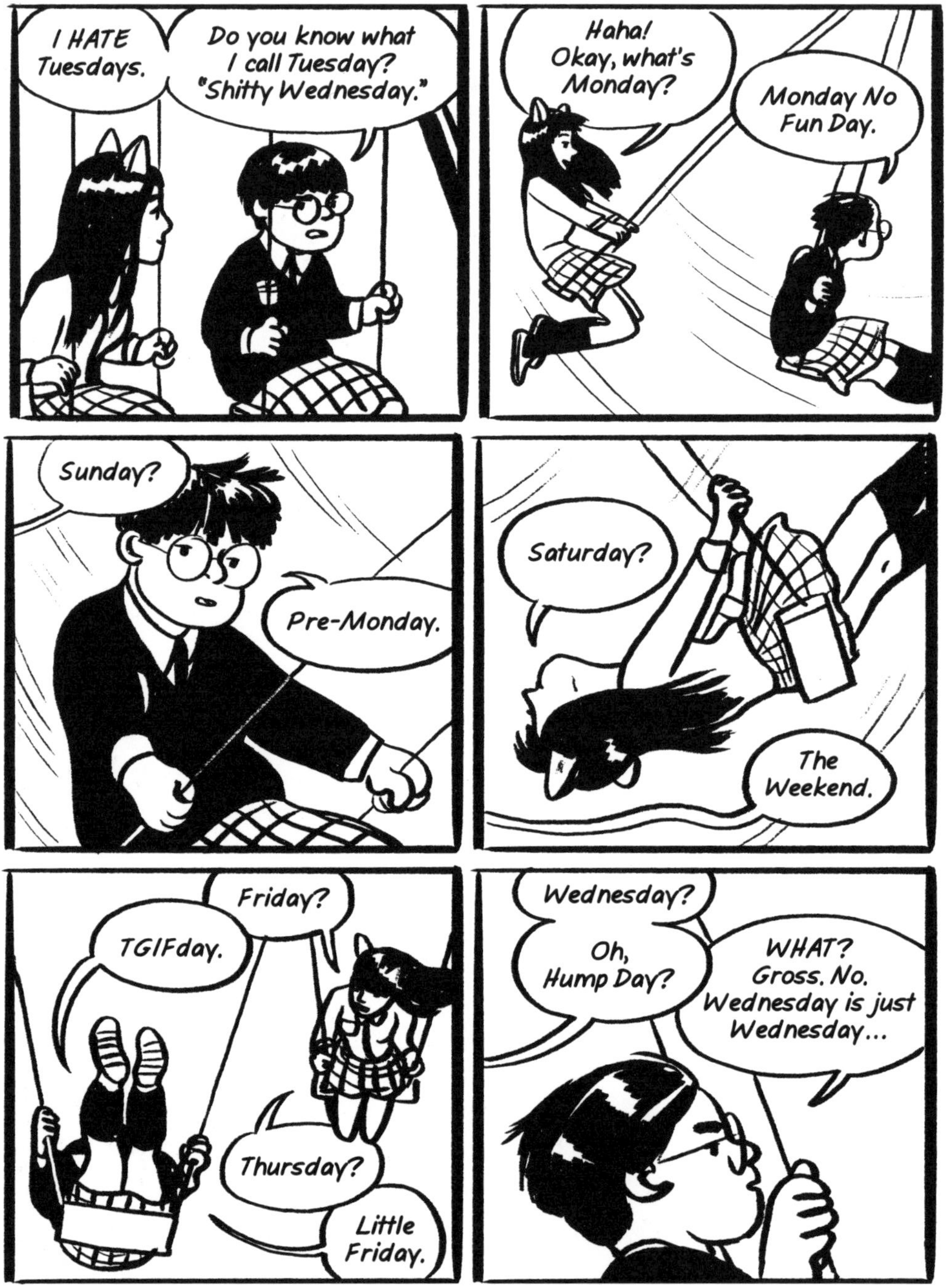
I HATE Tuesdays.
Do you know what I call Tuesday? "Shitty Wednesday."
Haha! Okay, what's Monday?
Monday No Fun Day.
Sunday?
Pre-Monday.
Saturday?
The Weekend.
Friday?
TGIFday.
Thursday?
Little Friday.
Wednesday?
Oh, Hump Day?
WHAT? Gross. No. Wednesday is just Wednesday...

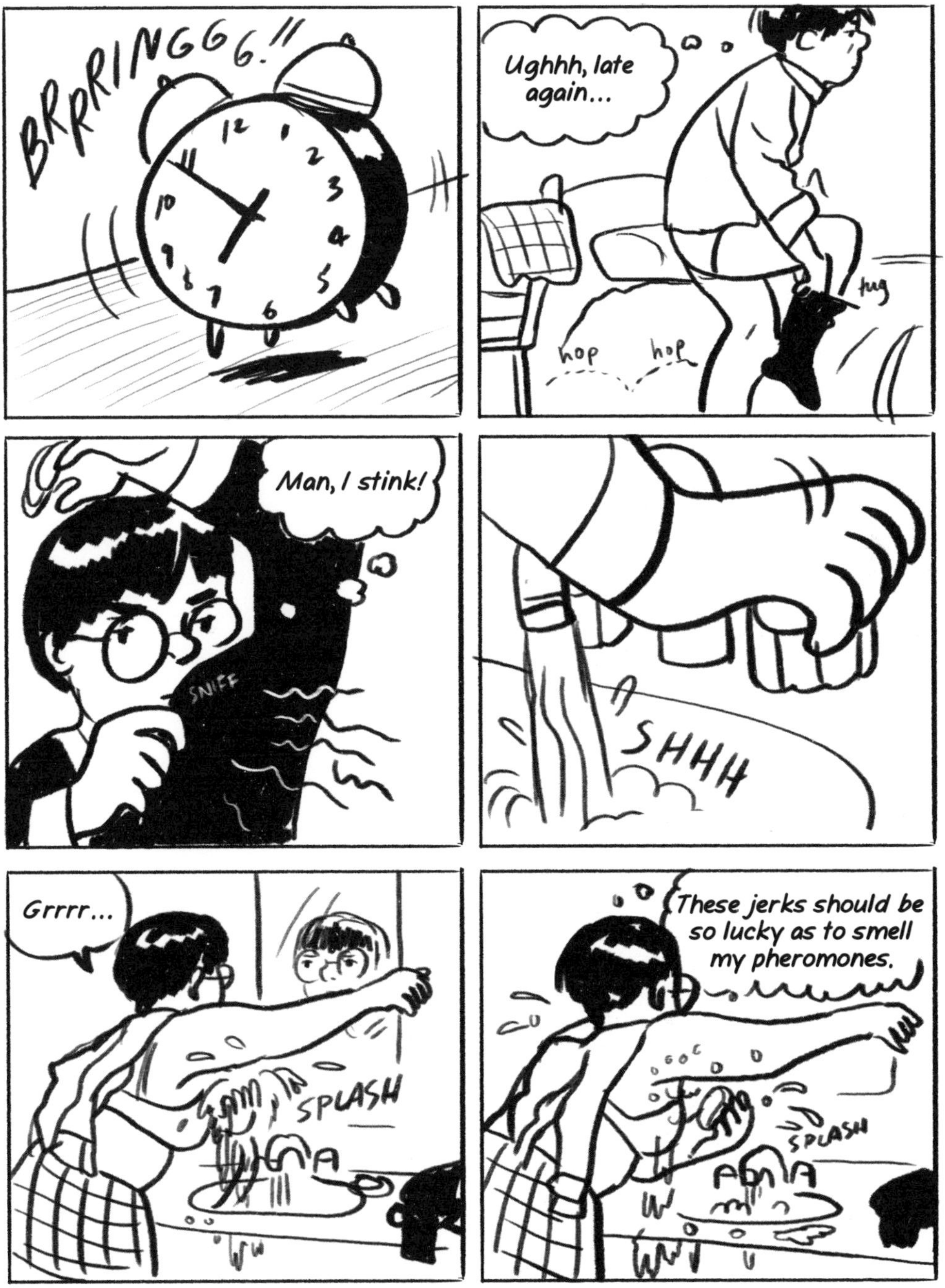
BRRRINGGG!!
Ughhh, late again...
tug
hop hop
Man, I stink!
SNIFF
SHHH
Grrrr...
SPLASH
These jerks should be so lucky as to smell my pheromones.
SPLASH

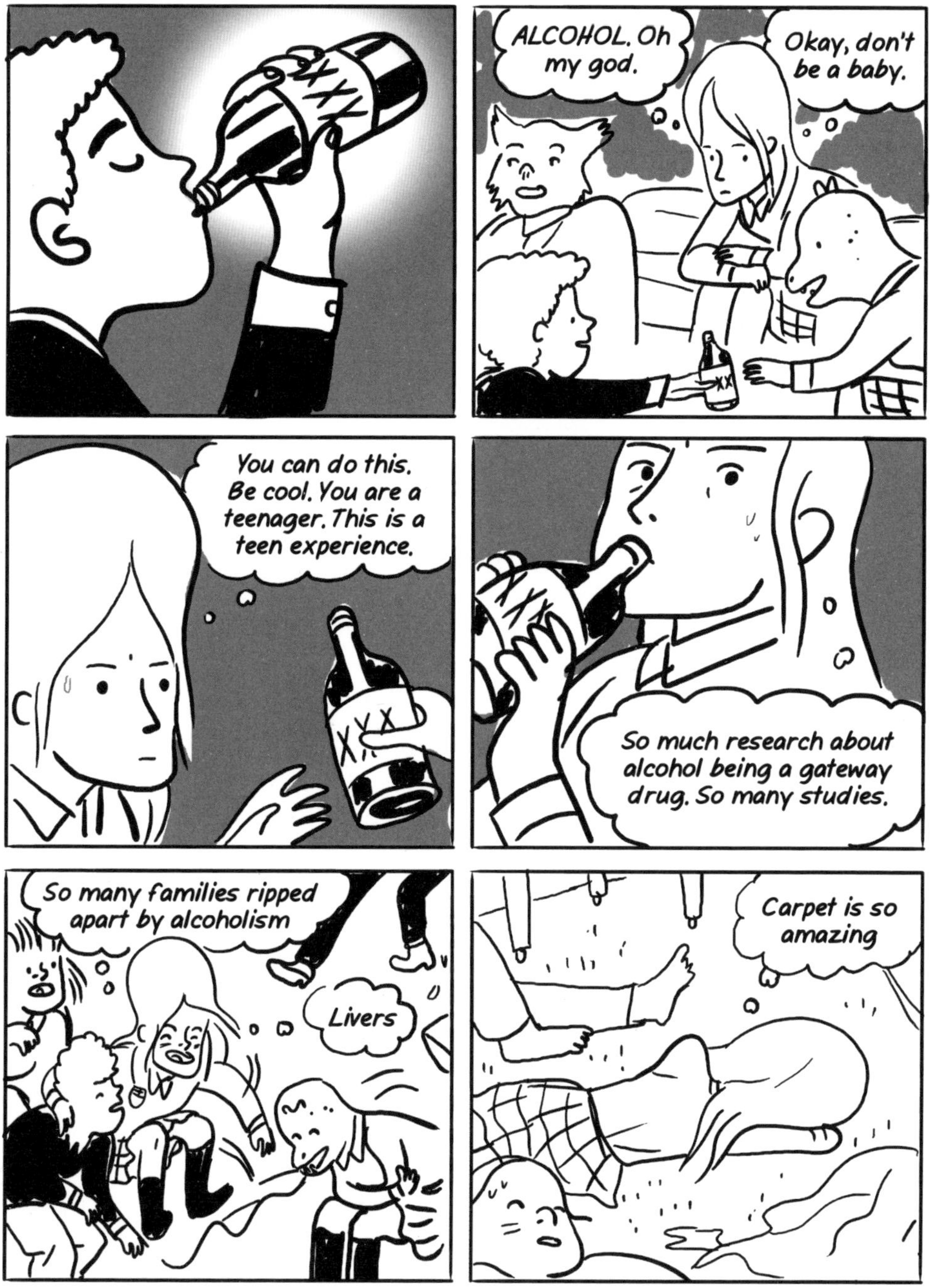
ALCOHOL. Oh my god.
Okay, don't be a baby.
You can do this. Be cool. You are a teenager. This is a teen experience.
So much research about alcohol being a gateway drug. So many studies.
So many families ripped apart by alcoholism
Livers
Carpet is so amazing

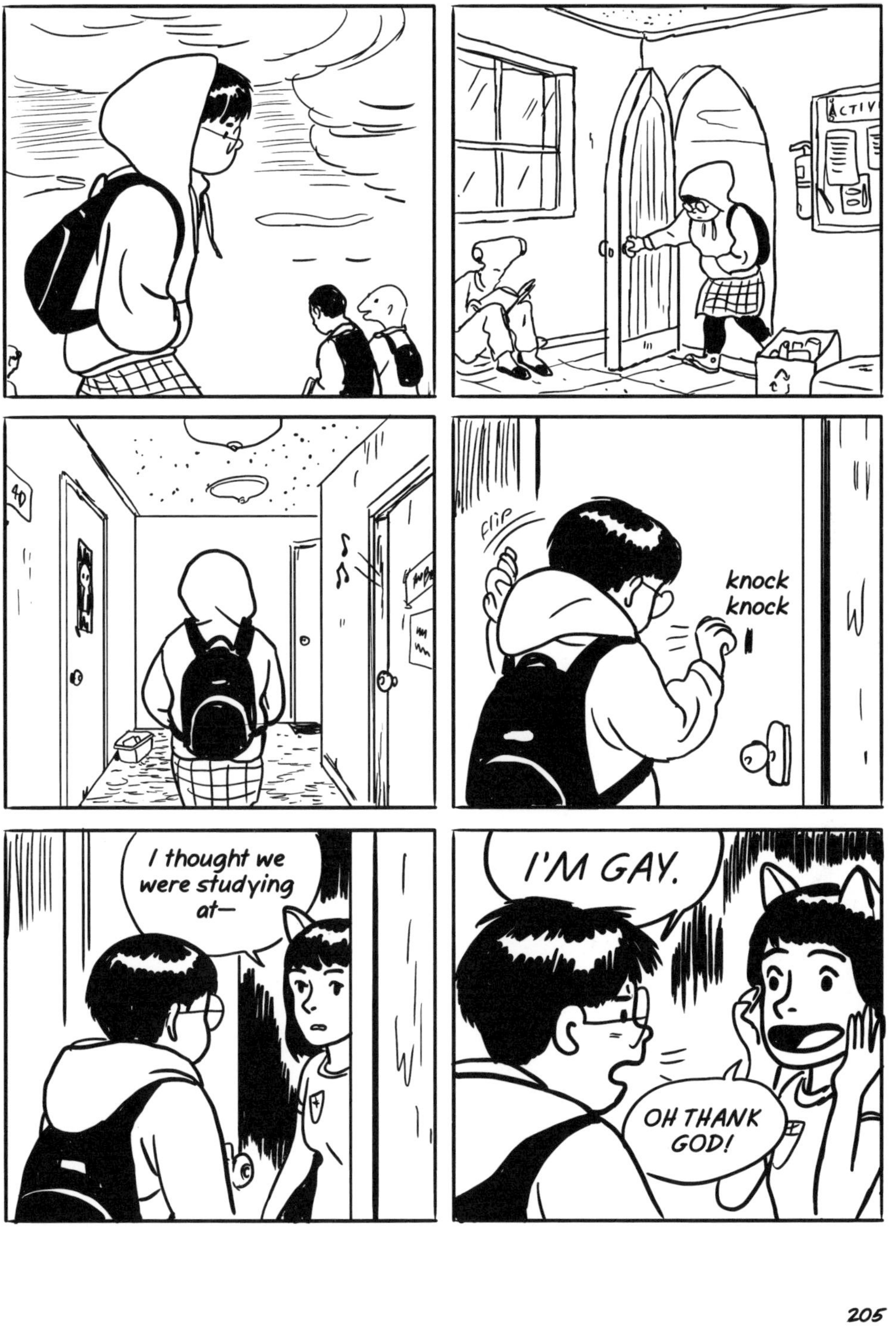
flip
knock knock
I thought we were studying at—
I'M GAY.
OH THANK GOD!

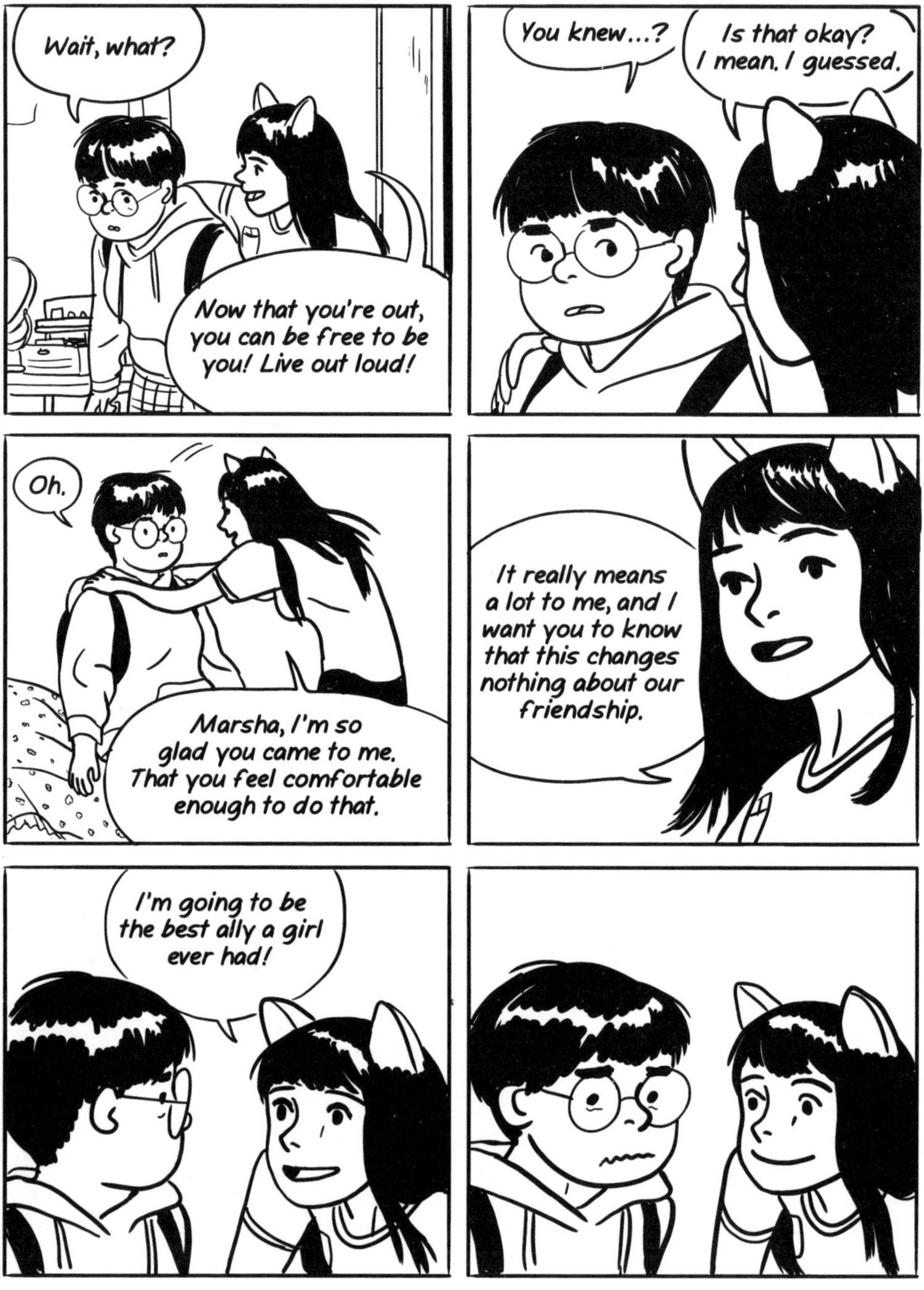
Wait, what?
Now that you're out, you can be free to be you! Live out loud!
You knew...?
Is that okay? I mean, I guessed.
Oh.
Marsha, I'm so glad you came to me. That you feel comfortable enough to do that.
It really means a lot to me, and I want you to know that this changes nothing about our friendship.
I'm going to be the best ally a girl ever had!

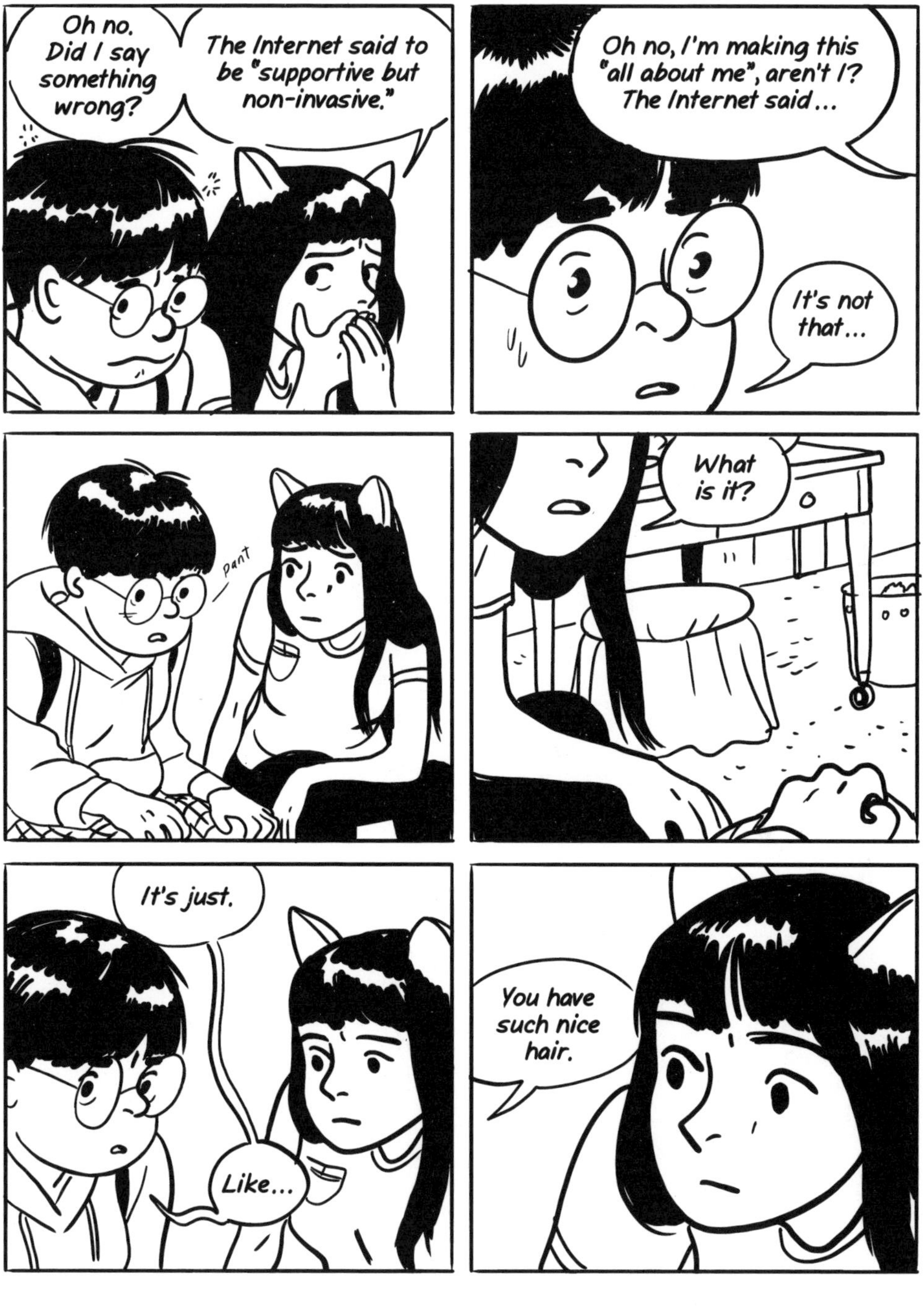
Oh no. Did I say something wrong?
The Internet said to be "supportive but non-invasive."
Oh no, I'm making this "all about me", aren't I? The Internet said...
It's not that...
pant
What is it?
It's just.
Like...
You have such nice hair.

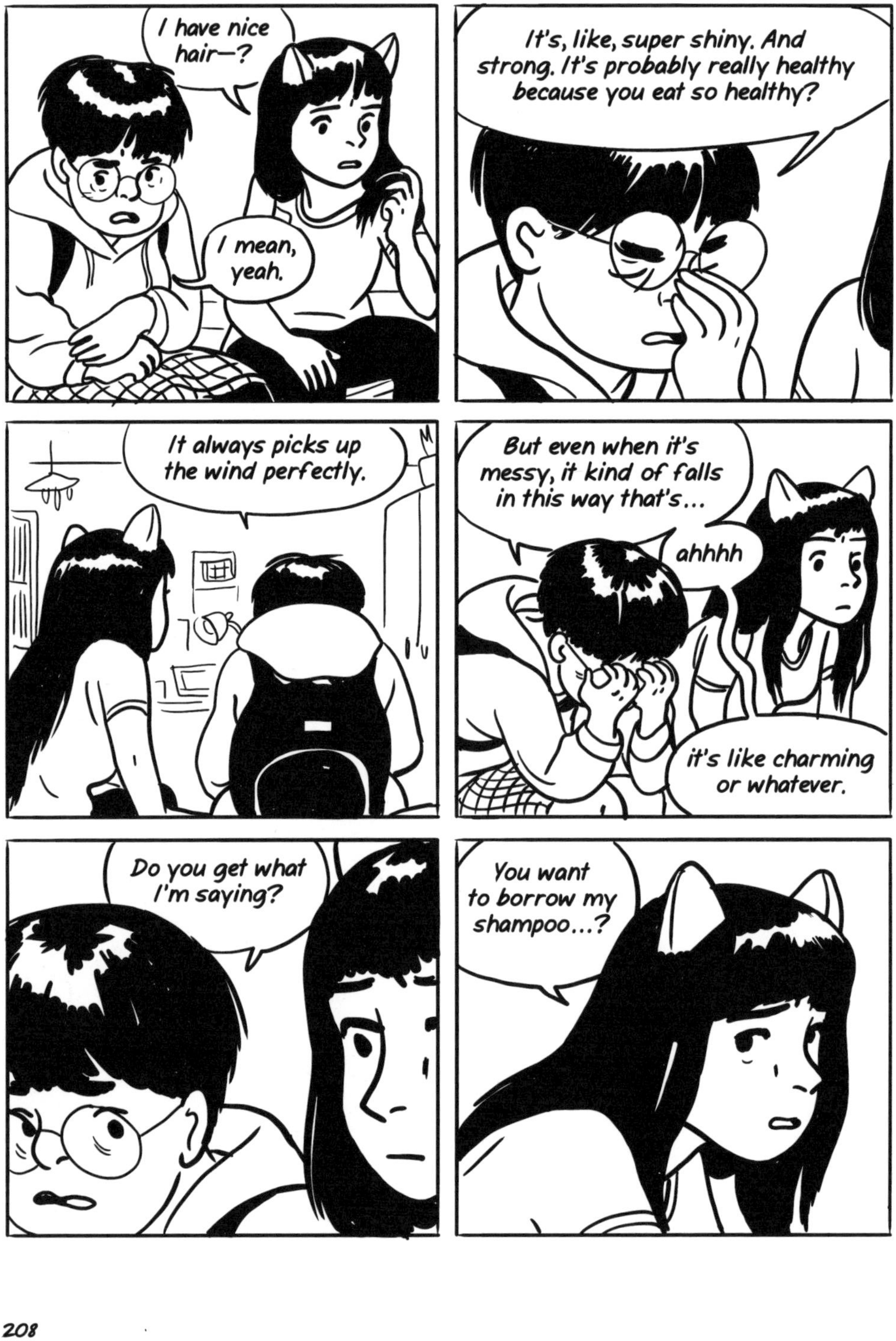

I have nice hair—?
I mean, yeah.
It's, like, super shiny. And strong. It's probably really healthy because you eat so healthy?
It always picks up the wind perfectly.
But even when it's messy, it kind of falls in this way that's...
ahhhh
it's like charming or whatever.
Do you get what I'm saying?
You want to borrow my shampoo...?

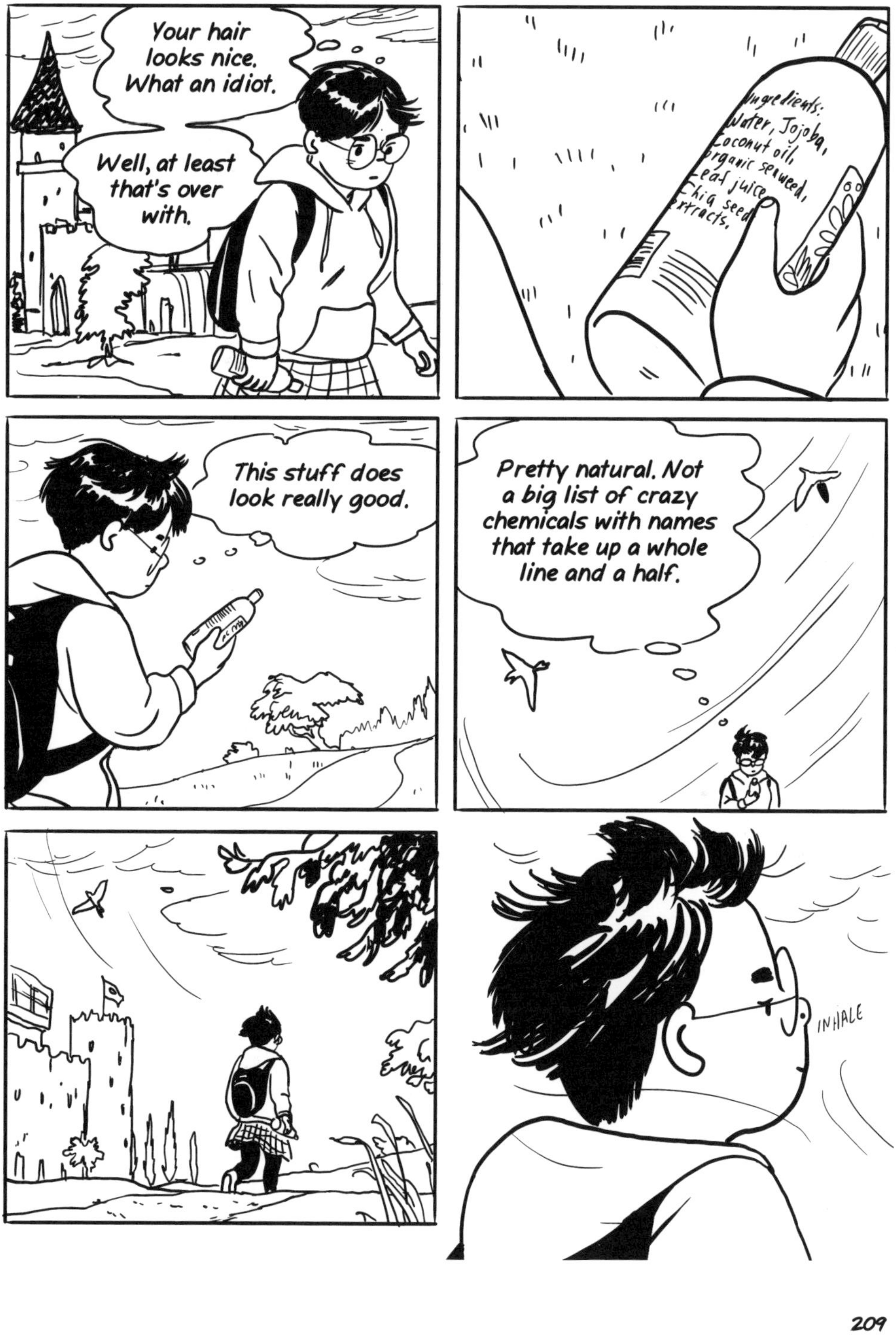
Your hair looks nice. What an idiot.
Well, at least that's over with.
Ingredients: Water, Jojoba, Coconut oil, organic seaweed, Leaf juice, Chia seed extracts.
This stuff does look really good.
Pretty natural. Not a big list of crazy chemicals with names that take up a whole line and a half.
INHALE

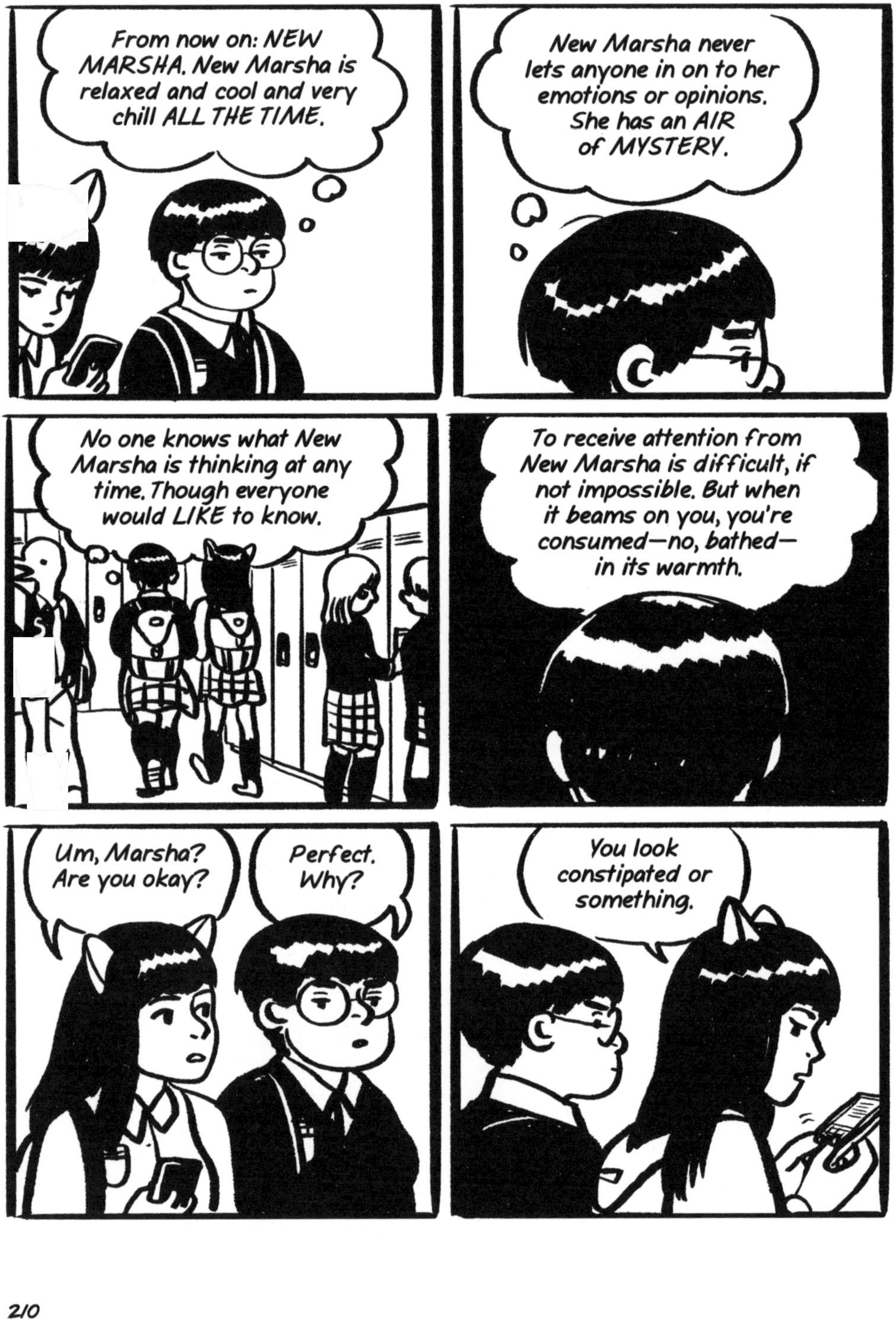
From now on: NEW MARSHA. New Marsha is relaxed and cool and very chill ALL THE TIME.
New Marsha never lets anyone in on to her emotions or opinions. She has an AIR of MYSTERY.
No one knows what New Marsha is thinking at any time. Though everyone would LIKE to know.
To receive attention from New Marsha is difficult, if not impossible. But when it beams on you, you're consumed—no, bathed—in its warmth.
Um, Marsha? Are you okay?
Perfect. Why?
You look constipated or something.

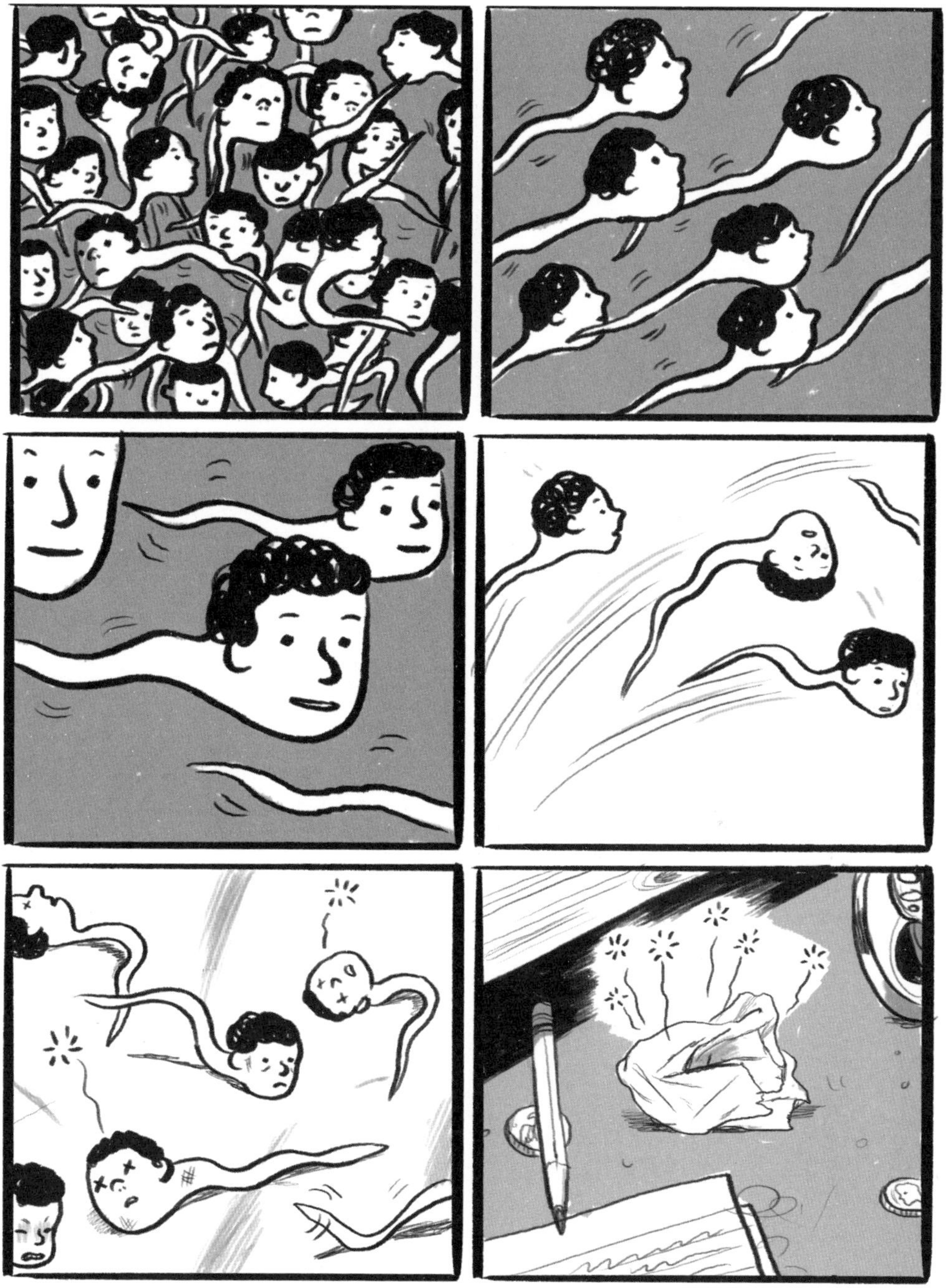

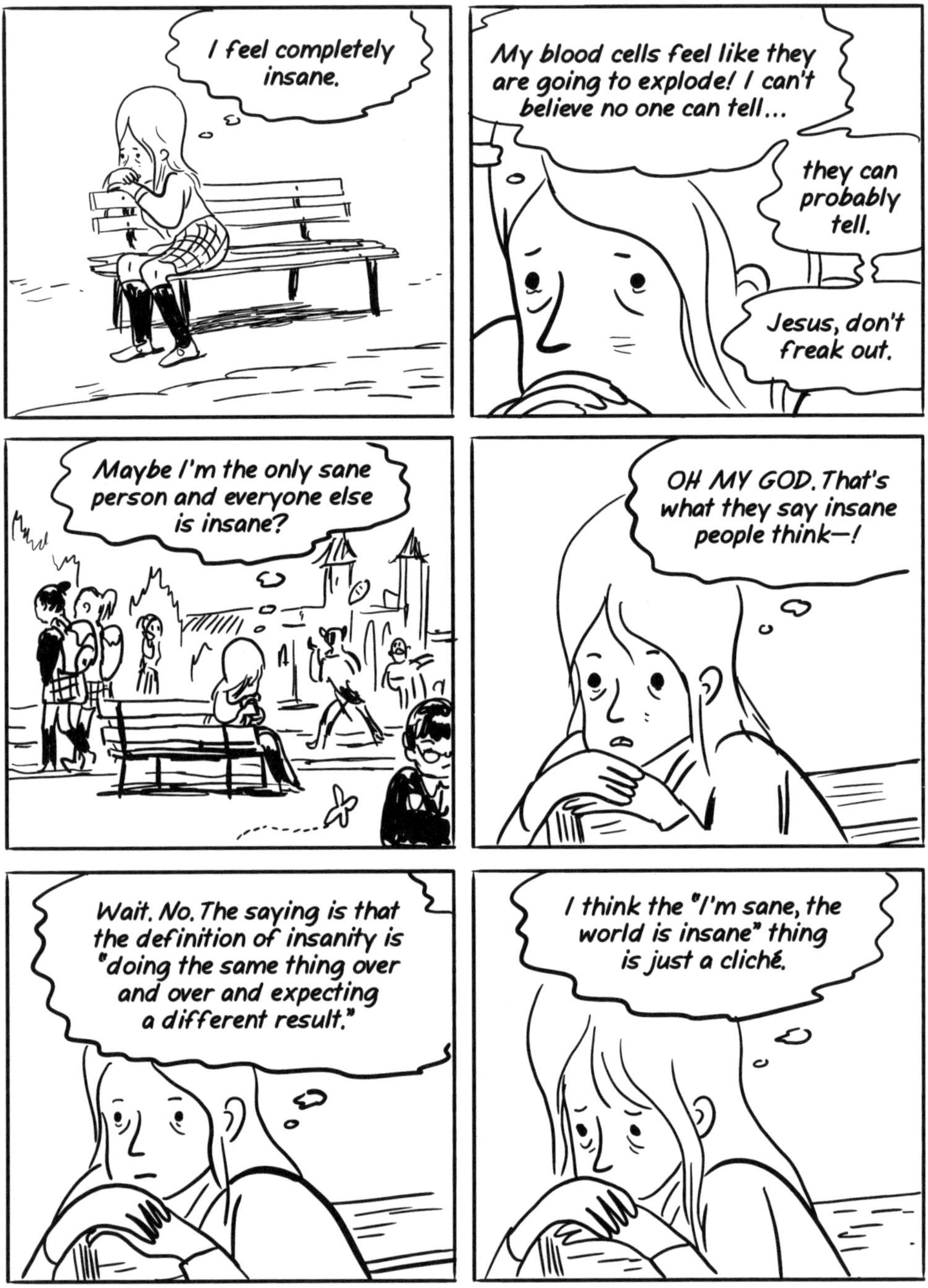
I feel completely insane.
My blood cells feel like they are going to explode! I can't believe no one can tell...
they can probably tell.
Jesus, don't freak out.
Maybe I'm the only sane person and everyone else is insane?
OH MY GOD. That's what they say insane people think—!
Wait. No. The saying is that the definition of insanity is "doing the same thing over and over and expecting a different result."
I think the "I'm sane, the world is insane" thing is just a cliché.

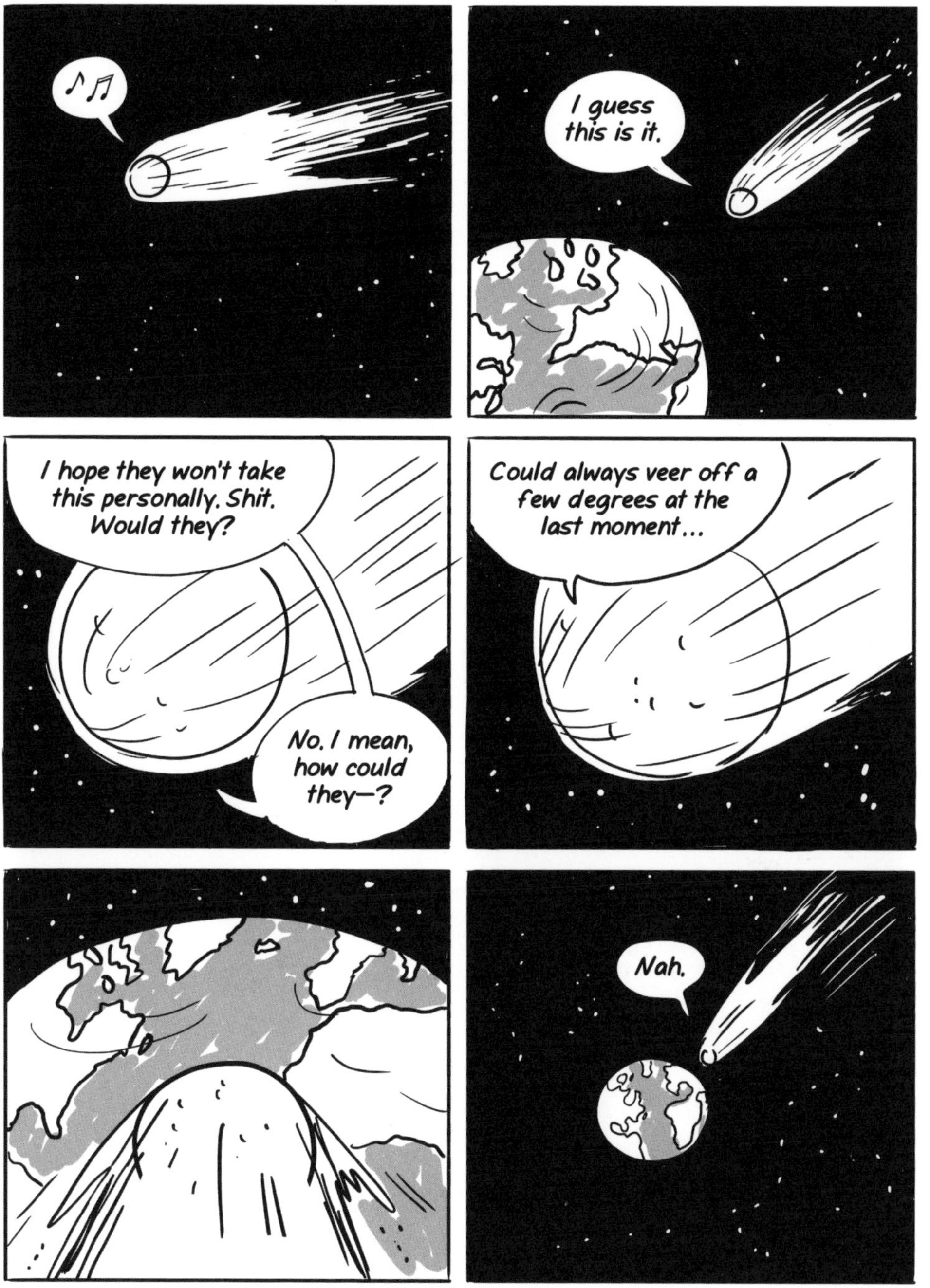
♪♫
I guess this is it.
I hope they won't take this personally. Shit. Would they?
No. I mean, how could they—?
Could always veer off a few degrees at the last moment...
Nah.

Weird to think that our whole species is gonna be extinct at some point and Nature isn't going to care a whit.
The whole thing could just start over again. A few million years and there'll be another advanced civilization on our planet.
They'll know we were here cuz of all our garbage. Maybe we'll be their mythology.
And then they'll die off too. Wash, rinse, repeat. It's probably happening all over the Universe.
And if the Universe is infinite, just think of the possibilities! Not that we're truly able to conceive of that type of time and space. But just think.
You're not special for pondering this shit, you know.
I guess not.
Wanna make out?
Maybe later.
But yeah. Probably.

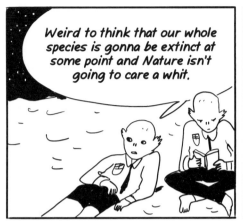

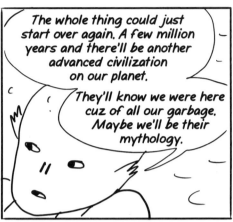

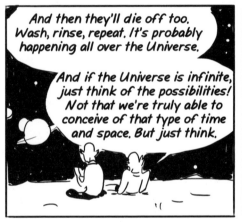

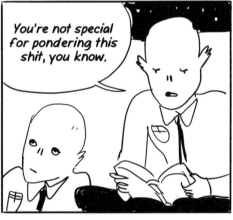

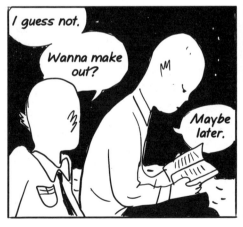

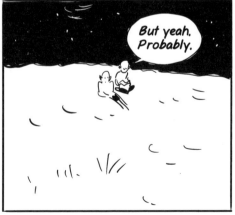

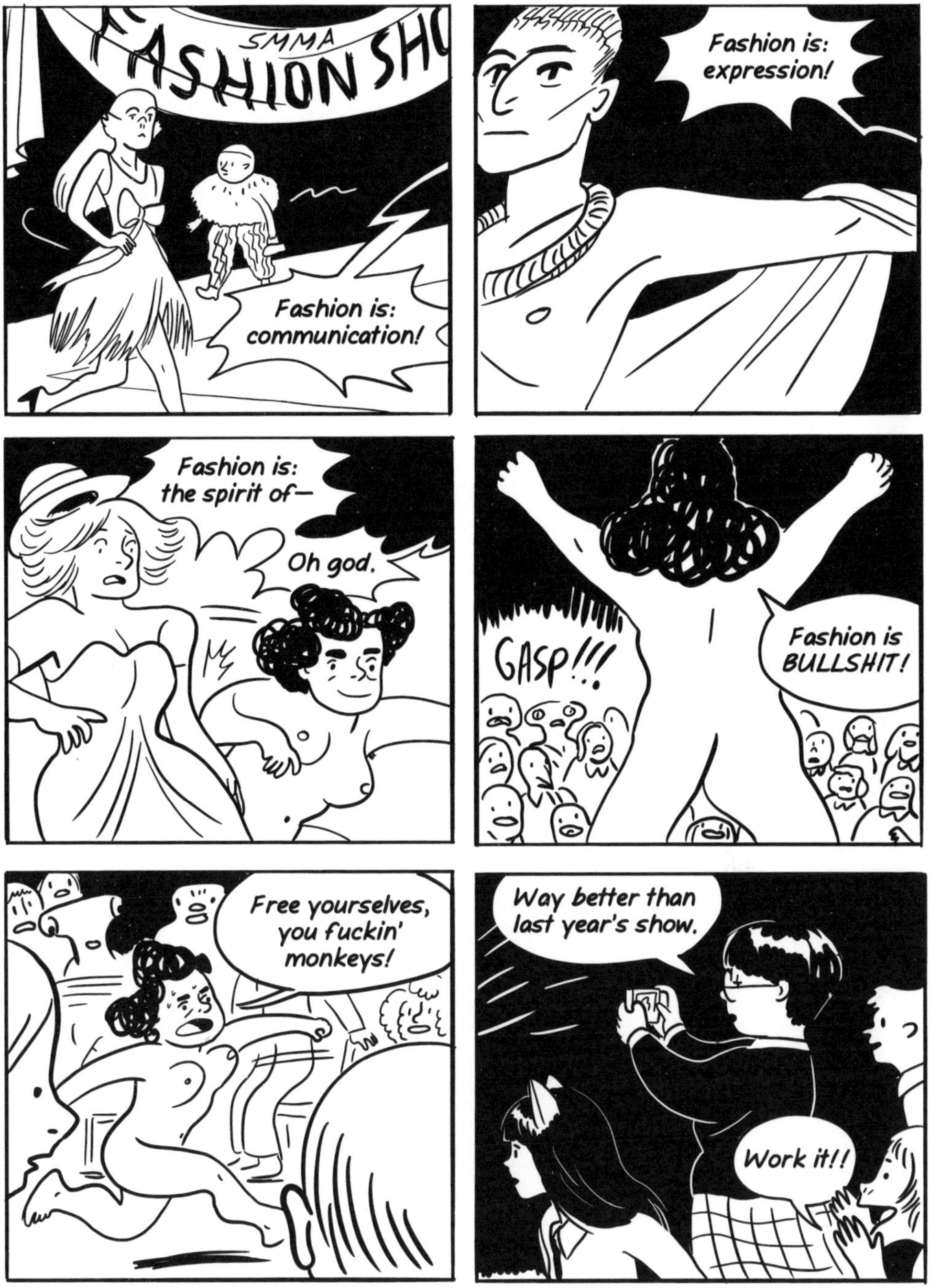
SMMA
FASHION SH
Fashion is: communication!
Fashion is: expression!
Fashion is: the spirit of—
Oh god.
GASP!!!
Fashion is BULLSHIT!
Free yourselves, you fuckin' monkeys!
Way better than last year's show.
Work it!!

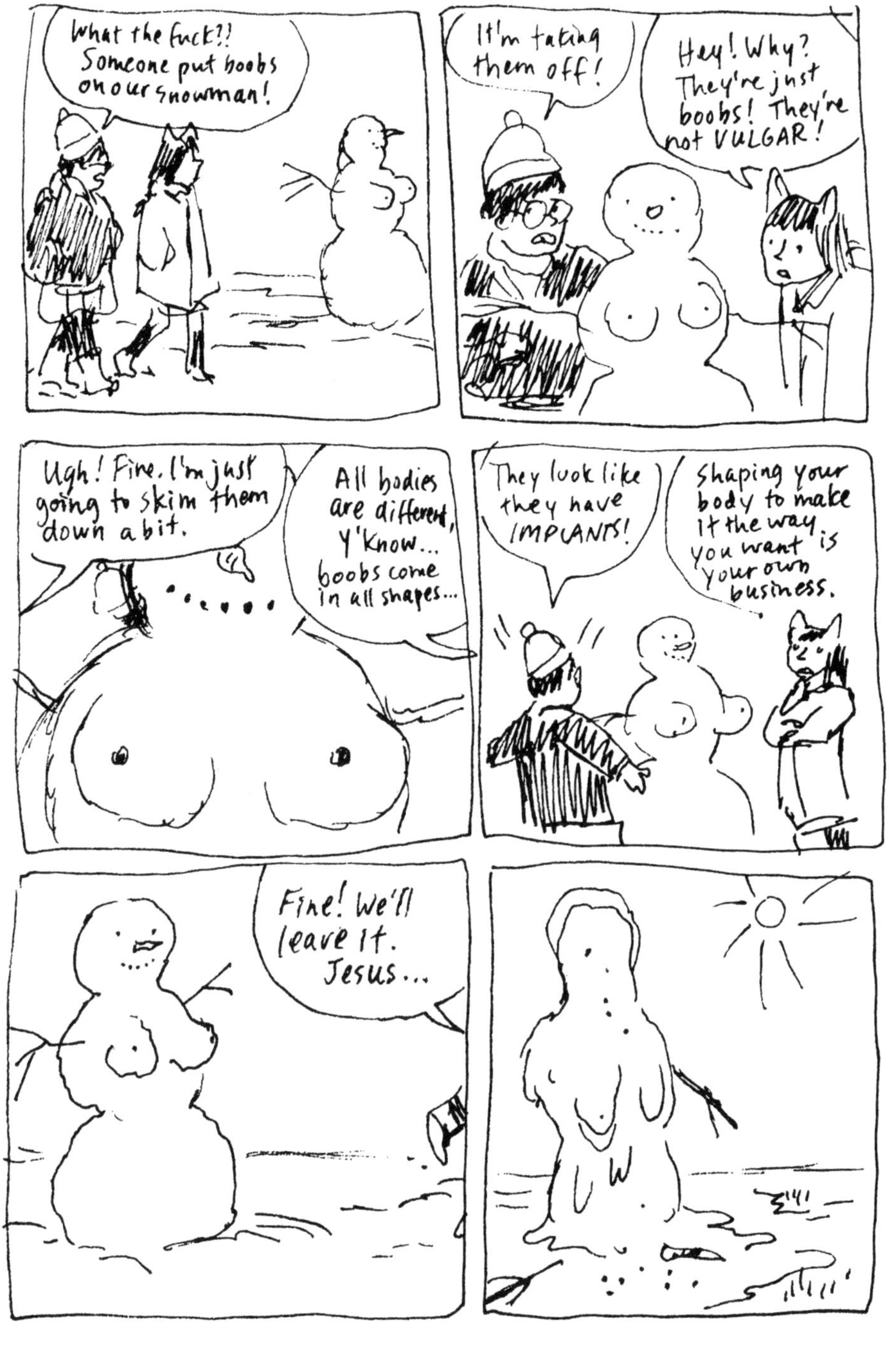
What the fuck?!
Someone put boobs on our snowman!
I'm taking them off!
Hey! Why? They're just boobs! They're not VULGAR!
Ugh! Fine. I'm just going to skim them down a bit.
All bodies are different, y'know... boobs come in all shapes...
They look like they have IMPLANTS!
Shaping your body to make it the way you want is your own business.
Fine! We'll leave it. Jesus...

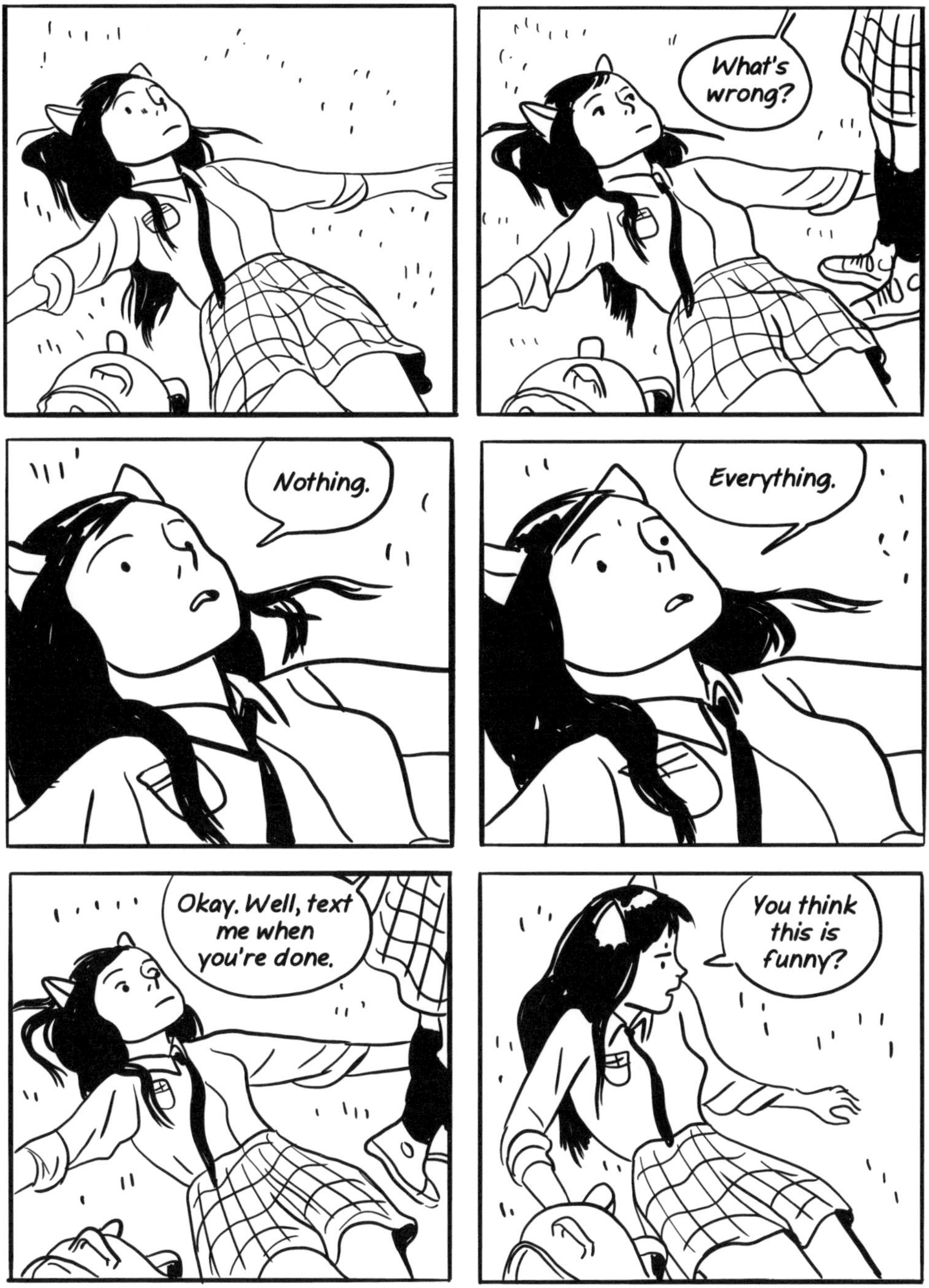
What's wrong?
Nothing.
Everything.
Okay. Well, text me when you're done.
You think this is funny?

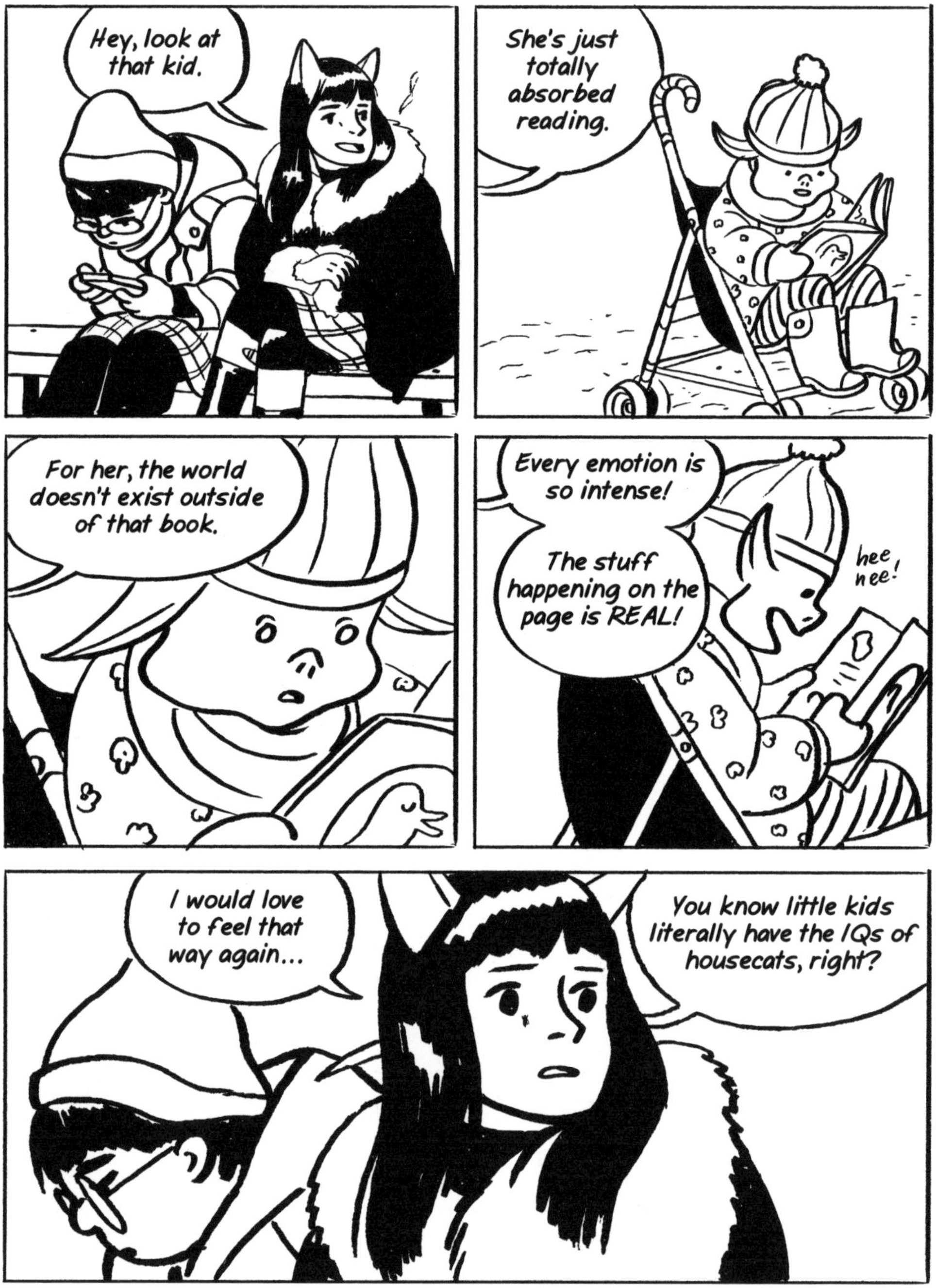
Hey, look at that kid.
She's just totally absorbed reading.
For her, the world doesn't exist outside of that book.
Every emotion is so intense!
The stuff happening on the page is REAL!
hee hee!
I would love to feel that way again...
You know little kids literally have the IQs of housecats, right?

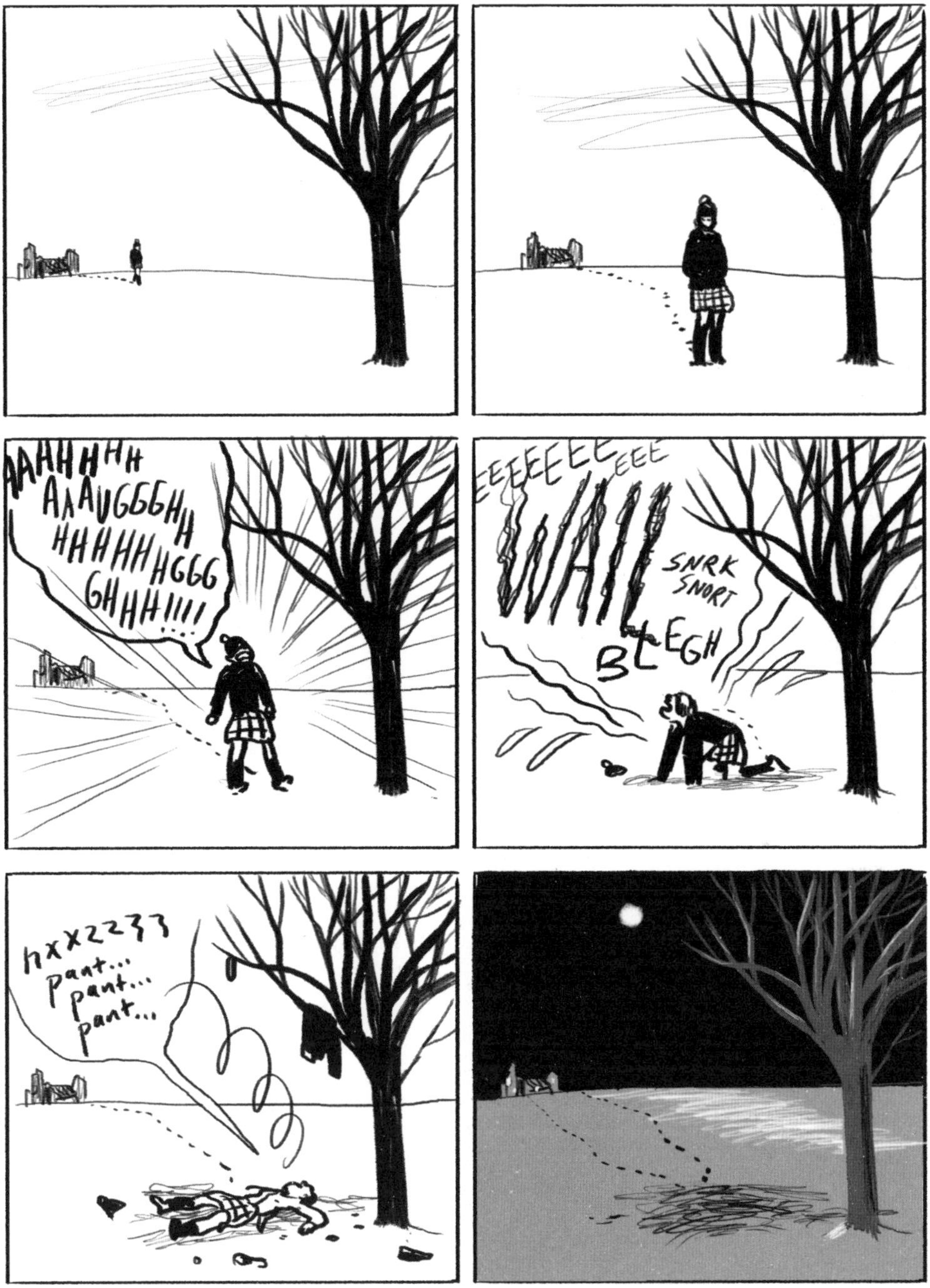
AAHHHHHH AAAUGGGHHH HHHHHHHGGG GHHH!!!!
EEEEEEEEEE WAIL
SNRK SNORT
BLEGH
hxxZZZZ pant... pant... pant...

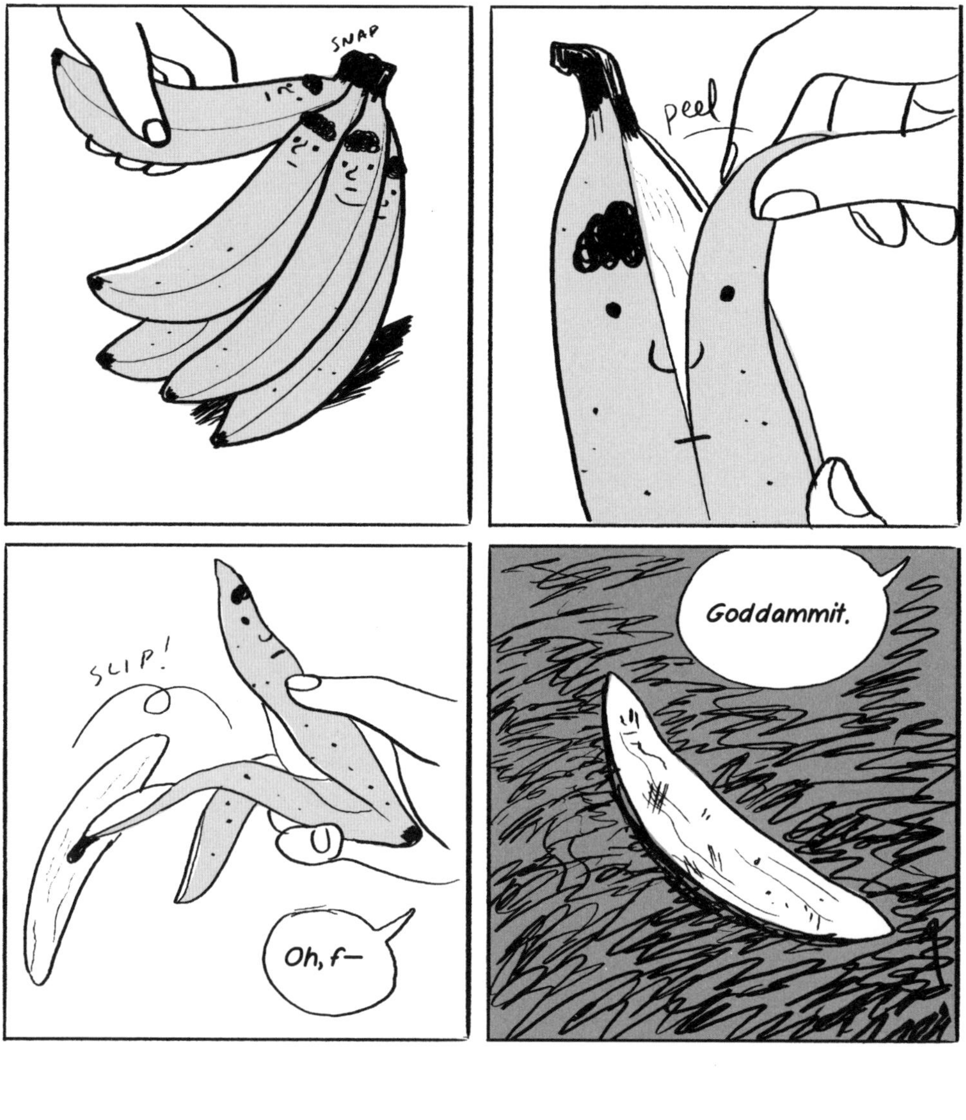
SNAP
peel
SLIP!
Oh, f—
Goddammit.

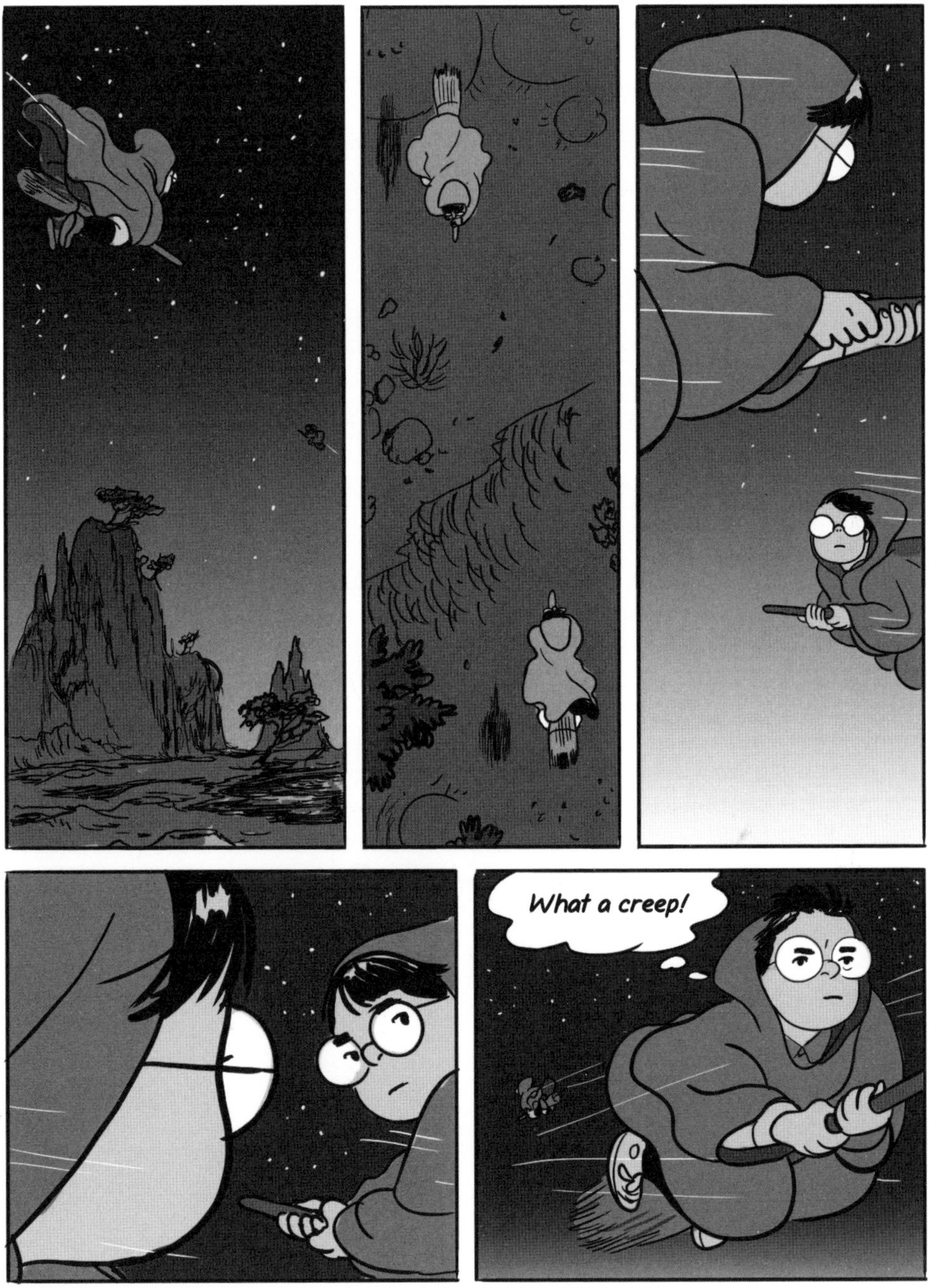
What a creep!

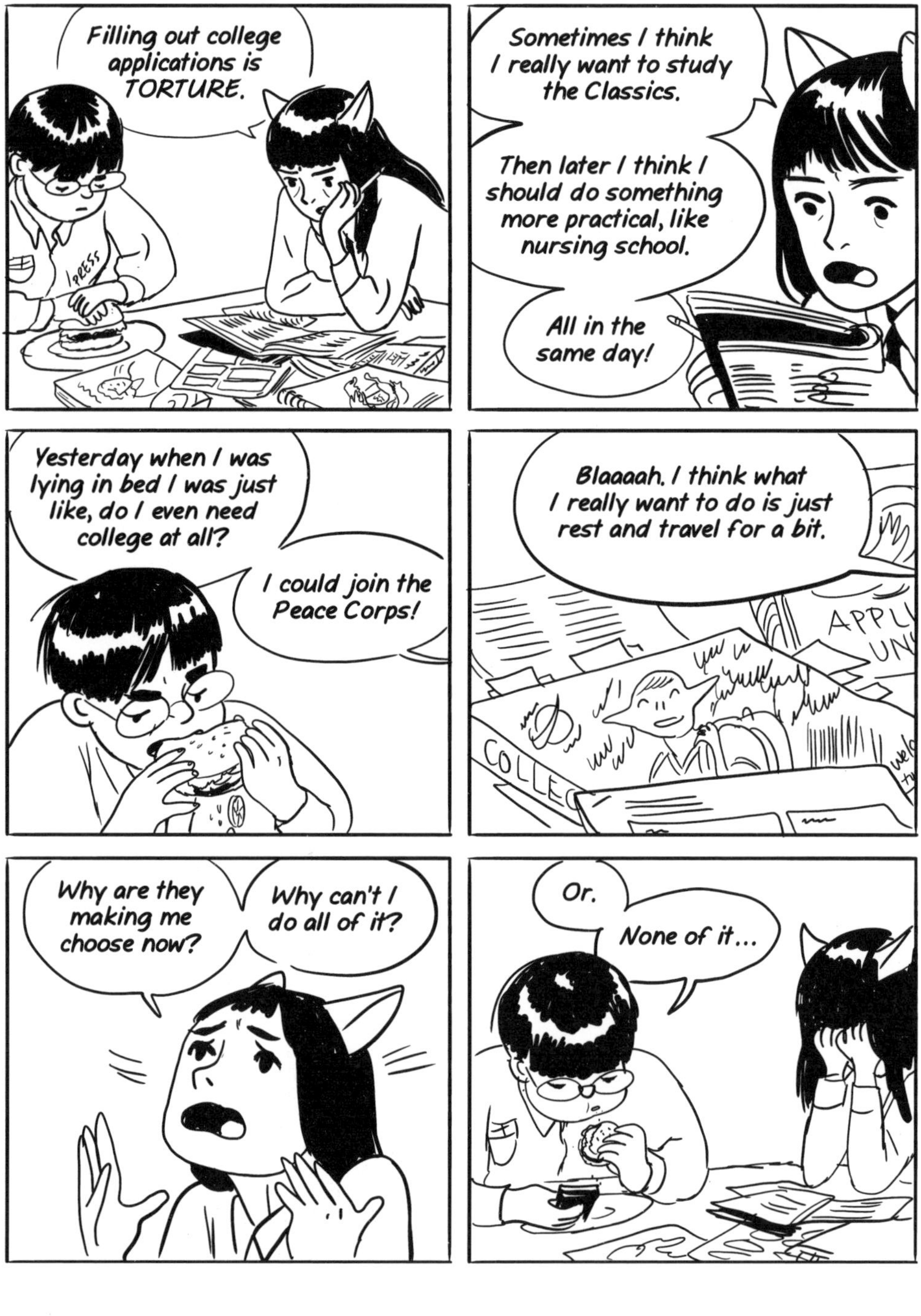
Filling out college applications is TORTURE.
Sometimes I think I really want to study the Classics.
Then later I think I should do something more practical, like nursing school.
All in the same day!
Yesterday when I was lying in bed I was just like, do I even need college at all?
I could join the Peace Corps!
Blaaaah. I think what I really want to do is just rest and travel for a bit.
Why are they making me choose now?
Why can't I do all of it?
Or.
None of it...

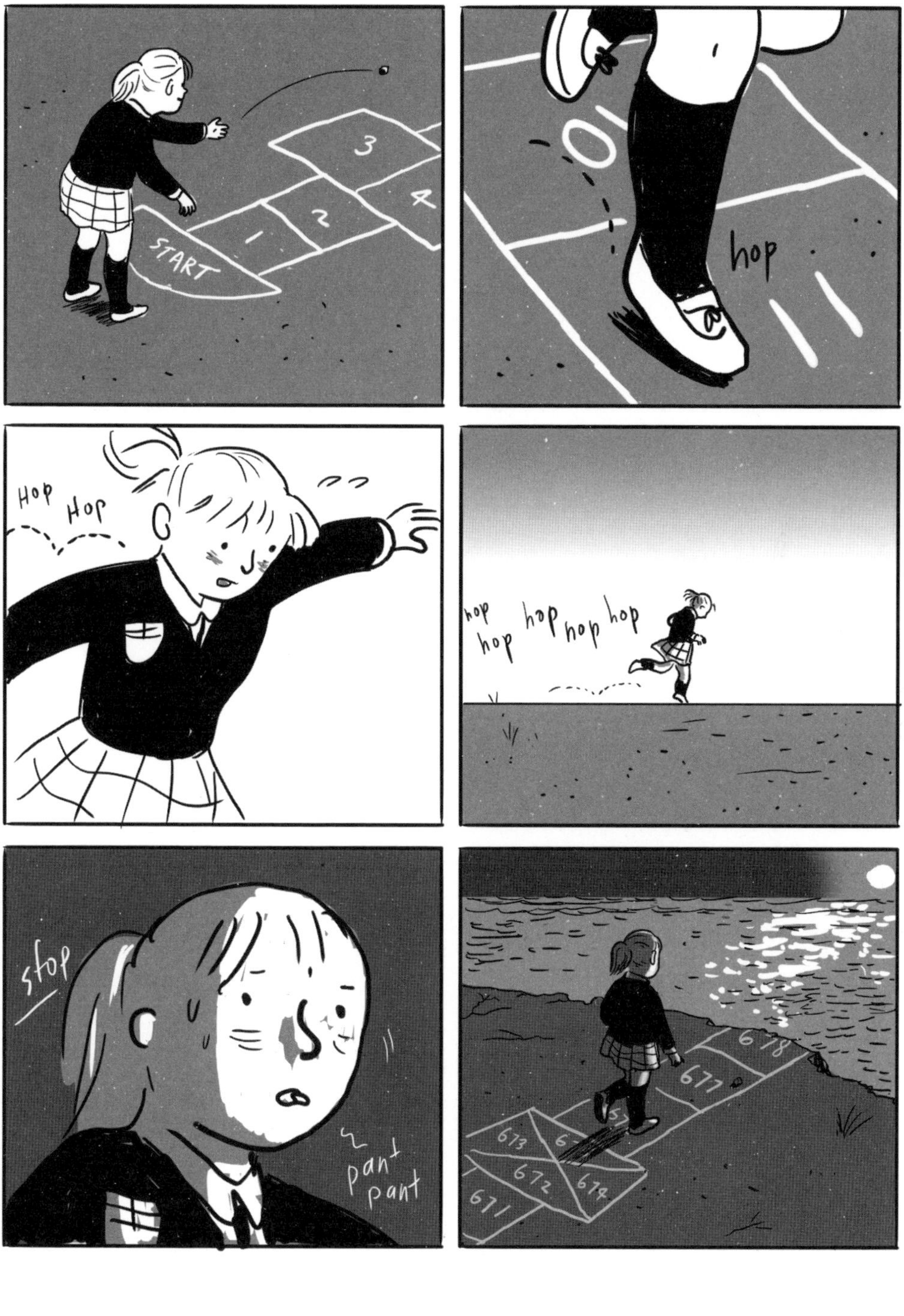

START
3
1
2
4
hop
Hop
Hop
hop
hop
hop
hop
hop
stop
pant
pant
671
672
673
674
677
678

I choose to live everyday.

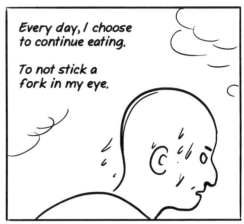

Every day, I choose to continue eating.

To not stick a fork in my eye.

I choose to not throw myself under a bus or drink antifreeze.

Or eat a bag of marbles.

And now, I choose to stop running

and lie down on this nice, cool grass.

TREVOR!

What the hell do you think you're doing, son?!

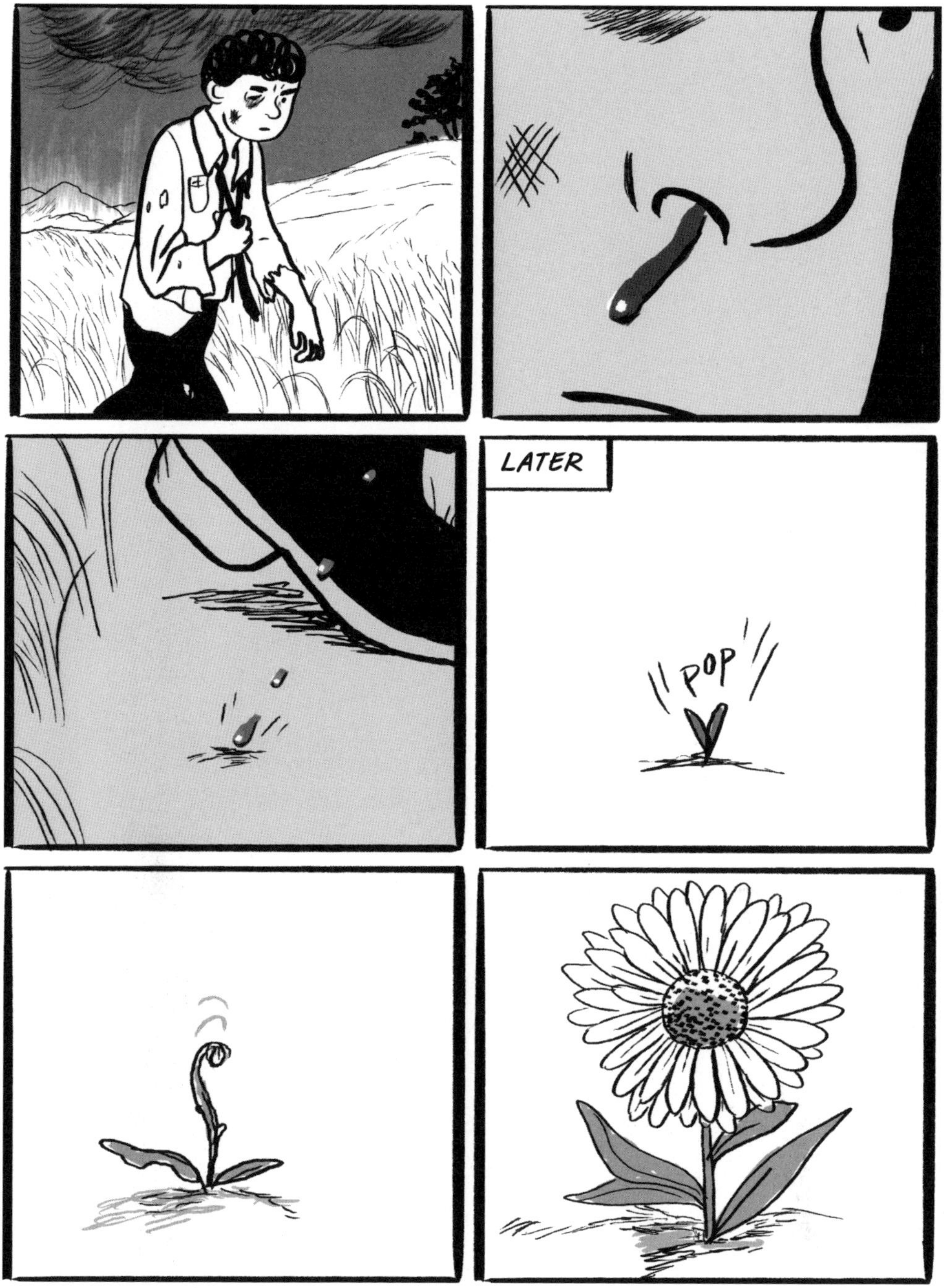
LATER
POP

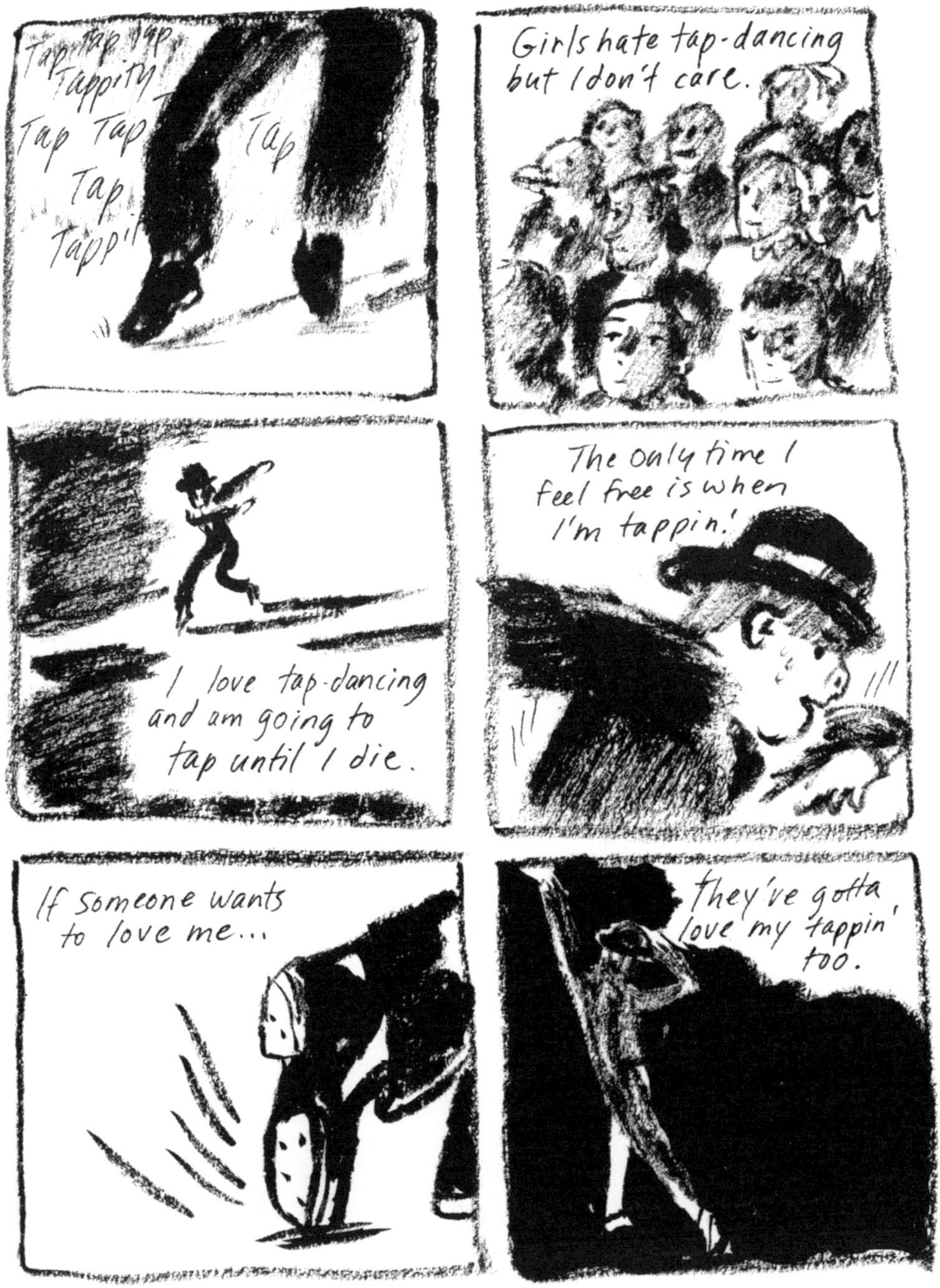

Tap Tap Tap
Tappity
Tap Tap
Tap
Tap
Tappi'
Girls hate tap-dancing but I don't care.
I love tap-dancing and am going to tap until I die.
The only time I feel free is when I'm tappin'.
If someone wants to love me...
they've gotta love my tappin' too.

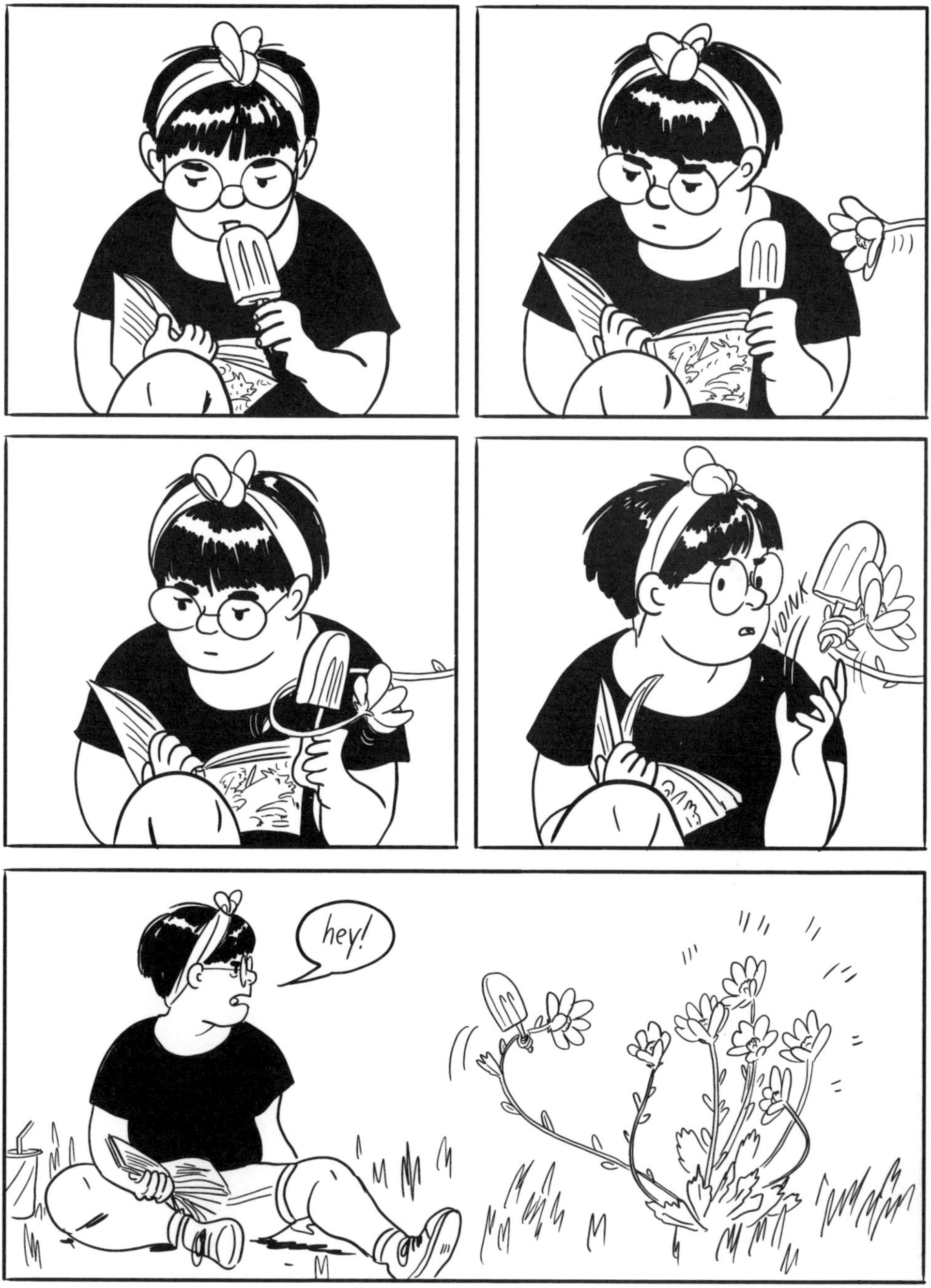
YOINK
hey!

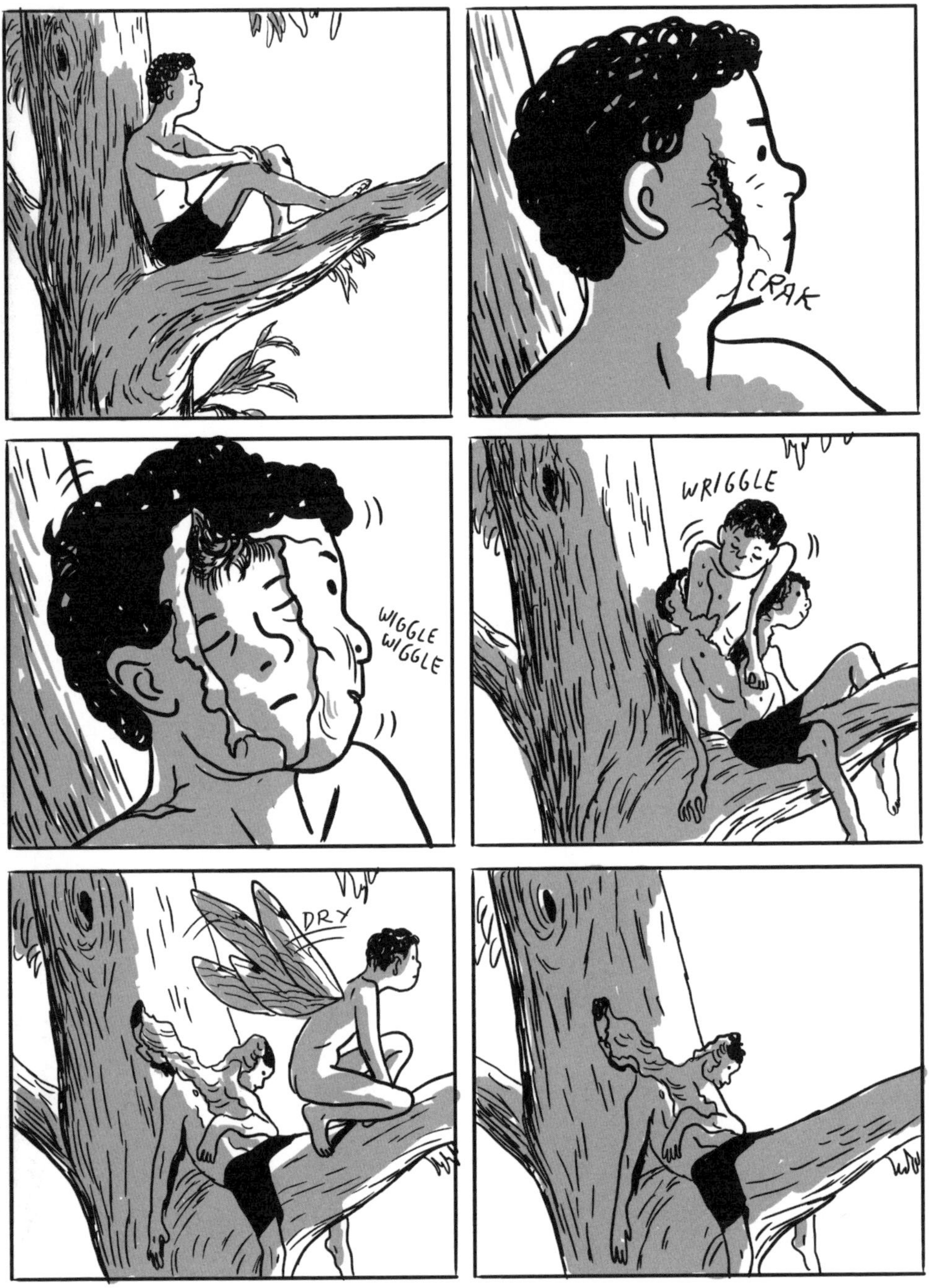
CRAK
WIGGLE WIGGLE
WRIGGLE
DRY

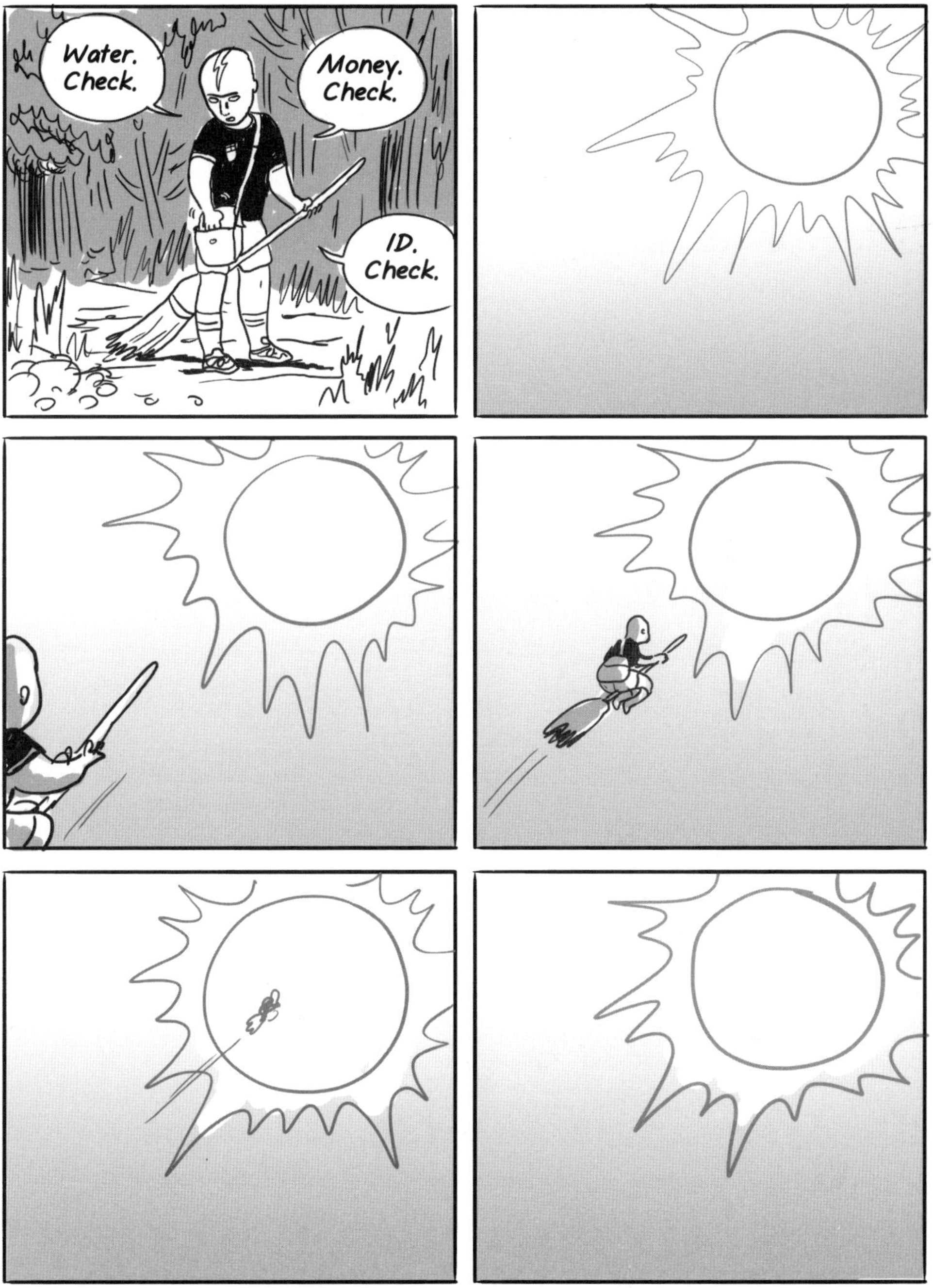
Water. Check.
Money. Check.
ID. Check.

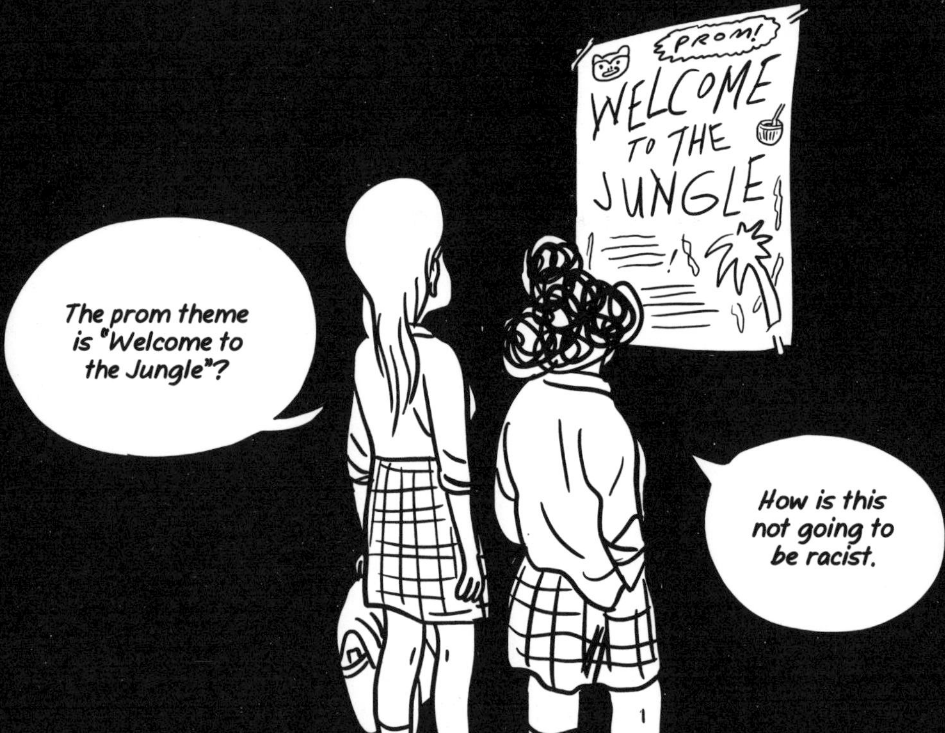
PROM!
WELCOME TO THE JUNGLE
The prom theme is "Welcome to the Jungle"?
How is this not going to be racist.

You can still come!
Just wear your regular clothes! No one will care!
I would rather jump out that window than go to prom.
I would rather club my own knees with a rusty pipe than go to prom.
Wendy, I would rather eat a plate of my own hair than go to prom.
UGH. Okay, I GET IT. Jesus.
No, this is fun.
I would rather eat a whole plate of corn and asparagus and beets and—
Oh my god, STOP.

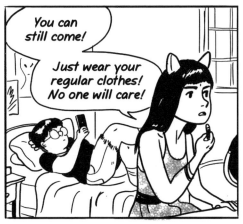

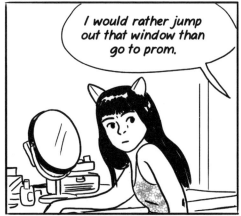

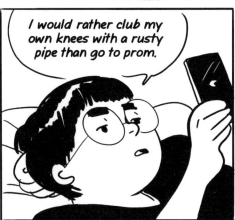

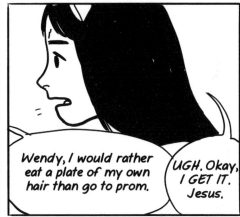

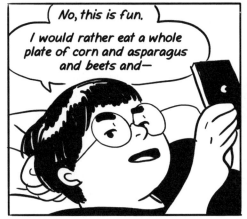

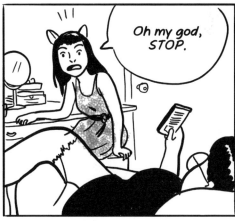

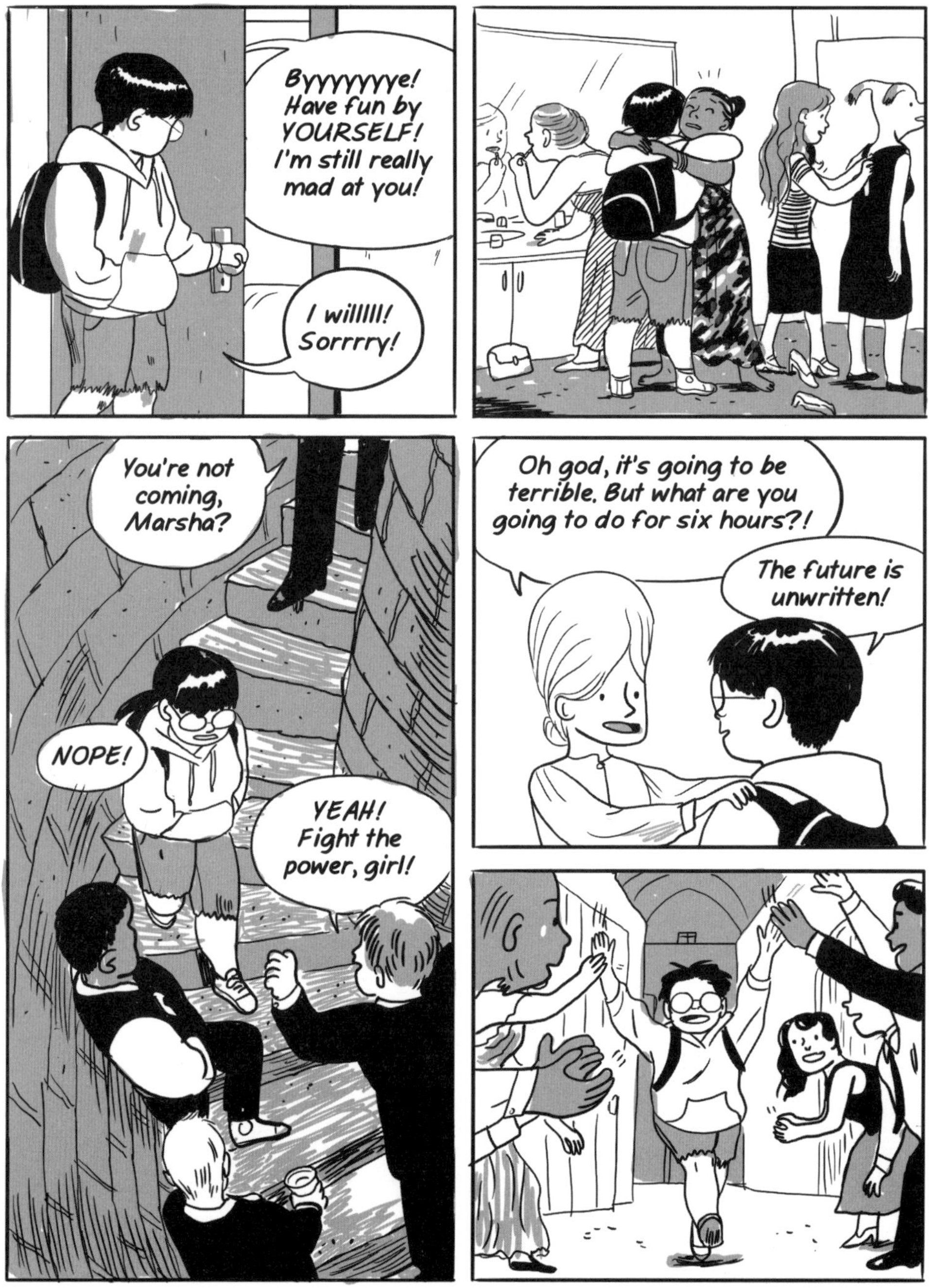

Byyyyyyye! Have fun by YOURSELF! I'm still really mad at you!
I willlll! Sorrrry!
You're not coming, Marsha?
NOPE!
YEAH! Fight the power, girl!
Oh god, it's going to be terrible. But what are you going to do for six hours?!
The future is unwritten!

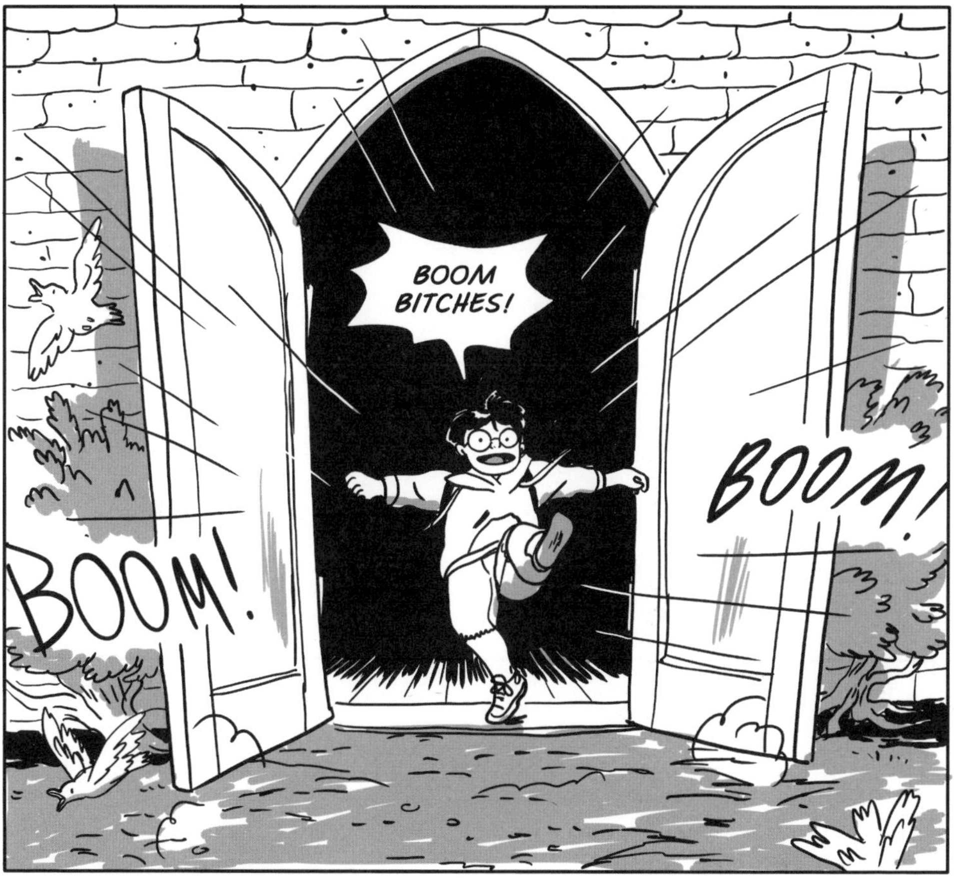
BOOM
BITCHES!
BOOM!
BOOM!

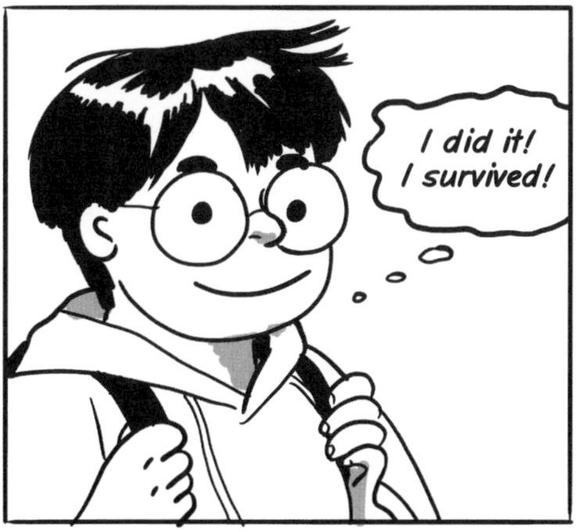
I did it!
I survived!

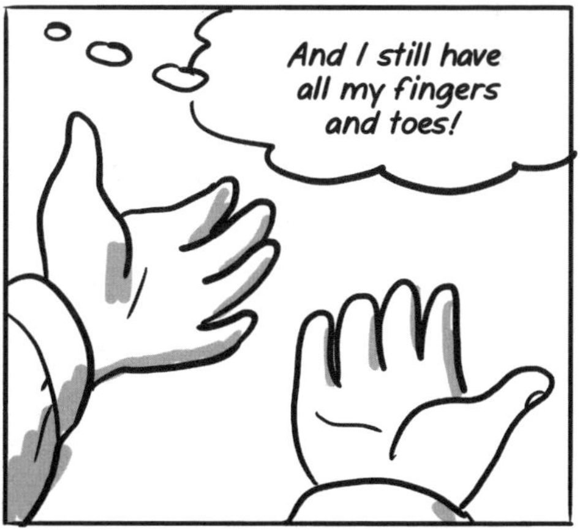
And I still have
all my fingers
and toes!

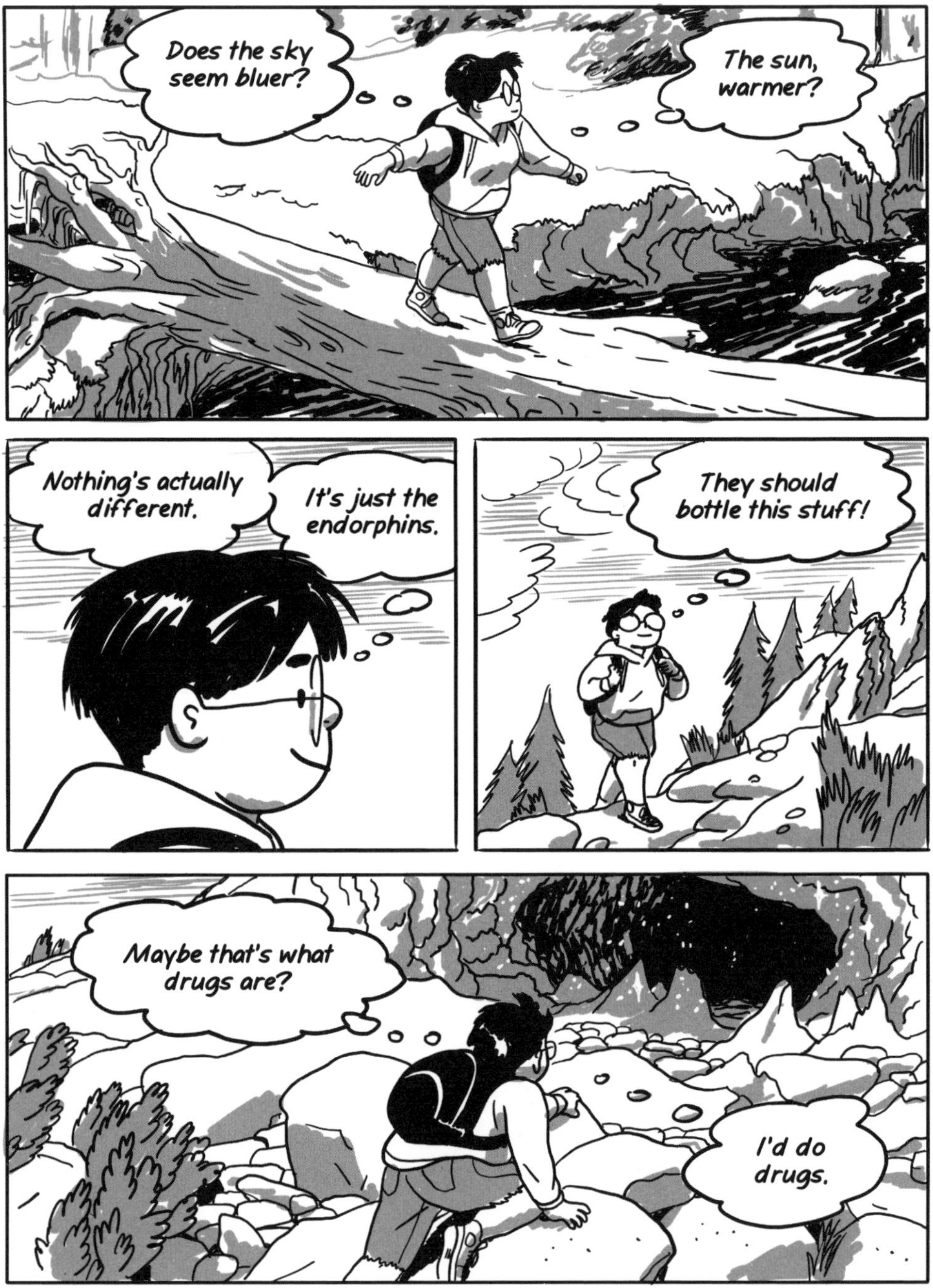
Does the sky seem bluer?
The sun, warmer?
Nothing's actually different.
It's just the endorphins.
They should bottle this stuff!
Maybe that's what drugs are?
I'd do drugs.

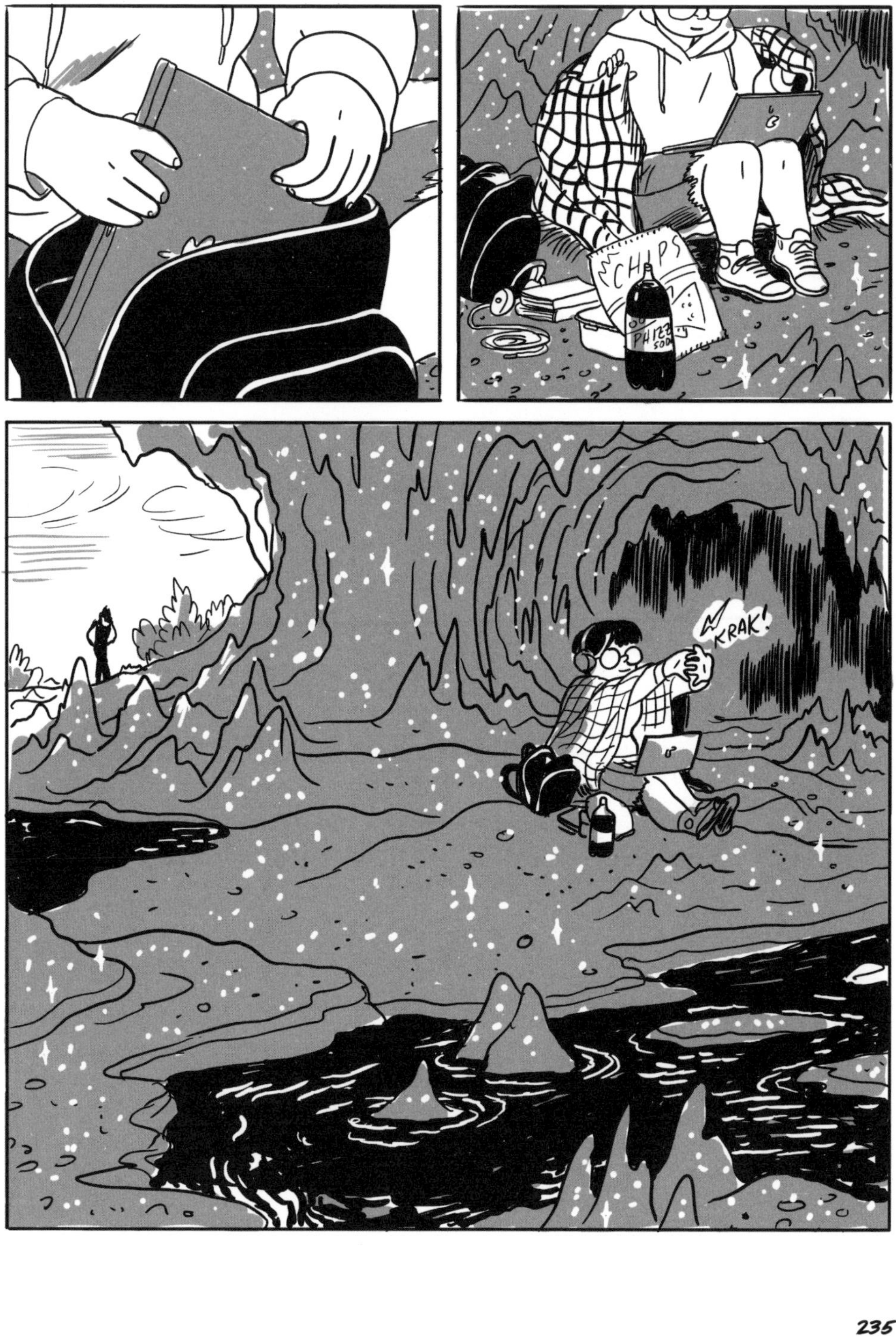
CHIPS
KRAK!

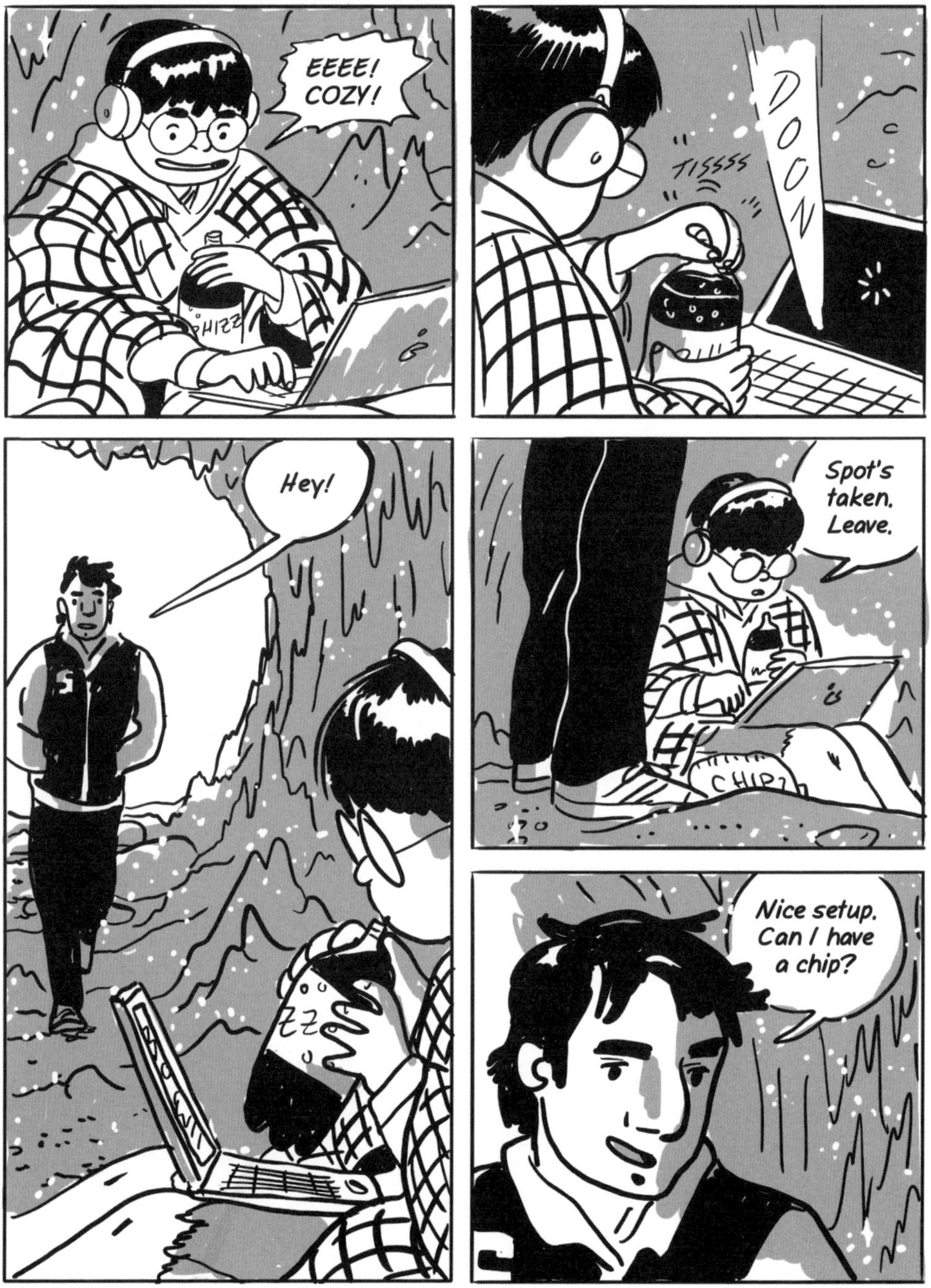
EEEE! COZY!
PHIZZ
TISSSS
DOOON
Hey!
Spot's taken. Leave.
CHIPZ
Nice setup. Can I have a chip?

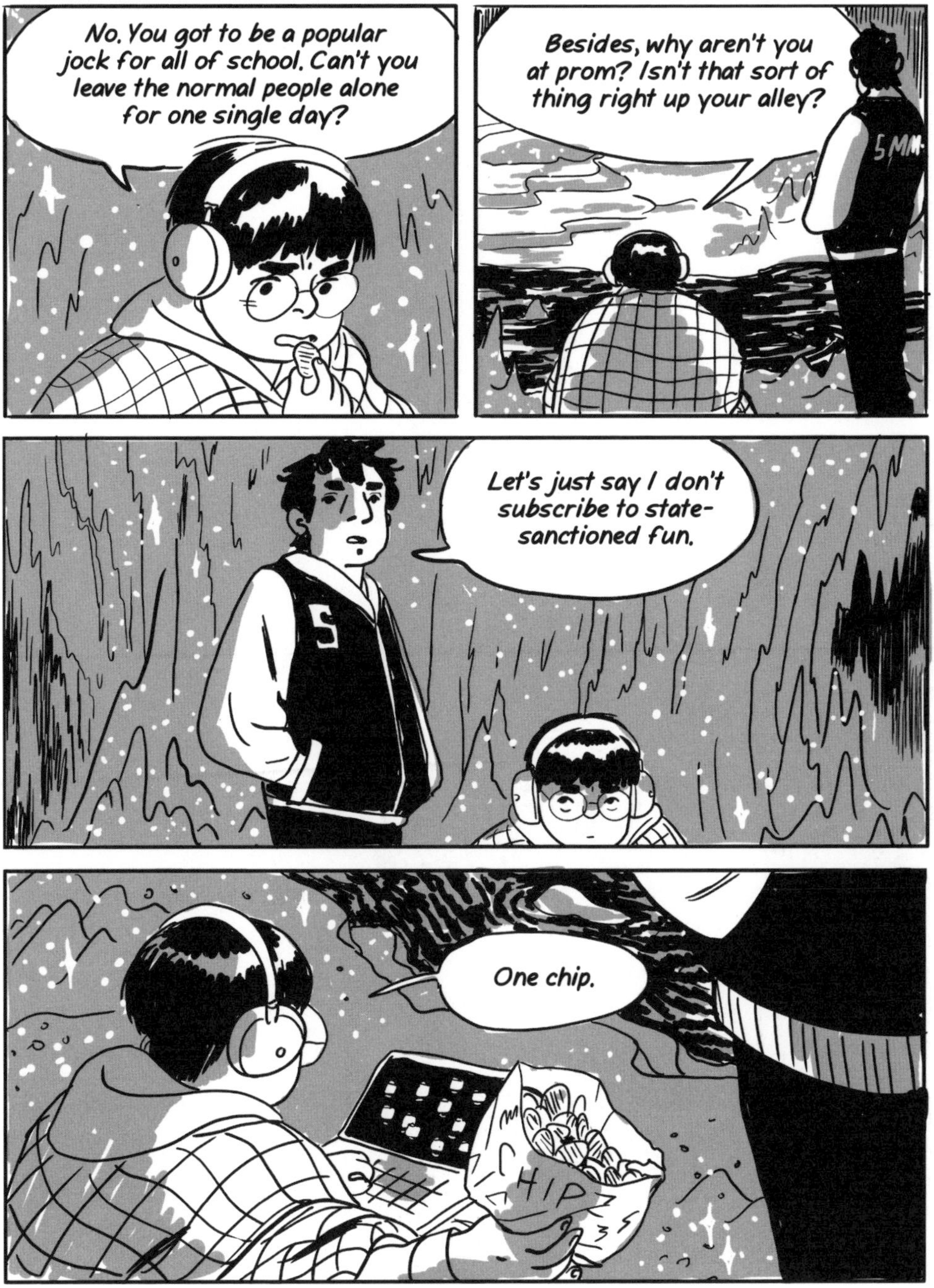
No. You got to be a popular jock for all of school. Can't you leave the normal people alone for one single day?
Besides, why aren't you at prom? Isn't that sort of thing right up your alley?
Let's just say I don't subscribe to state-sanctioned fun.
One chip.

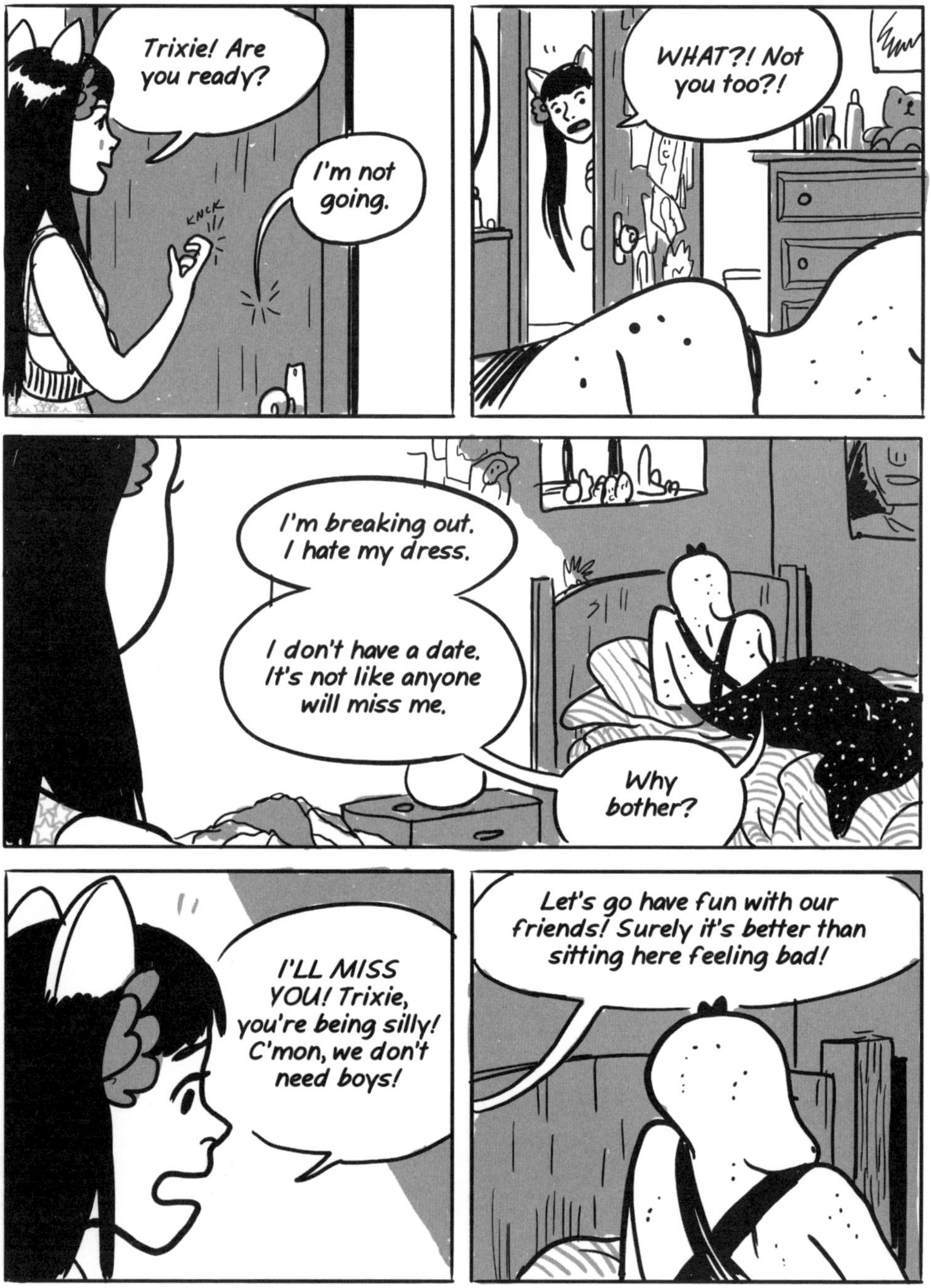
Trixie! Are you ready?
KNCK
I'm not going.
WHAT?! Not you too?!
I'm breaking out. I hate my dress.
I don't have a date. It's not like anyone will miss me.
Why bother?
I'LL MISS YOU! Trixie, you're being silly! C'mon, we don't need boys!
Let's go have fun with our friends! Surely it's better than sitting here feeling bad!

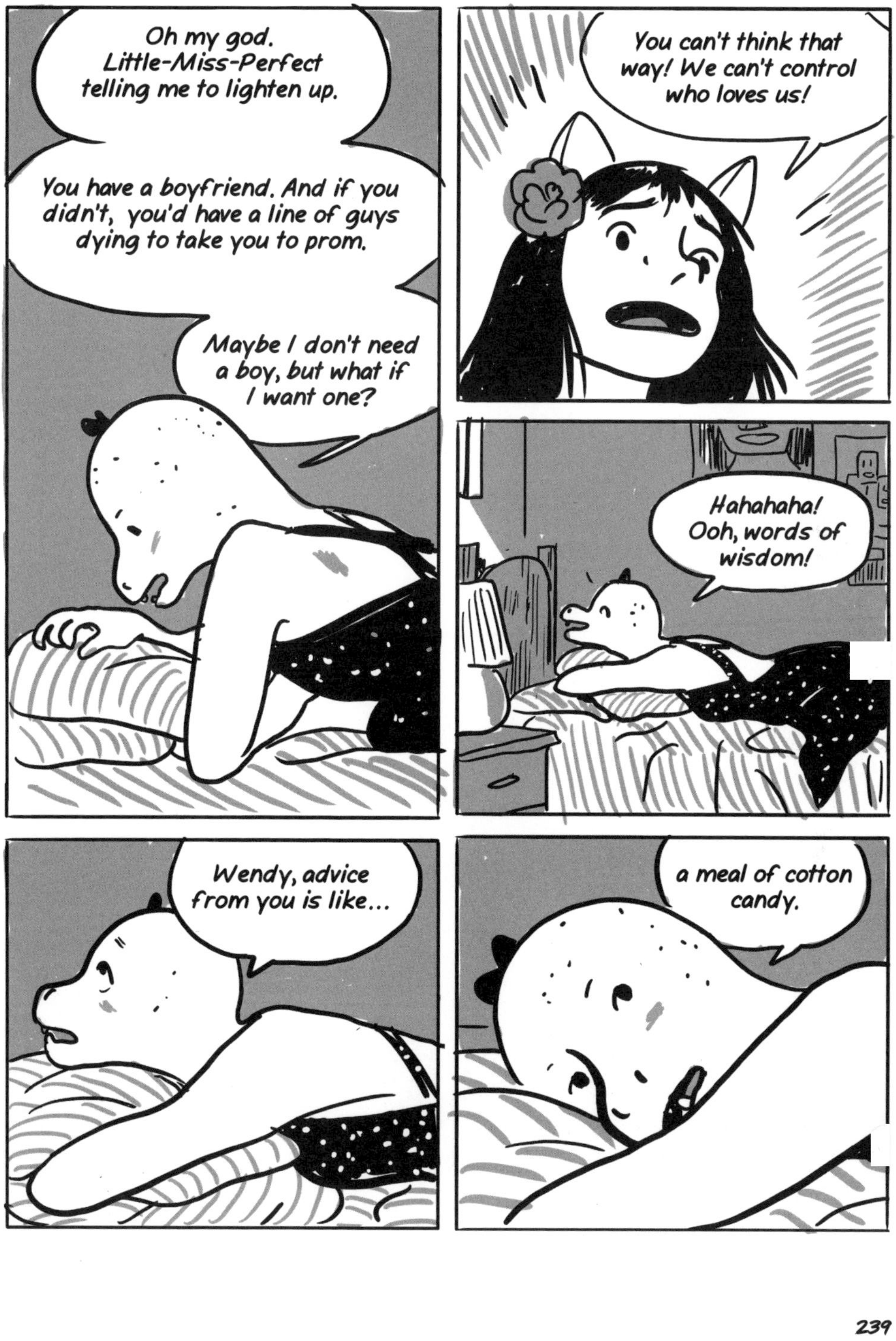
Oh my god. Little-Miss-Perfect telling me to lighten up.
You have a boyfriend. And if you didn't, you'd have a line of guys dying to take you to prom.
Maybe I don't need a boy, but what if I want one?
You can't think that way! We can't control who loves us!
Hahahaha! Ooh, words of wisdom!
Wendy, advice from you is like...
a meal of cotton candy.

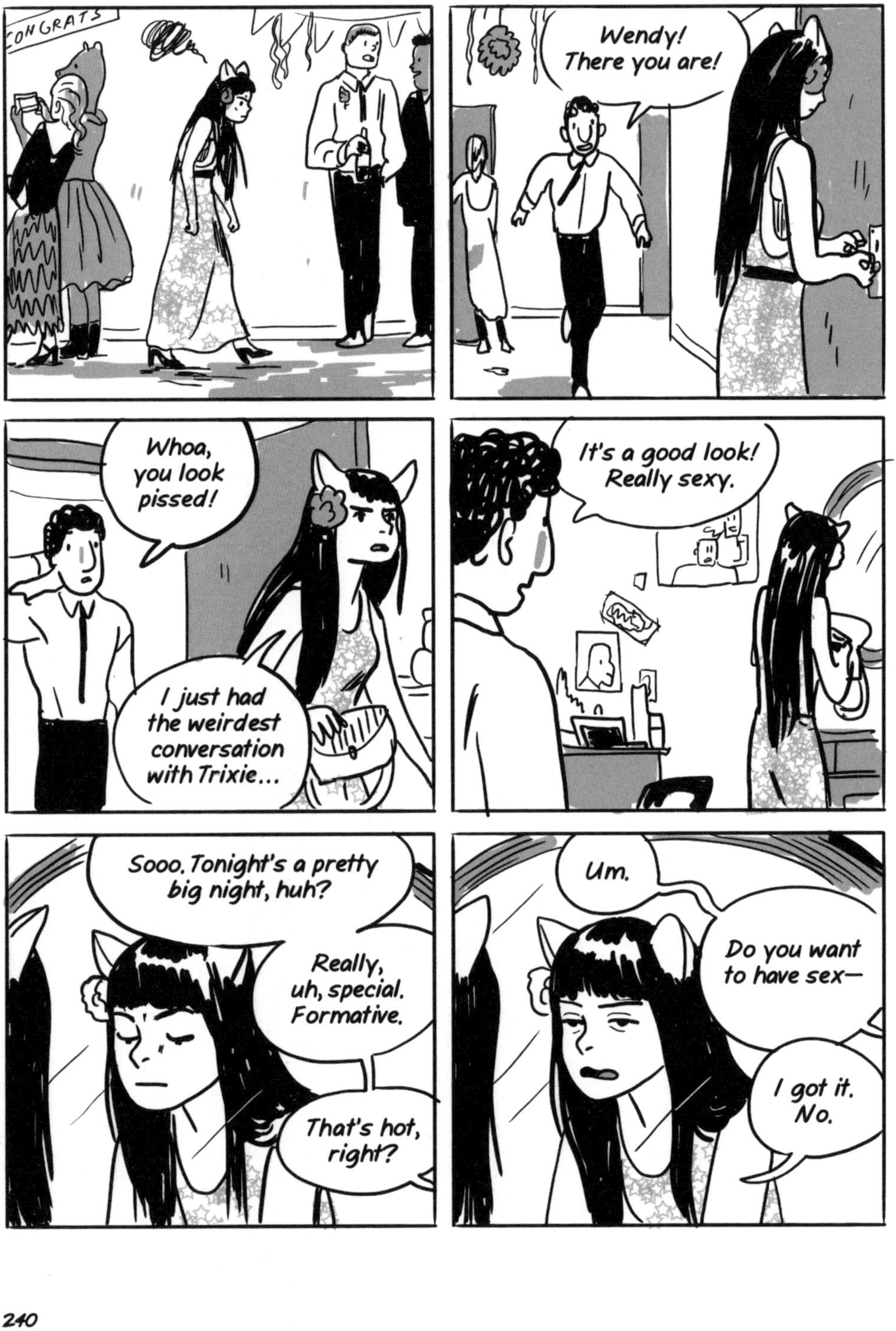
CONGRATS
Wendy! There you are!
Whoa, you look pissed!
I just had the weirdest conversation with Trixie...
It's a good look! Really sexy.
Sooo. Tonight's a pretty big night, huh?
Really, uh, special. Formative.
That's hot, right?
Um.
Do you want to have sex—
I got it. No.

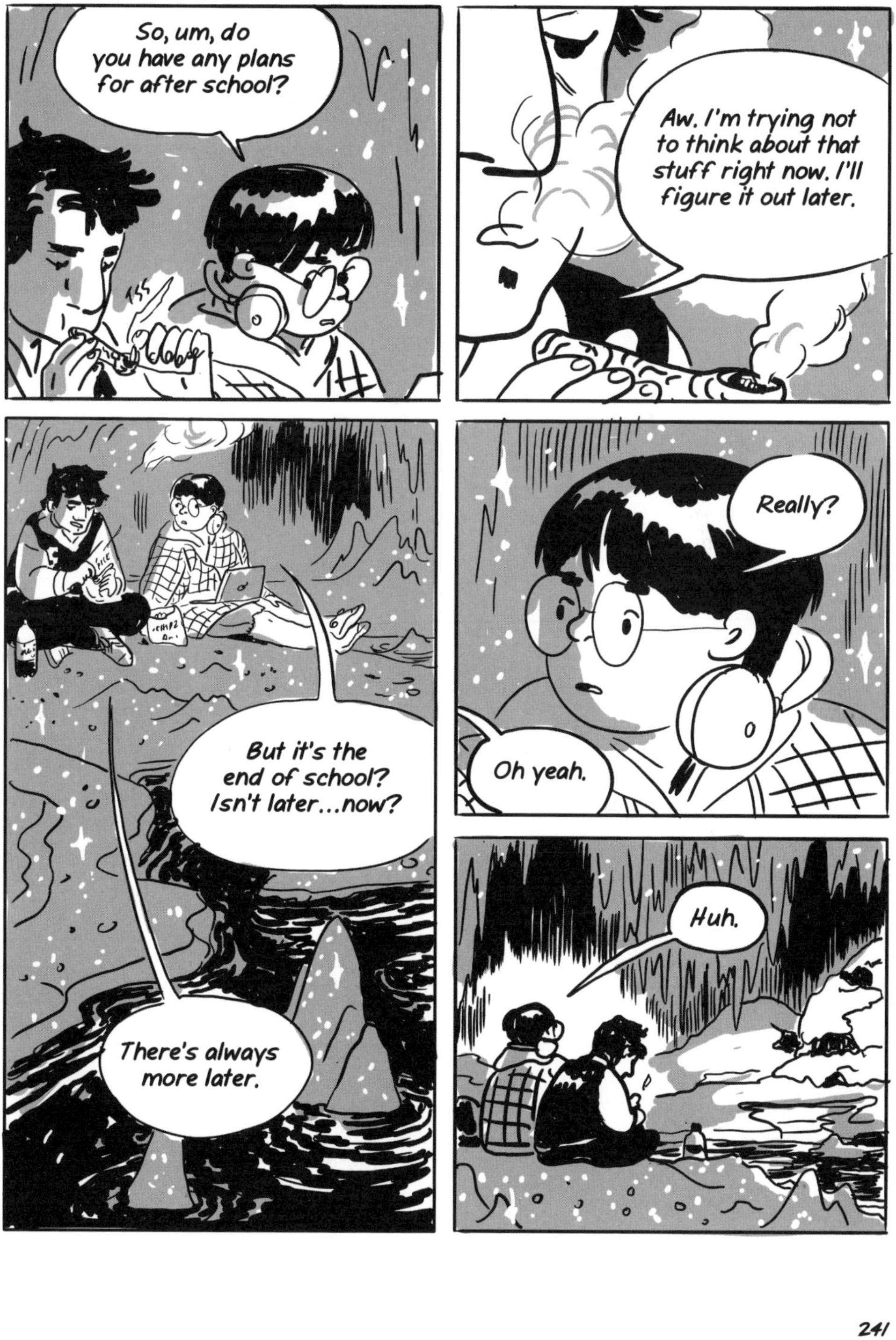
So, um, do you have any plans for after school?
Aw. I'm trying not to think about that stuff right now. I'll figure it out later.
But it's the end of school? Isn't later...now?
There's always more later.
Really?
Oh yeah.
Huh.

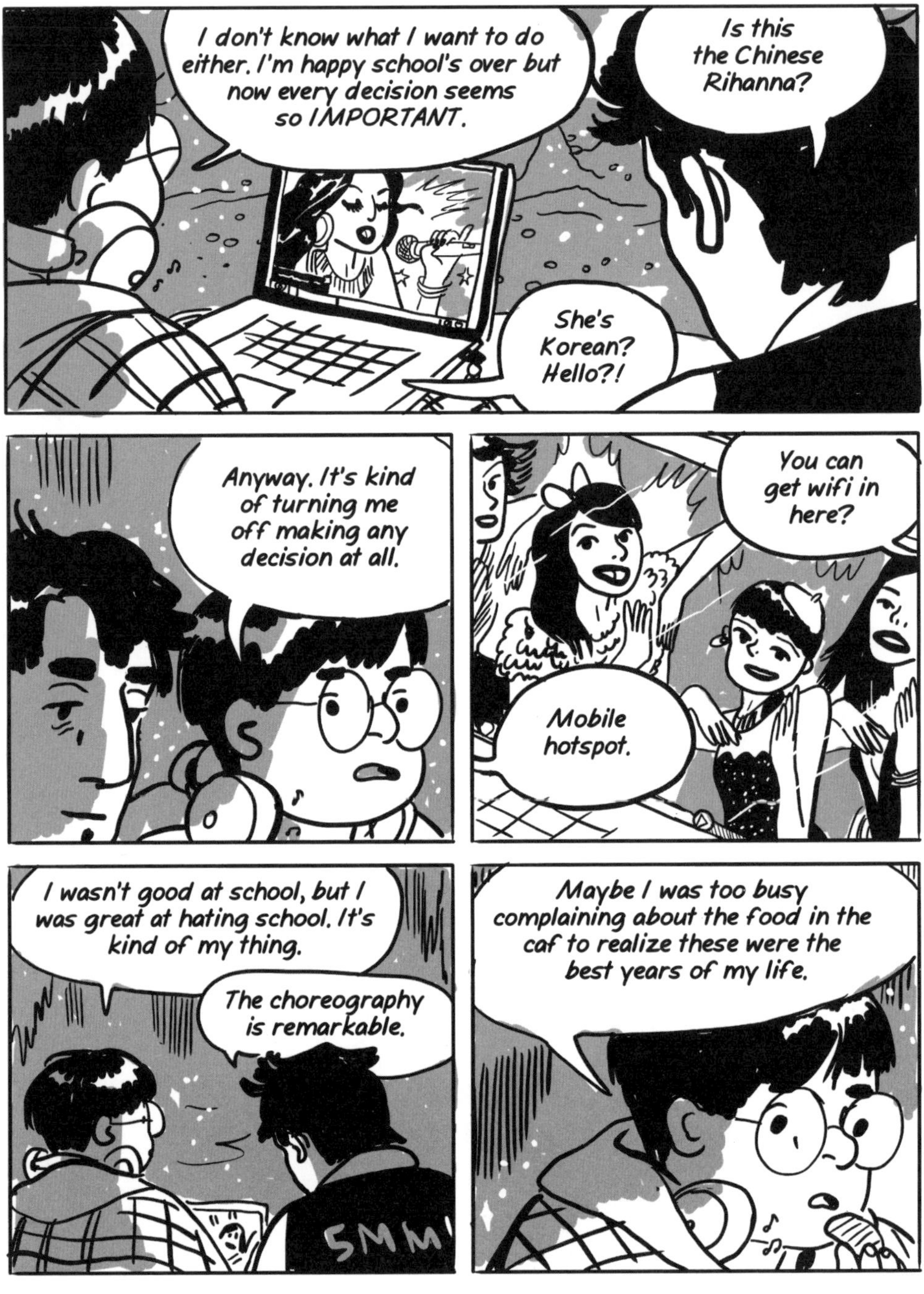
I don't know what I want to do either. I'm happy school's over but now every decision seems so IMPORTANT.
Is this the Chinese Rihanna?
She's Korean? Hello?!
Anyway. It's kind of turning me off making any decision at all.
You can get wifi in here?
Mobile hotspot.
I wasn't good at school, but I was great at hating school. It's kind of my thing.
The choreography is remarkable.
Maybe I was too busy complaining about the food in the caf to realize these were the best years of my life.
5MM

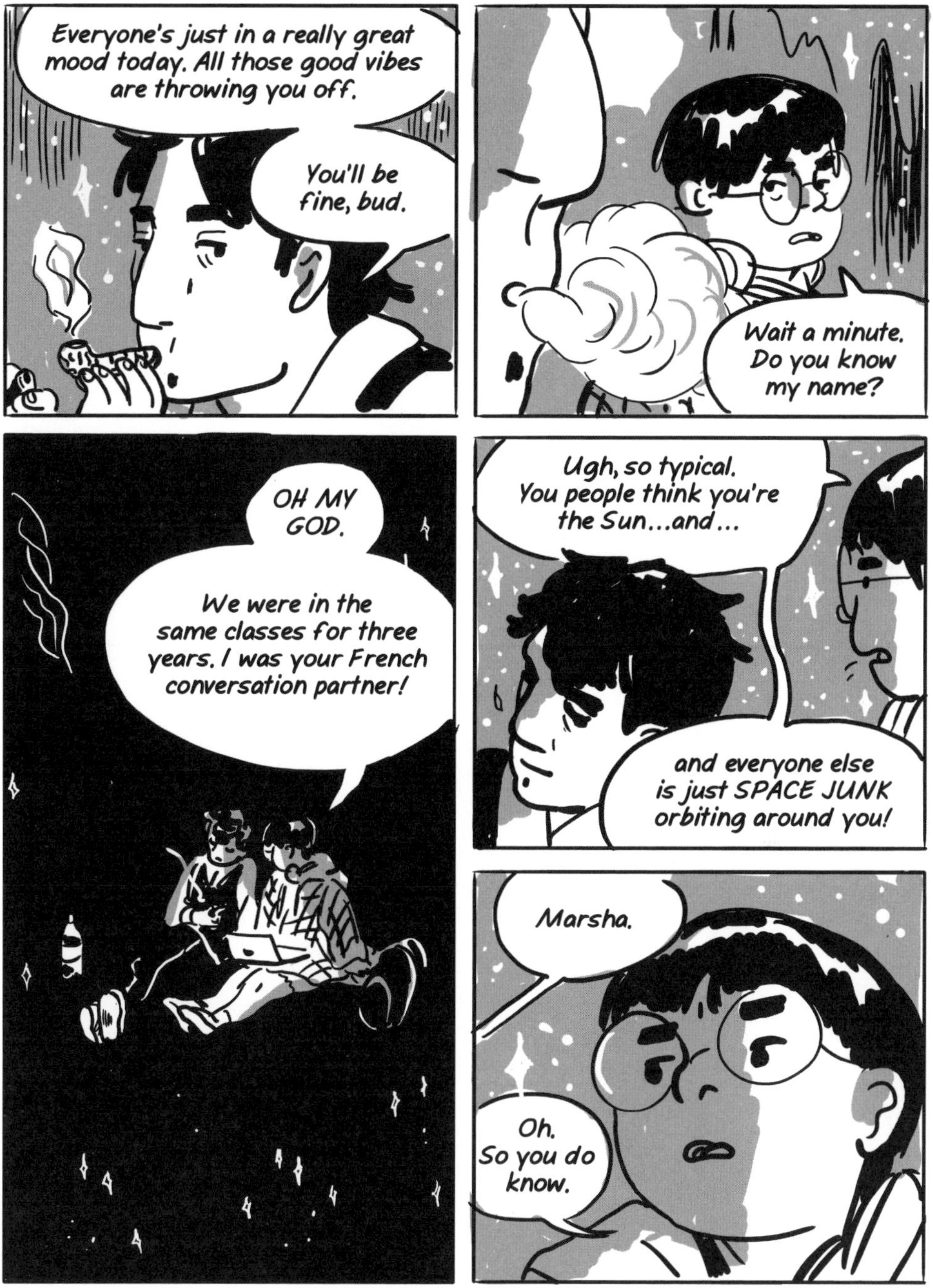
Everyone's just in a really great mood today. All those good vibes are throwing you off.
You'll be fine, bud.
Wait a minute. Do you know my name?
OH MY GOD.
We were in the same classes for three years. I was your French conversation partner!
Ugh, so typical. You people think you're the Sun...and...
and everyone else is just SPACE JUNK orbiting around you!
Marsha.
Oh. So you do know.

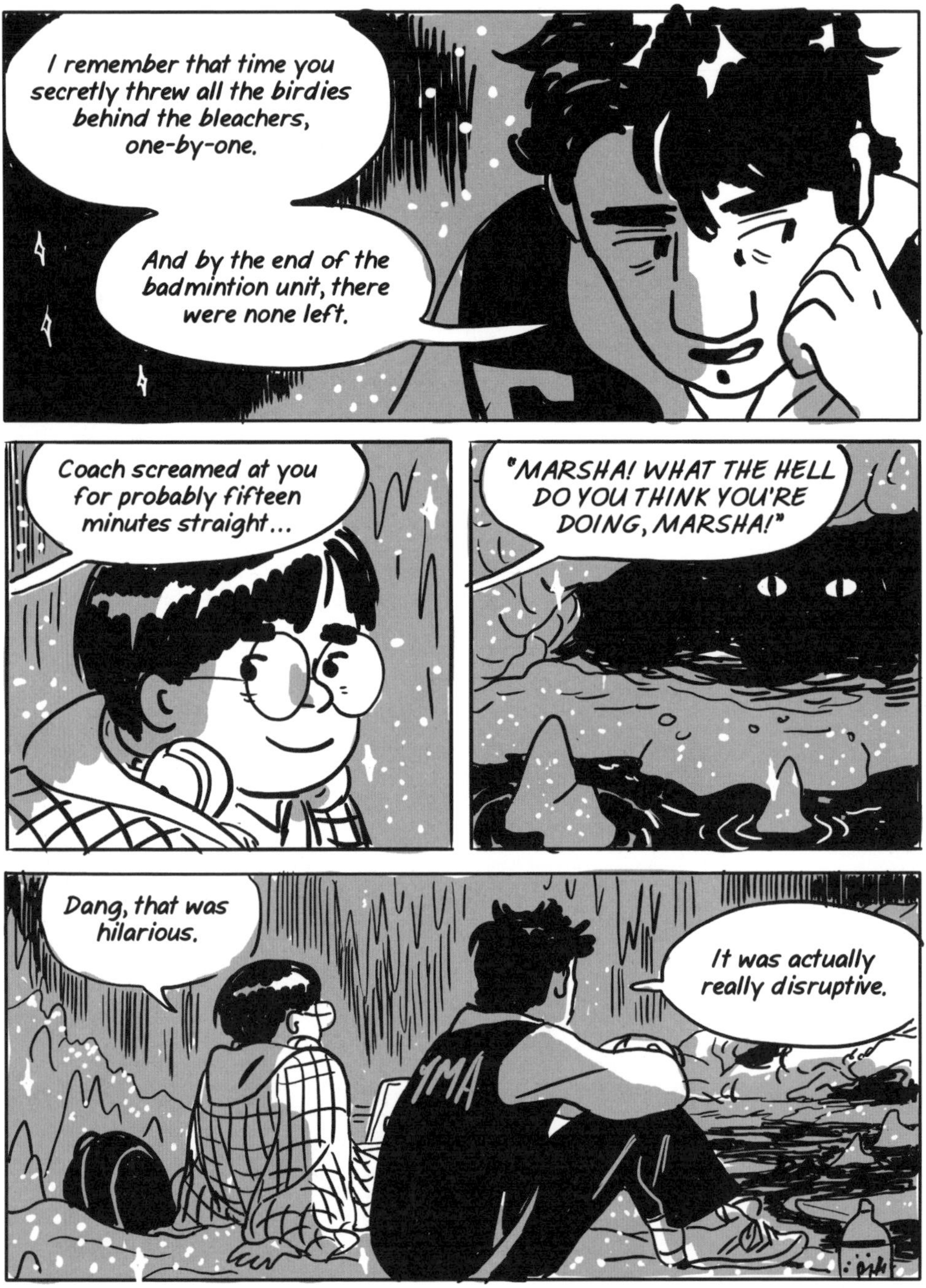
I remember that time you secretly threw all the birdies behind the bleachers, one-by-one.
And by the end of the badmintion unit, there were none left.
Coach screamed at you for probably fifteen minutes straight...
"MARSHA! WHAT THE HELL DO YOU THINK YOU'RE DOING, MARSHA!"
Dang, that was hilarious.
It was actually really disruptive.
YMA

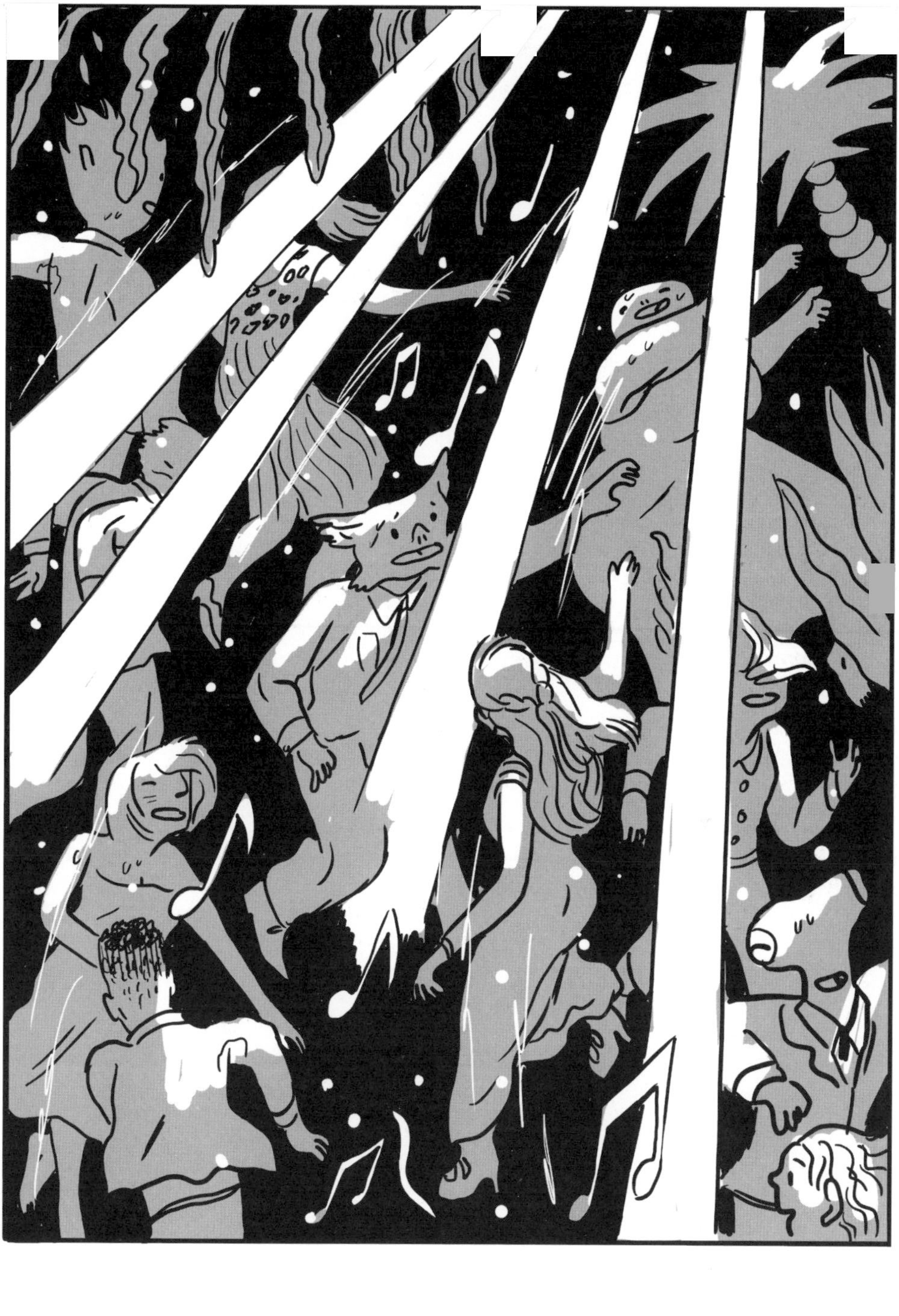

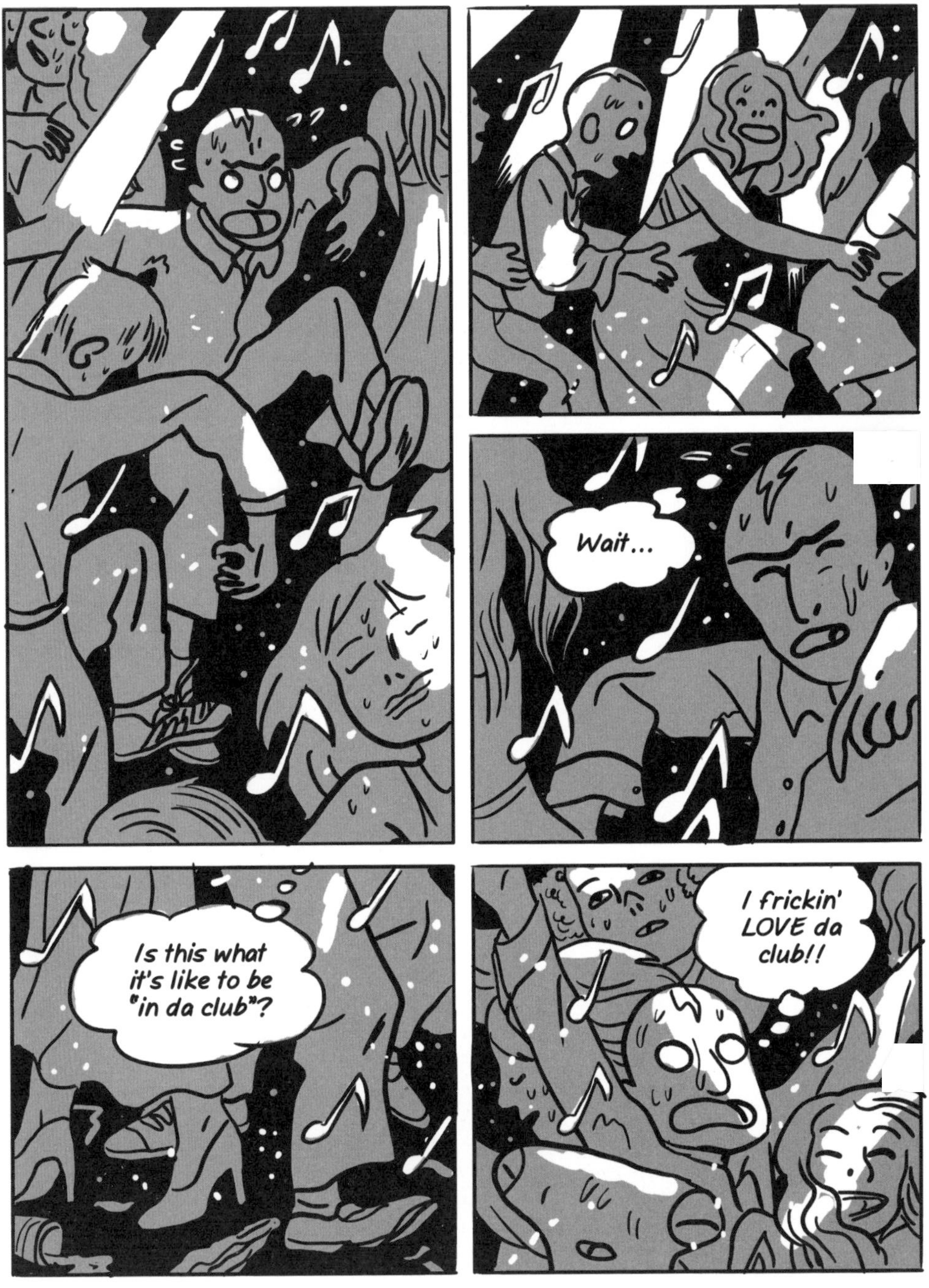
Wait...
Is this what it's like to be "in da club"?
I frickin' LOVE da club!!

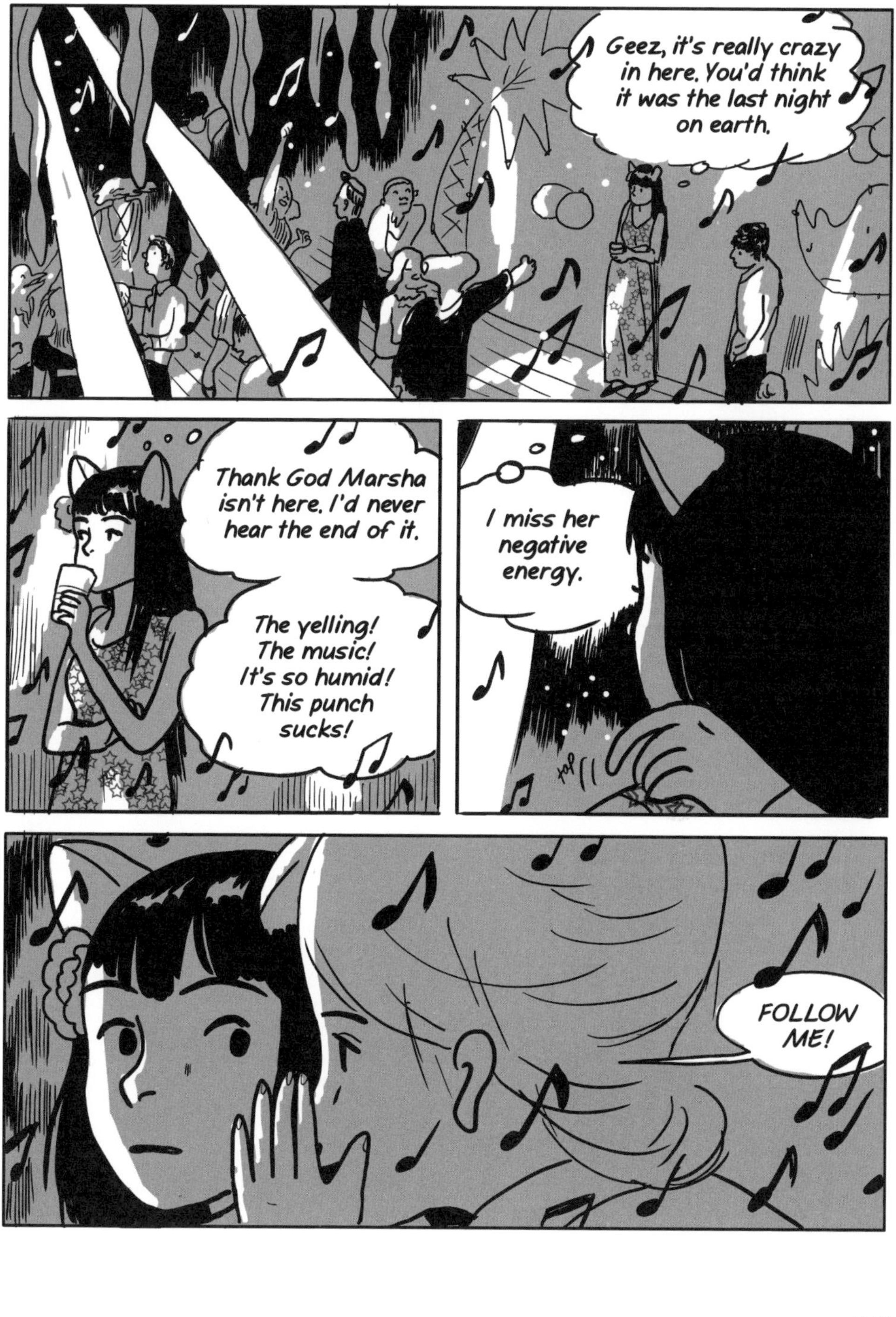
Geez, it's really crazy in here. You'd think it was the last night on earth.
Thank God Marsha isn't here. I'd never hear the end of it.
The yelling! The music! It's so humid! This punch sucks!
I miss her negative energy.
FOLLOW ME!

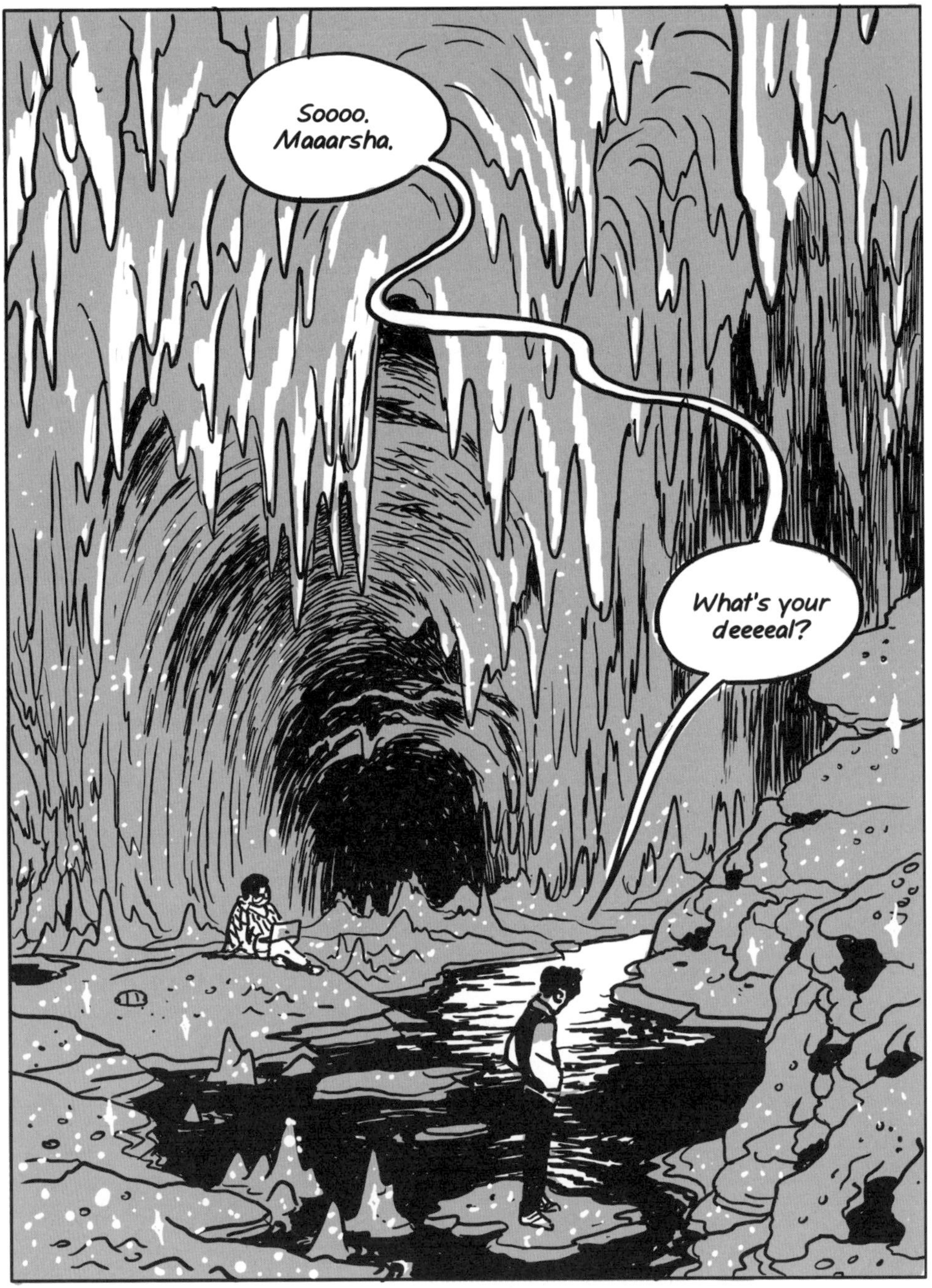
Soooo.
Maaarsha.
What's your deeeeal?

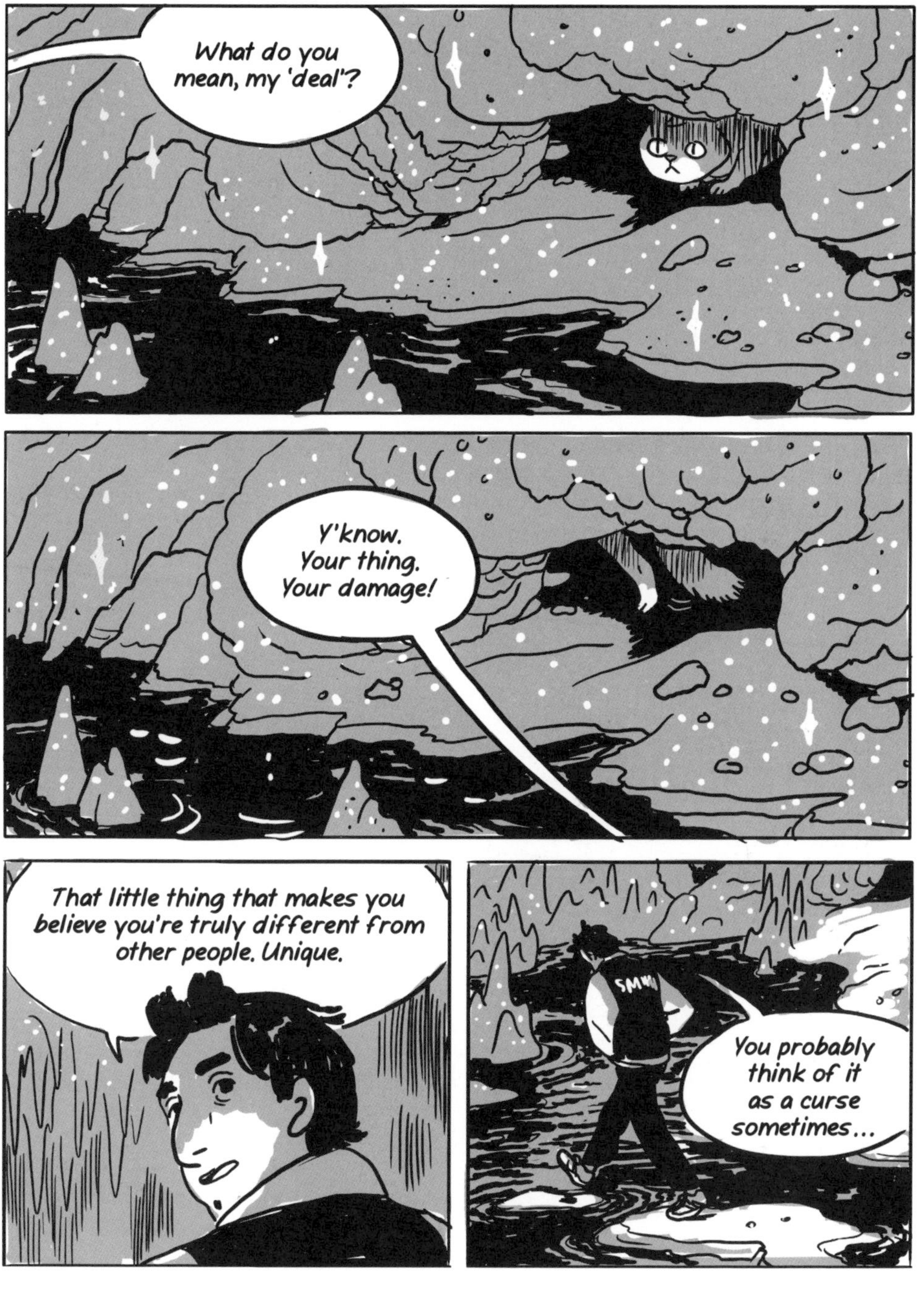
What do you mean, my 'deal'?
Y'know. Your thing. Your damage!
That little thing that makes you believe you're truly different from other people. Unique.
SMW
You probably think of it as a curse sometimes...

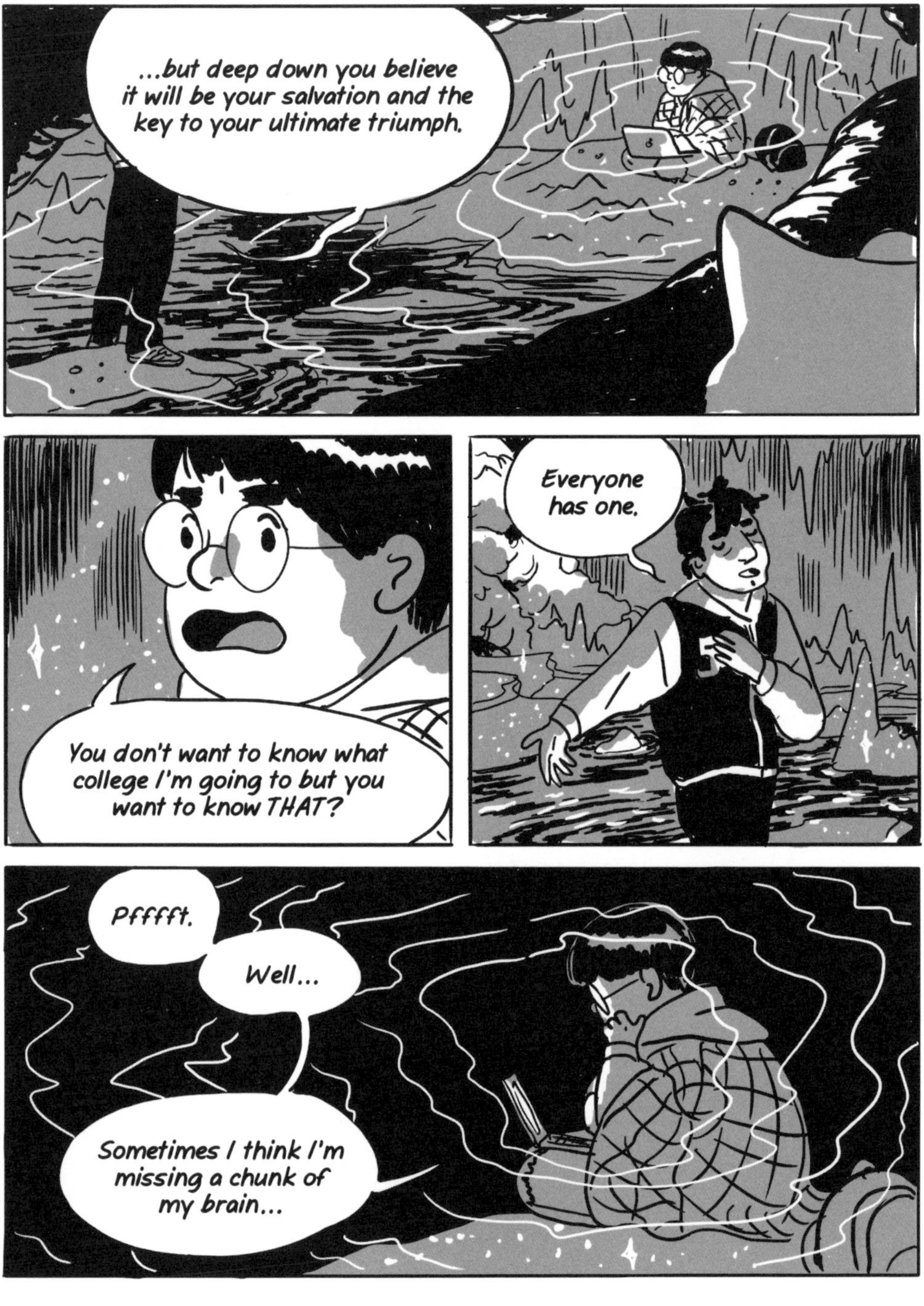
...but deep down you believe it will be your salvation and the key to your ultimate triumph.
You don't want to know what college I'm going to but you want to know THAT?
Everyone has one.
Pfffft.
Well...
Sometimes I think I'm missing a chunk of my brain...

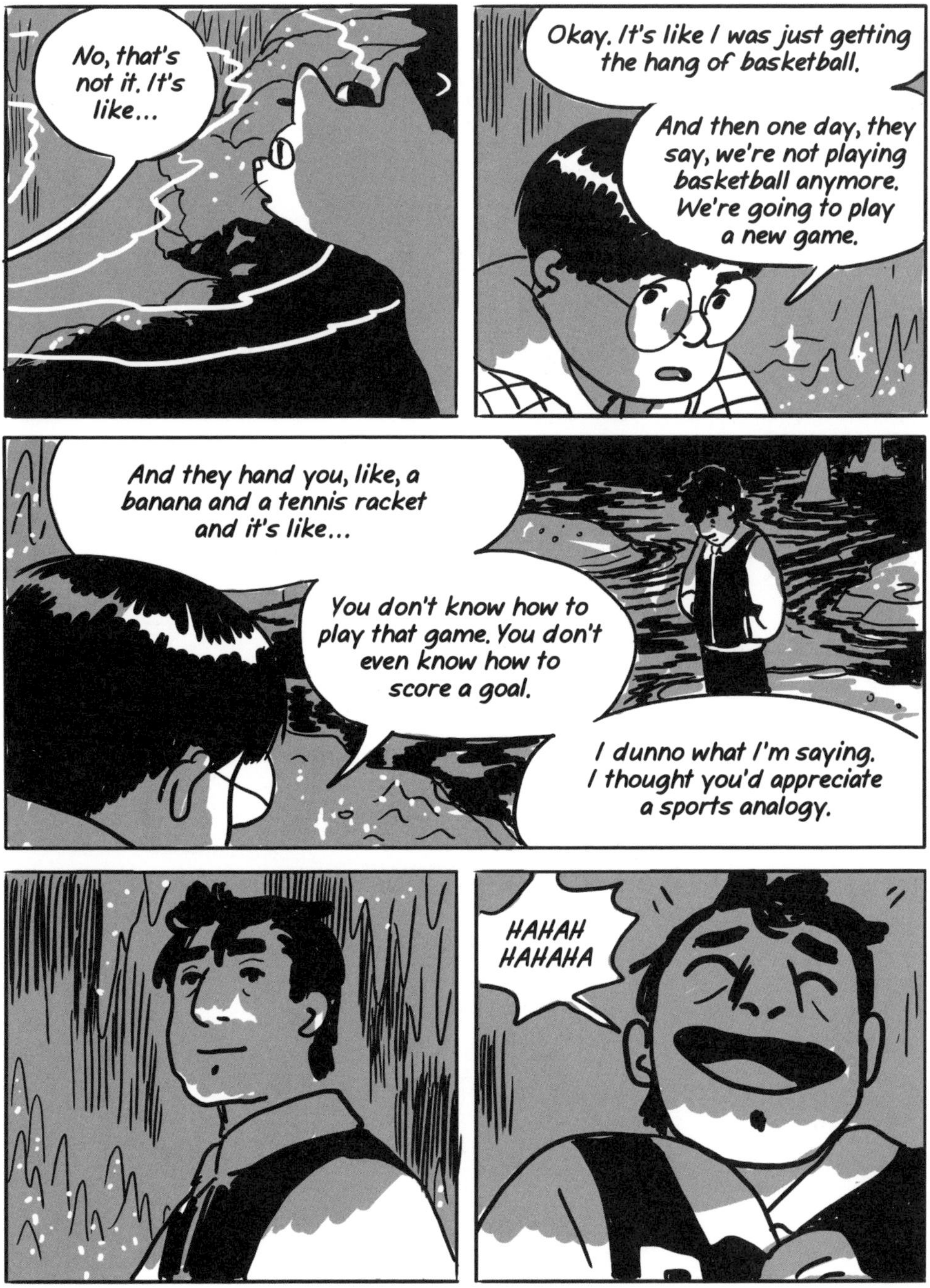
No, that's not it. It's like...
Okay. It's like I was just getting the hang of basketball.
And then one day, they say, we're not playing basketball anymore. We're going to play a new game.
And they hand you, like, a banana and a tennis racket and it's like...
You don't know how to play that game. You don't even know how to score a goal.
I dunno what I'm saying. I thought you'd appreciate a sports analogy.
HAHAH HAHAHA

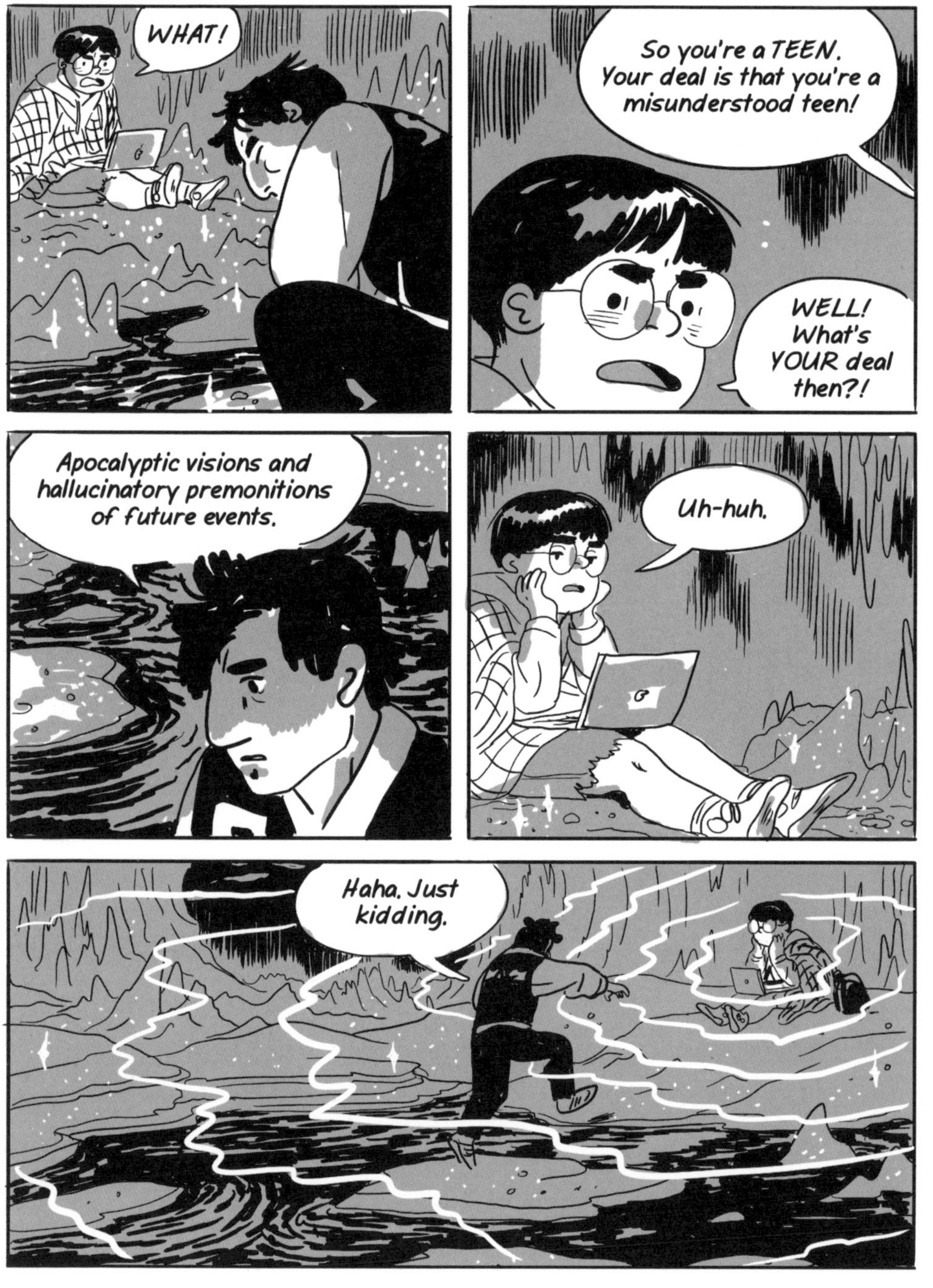
WHAT!
So you're a TEEN. Your deal is that you're a misunderstood teen!
WELL! What's YOUR deal then?!
Apocalyptic visions and hallucinatory premonitions of future events.
Uh-huh.
Haha. Just kidding.

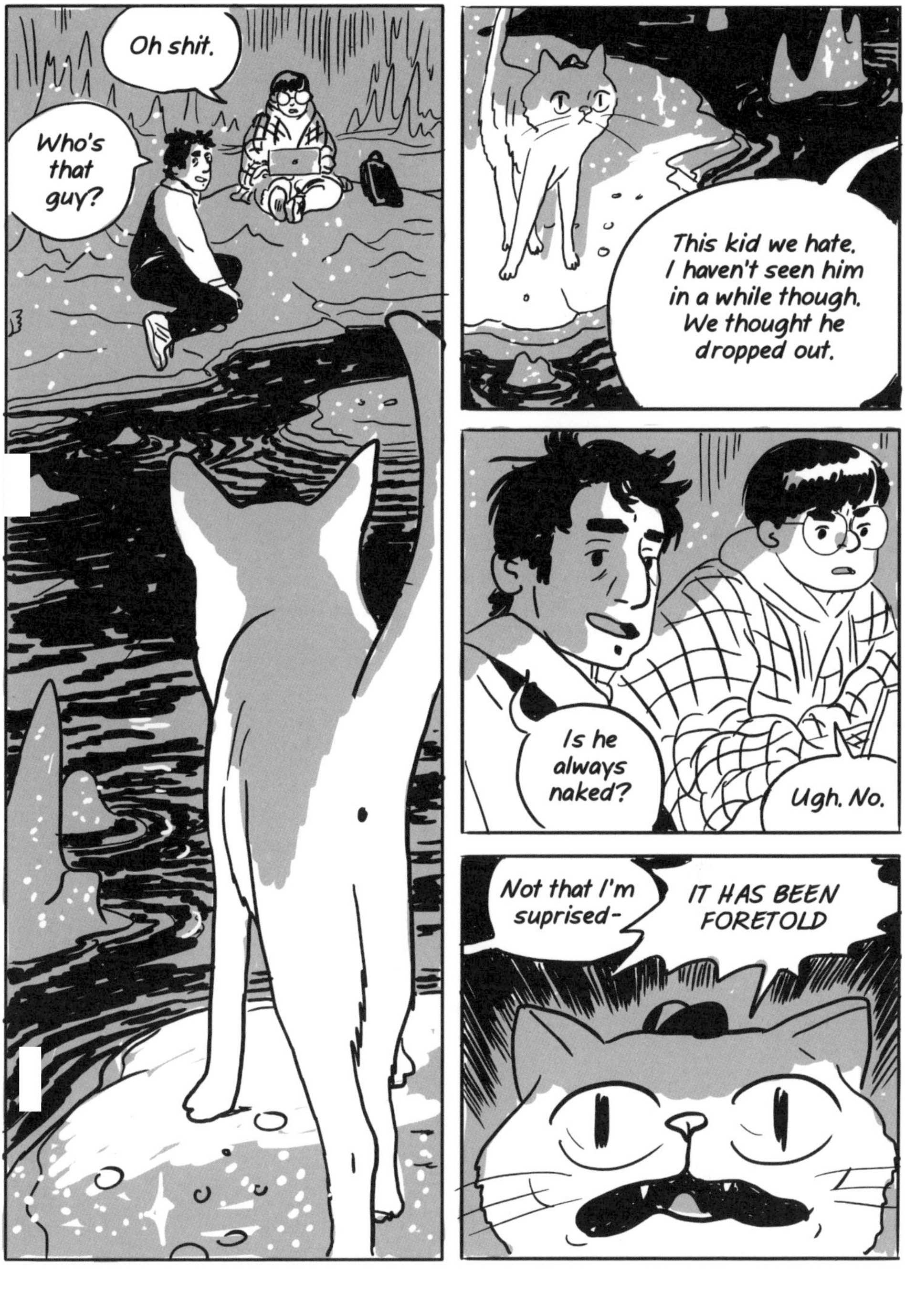
Oh shit.
Who's that guy?
This kid we hate. I haven't seen him in a while though. We thought he dropped out.
Is he always naked?
Ugh. No.
Not that I'm suprised-
IT HAS BEEN FORETOLD

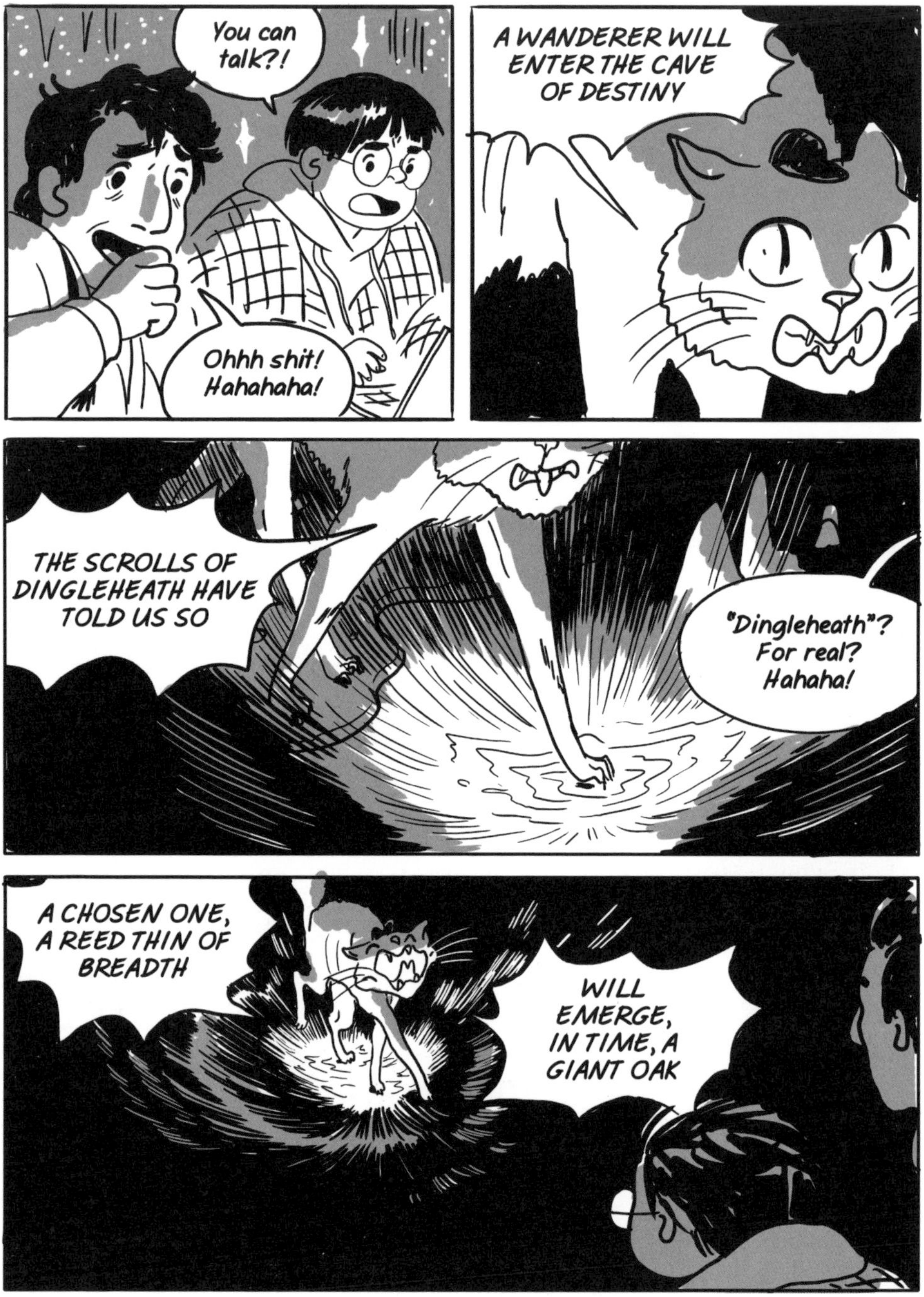
You can talk?!
Ohhh shit! Hahahaha!
A WANDERER WILL ENTER THE CAVE OF DESTINY
THE SCROLLS OF DINGLEHEATH HAVE TOLD US SO
"Dingleheath"? For real? Hahaha!
A CHOSEN ONE, A REED THIN OF BREADTH
WILL EMERGE, IN TIME, A GIANT OAK

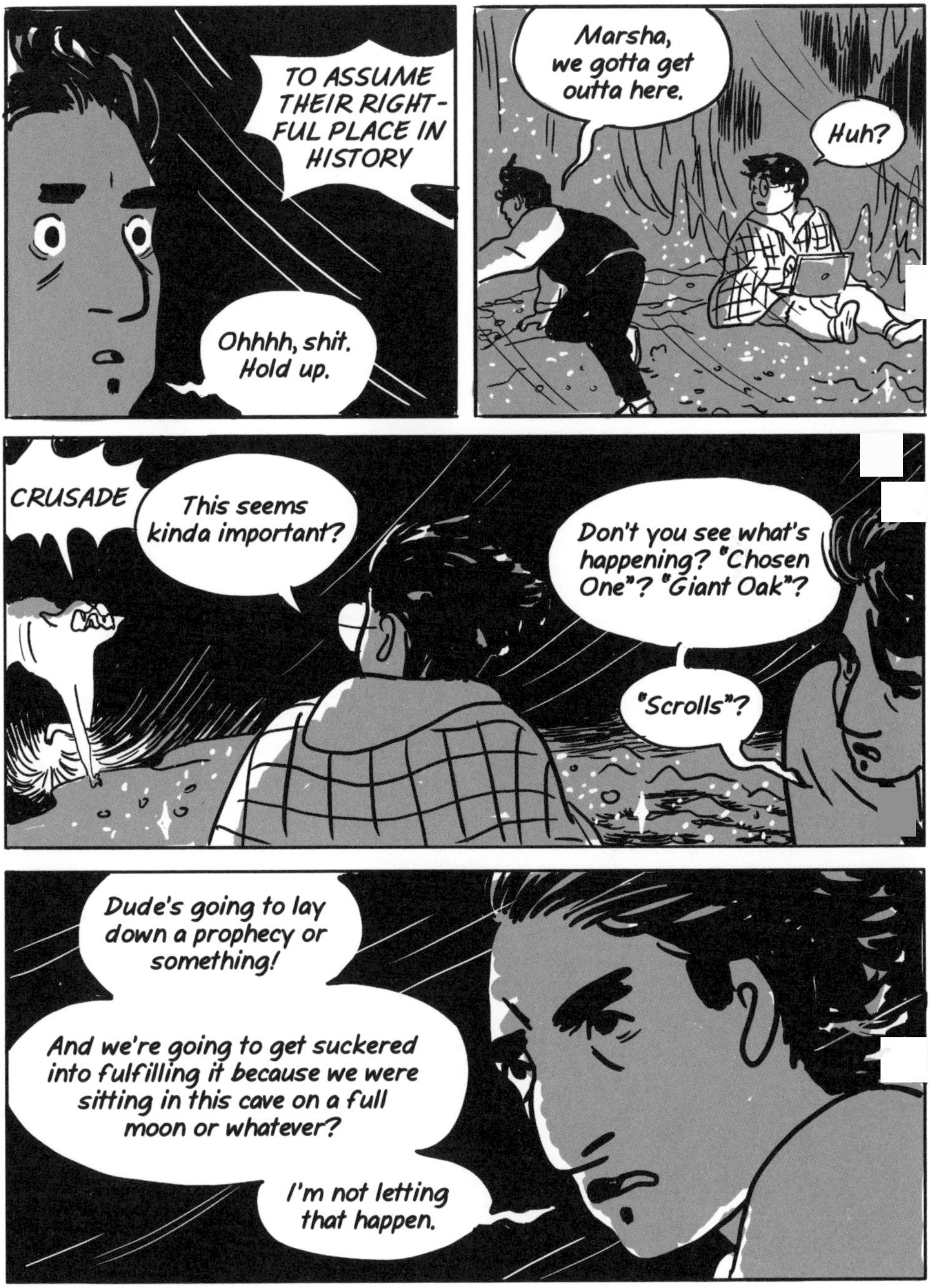
TO ASSUME THEIR RIGHTFUL PLACE IN HISTORY
Ohhhh, shit. Hold up.
Marsha, we gotta get outta here.
Huh?
CRUSADE
This seems kinda important?
Don't you see what's happening? "Chosen One"? "Giant Oak"?
"Scrolls"?
Dude's going to lay down a prophecy or something!
And we're going to get suckered into fulfilling it because we were sitting in this cave on a full moon or whatever?
I'm not letting that happen.

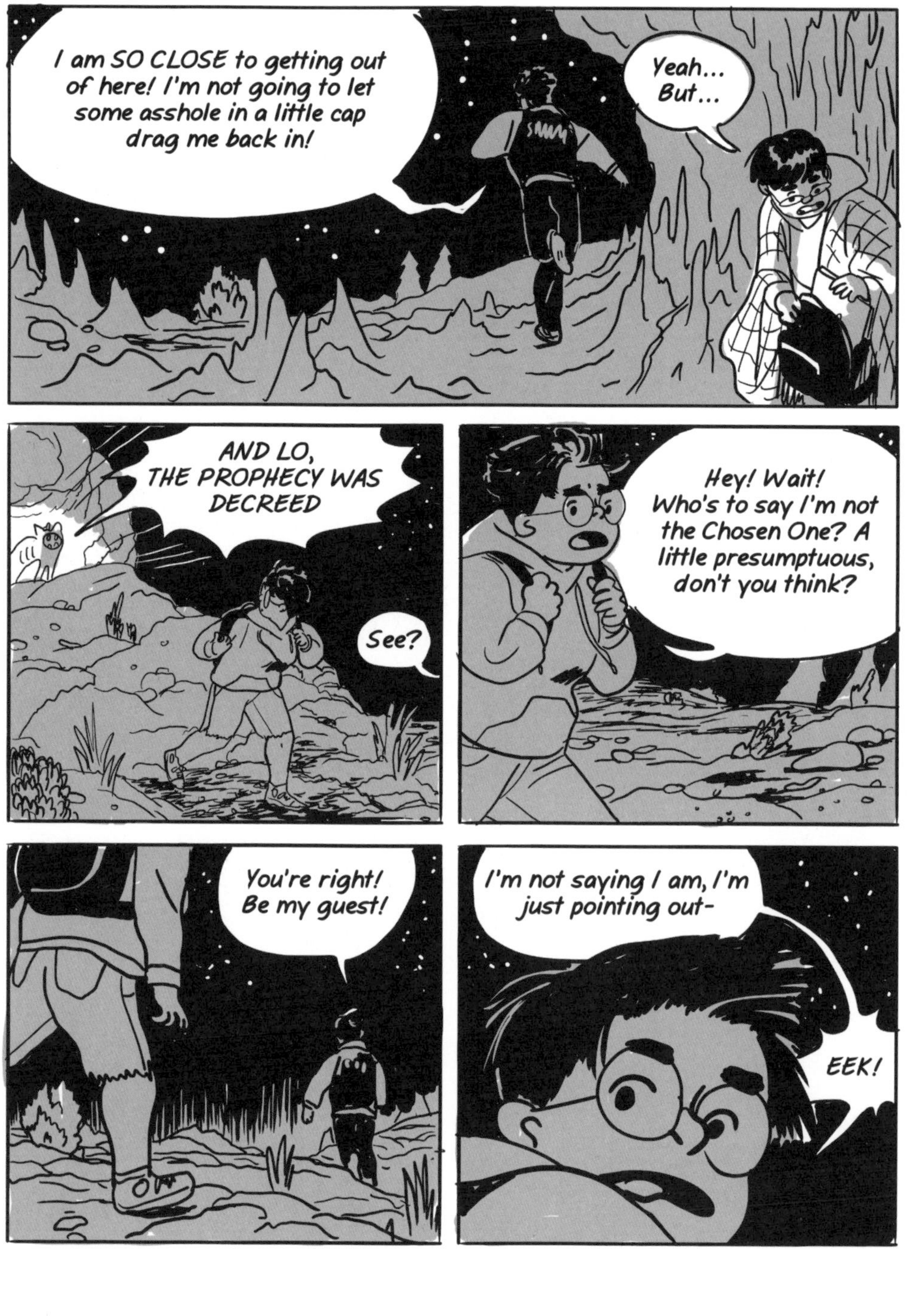
I am SO CLOSE to getting out of here! I'm not going to let some asshole in a little cap drag me back in!
Yeah... But...
AND LO, THE PROPHECY WAS DECREED
See?
Hey! Wait! Who's to say I'm not the Chosen One? A little presumptuous, don't you think?
You're right! Be my guest!
I'm not saying I am, I'm just pointing out-
EEK!

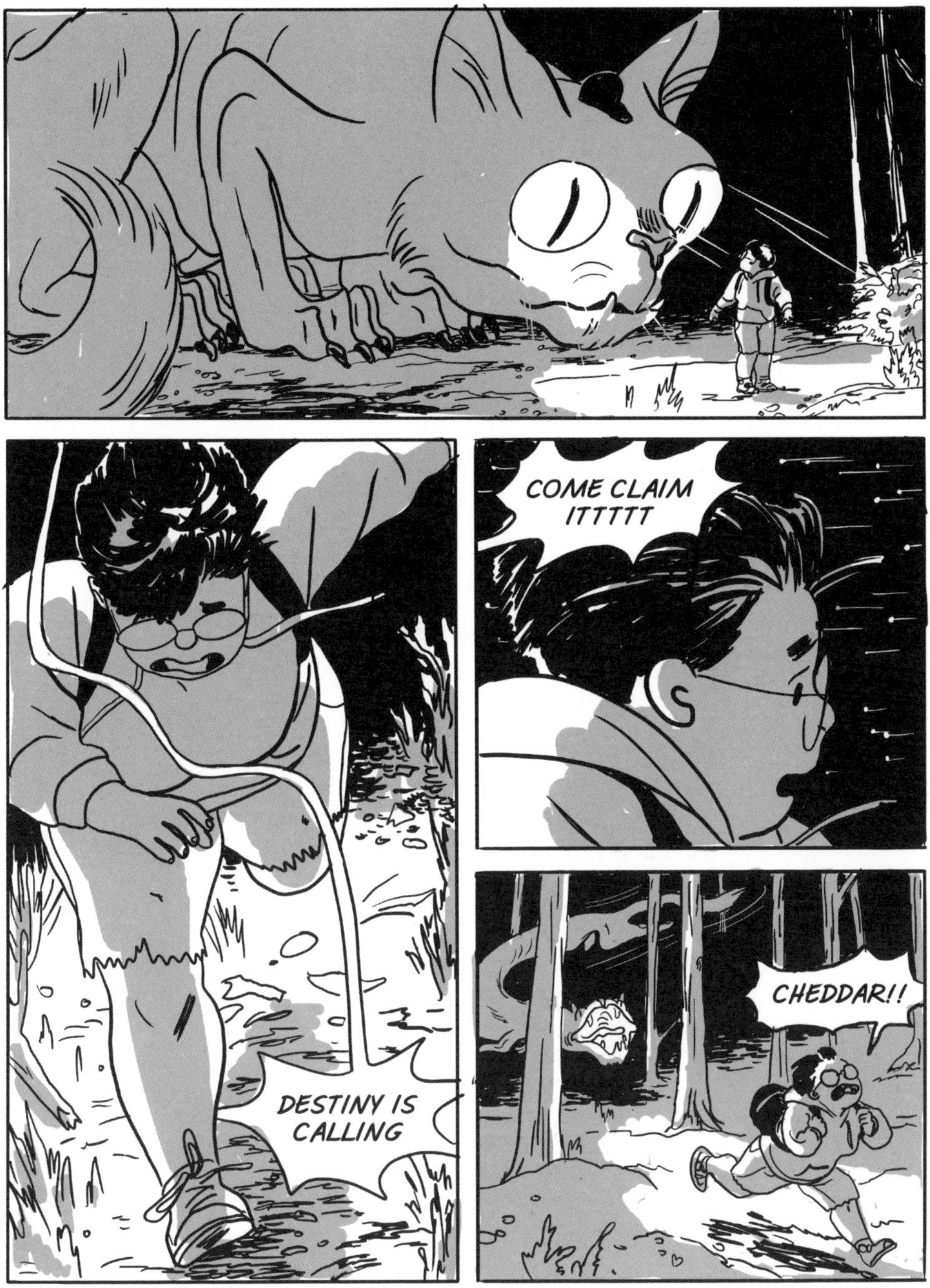
DESTINY IS CALLING
COME CLAIM ITTTTT
CHEDDAR!!

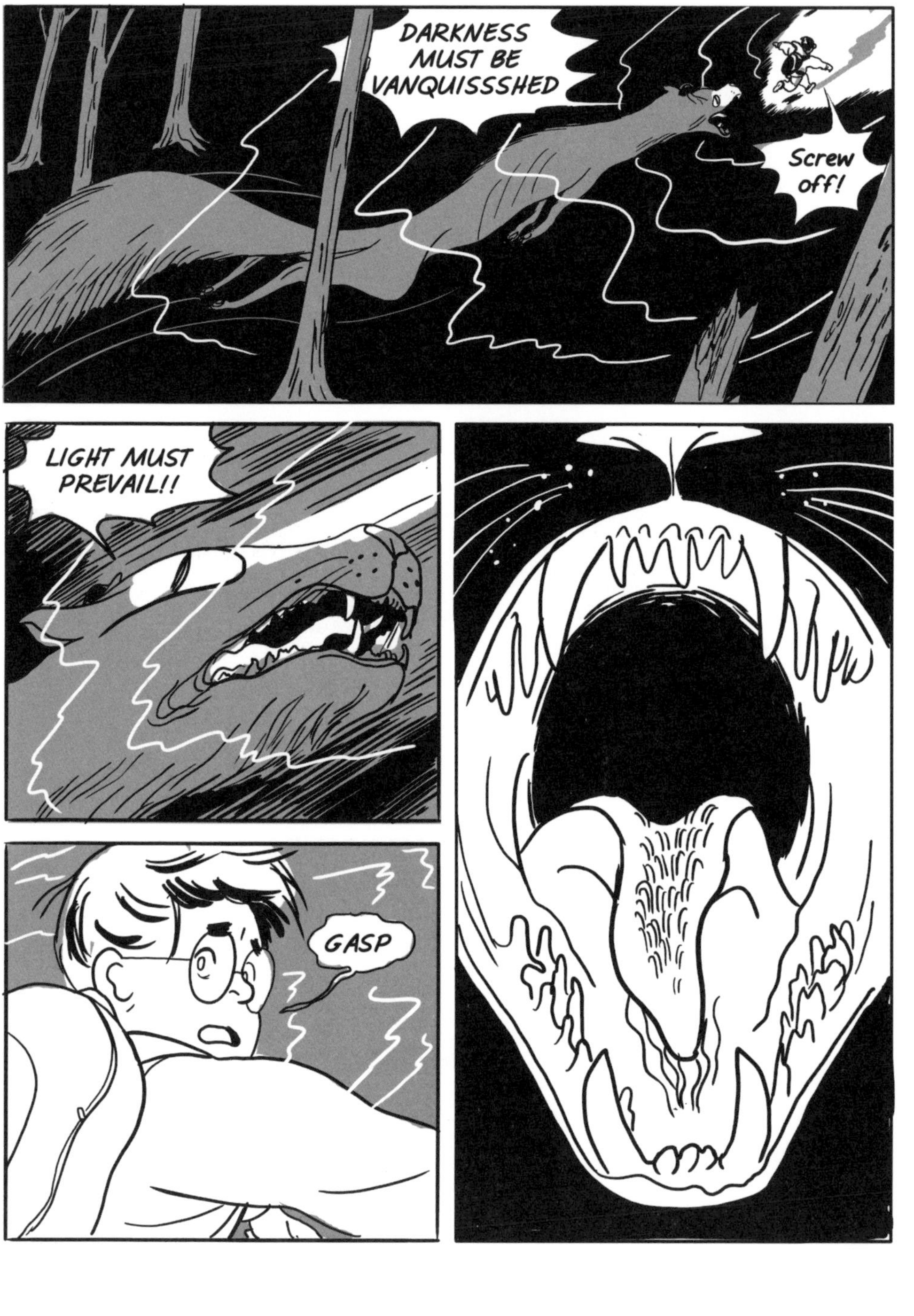
DARKNESS MUST BE VANQUISSSHED
Screw off!
LIGHT MUST PREVAIL!!
GASP

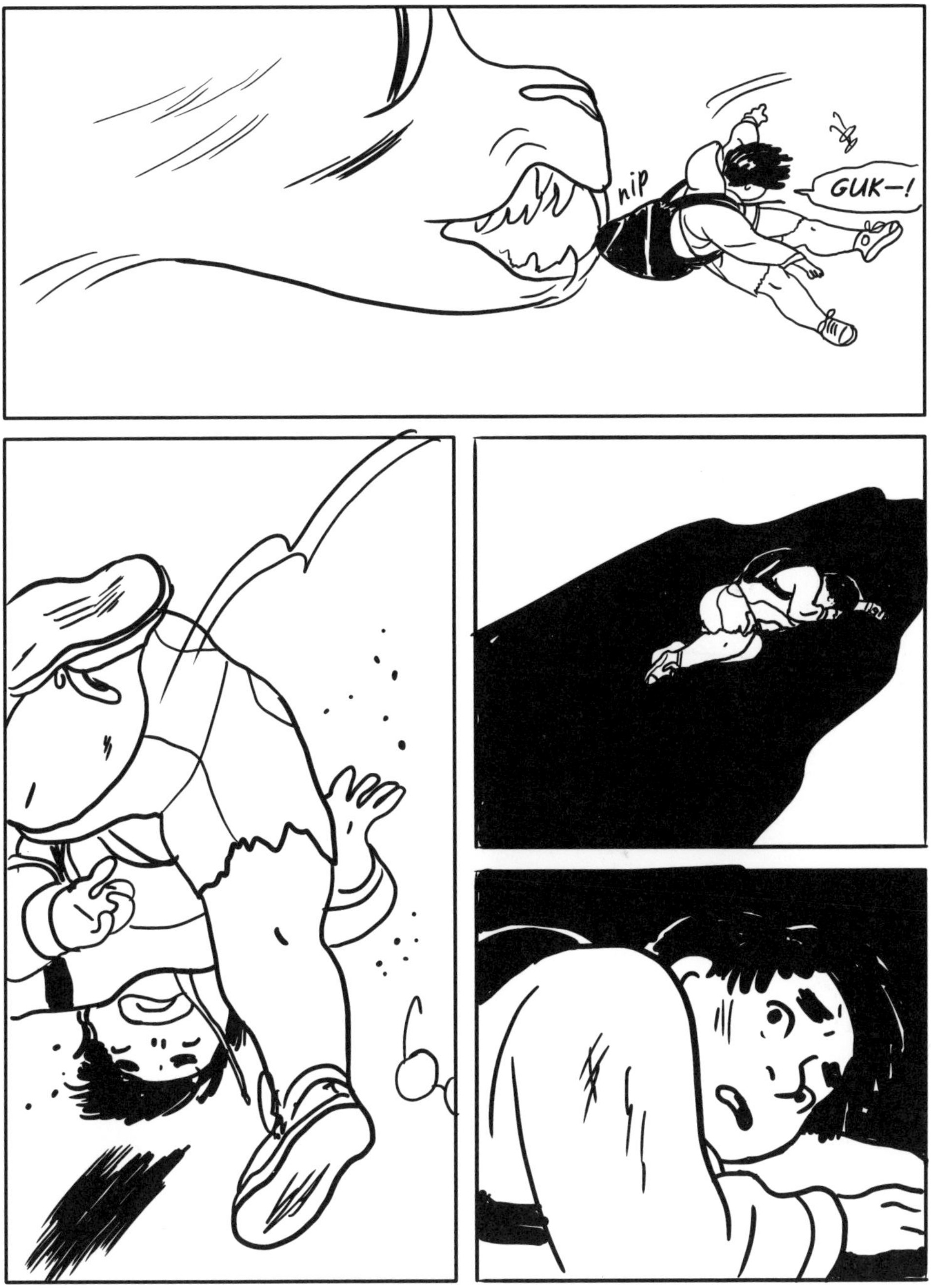
nip
GUK-!

THIS IS
SO UNFAIR...

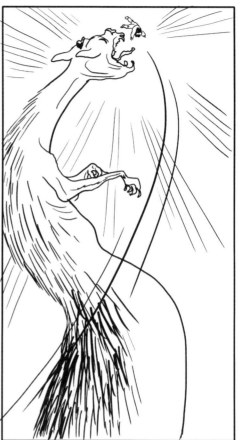

scoop

CHOMP

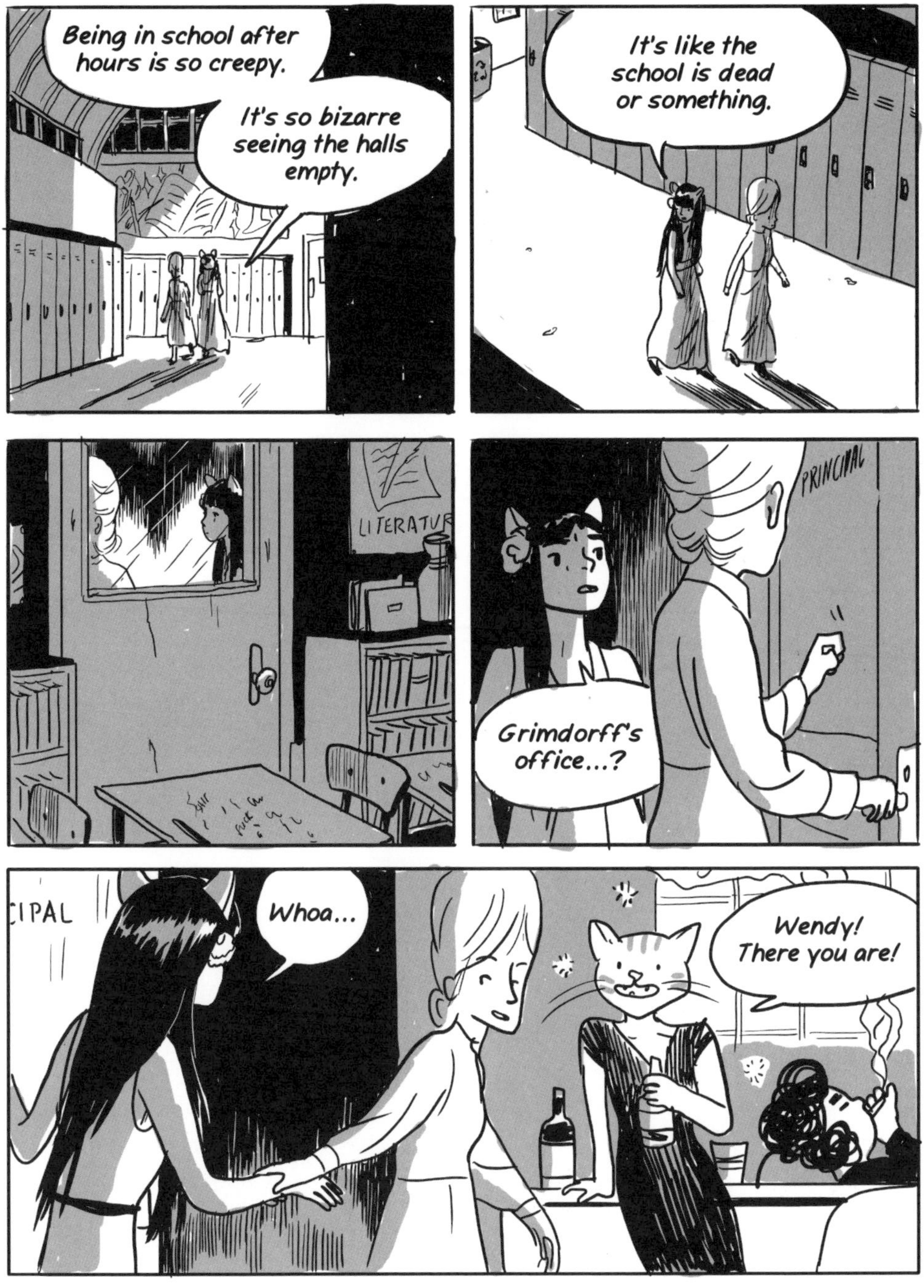
Being in school after hours is so creepy.
It's so bizarre seeing the halls empty.
It's like the school is dead or something.
LITERATUR
PRINCIPAL
Grimdorff's office...?
IPAL
Whoa...
Wendy! There you are!

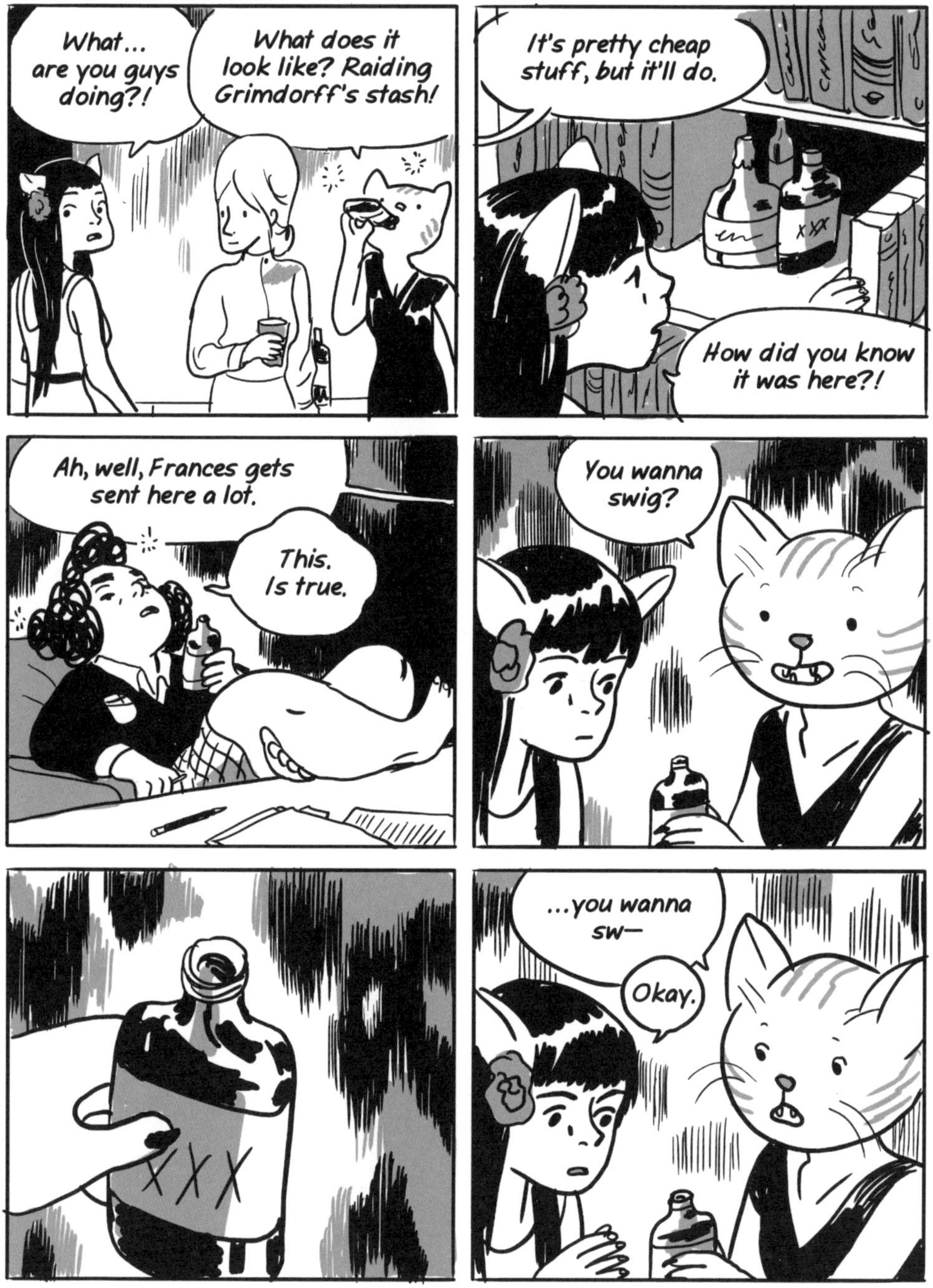

What... are you guys doing?!
What does it look like? Raiding Grimdorff's stash!
It's pretty cheap stuff, but it'll do.
How did you know it was here?!
Ah, well, Frances gets sent here a lot.
This. Is true.
You wanna swig?
...you wanna sw—
Okay.

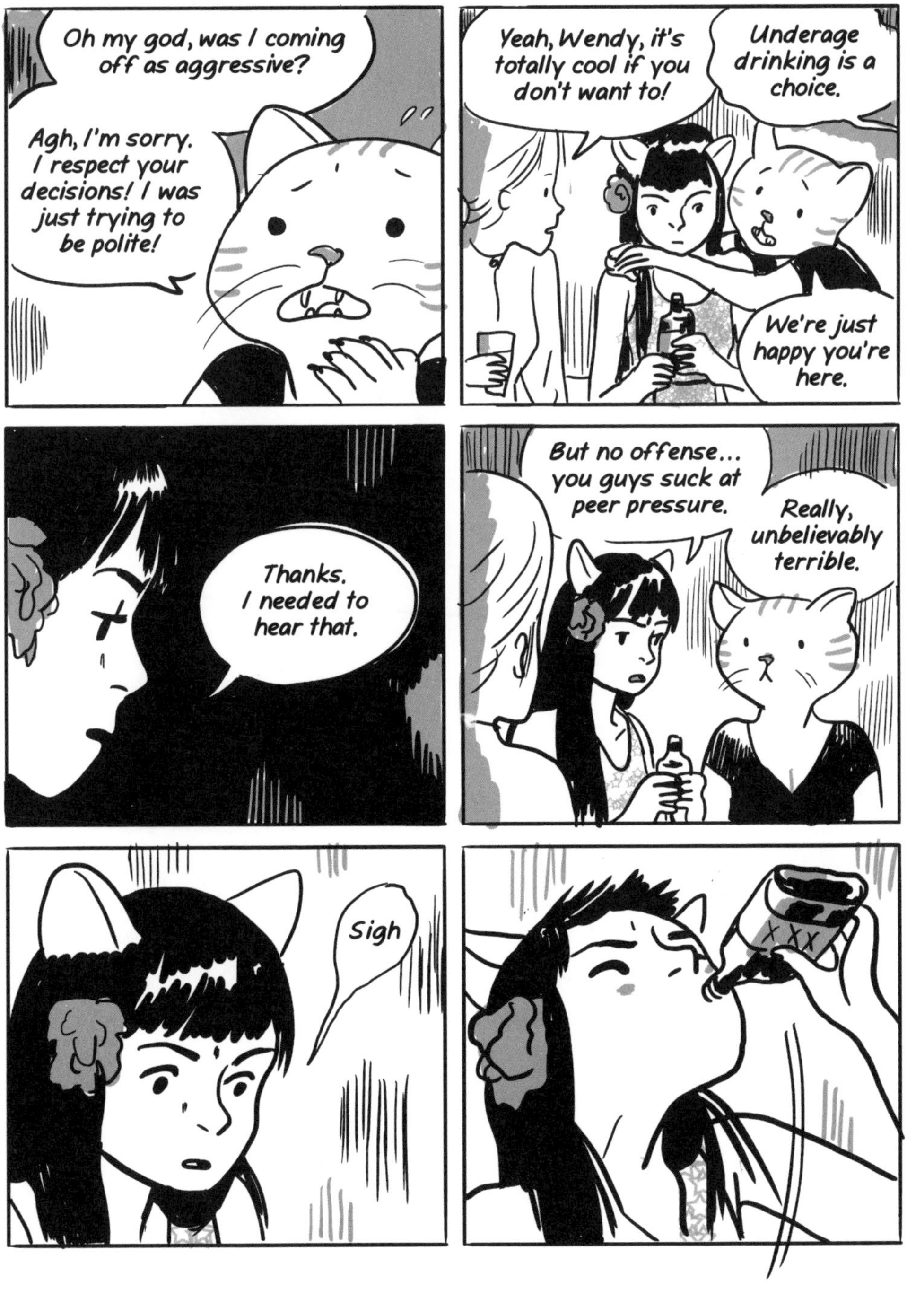
Oh my god, was I coming off as aggressive?
Agh, I'm sorry. I respect your decisions! I was just trying to be polite!
Yeah, Wendy, it's totally cool if you don't want to!
Underage drinking is a choice.
We're just happy you're here.
Thanks. I needed to hear that.
But no offense... you guys suck at peer pressure.
Really, unbelievably terrible.
Sigh
XXX

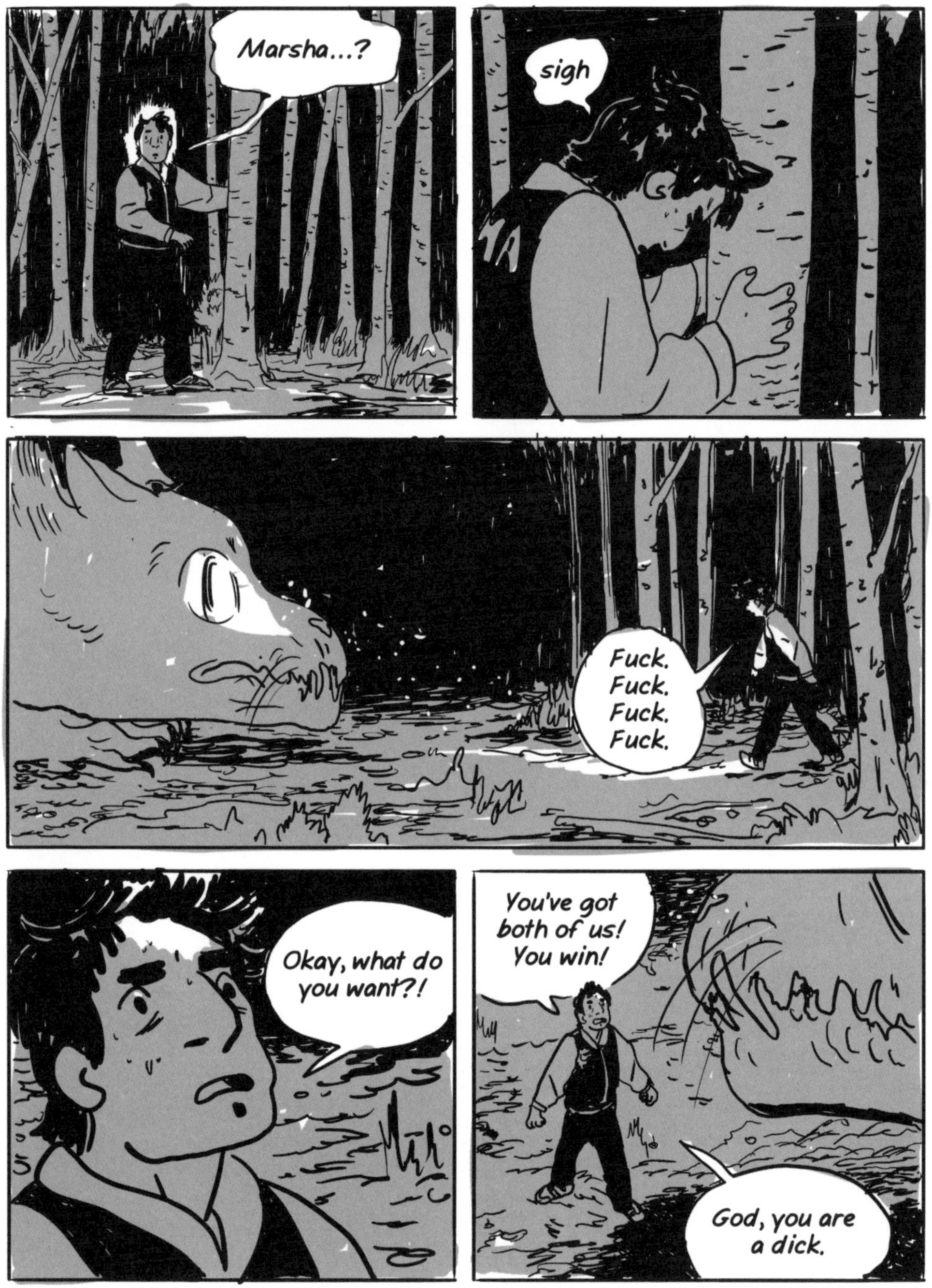
Marsha...?
sigh
Fuck.
Fuck.
Fuck.
Fuck.
Okay, what do you want?!
You've got both of us! You win!
God, you are a dick.

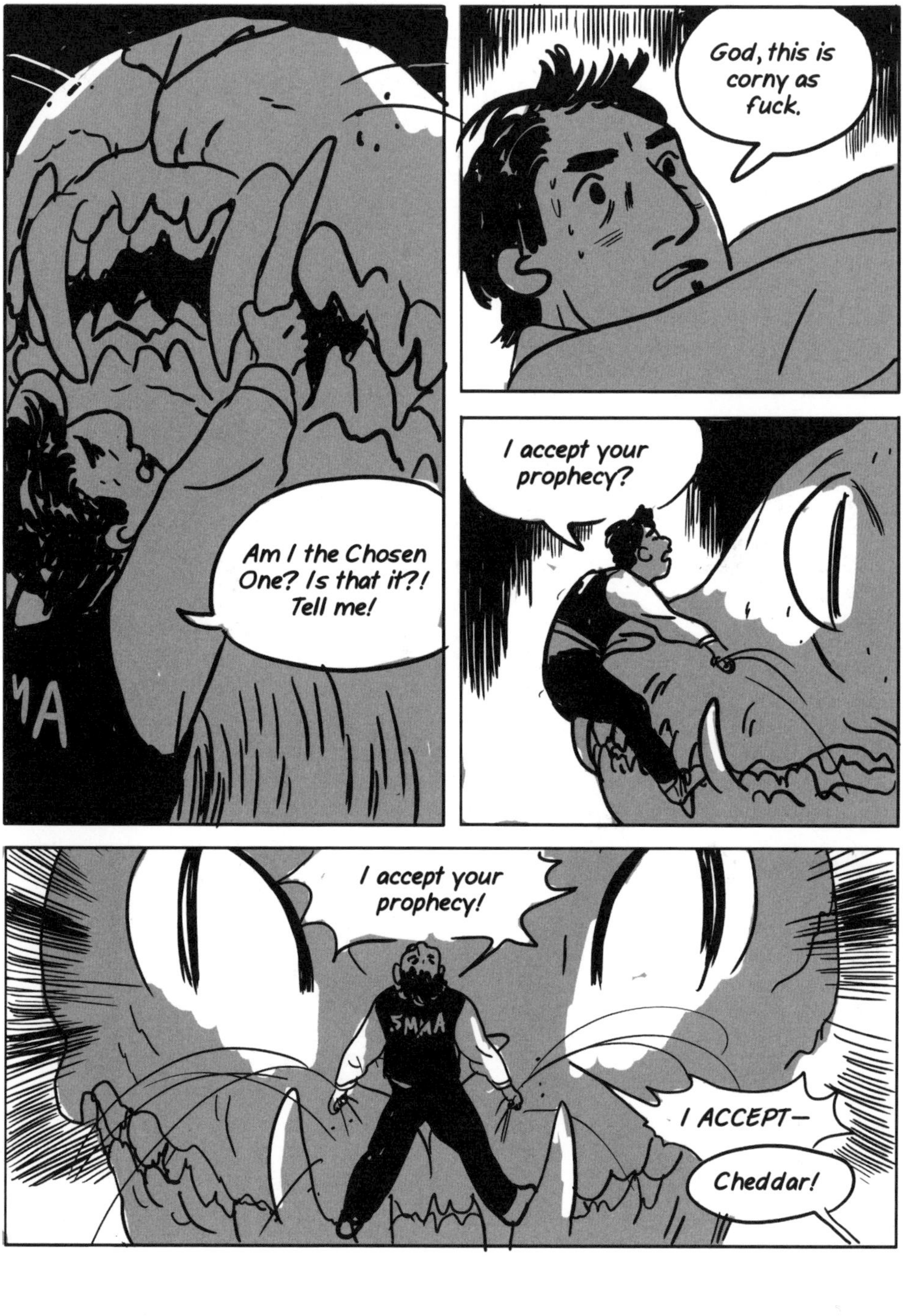
Am I the Chosen One? Is that it?! Tell me!
God, this is corny as fuck.
I accept your prophecy?
I accept your prophecy!
SMMA
I ACCEPT—
Cheddar!

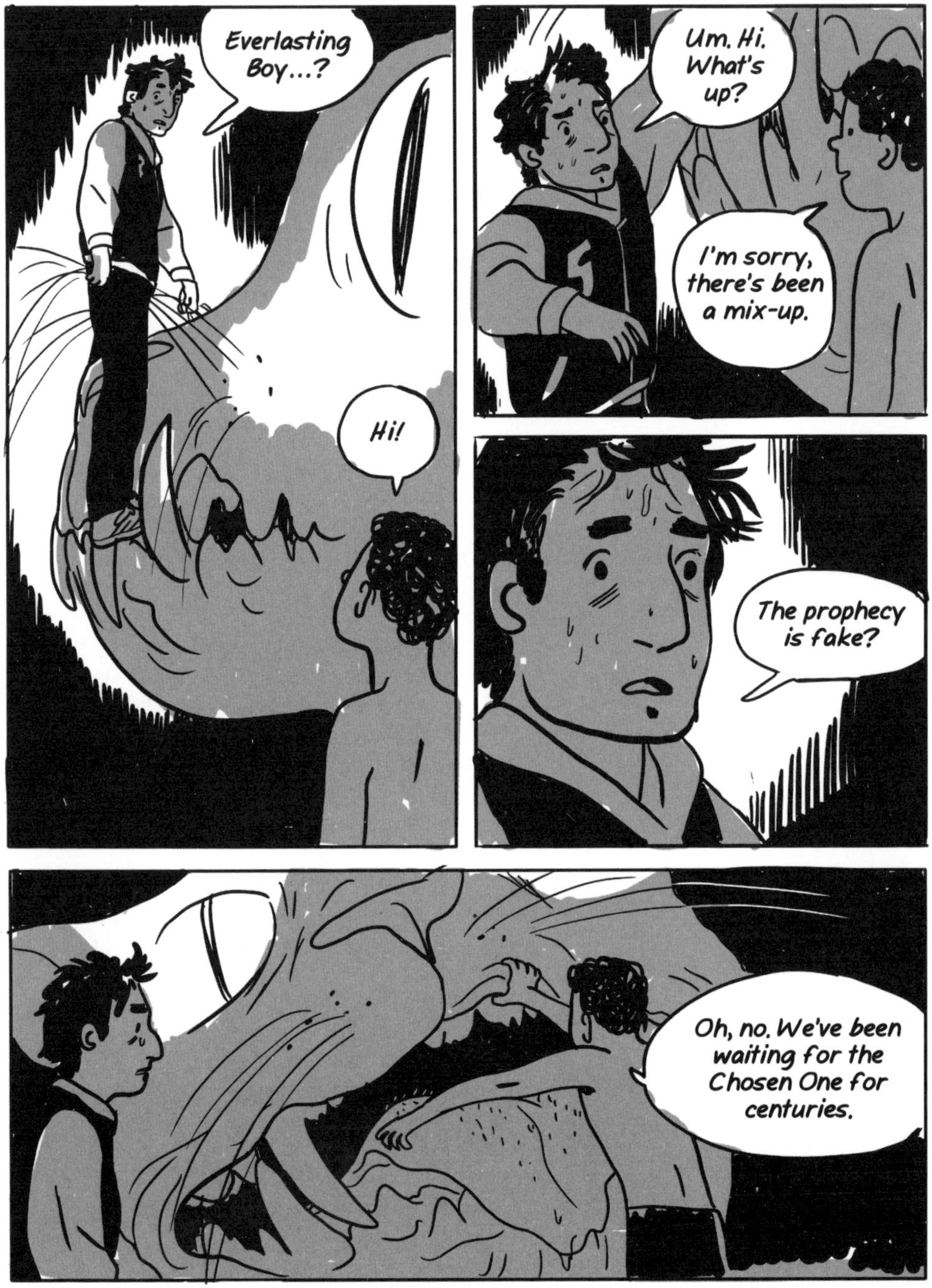
Everlasting Boy...?
Hi!
Um. Hi. What's up?
I'm sorry, there's been a mix-up.
The prophecy is fake?
Oh, no. We've been waiting for the Chosen One for centuries.

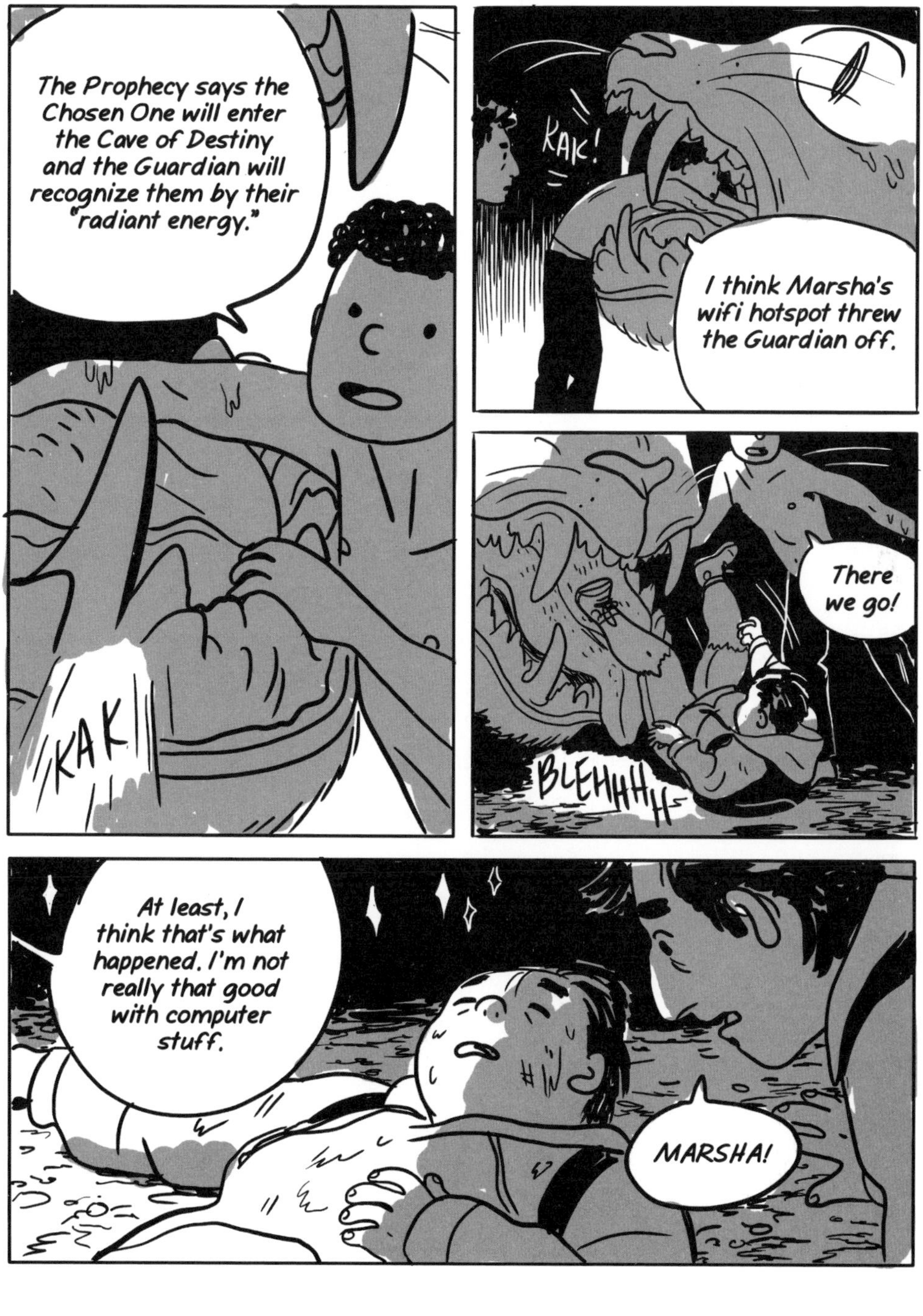
The Prophecy says the Chosen One will enter the Cave of Destiny and the Guardian will recognize them by their "radiant energy."
KAK
KAK!
I think Marsha's wifi hotspot threw the Guardian off.
There we go!
BLEHHHH
At least, I think that's what happened. I'm not really that good with computer stuff.
MARSHA!

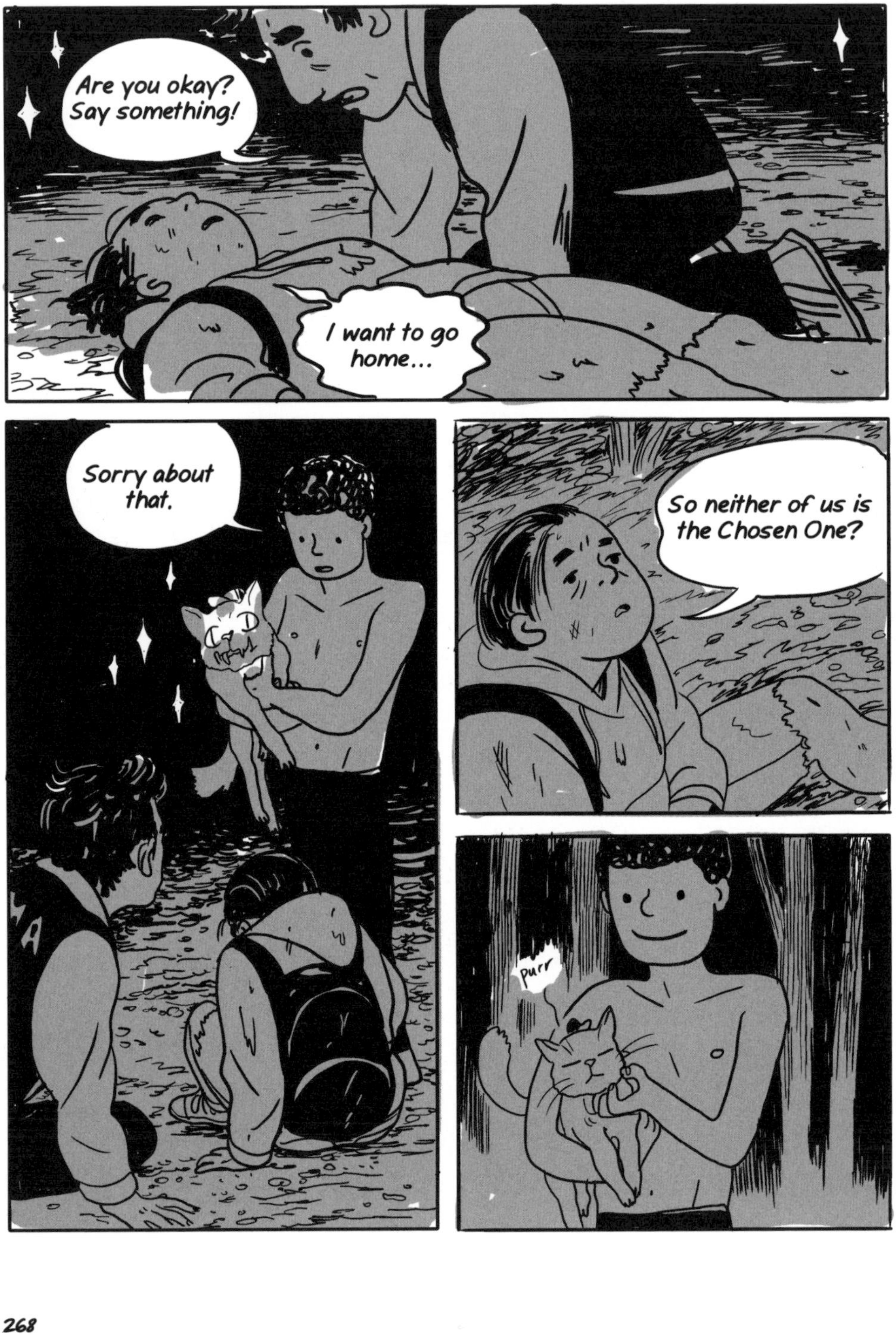
Are you okay? Say something!
I want to go home...
Sorry about that.
So neither of us is the Chosen One?
purr

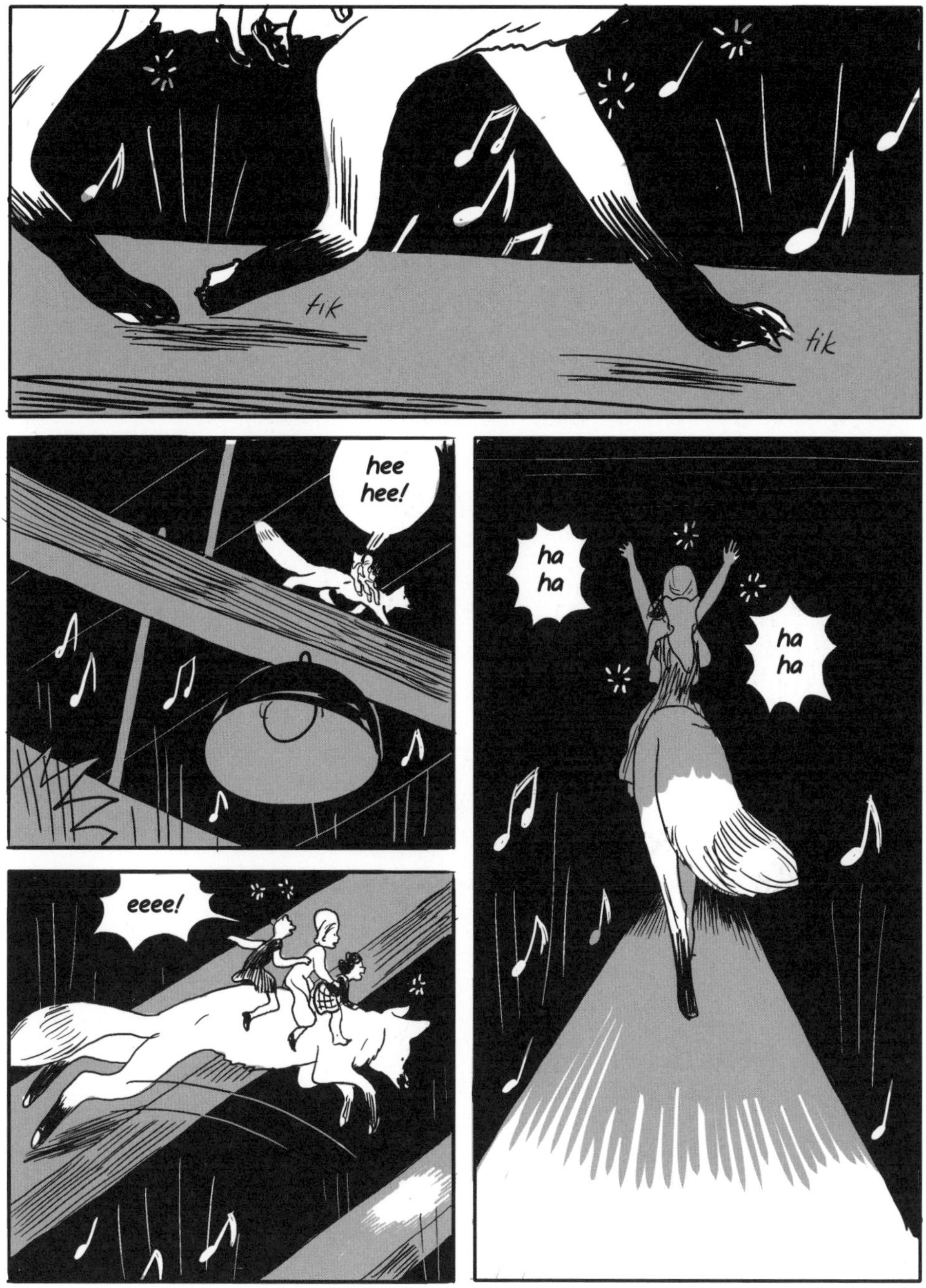
tik
tik
hee hee!
ha ha
ha ha
eeee!

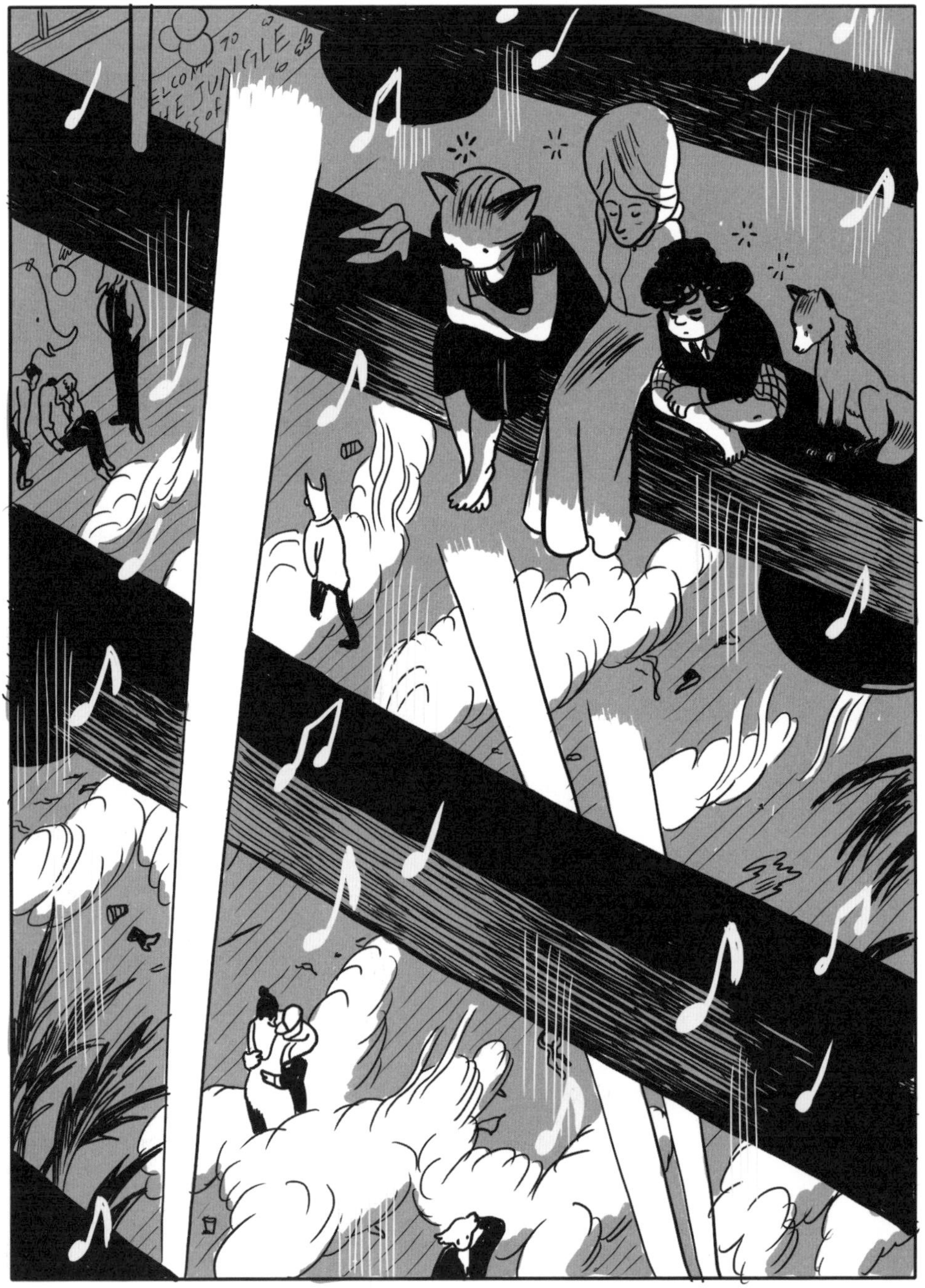
ELCOME TO
HE JUNGLE

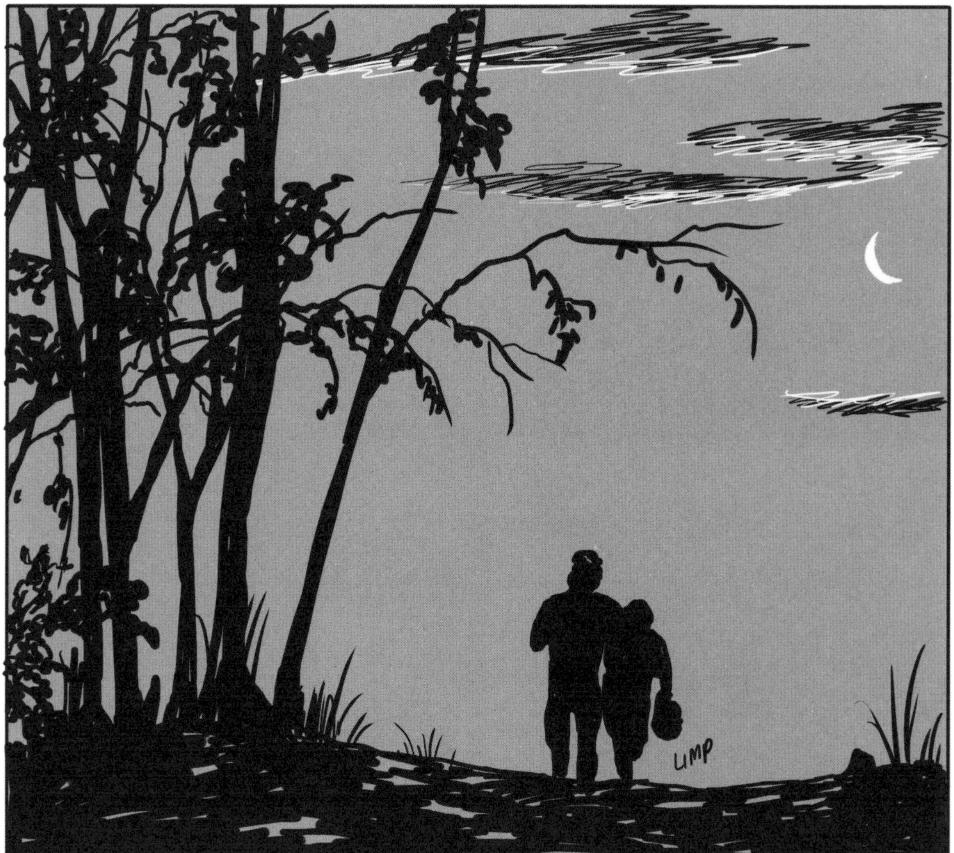
LIMP

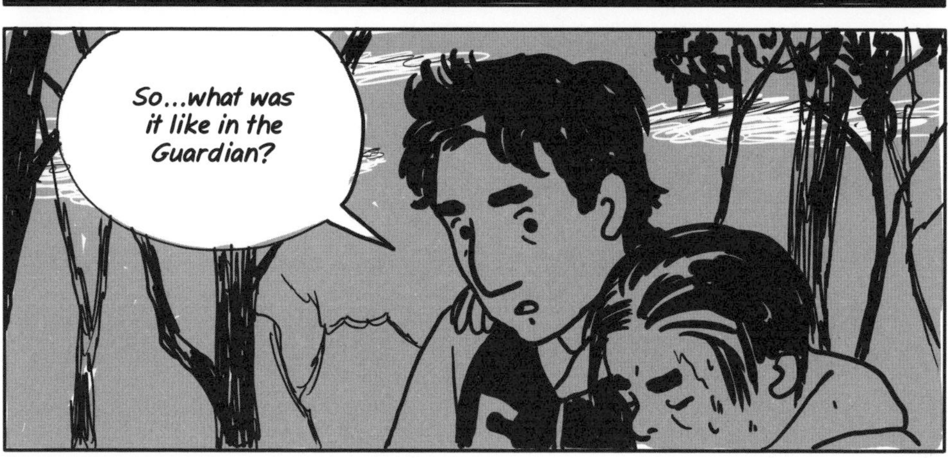
So...what was it like in the Guardian?

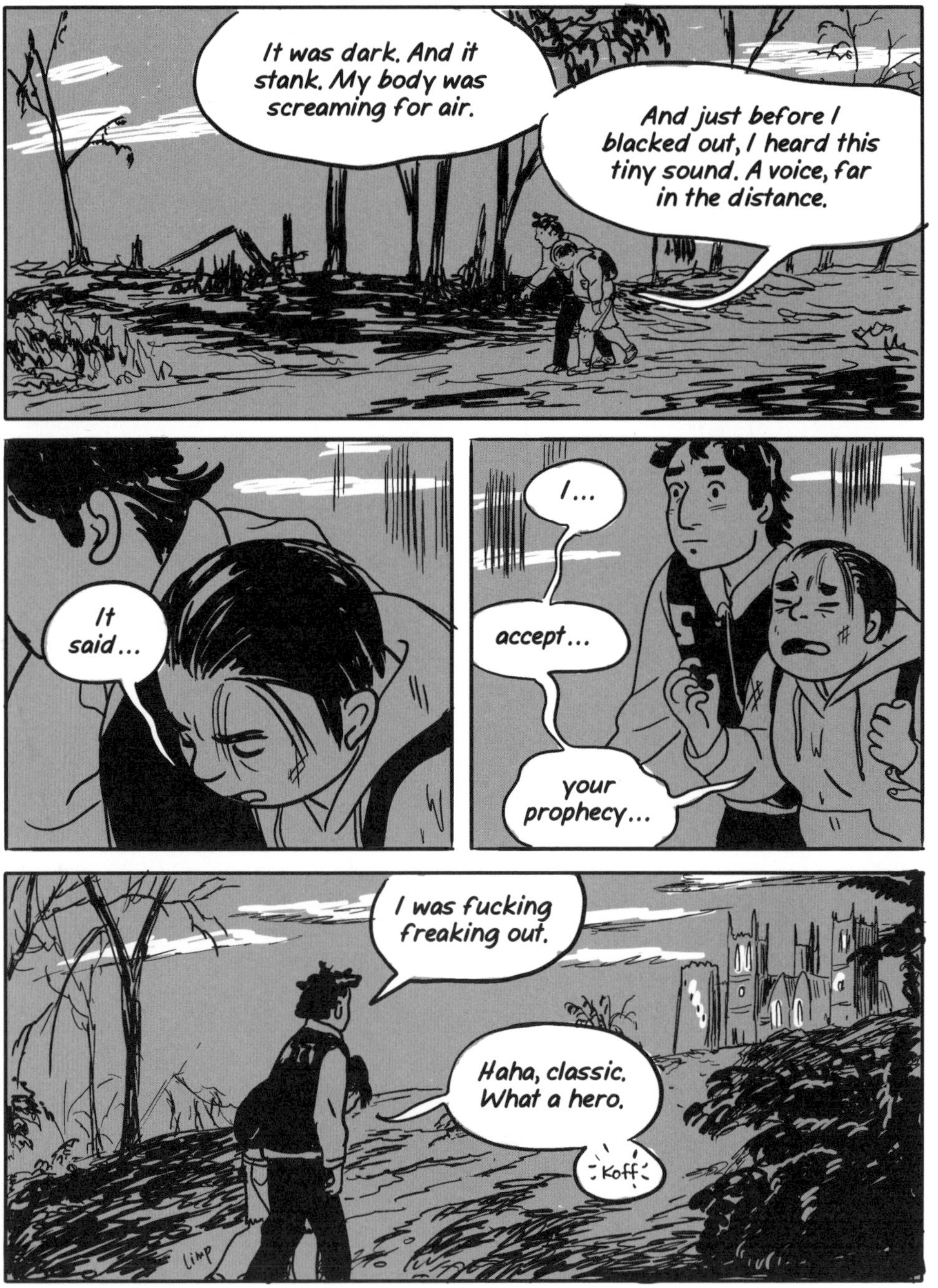
It was dark. And it stank. My body was screaming for air.
And just before I blacked out, I heard this tiny sound. A voice, far in the distance.
It said...
I...
accept...
your prophecy...
I was fucking freaking out.
Haha, classic. What a hero.
Koff
limp

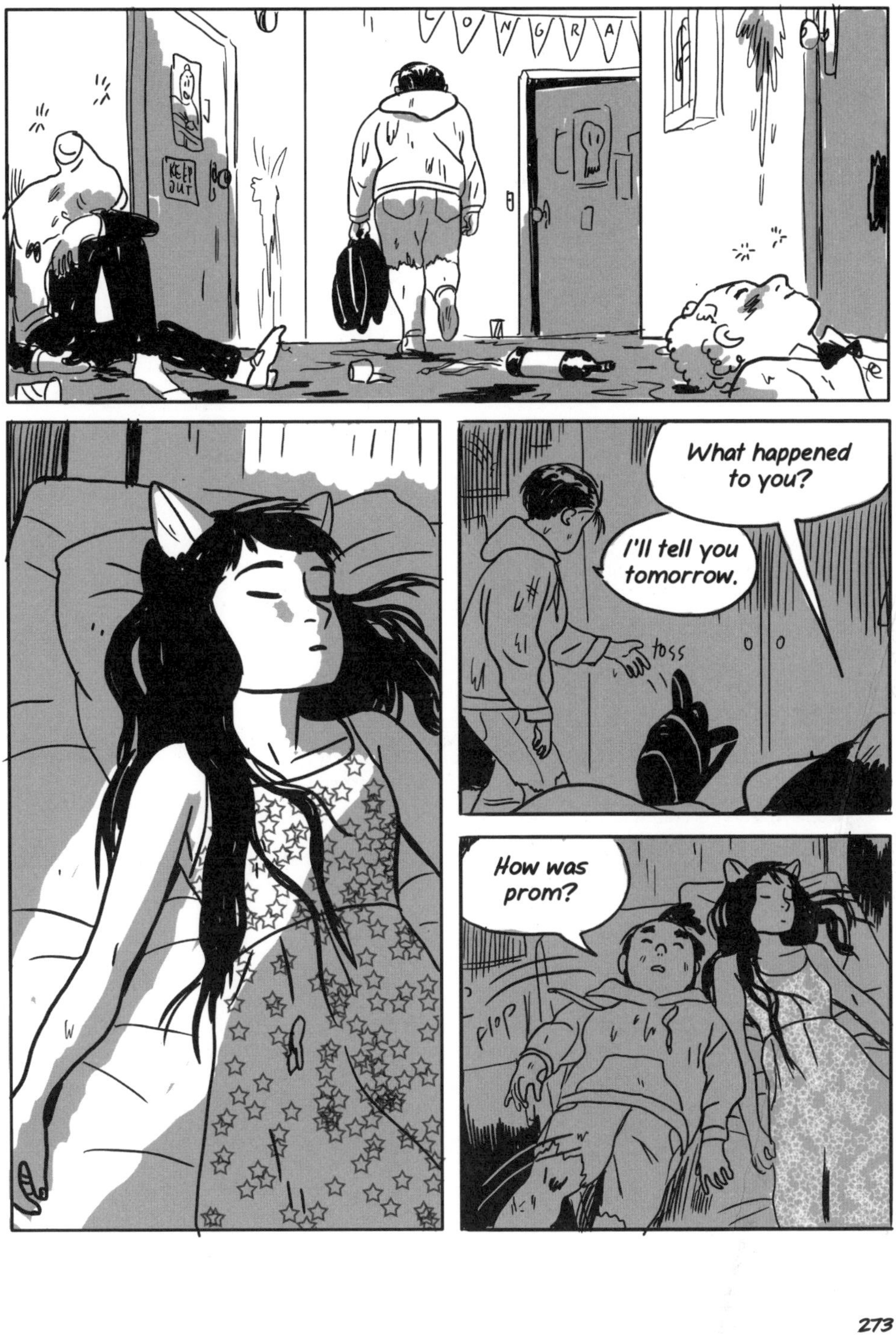
C O N G R A
KEEP OUT
What happened to you?
I'll tell you tomorrow.
toss
How was prom?
FLOP

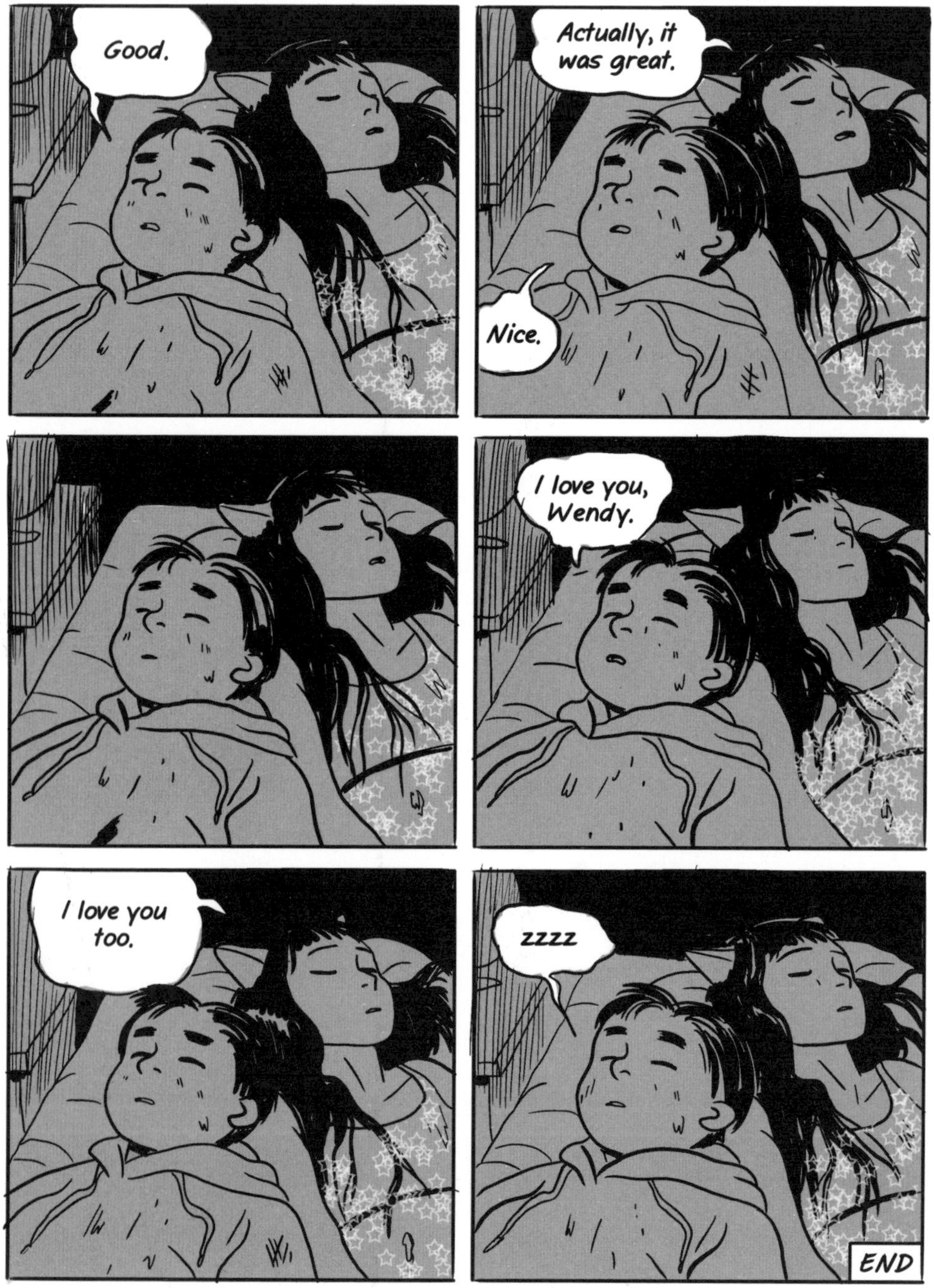
Good.
Actually, it was great.
Nice.
I love you, Wendy.
I love you too.
zzzz
END